D1265497

Local and Regional Government Information

How to Find It, How to Use It

Local and Regional Government Information
How to Find It, How to Use It

Edited by Mary Martin

GREENWOOD PRESS
Westport, Connecticut • London

Library of Congress Cataloging-in-Publication Data

Local and regional government information / edited by Mary Martin.
    p. cm.—(How to find it, how to use it)
    Includes bibliographical references and index.
    ISBN 1–57356–412–5 (alk. paper)
    1. Local government publications—United States—Handbooks, manuals, etc.
    2. Municipal government publications—United States—Handbooks, manuals,
    etc. 3. Public records—United States—Handbooks, manuals, etc. I. Martin,
    Mary. II. Series.
    Z1223.5.A1L63   2005
[JK2408]
015.73′053—dc22   2003061806

British Library Cataloguing in Publication Data is available.

Library of Congress Catalog Card Number: 2003061806
ISBN: 1–57356–412–5

First published in 2005

Greenwood Press, 88 Post Road West, Westport, CT 06881
An imprint of Greenwood Publishing Group, Inc.
www.greenwood.com

Printed in the United States of America

The paper used in this book complies with the
Permanent Paper Standard issued by the National
Information Standards Organization (Z39.48–1984).

10   9   8   7   6   5   4   3   2   1

Contents

Preface

When first discussing the idea of writing a reference book on local government information, it occurred to me that it would be impossible to do. Indeed, finding and listing local government information resources for the over 87,000 local government entities would be an impossible task. The sheer number of municipalities and counties in the United States makes it impossible to conduct a comprehensive listing of information resources about them. During the four years that this book was being written (1999–2003), a revolution in information dissemination of all kinds has been in progress. The Internet really grew at a phenomenal rate. And now, today, it is a really fast way to provide information about local government. Preliminary research indicated that there were few examples of books and many examples of Web sites that provide information about local governments. Many local governments produce brief pamphlets or flyers available locally. Unfortunately, visiting the locale is really the only way to find out about these things. Actually, touring the country as Alexis de Tocqueville (*Democracy in America*) did in 1831 would be a very interesting journey. It is a little easier to do so *virtually*, via the Internet. In fact, a Web site is a very inexpensive and easily accessible way for a city or county to provide information to its citizens.

There are thousands of Web sites that provide an astonishing array of approaches to providing information. There are also some books, but there are few that provide any sort of comprehensive access to local government information. There are some that do a creditable job if the focus is on a particular aspect of local government, or provide very brief, directory-type information. All of these types of information resources are mentioned as examples in this book.

The book is part of the "How to Find It, How to Use It" series formerly published by Oryx Press, now by Greenwood. The reason the book has assumed this format is because it really can only point the way and describe *examples* of local government information. It is not possible to be comprehensive and list all local government information resources. The book is not attempting to do that. What it attempts to do is provide a framework for understanding how local governments are organized, how they produce information, where that information may be located, and how to go about finding it and using it. There is really no intent to direct readers on how to substantively use government information. It is more like a blueprint, and does provide examples of how to use the resources found, be they in paper or electronic format. Although there is widespread belief out there that "everything is on the Web" and "you can find anything on the Web," those of us who work at library reference desks, or in any information-provider role, know differently. There are lots of experienced users who can't "find it on the Web." It may be there—but they can't find it. This book provides a framework for thinking about local government information that can serve as a pathfinder for anyone seeking such information.

The first three chapters of the book are general, describing certain germane issues related to use of local government information. First, the issue of access to government information is discussed. When looking at information on the local level, such as property taxes or business licenses, the issue of privacy becomes very real. Making such information readily available can possibly jeopardize a person's privacy. Possible issues and recent trends in policy are discussed. Second, local government structure is discussed. It is useful to know how a particular entity is organized before trying to look for information. For example, if one needs a copy of a particular will, it is necessary to know which court would have had jurisdiction over the matter. Third, local government archives are discussed. How and where local government records are routinely archived is essential to figuring out where these records, particularly if they are older, may be stored. These chapters were actually written by three separate authors who each brought a fresh perspective to the topics.

After writing 7 chapters alone, and taking about two years to do so, with 12 more chapters to write, I decided that it would be helpful to solicit the contributions of additional authors. I sent out a request for authors on Govdoc-L, an Internet Listserv created and maintained primarily for librarians in the government information field. I was overwhelmed with responses, so in order to give more people a chance to author a chapter, I paired authors, many times in opposite parts of the country. A few authors ended up working alone, as their partners had to withdraw. This brought an interesting perspective to the book. The authors provided examples of local government resources from their respective areas, bringing a wider regional flavor to the book. I enjoyed working with all of them, and I am very grateful, as without them this book would have taken much longer to write. I would like to thank first of all Henry Rasof (with Oryx Press), my first editor, who helped me hammer out the framework for the book; and my second editor, Scott Prentzas at Greenwood Press, who was always kind and patient. I would also like to thank Gail Cugno, a former library school student of mine, and a new librarian, for helping me with some of the final editing. My deepest gratitude also goes to Harriet Semmes Alexander, Mark Anderson, Maria Carpenter, Darcy Carrizales, Jim Church, Ann Ellis, Sherry Engle Moeller, Mark Gilman, Rich Gause, Joan Goodbody, Suzann Holland, Denise Johnson, Michael Kaminski, Anne Levy, Marianne Mason, Deborah Mongeau, Shawn Nicholson, Brian Rossmann, Marie-Lise Shams, and Dan Stanton. I couldn't have done it without you. Thanks for doing such an awesome job and being such great government documents librarians.

One of the most time-consuming and difficult things to do was to check Web sites, which are constantly changing Internet addresses. Surprisingly few actually disappeared, but many did move. It seems every time a Web site moves to a new server, the Web site changes its URL (address). I would like to offer a big thanks to those who provide links to the new URL. If a URL doesn't work, I found the surest way to find out whether the Web site relocated without leaving a forwarding address was to "Google it." I found the new Web site in many of the cases. This is sound advice whenever a Web site has moved.

I hope this book is useful to practitioners in the government documents field, and perhaps to those outside of the field in local government, who could use it as a resource when they are asked to locate some hard-to-find piece of local government information.

CHAPTER 1
Access to Local Government Information

Mary Martin and Richard Gause

MAJOR TOPICS COVERED

MAJOR RESOURCES COVERED

INTRODUCTION

Whatever policies were in place regarding access to public records prior to September 11, 2001, were forever changed by the events on that date. The destruction of the World Trade Center in New York City by terrorists, who developed their plans using fairly ordinary means to gather information, was definitely a wake-up call to those who collect, archive, and provide access to public records.

"May I have the city's 1966 tax report for 1234 East Park Street?"

"Here's the report you requested."

"Thank you."

It would be wonderful if all requests for local government information could be handled so easily. Unfortunately, many information seekers will encounter obstacles. Suppose the individual is trying to determine what the first-year property taxes were for his house when it was built. The county instead of the city may hold the specific property records. If the records still exist after several decades, they may be in remote storage. The 1966 taxes may have been assessed on vacant land, so he may actually need the 1967 record. He may encounter uncooperative or unknowledgeable staff reluctant to dig through old files.

This chapter identifies potential pitfalls and offers solutions to some general problems the researcher may experience in retrieving information. Methods of requesting information are discussed, including use of public records laws. Succeeding chapters will provide guidance for specific topics.

POTENTIAL BARRIERS TO ACCESS

Identification of Records and Issuing Agency

The first problem some researchers will encounter is determining the proper name of the records that contain the information they are seeking. Linked with identifying the name of the records is figuring out which agency produced them. Most agency staff should be willing to assist the researcher in identifying the appropriate records based on a description of the specific data sought. Such assistance becomes more difficult if the researcher wants to maintain secrecy regarding the specific data and the purpose of his request. If the initial records provided do not contain the needed information, the researcher could ask if there are any records related to those provided. A less revealing approach would be to ask whether the agency has a records inventory or some other list that identifies and describes all the records maintained by that office.

Another problem that may be encountered is that one agency may have obtained data initially compiled by other agencies. A school system may have requested crime data for a study of neighborhoods with at-risk children or transportation data for planning new bus routes. The second agency's analysis of the data may save the researcher's time by providing answers to questions or identifying the specific information held by the first agency. Citing the existence of data elsewhere may bolster the researcher's request to the first agency by demonstrating that it has already provided similar data to another agency.

Levels of Government

Even though local information is sought, the data may be collected and maintained by a regional, state, or federal agency instead of the local city or county government. The higher level of government office maintaining the local records may be in a different city. Such a situation may be beneficial by providing a centralized source with a standardized format for the researcher seeking comparative data from several different communities. An agency gathering data from multiple communities is more likely to have prepared an analytical report summarizing the data.

Geographic Boundaries

Unincorporated communities may not have clearly defined borders, making it difficult to correlate data gathered by different agencies. Municipal boundaries often change significantly over time, so care should be taken to gather appropriate collateral data to ensure that apples are compared with apples. Annexation of fully developed neighborhoods can significantly increase the population of a town overnight; the new residents are not sudden arrivals to the area, but they may create new demands on municipal services.

Special Districts

Some local services are provided by separate government entities whose records may not appear in centralized city or county files—especially since many are independent agencies and some special districts cross county boundaries. Common functions of special districts include community development, transportation, and water control; less expected functions occasionally covered by special districts include arts, educational facilities, health care, juvenile welfare, libraries, parking, and sports. Because special districts may be created and dissolved more easily than cities and counties, the records for the functions served by the special districts may be more difficult to track down. For example, of Florida's 1,100 special districts, 29 were created in 2001 and 13 were dissolved.

Joint Projects

When multiple agencies are involved in a project, they might each prepare their own reports, but it is likely that a single report will be published. Although each agency will probably be named on the report, organizations storing the report may identify only the lead agency for their filing system. If the report is no longer available at one agency, the researcher can seek a copy at the other agencies involved in the project. Even if a single local agency conducted the project, there may be interim status reports and a final report on file with a state or federal office if the project received external funding.

Reorganization

The issuing agency may change over time. When responsibility for providing certain services is transferred, the new agency may decide to discontinue gathering some portions of the data. The arrangement of the data may change significantly. The new agency might incorporate the information from the previous agency's publication as a section in its existing reports. The agency newly responsible might not want to make room for the previous agency's historical files, but the previous agency might not want to devote storage space for records about an activity in which it is no longer involved.

Nonexistent or Missing Records

Although disappointing, verification that records do not exist may save the researcher hours of fruitless effort. The search can then be turned to looking for alternate information.

Never Collected

It is possible that the information sought was never collected. Many people assume that the government has data to meet every possible information need. Even when a government agency has the ability to easily collect certain information, doing so might be considered a misuse of tax dollars if the information is not needed by the agency to fulfill its specific mission. Instead of using government records, the researcher may find that a trade association or nonprofit organization gathers similar information for its own purposes. Such organizations may compile data from various government agencies, as well as adding value through analysis of the data. The local realtors' association may have produced a list comparing the quality of schools and neighborhoods. Coincident with five of the last six decennial censuses, various religious bodies have cooperated to compile county-level data regarding church membership.

Dates of Coverage

Government records may exist for some time periods but not others. If the records seem to begin at a certain point, the researcher should determine whether any information was collected previously. Enabling legislation may indicate when the requirement to pro-duce the data began. The earliest record may specifically state whether it is the first issue or a continuation of previous efforts with a different title or by another agency. An anniversary issue may provide a history of the record. Gaps due to budget constraints, staff shortages, or other causes may be explained in the next available issue. Apparently missing data might be included in a combined issue. Raw data may exist for missing reports or for dates prior to the compilation of formal reports. The most recent information might be inaccessible until weekly, monthly, quarterly, or annual submissions are made to a central facility.

Missing Records

The original records may have been misplaced, lost, stolen, or destroyed by fire, flood, or mildew. An office with poor file-management procedures may not have a record of who has borrowed materials. A missing file might be sitting on a shelf in a commissioner's office, particularly if the information deals with a hot topic the commissioner is handling.

Copies of Records

Although potentially difficult to track down, copies of records may exist at other agencies or in the personal files of individuals responsible for either creating or using the information. The distribution list for the current edition of a report may help identify possible recipients of copies of a previous edition that is missing from the files. A report required of a local government agency may have been submitted to a state or federal agency; or it may move in reverse: Almost all of the population schedules from the 1890 federal census were destroyed in a 1921 fire, but the 1890 records for Washington County, Georgia, are still available because a copy was placed in the county records. Libraries, universities, or other research centers may have obtained copies of records. Other reports or journal articles may have been written that provide a synopsis of the data.

Exempt Information

Some information in government files is protected by privacy laws, discussed later in this chapter. Although specific information may be exempt from disclosure, many government employees mistakenly apply the exemption to entire documents. The researcher should request that the office withhold only the protected portion of the documents. The solution might be as simple as masking the Social Security number or similar sensitive-specific information prior to photocopying a requested document.

Retention Schedules

Most government offices do not have space to store files indefinitely. Retention schedules identify when and how offices can remove old records from their files. Some records are discarded, but others may be microfilmed or sent to an archival facility. Some offices recognize the historical value of certain records and either retain documents well beyond the retention schedule or turn them over to a local history center or museum. Staff in an efficient office meticulously adhering to retention schedules may no longer have the requested files, but may be the most knowledgeable source for identifying possible alternate locations for the information. It may be more difficult to search through poorly organized files in an inefficient office, but it might still have records that officially should have been thrown out long ago. A different kind of efficiency may cause access problems if the staff threw out entire file folders during spring cleaning without checking the individual records to determine any requirements for longer retention.

Off-Site Storage

Many counties throughout the United States have a central office through which some frequently requested public records are provided. If the volume of records exceeds the available storage, an office may move older or less popular records to another building. The request might still be processed at the central office, but retrieval from remote storage could add a day or more to turnaround time. Communicating with the office in advance of a visit may expedite delivery. The central facility may receive only summary records, so offices originating the records may have to be contacted for complete files.

Distance

Much research can be effectively conducted in online databases or through telephone calls, letters, or electronic mail. Conducting research long distance becomes more difficult for any portions requiring a personal visit to the office holding the records. Even if a researcher resides in the community being researched, some records may still be stored in another community or in an archive elsewhere in the state. Even if the records can be obtained without visiting

the office, the researcher may lose the serendipity factor of discovering nonrequested information during a visit. If it is not convenient for the researcher to travel to the government office, professional records retrievers are available for hire in most communities.

Format and Condition of Records

Is a certified copy needed? Does the researcher require paper printouts, or would other formats suffice, such as floppy disk, CD-ROM, magnetic tape, or microfiche? Perhaps the raw data are available in an accessible format. For electronic records, special software or a specific version of a program may be required. Some information might be stored on obsolete media, such as $5\frac{1}{4}''$ floppies, with no equipment readily available to run them. Audio or video recordings of meetings might be retained only until approval of the minutes. Even if recordings are retained, the quality of the tape will degrade over time. Older records may be faded, brittle, mildewed, or otherwise difficult to read, especially since preservation of records is not a high priority in many offices. Sometimes paper masters have been destroyed without checking microfilm or microfiche copies to ensure that the images are in focus and legible.

Indexing of Records

Records in one community will not necessarily be organized in the same manner as in another. Finding tools of some sort usually exist, but office staff may need to explain how to search effectively in their system. If there is no public access to the index, the research may suffer from a lack of expertise or diligence of a new staff member. The information within the records may use abbreviations and codes, so the researcher should also ask for a legend or list describing them. Older records may be organized in a cryptic manner that was understandable only to someone who retired 10 years ago. Some records may need the context of other records in a completely different file; but cross-references between the files may not exist, so the researcher somehow just has to know to ask for both records.

Costs

A few offices will provide basic information at no charge, such as photocopies of up to 10 pages free. Others may impose fees for staff time, as well as $1 or more per page for photocopies. Some public records laws allow the government offices to recover actual costs but not to charge additional fees. Even if charges are normally imposed, the researcher can ask about fee waivers. Large or repeated requests may qualify for discounts. Costs may be significantly less if the researcher can accept electronic or microfiche records and does not need paper copies. There may be no charge for looking directly at the records and hand-copying the needed information. If the researcher's time has value, it may prove more economical and fruitful to pay for access to a commercial database or to hire a professional information retriever rather than hunting through free resources.

Privatization

When private companies are engaged to provide public services, access to information crucial for public accountability may be impaired because many access laws do not specifically address this situation. The access problem has grown worse as more types of public functions traditionally performed by government employees have been privatized. Researchers may need to use government employees as intermediaries to obtain the desired information. Sometimes it may be necessary to seek a court order to gain access.

Uncooperative Record Holders

If the primary function of the government office is to maintain records and provide public access, the staff are more likely to be familiar with freedom of information (FOI) requirements. Reluctance to provide access is more likely when the target information is not commonly requested. The staff may first want to check with a supervisor to ensure that the records are not confidential. A staff member may fear repercussions if she is the one who releases information that ends up in a newspaper story about problems in her agency. Staff in centralized record offices have less personal attachment to the creation of the records. If the researcher seeks the records directly from the agency responsible for the functions reported, not only might staff be less familiar with their duty to disclose information, they might also have a tendency to circle the wagons to protect their office from intruders. In a small office, the problem might not be lack of cooperation, but simply that the individual who knows how to retrieve the specific records is not available because of vacation, illness, workshop attendance, or a meal break. If the office refuses to provide access, the researcher may need to assert his rights using the FOI

laws discussed in the next section. There are several interesting facts revealed in an article published regarding the availability of local public records. In "Hard to Open Records: Survey by 13 Papers Says Requests Denied Often," by David Noack, newspaper reporters found widespread denials of public records requests. Newspapers in other states have conducted similar surveys, with similar results, which brings credence to concerns over access issues.

FREEDOM OF INFORMATION AND PRIVACY LAWS

Background

FOI and privacy laws in the United States were enacted in the second half of the twentieth century to ensure that individuals had the right to know what personal information existed in government files and to balance that right of access with protection from inappropriate disclosure to others. Those laws will continue to change over the years as the pendulum of public opinion swings back and forth between outrage at government secrecy in hiding scandals and paranoia about invasions of personal privacy.

The Administrative Procedures Act of 1946 and the Federal Records Act of 1950 provided some congressional guidance about public access, but left federal agencies with much discretion for withholding information. The Freedom of Information Act (FOIA) of 1966 advanced public policy to a presumption that information must be disclosed unless specifically exempted. Following Watergate, the federal law was substantially amended in 1974 to narrow the exemptions. The Privacy Act of 1974 supplements FOIA regarding requests by individuals for records about themselves, as well as containing other privacy protections.

Some of the concepts behind the development of privacy procedures over the last 30 years can be seen in the 1973 Code of Fair Information Practices and the 1995 Principles for Providing and Using Personal Information. The Code of Fair Information Practices of the U.S. Department of Health, Education, and Welfare was the result of a project developed by a task force in response to concerns over the impact of computerization on medical records privacy. The code is based on five principles: (1) there must be no personal data record-keeping systems whose very existence is secret; (2) there must be a way for a person to find out what information about her is in a record and how it is used; (3) there must be a way for a person to prevent information about herself that was obtained for one purpose from being used or made available for other purposes without her consent; (4) there must be a way for a person to correct or amend a record of identifiable information about herself; and (5) any organization creating, maintaining, using, or disseminating records of identifiable personal data must ensure the reliability of the data for its intended use and must take precautions to prevent misuses of the data.

A 2002 article, "Access Wins in N.J.—After a Long Fight," by Amanda Lehmert, contends that various political forces are eroding public access to local government information. The New Jersey state legislature passed a new Open Public Records Act in 2002 that was rescinded after one day by a governor's executive order creating 583 exemptions to the act and requested that all levels of government withhold records that "materially increase" the risk of a terrorist attack. In response to public outcry, a subsequent executive order was issued after discussion between the governor's office and stakeholders that softened the effect of the original order somewhat.

Information Infrastructure, Policy, Security, and Information Privacy http://www.brint.com/NII.htm

There are many publications freely available online at this Web site. There is a nice "subject portal" arrangement, including such topics as e-government and privacy policy. This Web site has links to fascinating documents such as the white paper "Intelligence-Based Threat Assessments for Information Networks and Infrastructures," at http://www.aracnet.com/~kea/Papers/threat_white_paper.shtml, a very sophisticated assessment of risk measures surrounding the information infrastructure. Additional principles are outlined in the section of the document entitled "General Principles for All National Information Infrastructure (NII) Participants." One major point is that personal information should be acquired, disclosed, and used only in ways that respect an individual's privacy. It proposes certain strictures regarding collecting and storing personal information that encompass accuracy, completeness, judiciousness, reasonableness, relevancy, and confidentiality/protection.

State Laws

The federal FOIA usually applies only to records held by federal agencies. Nevertheless, it has influenced the development of many state laws. Discussion about the federal FOIA is also much more widely available and might provide useful advice for individ-

uals dealing with the laws of a state. Laws providing access to records at state or local government agencies now exist in every state, but vary greatly. In addition to the statutes of each state, case law and attorney general opinions have defined public records access on a state-by-state basis.

Tapping Officials' Secrets: The Door to Open Government in the 50 States and D.C. (Reporters Committee for Freedom of the Press, 4th ed., 2001) http://www.rcfp.org/tapping/index.cgi

This link is actually a Web page within a larger Web site, that of the Reporters Committee for Freedom of the Press, at http://www.rcfp.org, which has a complete compendium of information on every state's open-records and open-meetings laws. There is a search engine by topic and by state. One interesting feature is the "Compare" button, which allows a comparison of laws in a certain area, such as "records of executives" between states. Each state's section is arranged according to a standard outline, making it easy to compare laws in various states. The standard outline format often guides the user through specific questions such as, "Can the requester obtain a customized search of computer databases to fit particular needs?" The open-records section on this Web site covers basic application of the law, exemptions and other legal limitations, electronic records, open and closed record categories, and procedures for obtaining records, including a description of court actions. Lawyers in each state who use the open-records and open-meetings laws regularly write these guides. The online version provides a search function to quickly compare two or more states regarding a single outline item. The full compendium is available as a one-volume printed book or on a searchable CD-ROM. Even though the full text of this book is available for free online, paper copies for individual states are also available for purchase separately and can serve as a handy quick reference.

The Web site also provides regular news reports about FOI issues, as well as the texts of legal briefs and letters. It has published several other useful state-by-state guides with strategies for gaining access to various types of records, such as *Access to Juvenile Courts: A Reporter's Guide to Proceedings and Documents in the 50 States and D.C.* (1999) and *Access to Electronic Records: A Guide to Reporting on State and Local Government in the Computer Age* (1998).

Citizen Access Project (Brechner Center for Freedom of Information) http://www.citizenaccess.org

This online database is being developed by the Brechner Center for Freedom of Information at the College of Journalism and Communications, University of Florida, to "provide ratings, summaries and the legal language of open meetings and public records of the 50 United States and the District of Columbia." Users can compare specific provisions of access laws of 2 states or see comparative ratings for one access law category across the 50 states. Categories analyzed include whether or not the state law addresses indexing, delivery, and customizing of computer records as well as information in Geographic Information Systems. The database's resource library provides state-by-state links to statutes, legal cases, attorney general opinions, compliance audits, books, articles, and organizations.

National Freedom of Information Coalition's State and National Freedom of Information Resources http://www.nfoic.org/web/index.htm

This online resource directory provides legal code citations for each state's open-meetings and open-records laws. Also included are state contacts, form letters, lists of organizations, publications, and some links to court and attorney general opinions. A list of where to find code citations for FOIA laws in the various states is included. An index to pages with information about each of the 50 states is included. A table of code citations would look like this:

Publication Title	Title, Chapter or Section
Code of Alabama	§ 36-12-40 to § 36-12-41
Alaska Statutes	§ 40.25.110 to § 40.25.125
Arizona Revised Statutes	§ 39-121 to § 39-125
Arkansas Code	§ 25-19-101 to § 25-19-109
[California] Government Code	§ 6250 to § 6270
Colorado Revised Statutes	§ 24-72-201 to § 24-72-206
Connecticut General Statutes	§ 1-200 to § 1-241
Delaware Code	Title 29, § 10001 to § 10005, § 10112
District of Columbia Code	§ 2-531 to § 2-539
Florida Statutes	§ 119.01 to § 119.19
Georgia Code	§ 50-18-70 to § 50-18-77
Hawaii Revised Statutes	§ 92F-11 to § 92F-19
Idaho Code	§ 9-337 to § 9-349
Illinois Compiled Statutes	Chapter 5, § 140/1 to § 140/11
Indiana Code	§ 5-14-3-1 to § 5-14-3-10
Iowa Code	§ 22.1 to § 22.14
Kansas Statutes	§ 45-215 to § 45-229
Kentucky Revised Statutes	§ 61.870 to § 61.884
Louisiana Revised Statutes	§ 44.31 to § 44.37
Maine Revised Statutes	Title 1, Chapter 13, § 401 to § 410
Maryland Code	State Government, § 10-611 to § 10-628
[Massachusetts] General Laws	Chapter 66, § 10
Michigan Compiled Laws	§ 15.231 to § 15.246
Minnesota Statutes	§ 13.03
Mississippi Code	§ 25-61-1 to § 25-61-17
Missouri Revised Statutes	§ 109.180 to 109.190, § 610.010 to § 610.030
Montana Code Annotated	§ 2-6-101 to § 2-6-111
Nebraska Revised Statutes	§ 84-712 to § 84-712.09, § 84-1205.03
Nevada Revised Statutes	§ 239.005 to § 239.030
New Hampshire Revised Statutes	§ 91-A:4 to § 91-A:8
New Jersey Statutes	§ 47:1A-1 to § 47:1A-4
New Mexico Statutes	§ 14-2-1 to § 14-2-12
[New York] Public Officers Law	§ 84 to § 90
North Carolina General Statutes	§ 132-1 to § 132-10
North Dakota Century Code	§ 44-04-18
Ohio Revised Code	§ 149.43
Oklahoma Statutes	Title 51, § 24A.1 to § 24A.19
Oregon Revised Statutes	§ 192.410 to § 192.505
Pennsylvania Statutes	Title 65, § 66.1 to § 66.4
Rhode Island General Laws	§ 38-2-1 to § 38-2-15
South Carolina Code of Laws	§ 30-4-10 to § 30-4-165
South Dakota Codified Laws	§ 1-27-1 to § 1-27-3
Tennessee Code	§ 10-7-503 to § 10-7-507
Texas Statutes: Government Code	§ 552.001 to § 552.353
Utah Code	§ 63-2-101 to § 63-2-1001
Vermont Statutes	Title 1, § 315 to § 320
Code of Virginia	§ 2.2-3700 to § 2.2-3714
Revised Code of Washington	§ 42.17.250 to § 42.17.348
West Virginia Code	§ 29B-1-1 to § 29B-1-7
Wisconsin Statutes	§ 19.31 to § 19.39
Wyoming Statutes	§ 16-4-202 to § 16-4-205

State Freedom of Information Laws

Florida Government-in-the-Sunshine Manual (Tallahassee: First Amendment Foundation, Annual) http://legal.firn.edu/sunshine/index.html

The Florida Attorney General's Office updates this guide to Florida's open-meetings and open-records laws each year to incorporate new court decisions, attorney general opinions, and legislation. The statutory provisions are clarified by the discussion of case law and opinions from the attorney general interpreting and applying the law. An abridged version is available for free online. Similar guides are published in many other states by the attorneys general, press organizations, first amendment organizations, and bar associations.

Access Denied: Freedom of Information in the Information Age, ed. Charles N. Davis and Sigman L. Splichal (Iowa State University Press, 2000)

The state-by-state analysis in chapter 2 of *Access Denied* examines differences in access policy for electronic formats of information that are publicly available in print. Also discussed are issues of e-mail, software, fees, and customized records. Chapter 3 analyzes access laws in each state regarding public meetings that use media technology such as fax transmissions, e-mail, and video- and teleconferencing. Chapter 4 highlights the issues associated with privatization of government services. The remaining chapters provide a sense of how the policies are evolving, including coverage of issues such as public opinion, court rulings, and the difficulties of balancing access with privacy concerns.

The public access and privacy laws throughout the nation are influenced by events that sometimes cause a ripple effect from state to state. Florida's public records law was enacted in 1909 and is one of the oldest and strongest in the nation, but each year there are dozens of legislative bills proposed to modify it by providing additional exemptions or clarifying existing policies. Following Dale Earnhardt's auto racing death in 2001, the Florida legislature closed access to autopsy photographs, a change that may be replicated in other states.

Ease of searching for recent and proposed changes in the law varies from state to state. Florida's Online Sunshine Web site, http://www.leg.state.fl.us, the official site of the state legislature, provides the text of proposed bills, but sometimes the initial filing includes only a vague description of the bill. The actual text of the changes may be developed in committee, which means that public access and privacy advocates must be vigilant when the legislature is in session.

Compliance

Open Records Surveys (Freedom of Information Center, University of Missouri) http://foi.missouri.edu/openrecseries.html

State press associations, newspapers, and academic groups have conducted studies in many states to scrutinize the effectiveness of local open-records laws. Most studies have found that local officials routinely block access to records that by law should be open to the public. The linked surveys on this Web site describe the specific problems encountered by individuals seeking access. Most of the reports suggest that programs be implemented to educate government workers about the law.

Open Doors: Accessing Government Records (Society of Professional Journalists) http://www.spj.org/foia_opendoors.asp

This December 2001 study includes a list of red flags to watch for as indicators of problems with FOIA; for instance, "a government agency announces a new policy to close certain records or institute new procedures for requesting records." The FOIA "A to Z" section describes how various types of records or problems accessing them can be used as the basis for news stories. The Society of Professional Journalists works to maintain the flow of information in order to support a free press as "the cornerstone of our nation and our liberty." Through Project Sunshine, its volunteers "are on the front lines for assaults to the First Amendment and when lawmakers attempt to restrict the public's access to documents and the government's business."

Sample Freedom of Information Act Letters

State Open Records Law Request Letter Generator (Student Press Law Center) http://www.splc.org/foiletter.asp

This resource prompts responses to a series of fill-in-the-blank questions to create a letter customized to cite the appropriate public records law of a specific state. Users need to provide "a reasonable description" of the public records they are seeking and the name and address of the government official they "believe to be responsible for keeping those records." The Student Press Law Center also provides information, advice, and legal assistance at no charge to student journalists and the educators who work with them. The Web site includes legal research resources about access to records, meetings, and places or facilities. Other sample letters for specific states may be available from various organizations. Another FOIA letter generator is available from the Reporters Committee for Freedom of the Press, http://www.rcfp.org/foi_lett.html.

California First Amendment Coalition http://www. cfac.org/Law/CPRA/sample_request.html

This Web site lists some do's and don'ts in requesting records under the California Public Records Act and gives an example of what a letter should look like. A particularly expedient suggestion is, "I am sending a copy of this letter to your legal advisor to help encourage a speedy determination, and I would likewise be happy to discuss my request with [him/her] at any time."

Marion Brechner Citizen Access Project (University of Florida) http://www.citizenaccess.org

A similar Web address is provided for the state of Florida to assist the public in filing requests for public records under the state Public Records Act. Figure 1.1 is a sample public records request.

Guides to the Federal Freedom of Information Act

Tips for effectively using the specific public records laws of individual states may not be readily available. Even though federal laws may differ from those of individual states, researchers might glean useful advice from various guides that have been prepared regarding the federal FOIA.

How to Use the Federal FOI Act (Ed. Rebecca Daugherty; Reporters Committee for Freedom of the Press, 1998) http://www.rcfp.org/foiact/index. html

This online document and 33-page pamphlet provides practical guidance to journalists and others for using the federal FOIA as "an effective investigative tool." It includes sample letters and discusses fee waivers and expedited requests. Procedures described include a suggestion that the researcher first try informal means, such as a telephone call, before submitting a formal written request. It also recommends that separate letters be sent to agency headquarters and field offices, since a single request might limit the search to the central files.

A Citizen's Guide on Using the Freedom of Information Act and the Privacy Act of 1974 to Request Government Records (United States House of Representatives, House Report 107-371, 2002)

First issued in 1977, this report has been published during the first session of each Congress since 1987,

but was delayed until the second session in 2002. It provides guidelines for making requests, including sample request and appeal letters. An electronic copy can be retrieved from the Library of Congress/ Thomas Web site, http://thomas.loc.gov/cgi-bin/ cpquery/z?cp106:hr50.106, by searching for the phrase *freedom of information act* in the House Reports from the current or previous congressional sessions.

HOW TO OBTAIN A PUBLIC RECORD

Obtaining public records has become more complex than before, if that is possible. The trail that begins with birth and (sometimes) ends with death has become increasingly complex and voluminous. The definition of a public record is: "Those records maintained by government agencies that are generally open without restriction to public inspection, either by statute or by tradition" (Ernst et al. p.7). Accessibility varies, and it may be necessary to research the structure of the local government as well as the record-keeping practices of various agencies to determine where to go to find a public record.

Sourcebook to Public Record Information (4th ed., BRB Publications, 2002)

This is an excellent source of information about locating public records at all levels of government, from federal down to local. It is organized beginning with a few sections describing categories of public records and search tools. General information on obtaining public records is followed by information on finding electronic records. There is a chapter for each state, outlining state categories such as agencies, licensing boards, courts, county offices, and some municipal courts, although it does not go down to the level of individual municipalities. The usefulness of names and addresses of county courts will be detailed later in the present book. What makes the *Sourcebook* really valuable is the contact information provided. It is possible to obtain information using the Internet, but not all cities have an Internet presence yet. Also, while e-mail contact is very efficient, those seeking public records often need certified copies of original documents. It is often necessary to determine the type of record being sought in order to ascertain where it was produced and where it might be located.

Date
Records Custodian
Government Building
Anywhere, FL 54321

Dear Records Custodian,

Pursuant to the Florida Public Records Law, Chapter 119 of the Florida Statutes, I request access to review and photocopy: (List all records you wish to review, including any specifics such as governmental offices, public officials, issues of importance, names or dates. In this section, be as specific as possible in describing the records you want. This enables the custodian to process your request more quickly and avoids unnecessary costs associated with records searches.)

I am willing to pay all lawful and reasonable costs associated with this request. Please notify me in advance what those costs will be.

If you intend to deny this public request in whole or part, I request that you advise me in writing of the particular statutory exemption upon which you are relying, and an explanation for doing so, as required by Chapter 119 of the Florida Statutes. Additionally, if the exemption you are claiming applies to only a portion of a record, please delete the exempted section and release the remainder of the record as required by law.

In light of the nature and importance of the records requested, please make them available by (The public records law provides no definitive time limit for fulfilling records requests, but states that agencies must respond to records requests within a reasonable period of time.) If you have any questions about this request, please call me at (your number.)

Thank you in advance for processing my request.

Sincerely,

Concerned Citizen

Figure 1.1 A sample public records request letter.

This publication is also available online. A free demo is available at http://www.publicrecordsources.com.

Local Court and County Record Retrievers (BRB Publications, 2003)

This resource is a very nice, organized approach to finding record retrievers in local areas. Often it is not cost- or time-efficient to actually go to a remote area to retrieve a local government record. When the retrieval cannot be accomplished by mail, telephone, or fax, sometimes a personal visit is required. This book provides an alternative to a costly trip to obtain a public record. It is organized by state and lists names of firms or individuals, with telephone numbers, who will actually get the records, for a fee. There is also a profile of each firm or individual, providing contact information, what he or she will do, and what the cost will be in more detail. If a certain county does not have a record retriever, one in a nearby county may be helpful. The listings are geographical by state and alphabetical by the name of the record retriever.

ALTERNATE SOURCES OF INFORMATION

There are other sources of information to be considered when looking for local government records. Because of agencies changing over time, other government agencies may have information essential to the search. Public and academic libraries often have collections of local government documents. They do not usually systematically keep government records. Some are collected and held for their research value. Archives are described in chapter 3. Personal collections, as well as those of organizations, can also be consulted. For lists of libraries, do a Web search for *libraries* or *reference libraries*, for instance on Yahoo at http://dir.yahoo.com/Reference/Libraries. Listings of government agencies are referred to in several places in this book.

FOR FURTHER READING

Ciccariello, Priscilla. "Local Government Document Collections: Why, What, How, Whither?" *The Bookmark* 44 (summer 1986): 195–99.

Coyle, Karen. "Make Sure You Are Privacy Literate." *Library Journal* 127.16 (2002): 55–57.

Ernst, Carl, et al. *Sourcebook to Public Record Information.* Tempe, AZ: BRB Publications, 2002.

Gellman, Robert M. "Public Records—Access, Privacy, and Public Policy: A Discussion Paper." *Government Information Quarterly* 12.4 (1995): 391–426.

Lehmert, Amanda. "Access Wins in N.J.—After a Long Fight." *The Quill* 90.7 (2002): 25–26.

———. "Making Open Records a Right." *The Quill* 90.7 (2002): 28–29.

Minow, Mary. "The USA Patriot Act." *Library Journal* 127.16 (2002): 52–55.

Noack, David. "Hard to Open Records: Survey by 13 Papers Says Requests Denied Often." *Editor & Publisher, the Fourth Estate* 132.20 (1999): 20.

Strickland, Lee S. "Information and the War against Terrorism, Part IV: Civil Liberties versus Security in the Age of Terrorism." *Bulletin of the American Society for Information Science and Technology* 28.4 (2002): 9–13.

U.S. Dept. of Health, Education, and Welfare. *Secretary's Advisory Committee on Automated Personal Data Systems, Records, Computers, and the Rights of Citizens.* Washington, DC: U.S. Government Printing Office, 1973. viii.

CHAPTER 2
Forms of Local Government Structure

Marianne Mason

MAJOR TOPICS DISCUSSED

MAJOR RESOURCES

INTRODUCTION

The authority that a governmental body wields, the services it provides, and the method of gaining and spending its financial resources are often the best ways to identify government entities whether municipal, county, or intergovernmental/regional. Many of these responsibilities are outlined and defined through the individual state's code, as are options for types of government structure within the state. However, the codification of laws and constitution provide only broad brushstrokes in outlining governing provisions. Responsibility for providing services to the public may overlap geographic and jurisdictional boundaries and vary from one jurisdiction to another. Consequently, citizens may find it difficult to know which government entity to praise or blame for services rendered.

The purpose of this chapter is to describe the basic forms of local government, outline methods of identifying how government entities are organized, present the structure of a typical government organization, and describe selected resources for further exploration of issues relating to forms of local government. For background needed to understand these jurisdictions, scholars have attempted to explain the function, types, and structure of local government through journal articles, handbooks, and treatises. In addition, organizations that support practitioners of local government have provided a vehicle for communication, cooperation, and coordination of activities through research studies, program events, and other information-sharing mechanisms. The most important of these secondary sources are described within this chapter.

It is important to note that there are untold variations to the basic forms of local government. However, those described in this chapter are the acknowledged models upon which others are based.

GENERAL INFORMATION SOURCES

Forms of Local Government: A Handbook on City, County and Regional Options, ed. by Roger L. Kemp (Roger L. McFarland, 1999)

This volume combines basic information about the past, present, and future of local governments' structure with issues, studies, and examples of interest to local public officials and citizens. The goal of this publication is to address in a single volume all forms of government on the municipal, county, and regional level. Concepts of home rule, benefits and disadvantages of government structure options, efficiency and effectiveness of partnerships, models of governance, challenges presented by rural counties, and the woes of "suburbanites" are introduced and discussed, and the issues explained in a very user friendly format for local officials and concerned citizens.

State and Local Government: Fundamentals and Perspectives, by Michael Engel (Peter Lang, 1999)

This resource presents the study of local government through a political lens introducing theories and ideologies applied to the structure of local government and political action. The author presents political theories that may be applied to the understanding of local government functions and activities as a means to promote citizen advocacy. Policy issues of public finance, economic development, welfare, and education are addressed in comparison of conservative, liberal, and socialist ideologies.

State and Local Government on the Net
http://www.statelocalgov.net/index.cfm

Compiled by Piper Resources, this is an Internet directory of more than 7,000 links to government-sponsored resources. The goal of the site is to present a wide range of government information at all jurisdictional levels. Piper's criteria for inclusion is that the linked site be controlled or managed by the government agency that claims responsibility for the information provided and that the content be more substantial than that found in a brochure or telephone directory listing. The site is divided by broad jurisdictional categories, but of particular interest in the context of local government resources is the section of individual state links. The arrangement of subcategories is uniform for all states providing links to boards and commissions, regional organizations, counties, cities, related links, and a list of libraries within the state arranged by library type. Change is the only constant of the Internet, but a few of the most reliable Internet sites providing general links to state and local sources are listed here. These Web sites duplicate one another in some aspects but have individual strengths that the user must evaluate on the basis of information needed.

Local Governments and Politics http://www.lib. umich.edu/govdocs/pslocal.html

This Web site was created by Grace York at the University of Michigan Documents Center and includes links to directories, yearbooks, library holdings of specific publications, links to municipal codes, association and think tank Web sites, as well as subject-specific Web collections. An example of an interesting link is the one to the National Association of Government Archives Administrators, http://www.nagara.org.

State and Local Governments http://www.loc.gov/ global/state/stategov.html

This Web site, created by the Library of Congress, provides links to meta-indexes of government information, supporting organizations' sites, and individual states' government Web collections. An example of a particularly interesting link here is the "Local Government" page of GovSpot, at http://www.govspot.com/ categories/localgovernment.htm, which includes links to city, county, and state Web sites.

State and Local Task Force Information http://www. library.arizona.edu/users/arawan/stat.html

This is a Web site created by librarians at the University of Arizona on behalf of the American Library Association, Government Documents Round Table, State and Local Task Force, and it provides links to guides to sources, state documents checklists, bibliographies of resources, city and county directories, meta-indexes, and related sites. A Web page called Government Resources on the Web, at http://www. library.arizona.edu/library/teams/sst/pol/guide/metain dexes.html, provides links to a variety of resources such as the National Center for State Courts, http://www.ncsconline.org, and Government Redistricting Web Sites, at http://www.lib.purdue.edu/ govdocs/redistricting.html.

Please remember that, with few exceptions, the official and authoritative code for any jurisdiction *is still considered to be the paper version.* Check with your local government offices or library.

MUNICIPAL GOVERNMENT

The work of municipalities is to administer and finance services that directly impact the citizens who reside within their boundaries. Basic services that affect daily life such as primary and secondary education, public safety, sanitation, water, street maintenance, libraries, and parks and recreation are among those provided.

Authority to Govern

Municipal charters are granted through the state's legislature and specify the civic boundaries, governmental structure, and limits of municipal authority. The state code, which is the compilation of all state laws that are currently in effect, also outlines, describes, and defines the various forms of city-government organization options. The code may also identify appointed offices, specify elective officer posts, and prescribe their respective powers and duties. Generally, the text of a city charter can be found in the codification of municipal ordinances. Contrasting these two terms, the charter establishes the government, while ordinances are the issue-driven enacted local laws.

Home rule authority is also granted through the state code. The principle of home rule provides local government officials with discretionary powers to deal with matters of local importance without having to seek special grants of authority from the state. Although most state codes have given home rule authority to municipalities, not all municipalities exercise that authority. For many years, cities and towns were restricted by "Dillon's Rule," a court decision that allowed municipalities to do only those things specifically authorized by state legislative enactment.

Forms of Municipal Government

Mayor–Council

The elected mayor is the chief executive of the municipality who works in tandem with an elected council. Each branch of this type of government serves a two- or four-year term. Depending on the city charter, mayoral powers may vary in breadth of authority. A strong mayor has veto power over bills passed by the council, may have voting rights on council, appoints or removes department heads, and formulates the budget. The mayoral system is not as strong if responsibility for budgetary matters or the appointment of departmental administrators rests with council.

Council–Manager

The council form of government places primary authority with the elected council, which hires an appointed executive or manager. The manager is the professional administrator of the municipality, whose tenure is performance driven and who serves at the council's pleasure. The theory is that the manager is a nonpartisan professional administrator who conducts municipal affairs in a businesslike fashion, while the council members are responsible for policymaking and are more politically involved with the community. The mayor in these municipalities is a member of the council without veto or administrative powers but is the recognized political leader and spokesman for the community.

Commission

The commission form of government has no provision for a single executive. Voters elect a legislative body or commission, generally three, five, or seven members, who are responsible for all executive and administrative activities of the municipality. Each member also serves as an executive department head. The commission is presided over by one of its members, who often has the title of mayor. The mayor may be elected by the citizens or selected by the commission.

Town Meeting

In the town meeting form of government, an annual meeting in which all voters may participate is considered the legislative assembly and the attendees are the legislators who have the authority to pass bylaws and to deal with budgetary issues. At least one annual meeting must be held, but additional meetings may be held as needed. During the rest of the year an elected board of three or more selectmen manage daily municipal activities. A variation of this system is the *representative town meeting* form of government, in which voters elect a small group of citizens to represent the larger community. Meetings and debate are open to all, but only the elected representatives have voting rights.

Selected Sources of Municipal Information

The following resources are useful for obtaining information on local government issues, finances, and services.

Municipal Year Book (International City/County Management Association [ICMA], annual)

This annual publication provides practitioners and researchers with information on local government management issues, developments and trends in policy, intergovernmental topics, staffing and salary reports, and a directory of municipal officials. Published since 1934 under this title, it is considered the successor to the *City Manager Yearbook*, published from 1914 to 1933. The *Year Book* contains signed articles by local, state, and federal government agency experts; university scholars; and representatives of public interest groups. A significant component in each edition of the *Year Book* is the data compiled and analyzed by ICMA from its own surveys. Research questionnaires are distributed by ICMA annually to city and county managers, clerks, finance officers, personnel directors, police chiefs, and fire chiefs, among others, on a wide range of topics. The results are analyzed and represented as statistical reports. Recent editions include discussions of Supreme Court decisions and federal legislation impacting local government. Each annual edition is unique, with articles indexed through a cumulative index covering a discrete period of time.

Statistical Research Index (SRI) (Congressional Information Service [CIS], annual and online) http://www.lexisnexis.com/academic/universe/statistical

It is important to note that reports and articles containing statistical data are indexed through SRI, published by CIS, making individual reports accessible to a broad audience. The publication is not solely a source of municipal information, but a valuable source of county and regional government information as well. This publication is available through Statistical Universe at the Web address given.

Municipal Codes (Seattle Public Library) http://www.spl.org/selectedsites/municode.html

The Seattle Public Library maintains a Web site that has several links to other Web sites that have municipal codes available online. This list includes links to Municode, at http://www.municode.com, which is a source of free online municipal codes and a product of the Municipal Code Corporation, a major publisher of codified municipal laws and ordinances. There are, however, only selected cities with municipal codes available online. Municipal codes often include a description of the form of government of the city.

Supporting Associations and Organizations

International City/County Management Association http://www.icma.org

An organization that is equally important to both city and county governments is the ICMA. Its mission is to "enhance the quality of local government and to support and assist professional local government managers and administrators." Serving as an educational and professional development resource for professional administrators of local government, ICMA provides training materials and sponsors seminars and research on issues relating to local government management. The organization was formed in 1914 in response to the introduction of professional managers into municipal governments. As county government evolved to a more professionally managed system in the 1960s, ICMA broadened its mission to include support for county managers. This ICMA Web site is a significant resource for ICMA initiatives. Among the information available are documents published as issue papers on selected topics of importance to local government administrators. For example, forms of government are discussed in the "Issues Intersection" segment with several full-text documents related to understanding local government structure and responsibilities of the manager. With each brief topic description, links are provided to online discussion groups, news on legislative information, full texts of brief documents, access to the online catalog of publications for sale through ICMA, and links to related Web sites. The professional development portion of the site includes the calendar of seminars and workshops, preferred management practices, and references to training and assessment materials available through the ICMA bookstore. Of special note are the links provided to specific local government management associations and ICMA-affiliated organizations.

National Civic League. http://www.ncl.org

One of the oldest organizations supporting innovative problem solving in municipal government is the National Civic League (NCL). It was formed in 1894 as the National Municipal League in response to "widespread municipal government corruption," with its purpose being to "raise the popular standards of political morality." This nonpartisan, nonprofit organization takes a grassroots approach to government involvement by citizens and supports local government officials. The NCL continues to provide programs that foster principles of good government through technical assistance to communities, promotion of reform efforts, and publication of resource materials. The NCL's Web site includes the history of the league, its vision statement, organizational directory, membership information, publications list, and contact information. Publications may be ordered online, including the seventh edition of the Model City Charter. The NCL created the first Model City Charter in 1900 and is currently developing the eighth edition.

Local Government Institute http://www.lgi.org

The Local Government Institute (LGI) is a nonprofit organization whose mission is to improve the quality of local government in the English-speaking world. LGI provides technical assistance; develops reference resources including software, how-to guides and reference materials; and offers services such as consulting and advocacy on behalf of local governments, with a particular focus on municipalities. LGI's primary emphasis is on issues relating to human resources administration, governance, and community development. The contents of the LGI Web site include links to job postings in local governments, at http://www.govtjob.net, project proposals and initiatives listings, a consultants directory, related organizations, and an online bookstore for LGI practice-based publications.

National League of Cities http://www.nlc.org/ nlc_org/site

The purpose of the National League of Cities (NLC) is to strengthen and promote cities as centers of opportunity, leadership, and governance and serve as an advocate for cities and towns through lobbying activities. Its Web site provides links to organization leadership contacts, policy and legislative initiatives, programs, membership information, links to related state organizations, conference schedules, and the online newsletter *Nation's Cities Weekly*. An online service called CityNET is a password-protected information resource and message board for members to post questions and share information. The online publications catalog is topically arranged and describes NLC publications that are primarily issue based.

U.S. Conference of Mayors http://www.usmayors. org/USCM/home.asp

The U.S. Conference of Mayors (USCM) is a nonpartisan organization of elected mayors of cities with populations of 30,000 or more. The mission of USCM is to promote effective urban/suburban policy, strengthen federal/municipal relationships, ensure that federal policy meets urban needs, and provide mayors with leadership and management tools and a forum to share ideas. Contents of the USCM Web site include a best practices database, a directory of mayors, online bookstore of USCM publications, legislative updates, and descriptions of projects and services.

A Sample Government from Iowa: Iowa City

Each city's charter, which is found in the compilation of municipal ordinances, outlines the form of government for that particular municipality. So the search begins in the Iowa City Charter. There are two format choices for searching the *City of Iowa City Code*. The paper version is available at the city clerk's office and the public library, and the Internet version is on the city's Web site, http://www.icgov.org, under the "City Code" option on the home page. The site is updated every six weeks.

The charter is the first section within the codification of ordinances preceding Title 1 of the code. The charter is organized in three parts. The preamble states principles guiding the governance of the city, followed by a section of definitions and the eight articles of the charter:

Article I outlines the powers of the city.
Article II describes the city council, including general powers and duties.
Article III specifies election issues.
Article IV describes the city manager post, including appointment, removal, and duties.
Article V outlines the establishment, appointment, and rules of operation of boards.

Article VI governs campaign contributions and expenditures.

Article VII outlines electorate initiative and referendum options.

Article VIII describes options for amending the charter.

Iowa City is governed by an elected council and an appointed manager, a typical council–manager form of government. Article II specifies the composition of council; outlines districts; defines eligibility, terms, and compensation of council members; and describes the post of mayor.

COUNTY GOVERNMENT

The role of a county government is threefold. First, it carries out administrative duties required by the state and federal governments, which mandate programs related to health, welfare, courts, corrections, roads, tax administration, vital statistics, and elections. Second, counties provide municipal services for unincorporated areas, such as road repair, police and fire protection, and garbage collection. Third, county government often coordinates city services and programs across municipal boundaries. Services provided by the county include provision and administration of corrections facilities, courts, mental health programs, indigent health care, welfare programs, public health programs, property-value assessments, garbage disposal, pollution control, arterial and collector roads, vital statistics/records, and regulatory standards. The county code identifies the type of governing board established for that particular jurisdiction.

Authority to Govern

Elected county officers, frequently referred to as row officers, are in place as mandated by the state code, which outlines corresponding responsibilities. The term *row officer* refers to organizational charts that list row after row of titles. These officers could include the assessor, attorney, auditor, clerk, coroner, district attorney, election supervisor, prosecutor, recorder, sheriff, superintendent of schools, and surveyor.

Forms of County Government

Commission Form

Sometimes referred to as a *plural executive* form of government, this government structure is characterized by a governing group of members, usually three or five individuals, who typically have been elected by a district. Most commonly, this group is known as a board of commissioners or supervisors, council, county court, or levying court. The board has varying degrees of executive and legislative powers and its members serve either a two- or four-year term of office. Executive powers may include administration of local, state, and federal policies, appointment of county employees, and supervision of road maintenance. Legislative authority may include enacting ordinances, levying special taxes, and adopting budgets. The board usually selects one of its members to serve as the presiding officer; however, no single administrator is responsible for all county operations. Most often, each board member serves as a department head and shares administrative duties with independently elected office holders (row officers).

Council–Administrator Form

Trends toward adopting more professional management strategies in counties have led to the development of this form of government structure, in which a county board is elected and an administrator is appointed by the board. Other titles for the administrator include chief administrative officer or county manager. In this type of governance, the board has legislative and policymaking functions, while the administrator is responsible for important staff and administrative functions. The responsibilities of the board include adopting ordinances and budgets and setting policy, while the administrator drafts ordinances, proposes and implements budgets, and recommends policy. With the title of county administrative assistant, however, a manager may have her responsibility limited in county operations and hiring practices.

Council–Elected Executive Form

This form of county government represents a parallel to the elected mayor and elected council on the municipal level, with similar separation of powers representing the executive and legislative branches of government. Because the executive is elected, that position holds more political clout than in the council–administrator form. The executive administers county business, appoints department heads, recommends public policy to the council, prepares the budget, enforces county policy, has veto power over council decisions, and is considered the formal county representative. The council adopts policies, approves the budget, audits financial performance of the county, and may override the executive's veto.

Other County Government Structures

City–County Consolidation

Consolidation provides a joint governing body for all government services in the combined city and county area. The goal is to increase services, efficiency, and cost saving. In consolidated government, the mayor may speak for the region.

Home Rule or Charter Form

County voters are granted the right to adopt, amend, revise, or repeal a county charter through provisions established by the state's constitution or by statute. Although home rule does not free counties from obligations required by state law, it allows for local citizens to provide solutions to their unique problems without excessive state involvement.

Community Commonwealth

Adjoining jurisdictions including counties, municipalities, and/or townships within the county may unite to form an alternative government to make more efficient use of their resources.

Multicounty Consolidation

Two or more counties may merge as a single organization while retaining their original geographic boundaries, with governing officers drawn from each county. The goal is increased efficiency resulting in more cost-effective provision of services.

Township Board/Trustees

In this type of county government, the township supervisor serves as the township administrator as well as a member of the county board of supervisors.

Selected Sources of County Information

Some older works often cited and considered research classics in the literature of county government are worthy of note, even though they are no longer in print.

County Government in America and *Modern County Government*, by Herbert Sidney Duncombe (National Association of Counties Research Foundation, 1966 and 1977, respectively)

These two classic publications trace the origins of county government, the evolution and reforms that have taken place in the United States in the twentieth century, political aspects of local government, service to the public, and how services are financed. Charts, diagrams, statistical tables, and case studies abound in both publications.

County Year Book (National Association of Counties and International City/County Management Association, annual)

The *County Year Book* called itself "the authoritative source book on county governments" during the four years it was published, from 1975 through 1978. Jointly published by the National Association of Counties (NACo) and the ICMA, this resource is similar in format to the *Municipal Year Book* described in the previous section. Many of the articles are based on the results of annual surveys completed by county officials that are presented and interpreted by NACo. Signed articles by researchers and scholars on issues ranging from basic concepts of government organization to federal actions that affect county government are a major component of the publication. Profiles of individual counties through charts, graphs, and tables are abundant. Each volume shares a similar format with data specific to that year, but articles are unique to each edition, making the cumulative index at the back of each year particularly useful.

County Government Structure: A State by State Report, by Blake R. Jeffery (National Association of Counties, 1989)

Unique in coverage, this heavily cited work is a comprehensive documentation of the government structure for every county in the United States through narratives, tables, and graphics. Included is a brief historical overview of county government with explanatory notes of basic forms. Important principles and terms are defined in a succinct narrative. Row officers are given particular attention through an overview description followed by state-by-state enumeration of officers. A table outlining county government structure is followed by a detailed state-by-state county government summary. This publication is currently available for purchase at the NACo Internet site: http://www.naco.org.

The American County: Frontiers of Knowledge, ed. by Donald C. Menzel (University of Alabama Press, 1996)

The American County: Frontiers of Knowledge is a volume that takes a broad view of issues relating to county government, including the history and development of the current forms of government. It reviews current issues of concern to counties and provides the basic knowledge for understanding county government while identifying areas that need to be further addressed. Categories of change, structure and governance, management, fiscal policies, and trends provide the foundation for the text while providing ample references for further exploration of the subject by citizens, practitioners, and scholars.

Supporting Associations and Organizations

National Association of Counties
http://www.naco.org

The NACo is the only national organization that specifically supports county governments and serves as an advocate for legislative, lobbying, educational, programming, technical support, and research endeavors. Its Web site describes membership services that include an overview and history of the organization, contact listings, access to the NACo publications catalog, descriptions of projects and programs, calendar of seminars and events, and links to individual county associations in 48 states and affiliate organizations. Caucuses, which are independent of NACo but whose membership meets during its conferences, were formed to promote discussion of the special needs of urban, rural, minority, and political groups in county governments. Several publications are available online, including *County News*, the NACo's biweekly newspaper containing news that affects county government, ranging from federal legislation to county-level news; *Legislative News*, the weekly legislative report issued when Congress is in session; *Leadership Letter*, a biweekly newsletter of programs and activities; *Coast to Coast*, county news published every two months; and *County Environmental Quarterly*, on these programs.

NACo is the parent organization of four subsidiaries: (1) the NACo Research Foundation, which sponsors management and servicing of federal grants and contracts; research and training; satellite- and videoconferencing; corporate member program; premier member program; the Information Technology Center for Counties, and publication of *County News*; (2) the NACo Service Corporation, which is responsible for development, management, and oversight of public/private partnerships; (3) the NACo Financial Services Corporation, which provides products and financial services to governments and its employees;

and (4) the NACo Financial Services Center, which provides services in insurance, employee retirement, banking, and public finance to counties and their employees.

Previously described as a supporting organization for municipal government, NACo is equally valuable to the county manager, particularly in the council–administrator form of government.

The Innovation Groups http://www.ig.org

The Innovation Groups (IG) is a nonprofit, membership-based organization that supports communication and information sharing between city, town, and county governments. Online member services are available through the IG Web site and include an electronic bulletin board, consulting services, and an online library of IG publications and access to shared local documents. IG sponsors two monthly publications. The *IGnewsletter* provides local government news, product information, and management perspectives. Another publication, *Inews*, publishes articles that are issue based, distributed by e-mail to IG members. Meetings, workshops, and satellite conferences are held throughout the year on issues related to local government.

A Sample Government from Iowa: Johnson County

Beginning a search for county government information is often a coin toss. The state code, which defines the various forms of county government sanctioned by the legislature, may be the best source to consult to build a vocabulary of forms of government and get information regarding the responsibilities of counties in general. On the other hand, only the county code of ordinances can identify what choice of government organization the county has selected within the state's parameters. Muddying the water further is the fact that the county code, which will always identify the type of county governance, may not include a charter document that specifically defines the governing body. Johnson County, Iowa, is one such county. The *Johnson County Ordinance Book* (in two volumes), which is housed in the county auditor's office, identifies the board of supervisors as the governing body in Johnson County (chapter 1:1). The board of supervisors form of government was established by resolution, although no reference to the specific resolution has been found. Resolutions, meeting minutes, and the ordinance book are maintained in the county auditor's office with records dating from the mid-1830s. Records are chronologically arranged but not indexed by subject. The spidery web of the various forms of record keeping are fascinating to observe, but difficult to decipher. Records from some years are missing as the result of housekeeping decisions made long ago. Instead of relying on official records, the *Johnson County Home Page*, at http://www.johnson-county.com, answers the basic questions about the structure and form of local government. At the *Johnson County Home Page*, select "Departments" and then "Board of Supervisors" to find organizational information about the workings of the board. Among the many links provided are "Meet the Board of Supervisors," "Meeting Information," "Minutes and Agendas," "Duties of the Board of Supervisors," and the "Johnson County Organizational Chart."

The description of the responsibilities of the board of supervisors found on the Web site is as follows:

The Board of Supervisors is composed of five members, elected at large, with each serving a four year term. Any vacancy occurring in the Board in the interim between elections is filled by appointment by a committee of the County Auditor, the County Treasurer and the County Recorder. The Board is the legislative body of the county and is empowered to:

Make appointments to non-elective county offices and to county boards and commissions.
Fill vacancies in elective county offices occurring in the interim between elections except vacancies occurring in its own membership.
Approve compensation for county employees other than elected officials and, subject to the limitations imposed by the Compensation Board, approve compensation for elected officials.
Allow claims against the County and order payment of those claims.
Enter into contracts in the name of the County for the purchase, sale, or lease of property, including real estate, and for the purchase of services.
Require reports of county officers on subjects connected with the duties of their offices.
Approve budget proposals of county offices and levy property taxes to raise revenues.
Manage all county buildings and grounds.
Supervise construction and maintenance of the secondary roads system. Establish building zones for unincorporated areas of the County.
Make official canvass of votes cast in the County for elections.

Approve applications for beer, liquor, and cigarette sale permits for establishments outside incorporated areas.
Approve homestead tax credit applications and military service tax credit applications.

Links to information about current supervisors are provided here as well.

Although there are two volumes of the *Johnson County Ordinance Book*, only volume 2, at http://www.johnson-county.com/zoning/ordinances.shtml, which covers property and land issues, is on the Web and is available through the site index page under the heading "Code of Ordinances." Volume 1 is housed in the auditor's office.

REGIONAL GOVERNMENT

Due to increased federal and state regulatory demands placed on local jurisdictions, cooperative partnerships are often the most efficient and cost-effective means of compliance. Complexities of providing services to diverse populations create an additional impetus to share financial resources, technical expertise, and organizational clout. City to city, city to county, county to county, state to state, and other configurations of partnerships provide the means to deal with interjurisdictional issues such as the environment, transportation, economic development, employment training, housing, disaster preparedness, and community planning. These regional partnerships may be referred to as development districts, intergovernmental councils, councils of governments (COGs), or metropolitan planning organizations (MPOs), depending on the jurisdictions involved.

Authority to Govern

As with municipalities and counties, joint governmental activities are outlined through the state's codification of laws. However, the code often provides more detail in specifying the organizational structure and authority of regional organizations and special districts. Whether these entities are joining forces to provide a specific public service, establish a regional planning council, or form an advisory body, the code specifies among other things the purpose, composition, and powers of the governing body and membership of the organization. At the same time, intergovernmental organizations are given wide authority to address issues of mutual interest.

Forms of Regional Government

Regional Planning Commission

This type of organization may be composed of a single county, a multicounty entity, or multiple jurisdictions and is governed by a board composed of citizens who may include elected officials from each county/jurisdiction. These commissions exist to prepare plans, provide technical assistance, and administer regulations as required by the state or federal government. Multiple states may also form regional planning commissions, which may require congressional approval to be formed.

Councils of Governments

COGs may carry out planning activities, but their responsibilities extend to any service needed by a member government, provided the entire membership agrees upon that action. The structure usually involves appointed representatives from each member government but may also include representatives from relevant organizations in the region.

Metropolitan Planning Organizations

MPOs are concerned with interagency programs such as transportation, economic development, and comprehensive planning issues in adjoining urban areas. Often, MPOs allow local officials to have greater control over federally mandated programs that affect their communities than communities that do not have MPOs.

Selected Sources of Regional Government Information

Substate Regionalism and the Federal System. Vol. 1, Regional Decision Making: New Strategies for Substate Districts (United States Advisory Commission on Intergovernmental Relations [USACIR], 1973–74)

Among the many publications issued by the USACIR, this is the most directly relevant to the topic of forms of regional government. Although rather dated, this publication is still a valuable resource.

The contents include a regional council profile and a general discussion of regionalism, special districts and authorities, and federal programs supporting regionalism. This publication is out of print but may be located in many research libraries. To see a complete bibliography of USACIR publications, go to http://www. library.unt.edu/gpo/ACIR/acir.html, which is described in the following section.

Supporting Associations and Organizations

United States Advisory Commission on Intergovernmental Relations http://www.library.unt.edu/gpo/ ACIR/default.html

Although no longer in existence, the USACIR is an important component in the study of regional governments. During its half century of activity, its mission, as established by the federal government, was to "strengthen the American federal system and improve the ability of federal, state, and local governments to work together cooperatively, efficiently, and effectively." For more information about the organization and its history, a bibliography of publications, and relevant resources, see the USACIR Web page. This site is made available through a partnership of the U.S. Government Printing Office and the University of North Texas Libraries' Government Documents Department "to provide permanent public access to the electronic Web sites and publications of defunct U.S. government agencies and commissions."

American Council on Intergovernmental Relations http://www.library.unt.edu/amcouncil/index.html

Designed as a successor to USACIR, the American Council on Intergovernmental Relations (ACIR) is a nonprofit organization established for charitable and educational purposes, serving as a nonpartisan research body and policy forum. Unlike the Advisory Commission, the Council is not a governmental entity and receives no federal funds. Operating funds are dependent on contributions, grants, contracts, and product and service fees. The publications and other information sources of the USACIR have been acquired by the Council and will remain under its protection. Information about the Council may be accessed through its Web site.

National Association of Regional Councils [NARC] http://www.narc.org

This is a nonprofit organization that promotes and fosters cooperation among regional communities through advocacy, educational programming, research, and outreach activities. Its membership is not limited to intergovernmental agencies but includes public, private, academic, nonprofit, and civic regional organizations. NARC monitors legislative and regulatory activities that impact regional programs on the state and federal level through lobbying efforts. Educational programming includes sponsorship of conferences and training workshops. In addition to the Annual Conference and Executive Directors Conference is the Washington Policy Conference, which provides an opportunity for regional leaders to meet and discuss the NARC federal legislation and policy agenda for the coming year. During the same week, the National Regional Summit convenes to discuss regional issues and initiatives. NARC's Web site provides links to conference calendars and agendas, topical pages with related links, an online bookstore of NARC publications, an annotated list of suggested reading, and a Regional Information Clearinghouse, which provides a profile of regional organizations throughout the United States.

A suborganization of NARC is the Institute for The Regional Community (ITRC), which serves to broaden the knowledge of regionalism and promote collaboration among public, private, and civic organizations. As an outreach vehicle, ITRC sponsors the Regional Agenda at NARC's annual Regional Summits and produces the newsletter *The Regionalist*, cosponsored by the University of Baltimore and the Schaefer Center for Public Policy. More information about ITRC can be found at the NARC Web site.

Association of Metropolitan Planning Organizations [AMPO] http://www.ampo.org

This is a nonprofit membership organization that provides technical support to MPOs that have responsibility for planning, programming, and coordination of federal highway and transit investments. The AMPO Web site provides links to related organizations, policy statements and best practices white papers, suggested readings, online newsletter, publications catalog, and calendar of events.

Regional Government Associations

The search for this type of information can begin with the question, "Is there a regional organization in my area and what does it do?" For the sake of a sample search, Johnson County, Iowa, is the local community targeted.

An Example from Iowa: East Central Iowa Council of Governments (ECICOG)

The official point of entry in finding the answer is through the Code of Iowa, the laws that are currently in effect for the state. The index volume is the logical and appropriate first step in the search, under the headings "Regional Planning Commissions" and "Planning Commissions." Under the broad subject of "Planning Commissions," several subheadings are listed, followed by the section in the code where the full text of the law can be found. The relevant subheadings follow:

Powers of Joint Agencies (Iowa Code, ch 28E.15): The broad purpose of such organizations is defined as "comprehensive planning for its area for the purpose of carrying out the functions as defined for such [agencies] by federal, state and local laws and regulations."

Council of Governments (Iowa Code, ch 28H): Specific reference is made to COGs in the "establishment by executive order...of the East central Iowa council of governments serving Benton, Iowa, Johnson, Jones, Linn, and Washington counties" (ch 28H.1). The sections following in ch 28H refer to coordination of a work program (ch 28H.2), duties of the council (ch 28H.3), membership and liability of members (ch 28H.4), and agreements with other agencies (ch 28H.5).

After discovering that, yes, there is an organization that serves the East Central Iowa Council of Governments (ECICOG), the next step is to learn more about the organization. An Internet search for "East Central Iowa Council of Governments" returns the ECICOG home page, http://ecicog.org, and further information about the services provided.

National Association of Regional Councils http://www.narc.org

An alternative method of discovering information about the ECICOG is through a secondary source, such as a Web site of an organization or association supporting regional governments. The NARC Web site provides a state-by-state listing with corresponding links to targeted organizations. The welcome page of the ECICOG site confirms that the organization came into existence through the previously cited provisions of the Code of Iowa.

The next question to be answered is, "What exactly does this organization do?" The ECICOG welcome page, http://ecicog.org, explains that it was "created to promote regional cooperation and to provide professional planning services to local governments." The composition of the governing board is described, jurisdictions involved are listed, and programs are outlined. As a Census Data Affiliate, one of the primary functions of the ECICOG is to make reference materials available to the public on topics of land use practices, government finances, and environmental conditions. As liaison to state and federal agencies, it assists local governments in understanding and complying with regulations and mandates. The *ECICOG Express* is its bimonthly newsletter that provides information on programs and projects. In the area of community development, ECICOG provides technical assistance on land use planning, zoning and subdivision regulation, and local government financing and assists cities in revising their ordinances as required. ECICOG also secures and administers state and federal funds for local infrastructure improvement and community facility projects and assists communities in addressing local housing needs such as rehabilitation, adaptive reuse of existing structures, and new

housing development. Solid-waste management programs that develop and improve recycling and waste-reduction and environmental-education programs in local communities are part of the ECICOG mission. Environmental legislation and new state and federal programs are tracked by staff who are responsible for the area's comprehensive plan. This COG works closely with local jurisdictions to implement federally funded transportation projects and improvements and is also responsible for the regional transit system. The Web site includes Community Development Block Grant opportunities, which are listed along with ECICOG's seven-year funding history.

This is a brief summary of resources relating to the structure of local government. Of course, the best information about any particular local government is the government itself; however, some of these general and specific resources will be helpful.

CHAPTER 3
Municipal, County, and Regional Government Archives

Suzann Holland

INTRODUCTION

Researchers working with local government information will need to dig into the past. Most quests for older local records will eventually lead to an archival facility. This chapter is designed to educate the reader about archives and the issues that shape them. Researchers visiting archives will find a wide variety of policies and practices that will translate into vastly different experiences among institutions. Information provided in this chapter will assist readers in creating a strategy for research as they seek out the resources described in the latter portion of this book.

The information presented in the previous chapter briefly explained the structures of local, county, and regional government. The records produced by the different parts of these structures are generally collected through one of three basic strategies: (1) a records management plan guiding the collection of records in a central location, (2) simple storage within individual divisions (with or without benefit of a records management plan), or (3) surrender of materials to an outside party, such as a professional or dedicated archive. Each strategy differs from the others in preservation, policy, organization, responsibility, and ultimately, accessibility. A brief overview of records management is necessary to preface the explanation of these strategies and how they affect the research process.

RECORDS MANAGEMENT

Ideally, the government entity from which the researcher seeks records will have a concrete records management plan. Localities inevitably produce hordes of paper documents. A records management plan, which is often adopted by ordinance, helps tame what can be an overwhelming problem: what to do with it all. A typical records management plan begins by defining *records* for the locality, which usually consist of any and all documents created or received by it, regardless of format or public accessibility. For legal reasons, such records are usually declared to be public property, thereby under the control of the locality. A person or team is designated to be in charge of executing the policy, and their duties are outlined.

Records control schedules are the most important part of the records management plan. These documents determine what is to be retained, where it is to be kept, for how long it is to be retained, and how it will eventually be disposed of. Think of how you've heard it suggested that you keep your tax returns and supporting documents for seven years. After those seven years are up, you gladly throw them out. What we think of as a rule of thumb is in actuality a records control schedule. If you had a similar plan for all the material that came into your home, you would essentially have a records management plan for your household. The concept works much the same way at the government level, though obviously on a much larger scale. In theory, after a records management plan is adopted and implemented, the employees know what to do with their paper records.

Many localities formulate their records management plans to collect documents in a central location. If the quantity of records is especially large, it is usually cost-efficient to have a single records department with dedicated staff. This is often the city or county clerk's office, particularly for recent records. In an age of common litigation, localities save more of the paper they generate than they did just a generation ago. For major metropolitan areas, the quantity of records can be so massive that the records need to be stored at an off-site facility run by a private company experienced with matters of preservation, security, and ideally, access. Off-site storage is still overseen by the locality's records management staff. Centrally located records can ease the task of the researcher, as the staff should be used to requests, familiar with accessibility policies, and able to find the requested records in an expedient manner.

Some records management plans dictate that records remain in the departments that created them, a policy typical of small localities or those with extremely tight budgets. Self-storage also commonly exists in localities without a records management plan in place. This method can work for or against the researcher. Because there is no dedicated staff to handle records requests, employees of the department may have little or no time to deal with them. Research requests can feel like a hindrance to completing "real work" by clerks. However, because employees of departments implementing self-storage are very familiar with the records being sought, they are usually aware

of policies regarding public access, the range of records available, and where any older transferred records are now housed. There is a mandate and a duty to provide public access to these records.

The third strategy, surrender of materials to an outside party, generally occurs in two situations. Mandated transfer is required by law and is usually hierarchical in nature. For example, each state requires that events such as births and deaths be recorded. Some states gather this information directly, while others rely on the localities to collect it. In the case of the latter, the state is the custodian of records originating at a local level. Some localities may maintain duplicate documentation for their own purposes, but most surrender such materials to the state without doing so and are pleased not to be burdened with such matters.

The other type of surrender of records involves donation to another facility, typically a public or college library, historical society, museum, or a regional or state institution. The decision to voluntarily surrender materials involves a number of factors, which may include increasing accessibility to the public, easing workload at local government offices, and addressing preservation concerns. As governments grow increasingly aware of the historical value of the paperwork generated by administrations of the past, concern for the care of these records has increased as well. The receiving institution takes responsibility for how the records are used and cared for.

Why not just store the records at an archival facility, rather than donating them? Archivists are reluctant to provide care for and provide access to record groups they do not control. Suppose that a particular city wishes to store its records at the public library in the interests of local history. One of its past mayors is still alive and insists that the records of his administration be closed to the public, though they are by law public documents. Researchers wishing to reproduce photographs or other materials must be referred to the city for permission, a frustratingly tedious process. Some of the records the city wishes to turn over involve sensitive information about living persons. Such a situation would put the library in the position of doing all of the work but maintaining no control over the collection. Professional archivists are well trained to deal with issues such as privacy, copyright, and accessibility. With no training in the area, employees of localities are unlikely to understand exactly how archives operate and how researchers use them. For these reasons, storage of records without transfer of ownership can be a logistical nightmare, and is rarely undertaken.

Record Group Splits and Overlaps

The three previously outlined records management strategies are often used in combination. Interrepository relationships evolve when record groups must be divided or overlapped between localities and institutions. The decision to split or overlap record groups is typically based upon the age of the records involved, and/or the patterns of their usage (by the creator and the researchers).

Splits are quite common. For example, vital records created after the date of statewide mandate of such records are typically held by a state agency, with any earlier records remaining with the local government or turned over to a historical society or other institution. Interrepository relationships based upon an anticipated usage pattern are similar to those based upon age. To illustrate, court records that are a hundred years old are unlikely to be used by the court itself. The anticipated users are researchers with historical or genealogical interest. Because the anticipated usage pattern is independent of the court, it is reasonable to send such records to another location. Conversely, the current mayor's administration will need to refer to the records of the preceding mayor's administration. Those records need to remain accessible to city employees, who need them to carry out their duties. In such a situation, researchers would need to approach the mayor's office for access to the records.

Just as splits within record groups are common, overlaps in record possession also abound. Record overlaps may seem confusing at first, but they may benefit the researcher. They increase accessibility to records, giving researchers a choice of institutions in which to review records. In addition, the preservation and duplication of valuable historical information have become widely implemented practices; a legacy of the destruction of local records wrought by late-nineteenth- and early-twentieth-century disasters, which will be discussed later in this chapter. Though not as likely as in the past, disasters still can and do strike. For example, the Dunkerton, Iowa, city hall was destroyed by flood in May 1999. Municipal operations were moved to a temporary building, which was leveled by a tornado in May 2000.

Two Hypothetical Extremes

Discovering the mere existence of a local or regional government records "stash" may lead a researcher to believe that finding needed information will be simple, but this may not be the case. Many government archives are informal and poorly organized, which can hinder accessibility. As the following two hypothetical examples demonstrate, the structure (or lack thereof) of the archives' operations has major impact on the accessibility of the records, primarily the ability of the entity to locate requested records.

Orbach City

Orbach City's records are a complete disaster. The so-called archives consist of a corner of a back room in the courthouse basement, which has been designated as the City Archives, though the county runs the courthouse. The records have been stored in acid-free boxes, but there have been no preservation attempts as yet on the paper. No records management policy exists for the paper records or those of other formats. The mayor has asked the director of the county library to appoint a librarian to head a city archives committee, an idea that was raised over six months ago, with no constructive steps having been taken to date. The city has very little money to spare and cannot hire a consultant, much less staff to set up a proper facility. No one on staff is knowledgeable about the preservation issues involved. Although the mayor's intentions are good, the current situation is unmanageable. Researchers wishing to access the records are systematically discouraged because there is no staff to assist and it is unlikely that the requested material can be located in the room full of boxes. The records are rapidly deteriorating due to the dampness of the environment. There are no duplicates of the oldest records, and no one on the city's staff has had the time to respond to the State Historical Society's request for Orbach City to send its oldest vital records to the capitol for inclusion in the new local history microfilming project.

Safford County

Safford County's records are numerous but well organized. A special committee drafted a records management plan more than a decade ago; and with a few exceptions, it has been smoothly implemented. Safford County recognized the value of the documents of its past but had little money to spare for archiving efforts. It solicited help from the small archives of the nearby university. The archives staff helped Safford County organize a small group of volunteers to write a grant proposal to the National Archives and Records Administration (NARA). The resulting small influx of funds helped finance a joint effort between the county and the university. The university's archives conducted the preservation operation and also microfilmed the majority of the oldest records. A complete run of duplicate reels was sent to both the state archives and the public library. This has helped ease the burden that Safford County employees felt in trying to make the records accessible to requestors. When researchers ask for old materials, they are generally referred to the university's archives or the library. Researchers from outside the immediate area are well served, as the archives are able to fulfill copy requests via fax or mail for a small charge.

Reality—Somewhere in the Middle

Again, the above hypothetical examples are at the extreme ends of the spectrum. But each of them is probably a fairly accurate representation of a locality somewhere in the United States. Though Orbach City could certainly take a few cues from Safford County, its best path toward the same result is unlikely to be the same. The examples are intended to help readers understand just a few of the typical difficulties that localities may face in dealing with their records and possible solutions available to them. An excellent example of an archival storage facility that has a good organizational plan is the Tennessee State Library and Archives. An example of its organization chart is provided on the Web site, at http://www.state.tn.us/sos/statelib/techsvs/sitemap.htm.

FINDING ARCHIVES

Repositories

How do researchers know where to find archival facilities? Often, municipal departments can direct researchers to the appropriate repositories. Each state has a historical society or state archives of some type; many states have both. But first, researchers can benefit by seeking the treasures of smaller, local facilities.

Resources

Repositories of Primary Sources http://www.uidaho.edu/special-collections/Other.repositories.html

This database, maintained by Terry Abraham at the University of Idaho, is so highly regarded that the Library of Congress links to it, rather than attempting to emulate it, in its *National Union Catalog of Manuscript Collections*. Encompassing the entire world, the site links to repository Web sites rather than describing them. Repositories in the United States are grouped by state. For example, if "State," then "Arizona," then "Mesa Public Library" are chosen, valuable information is provided about services and collections there.

This database is constantly updated with new or changed entries. This is an excellent resource for seeking out very old records that may be in the custody of historical societies or university archives.

The Librarian's Guide to Public Records: The Complete State, County, and Courthouse Locator, ed. by Michael L. Sankey and Carl Ernst (Business Resources Bureau Publications, 2000)

This thick paperback provides direct access information for over 11,500 public record locations at the federal, state, and county levels. While it does not provide information for municipalities, it offers a quick way to find county-level agencies and provides addresses, phone numbers, and Web site addresses when available.

Records Management: A Practical Guide for Cities and Counties, by Julian L. Mims III (International City/County Management Association, 1996)

This volume provides detailed information on how localities should manage their records. The included sample plans will give the user an introduction as to what to expect when the localities still hold the records the researcher is seeking. The volume may be growing a bit outdated, as it only briefly touches upon the problems that electronic records create, but it represents the best print overview available at this time.

Libraries

Perhaps the most effective tool for learning about the archival facilities in a particular area is simple word of mouth. Archivists in one facility are likely to be familiar with other area archives and their respective holdings. Librarians, avid genealogists, and college faculty may also prove quite helpful, depending on the arena in which the researcher's quest originates. Suppose a couple wanders up to a desk in a public library seeking information on the 1924 murder of an ancestor. The librarian helps them find a newspaper account of the murder, using the date of death that they provide, then suggests that the coroner's inquest report, police records, and trial information might be available. After being directed by the librarian to the appropriate local government agencies, the pair finds that the coroner's records before 1948 were destroyed, but they get trial records and a lead on finding arrest information. An enthusiastic, knowledgeable professional can help formulate a research plan to help avoid wasting time.

USING ARCHIVAL FACILITIES

Researchers who have never used an archival facility may not know what to expect, and therefore may be unprepared on their initial visit. An archive is quite different from a library, even if it is housed in one. The storage areas for the materials are closed to the public. Instead, requested materials are brought to a reading room for the researchers' use. A few basic guidelines follow to introduce the "newbies" to this arena and help those who refer them remember to mention the things that more experienced users take for granted. While these policies do not exist in every repository, they are assuredly the norm.

Security is a priority for archives, owing to the irreplaceability of their collections. Researchers will be expected to sign in, provide photo identification, and sign a form agreeing to adhere to the rules of the archives. At larger institutions, visitors may be required to apply for a research pass, sometimes for a nominal fee. Be prepared to leave most personal belongings outside the facility, often including purses and briefcases. Any portfolios, notebooks, or folders that are brought into the facility are subject to search upon the researcher's exit. Many materials in archives have high monetary value; staff members have good reasons for such scrutiny.

The fragility of many records necessitates making rules for how they are handled. Cotton gloves may be provided. Some items may be encased in Mylar sleeves sealed on all sides. This preservation method is called encapsulation, considered superior to lamination because it is reversible. Prohibition against photocopying of especially fragile materials is common, as the light involved in the process may further degrade the documents. Many materials are in book or ledger form, and bindings can be damaged in an attempt to lay them flat for the photocopying process. Plan on doing a fair amount of transcription by hand. Only pencils will be allowed into the reading room, although some facilities allow laptop computers, which can save tremendous amounts of time for adept typists.

Many archives can arrange to have visual and sound materials reproduced for researchers. This can be expensive, as it generally requires valuable time from the professional staff. The archives should be well acquainted with any copyright issues involved and can distinguish between the assorted types of use referred to in applicable copyright law.

SPECIAL LOCAL RECORDS ISSUES
The Value of Local Records

The methods by which archivists and individual researchers appraise records differ, just as their purposes differ. Professional archivists are trained to assess a record group's value as they make acquisitions

Archivists are concerned with two basic record-value categories as they appraise: primary values and secondary values. Primary values are those for which the records were created. These include administrative value, which supports the operation of the creator; fiscal value, which is crucial to the financial dealings of the creator; and legal value, which may be needed to establish rights and responsibilities under the law. Primary values are essentially a concern of records management rather than of archives. By the time records are archived, their immediate primary value has likely ceased.

Secondary values represent the midlife career change, so to speak, of local records. Once record groups are no longer needed for their original purpose, their value is limited to evidential and informational values. Evidential value is the potential for the records to provide documentation about the history of the creator or act as evidence of the actions of the creator. Informational value adds to an existing big picture, often outside the scope of the locality. Often, these two types of value coexist within the same record group. For example, the personal papers of a Negro Leagues pitcher hold evidential value for the particular player's life and informational value for the Negro Leagues.

Resources

Local History Collections in Libraries, by Faye
  Phillips (Libraries Unlimited, 1995)

This comprehensive manual of operations for managing local history material within the administrative framework of a library covers issues of administration, acquisitions, access, and use of all formats of material. Information on continually changing areas such as preservation, copyright and other legal concerns, computer applications, and national databases is also addressed, along with public relations roles and outreach activities for local history collections. Guidelines for administration of nontraditional library material (e.g., manuscripts) will be especially helpful to librarians. Archivists will value the manual as one of continuing practical education and theoretical development, as exemplified by the Society of American Archivists' Basic Manual series and Archival Fundamentals series. Manuscript curators, students, and administrators will also benefit from this book.

Archives and the Public Good: Accountability and Records in Modern Society, by Richard J. Cox and David A. Wallace (Quorum Books, 2002)

This volume widens the perspective of the roles that records play in society. As opposed to most writings in the discipline of archives and records management, which view records from cultural, historical, and economical/efficiency dimensions, this volume highlights that one of the most salient features of records is the role they play as sources of accountability—a component that often brings them into daily headlines and into courtrooms. Frequent struggles over their control, access, preservation, destruction, authenticity, accuracy, and other issues demonstrate time and again that records are not mute observers or mere objects upon which the record of some activity has been engraved. Rather, they are key components of memory formation and erasure.

Archival Theory, Records, and the Public, by Trevor Livelton (Scarecrow Press, 1996)

This book considers the nature of public records from an archival perspective, analyzing concepts rather than the daily realities with which public records archivists deal. Trevor Livelton is an archivist with the city of Victoria, British Columbia, and has worked with public and private records in a variety of settings. His carefully reasoned conclusions provide a strong foundation on which principled, rather than ad hoc, decisions can be made, and so will be of interest to teachers, students, and practitioners of archival science. The author presents a general or theoretical view of public records as documents made or received and preserved by the sovereign or its agents in the conduct of governance. This analysis is illustrated by a variety of examples and a discussion of freedom of information.

For users of local records, a record group often holds appeal for a variety of research interests. Individuals using local records do not go through the same type of process in assessing a record group's value.

They evaluate the quality of local records, both in physical terms and in how useful the records are. Two of the characteristics that help patrons of archives assess research value are completeness and legibility. Very little assurance exists that a particular record group is complete. Gaps often exist for a variety of reasons. A section of the overall group may have been stored elsewhere or discarded, or records simply were not kept for certain periods of time. Genealogists are familiar with strange policy changes in keeping nineteenth- and early-twentieth-century vital statistics. Marriage records might be available from as early as 1832 in a particular county, only to have no records kept at all for a later 30-year period. Staff changed frequently in the past, as did priorities. Bear in mind that an absolutely complete record group is a rarity, for whatever reason.

Two issues of legibility cause difficulties when working with old government records. The records may be physically damaged, often through moisture, mold, or sunlight exposure, all of which lead to paper deterioration. In desperate situations, working with a photocopier's lightness and darkness settings to adjust the contrast can sometimes make text discernible. Legibility issues caused by damage further illustrate the importance of duplicating and preserving older records stressed earlier.

Typical penmanship has undergone changes over the years, leading to legibility problems of a different sort. The older the record, the more likely users are to have trouble deciphering the handwriting.

Reading Early American Handwriting, by Kip Sperry (Genealogical Publishing Company, 1998)

This book is designed to teach you how to read and understand the handwriting found in documents commonly used in genealogical or historical research. It explains techniques for reading early American documents; provides samples of alphabets and letter forms; defines terms and abbreviations commonly used in early American documents such as wills, deeds, and church records; and presents numerous examples of early American records for the reader to work with. Each document—nearly a hundred of them at various stages of complexity—appears with the author's transcription on a facing page, enabling the reader to check his own transcription. Also covered in the work, with particular emphasis on handwriting, are numbers and roman numerals, dates and the change from the Julian calendar to the Gregorian calendar, abbreviations and contractions, and standard terms found in early American records.

Preserving Archives and Manuscripts, by Mary Lynn Ritzenthaler (Society of American Archivists, 1993)

This book is the standard general preservation guide for archivists. It provides valuable information about the world of preservation techniques that are designed to ensure that local records remain for future generations to refer to. Skimming this title will help the reader understand why certain access policies exist.

Providing Reference Services for Archives and Manuscripts, by Mary Jo Pugh (Society of American Archivists, 1992)

Part of the Society of American Archivists' Archival Fundamentals series, this title is an excellent resource for those preparing to visit an archive. The overview of reading-room policies is invaluable in understanding what an archive can and cannot provide. By understanding the standards expected from the archivist's professional organization, researchers will have a good idea of what to expect from those providing reference service.

How accurate are records generated by local governments? Accuracy can vary widely; a good rule of thumb is to take nothing as gospel. Look for red flags, such as obvious errors in spelling, impossible dates, and records that are inconsistent in format from one to the next. The ideal method for verifying the accuracy of a given record is to compare it with another record of the same event. Sometimes the end result of such a comparison is verifying that you *don't* know something. My long-dead grandfather had five different birth dates on five different documents: the family bible, his birth record with the county, Social Security number application, marriage license, and death certificate. Apparently, he was confused, too! I still don't know which date, if any, is correct; but because of the discrepancies, I have not mistakenly accepted as gospel the county birth record. Consider which areas of government would have an interest in the event you are researching. The net can often be cast wider than we realize.

Missing Records

Researchers seeking local materials are often told that there are no records left. This is often true, as a tragic percentage of yesteryear's documentation is gone

forever. Few things are as frustrating as desperately needing a record that no longer exists. How can the records be gone? Strangely enough, sometimes it is the result of a long-ago conscious decision. As noted earlier, the archives movement grew steadily in the twentieth century. In our nation's early days, many local officials did not realize the value of decades-old ledgers and brittle court documents. Growing governments needed room for newer documents, and that extra space was often acquired by discarding the older records, deemed useless. It would be unimaginable for a discard of this nature to occur today. But researchers must still deal with the damage of yesterday's ignorant decisions.

When records are gone, researchers will find that the most common cause is a disaster of some type. Destruction of records by flood has occurred many times, but the ravages of fire have obliterated far more records than people realize. Many are familiar with the Washington, D.C., fire that left only a few fragments of the 1890 census, but few realize how common fires were in courthouses and city halls up until the mid-twentieth century. Consider the unfortunate county of Hamilton, located in the southwestern corner of Ohio. Its residents saw four courthouses burned to the ground before the construction of the present building in 1884. Virtually all of the original records were lost, though a few have been reconstructed from other sources.

Burned Record Counties Database http://www.lva. lib.va.us/whatwehave/local/burned/index.htm

The Library of Virginia has begun a project that should serve as a model for other institutions around the nation. Wars, natural disasters, and fires have hit the original local records of Virginia hard. A full quarter of Virginia's 95 counties have lost records through disasters, descriptions of which are fully documented by the library. Hence, it maintains this database. It is important to not assume that records are lost forever due to a disaster—verify that they truly do not exist in any other form.

Check for duplicates or abstracts in other repositories. Generally speaking, the more recently the records were discarded or destroyed, the more likely it is that duplicates exist elsewhere. When there are no duplicates or backup copies to work from, records can sometimes be partially reconstructed through the use of alternative resources. For example, information in destroyed property records may have also appeared in the local paper. The Burned Record Counties Database is starting to reach beyond its original purpose, now offering suggestions for alternative resources to capture missing information. The use of alternative resources often requires a great deal of additional work, but it may be the only option for certain information.

Be forewarned, though, that every researcher must be prepared to face disappointment. Some information is simply lost to history; some questions will remain forever unanswered.

FOR FURTHER READING

Cox, Richard J. *Documenting Localities: A Practical Model for American Archivists and Manuscript Curators*. Lanham, MD: Scarecrow Press, 1996.

Miller, Fredric M. *Arranging and Describing Archives and Manuscripts*. Chicago: Society of American Archivists, 1990.

National Historical Publications and Records Commission. *Directory of Archives and Manuscript Repositories in the United States*. Phoenix, AZ: Oryx Press, 1988.

O'Toole, James M. *Understanding Archives and Manuscripts*. Chicago: Society of American Archivists, 1990.

Phillips, Faye. *Local History Collections in Libraries*. Englewood, CO: Libraries Unlimited, 1995.

Wilsted, Thomas, and William Nolte. *Managing Archival and Manuscript Repositories*. Chicago: Society of American Archivists, 1991.

CHAPTER 4
Finding Local Government Information in General Indexes and Bibliographies

Harriet Semmes Alexander

TOPICS DISCUSSED

Local Publications
  City and County Documents
  Newspaper Sources
  Other Local News Internet Sources
National and Regional Sources
  Regional Library Networks
  Databases
  Public Affairs Information Service
    (PAIS)
  Internet Resources
Academic and Research Sources
Federal Government Resources

MAJOR RESOURCES COVERED

Index to Current Urban Documents and Urban Documents Microfiche Collection
Index to Current Urban Documents Online
State and Local Government on the Net
Official City Sites
National Newspaper Index
LexisNexis Academic
Newsbank
WorldCat
Sage Urban Studies Abstracts
FirstGov: Local Governments
FirstGov

LOCAL PUBLICATIONS

City and County Documents

Indexes

Index to Current Urban Documents and Urban Documents Microfiche Collection (Greenwood Press, annual)

This is an index to any documents produced by a local government as its primary records. Since 1972, the *Index to Current Urban Documents* has provided a listing and access to publications from approximately 500 cities/counties across the United States and Canada. Traditionally, prior to September 2000, Greenwood Press published annual indexes to a collection of documents on microfiche. On September 8, 2000, the index became Internet accessible, at http://www.urbdocs.com/, with PDF files of full-text documents available. More than 2,400 documents are added yearly, generally averaging only 4 to 5 per location (2,400 documents/500 cities). Obviously

some locations are more generously represented than others.

Greenwood Press provides subscription options to the index only, regional indexing and documents, or full indexing and documents. The press acquires its documents through a network of North American public/academic libraries, which provide information and copies of their documents per agreement. Topics include many aspects of city/county government, from hospitals, mental health care, schools, police, transportation, and budgets to neighborhoods, museums, libraries, and environmental and cultural concerns. Multiple subject headings are assigned as well as a geographic locator. Print volumes have separate subject indexes and geographic indexes. Appendices include lists of libraries, agency and organizational contributors, regional councils of governments represented, and cities/counties included in the series. The geographic index of the annual print volume, which continues to be issued to online subscribers, contains the most complete information on the documents in the series. Entries contain annotations that characterize the actual documents, including a description of the subject matter of documents when the titles are unclear or incomplete and/or more than one document is present on the fiche. Geographic entries are alphabetical by the name of the city/county and subarranged by the name of the corporate entity producing the documents, such as city of Chicago, Department of Buildings, mayor's office, public schools, state agencies, and universities. Accession numbers precede each entry in the geographic index.

For more highly represented localities, which are generally the larger cities (producing more than 20–30 documents/year), the subject index is probably the more efficient approach to locating specific topics. Document fiche numbers are alphanumeric, containing a three- to four-letter alphabetical designation for the city/county, and a four-digit number corresponding to the number of items within the document series under the specific location (e.g., SEWA-0669 and SMN-0669 mean that Seattle, Washington, and St. Paul, Minnesota, respectively, have 669 documents; HOTX-0115 means that Houston, Texas, has 115). As one would expect, New York City, Chicago, and Los Angeles are all well represented.

Index to Current Urban Documents Online [ICUD]
  http://www.urbdocs.com

This database contains documents added to the collection beginning with volume 29 (years 2000–2001) of the print index. Date of most recent database update and total number of documents in the online database presently appear at the top of the search page, to the right of the heading. Search methods are simple, including a dialog box into which to enter keywords or phrases for searching and menus for selecting supplied subjects, municipalities, or states. Two major additions are provided to the entries—PDF-formatted copies of the documents and the Web address for the document provider. Web links allow access to other documents on topics or locations covered by retrieved documents or by location. A new feature has been added to the thesaurus: "Internet Access to This Document." The purpose of this heading is to convey that copies of the documents are available at the Web site address provided as well as in PDF format on the ICUD database. As of 2002, only 25 documents are listed under this subject heading. The Internet is becoming accessible to larger portions of the general population and the Web the preferred and most cost-effective mode of publication for city and county documents that are of interest to limited audiences. Direct Web addresses for documents are frequently given in the supplemental text of the entries. Online subscriptions presently include print copies of indexes and microfiche copies of documents.

Library Literature http://www.hwwilson.com/
  Databases/liblit.htm

Library Literature is a database that indexes journals from the area of library and information science. Reflecting the latest trends in a rapidly evolving field, this database indexes English- and foreign-language periodicals, selected state journals, conference proceedings, pamphlets, books, and library-school theses, plus over 300 books per year. This resource delivers full-text articles from over a hundred select publications. PDF page images of the full-text articles bring researchers charts, graphs, photos, and other valuable graphical information. It is useful as it provides subject cataloging for articles and books about local government information, often written by librarians and archivists. This database also contains links to sites mentioned in articles, pointing users to valuable information on the Web. It is available through H. W. Wilson's Wilson Web and OCLC's FirstSearch electronic database search interfaces, as well as on CD-ROM. It is available through most large university libraries and through individual subscription.

Journal Lists

Two journals frequently contain bibliographies of local government documents. They are *Journal of Government Information* (Elsevier, bimonthly) and *Dttp* (aka *Documents to the People*) (American Library Association, quarterly); following are some examples of articles from these journals that contain such bibliographic lists (excerpted below).

Hutto, Dena Holiman. "Recent literature on government information. Items published, indexed, or reviewed May-November 2000." *Journal of Government Information* v. 28 no2 (Mar./Apr. 2001) p. 185–240.

Farmer, L. S. J. (2000). The cost of getting digitized. *Book Report, 18* (3), 49–51. California government provides grants to school libraries.

Gostyla, S. (2000). Developing responsive services online. *American City and County, 115* (4), 10.

Greenberg, P., & Morton, H. (2000). *1999 information technology and internet laws.* Denver, CO. National Conference of State Legislatures.

A guide to government and e-commerce: the digital future of government, (2000). *Public Management, 82* (7) inserts 1–8, following p. 32. Initiatives by local government.

Gunnes, A. E., & Kovel, J. P. (2000). Using GIS [geographic information systems] in emergency management operations. *Journal of Urban Planning and Development-ASCE, 126* (3), 136–149. In Douglas County, KS.

Letson, R. (1999). Small government agencies solve big problems. *Imaging and Document Solutions, 8* (4), 20–22, 24, 26, 28. Four state or local government agencies implement document management solutions.

Parsons, Kathy A. State and local documents bibliography: June 1999. *DttP* v. 27 no4 (Winter 1999) p. 13–14.

Anthes, Gary H. "A Tale of Two Cities." *Computerworld* 32:2 (1998); 69–71.

Baker, Paul M. "Local-Government Internet Sites as Public Policy Innovations." Ph.D. Dissertations. George Mason Univ., 1997. 177p.

Berinstein, Paula. "The Numbers Game: The Top 10 Sources for Statistics." *Online* 22:2 (Mar.-Apr. 1998); 61–65.

Boland, Joseph B., et al. *Local Area Data for Oregon: A Bibliography of Sources.* 2d ed. Eugene, Ore.: Univ. of Oregon Library, 1998. http://libweb.uoregon.edu/ govdocs/localdat.html

Bourquard, Jo Anne, Pam Greenberg, and Anneliese May. *Electronic Access to Legislative Information.* Denver, Colo.: National Conference of State Legislatures, 1996. 44p.

Bowser, Brandi. "Opening the Window to On-Line Democracy: www.local-government.com." *American City & County* 11:1 (1998): 32–38.

Clark, Cynthia D. and Judy Horn, compilers. *Organization of Document Collections and Services. SPEC Kit 227 and SPEC Flyer 227.* Washington, D.C.: Association of Research Libraries, Office of Leadership and Management Services, 1998. 123p. ED418724.

Access to these and other library publications online through indexes such as Library Literature, available through OCLC, allows one to identify specific issues of these publications and others containing municipal and local government publication bibliographies. Documents listed in both of these journals are selected and described by librarians.

Web Sites (General)

State and Local Government on the Net (Piper Resources) http://www.statelocalgov.net

Other locally produced documents are the official and unofficial city Web sites springing up on the Internet. The nature of the Internet frequently makes it difficult to determine which local sites are officially produced by government agencies and which are produced by well-wishers, dot-coms, the media, or political interest groups. This site, produced by Piper Resources, an Internet publishing firm, leads users to the sites produced or sanctioned by state and local governments. At present, links are provided to more than 7,000 sites, a factor which indicates the significance of this product and continuing time-consumption for the Webmaster. Other sites (such as Official City Sites, listed below) may presume to be as extensive, but the producers' lack of publishing background/ability to limit the site's scope makes Piper's not only the more reputable site but also the more reliable one.

Official City Sites http://www.officialcitysites.org

This database was awarded the Silver Platter Site Award by the Ask Jeeves search engine. Official City Sites attempts to locate not only those sites produced and/or sponsored by city governments but also sites provided by commercial and business organizations (such as chambers of commerce) and sites that represent community and economic development and travel and tourism. An impressive and exhaustive list of links is provided for all cities and county names for each state in the United States. However, frequently, the links lead nowhere after one has initiated a search. And while the directory search frequently picks up overlooked official city sites, the pages on which such links are expected to appear are blank, indicating to the unwary user that an official site is unavailable. Despite the .org ending on this site, it is highly commercialized, carrying a disconcertingly large number of advertisements. Much has been attempted here, and it is not surprising that the results are somewhat disappointing, despite the large number of links on the site.

Newspaper Sources

Indexes

While *Index to Current Urban Documents* is a highly appropriate source of information on local government, only larger libraries and those focusing on urban planning and programs may be able to allocate funds for this specialized collection. It is also very selective, currently covering documents from only 500 cities. Other than government publications, the most prominent form of current local government information is the newspaper. Newspapers not only indicate what governments plan and legislate, but also why they do so, how they apply plans and laws, and how the local populace reacts to their work.

Before the Internet age, indexes covering newspapers were rare and limited to the more prestigious titles, such as the *New York Times*, the London *Times*, the *Washington Post*, and the *Los Angeles Times*. University Microfilm, Inc. (UMI) has a series of paper indexes and/or a series of microfilmed newspapers (formerly published under the name of their parent company, Bell and Howell) beginning in 1972. Seven city newspaper titles are currently indexed via CD-ROM: *Los Angeles Times*, *Washington Post*, *Atlanta Journal-Constitution*, *Chicago Tribune*, *Boston Globe*, and *New York Times*. Print indexes are also available for the *Denver Post*, *Washington Star-News*, New Orleans *Times-Picayune*, *New York Times Tribune* (1875–1906), *Minneapolis Star and Tribune*, *St. Louis Post-Dispatch*, *Nashville Banner–The Tennessean*, *Houston Chronicle*, *Cleveland Plain Dealer*, and *Philadelphia Inquirer*.

National Newspaper Index (Gale Group/Thomson)
     http://library.dialog.com/bluesheets/html/bl0111.
     html http://www.gale.com/customer_service/
     sample_searches/nni.htm

This resource is an online index to five major newspapers: *Christian Science Monitor*, *New York Times*, *Washington Post*, *Wall Street Journal*, and *Los Angeles Times*. Since the text is not provided, it is necessary to consult microfilm copies of the newspapers (available at libraries) or consult online Web sites (e.g., washingtonpost.com, latimes.com) to obtain copies of articles.

Newspapers of smaller cities/towns tend to be indexed only locally, and availability of indexing is geographically limited to the locale producing the index, often a public or university library. The Memphis Room of the Memphis/Shelby County Public Library and Information Center contains a clippings file from the local newspapers dating back to the 1930s, and the University of Memphis provided a selective subject index in the form of a card catalog to both the morning (*Commercial Appeal*) and evening (*Press-Scimitar*) newspapers published in Memphis until on-

line sources were provided on a continuous basis through Academic Universe and the *Commercial Appeal* site, *GoMemphis*. Subject coverage is limited to local information only, and this card index remains the sole subject access to developments in Memphis and neighboring municipalities in Mississippi, Arkansas, and Tennessee for the period from 1964 to 1993. When local indexes are not available, access to newspapers is limited to information from local newspaper morgues (or archives) or through secondary documentation, such as local histories.

Full-Text Sources

GoMemphis http://www.gomemphis.com

This is the Web site for the Memphis *Commercial Appeal* and is similar to those for other newspapers published in the United States. As computer access becomes more widely available, more newspapers are publishing Web sites containing local information, including archival records (news articles more than two weeks old). Searching the archives is free, but end users are generally charged on a per item basis for the articles that result from their searches (presently $1.95/article for *Commercial Appeal*, $2.50/article for *New York Times* [http://www.nytimes.com] and *Los Angeles Times*). Abstracts or parts of the article are presented to the end users to identify articles of interest. Page numbers and section numbers are not supplied, so that while the Internet source allows one to find the right date, entries give no other pertinent information; one may not use the Internet to find specifics in a print/microformat edition of earlier issues of the newspapers. See Newsdirectory.com, discussed later, to find local newspaper Web sites when the name of the local newspaper is unknown.

LexisNexis Academic http://www.lexisnexis.com/
     academic/1univ/acad/default.asp

This database is the Internet-accessible form of the LexisNexis database made available to academic libraries. LexisNexis Academic provides business information and legal information as well as the general news sources provided by newspapers. However, since the legal information provided is national and state, not local, the primary emphasis of this discussion will be the information provided in the news section of the database. Excluding the *Wall Street Journal*, for which abstracts only are provided, LexisNexis Academic provides access to about 150 local newspapers throughout the United States. The most outstanding factor is that the full text—and only the text—of the articles is provided in this online database; sponsoring and classified advertisements have been excluded. However, many first-time users are unaware of the difficulties surrounding search methods for a full-text database in which subject headings are not provided. Databases that provide only keyword-type access to citations are difficult because searchers have to develop an internal lexicon of alternate phrases that mean essentially the same thing, such as "death penalty," "capital punishment," and "execution." With full text added, users must add to this lexicon alternate meanings or uses of search words, because not only people, but also laws may be "executed." And if one is looking for cases in which the death penalty or capital punishment has been applied (by far the best use of newspapers for this topic), the best term is a form of the word "execution." Finding articles that mention the mayor may not be difficult, but narrowing these articles down to those that discuss the mayor as an official of the city may be more difficult than expected. Mayors commonly appear at cultural and social functions and are frequently used as spokespersons for any local coverage of an event, whether local or national in origin. In many cases news may be carried verbatim from one of the wire services, such as Associated Press or Reuters. LexisNexis Academic also carries these news services and large newsmagazines. In many cases there may be more than 200 similar articles reporting the same event on the same day. Add follow-up, and the amount of information surrounding events can become overwhelming. Consider the events of September 11, 2001, and the frequency with which the mayor of New York's title and name were mentioned afterward, even in local papers across the United States, and one begins to see the difficulties that searches on local government in another city may entail. This duplication also has much to do with the format for searching LexisNexis Academic.

On the LexisNexis Academic Web site, news is subdivided into "General News," "Today's News," "U.S. News," "World News," "Wires," "Transcripts," "Arts & Sports," "Campus," and "Non-English Language News." While the "General News" subdivision allows users to search "Major Newspapers," most local news sources are found in the "U.S. News" subdivision. The basic search format requires that three areas be selected/filled in. A keyword dialog box allows the insertion of any word or words appearing in the headline or first paragraph of the article. Second, a location, either a region (Midwest, Northeast, Southeast, or West) or state must be chosen. This location refers to the place in which the newspapers are published, not necessarily the place that is the topic of the articles listed therein. And third, a date must be chosen. The dialog box provides varying choices between "Today" and "All Available Dates," with "Previous Six Months" the default time period. Despite the choices, text of few newspapers prior to the 1990s is included, with a few exceptions from the major newspapers, such as the *New York Times*, *St. Louis Post-Dispatch*, *Miami Herald*, and *Los Angeles Times*. The longest representation of a newspaper is that of the *New York Times*, for which holdings begin in 1980. A second dialog box following that in which keywords from the headline or first paragraph are searchable allows the insertion of words that may appear in the same location or elsewhere in the text of an appropriate article. Any search returning more than 1,000 documents results in an error message stating, "This search has been interrupted because it will return more than 1,000 documents. Please edit your search and try again." Several suggestions are made for narrowing the scope of the search. Guided searches allow more alternatives to users, providing three dialog boxes that can be dropped down to search "Headline," "Headline and Lead Paragraph," "Full Text," "Author," and "Caption." The tips section at the bottom of this page provides a wide range of Boolean search possibilities, from the frequently applied "and" and "or" to the more-limited-use "w/p" (within the same paragraph) and "w/s" (within the same sentence.)

LexisNexis Academic is an expensive database that is really affordable for only large libraries and libraries with consortial buying arrangements, in which a group of libraries pay less each because a number of them subscribe. There is a commercial LexisNexis product that is very expensive.

Newsbank http://www.newsbank.com

Newsbank is a pay-for-use database containing the full text of articles from newspapers. Developed for a variety of users, from public schools and public libraries to colleges and universities, the hallmark of Newsbank is its ease of use. A basic, or keyword, search involves typing the intended search term into a dialog box and clicking the search button. Articles from over 200 U.S. newspapers are currently selected, indexed, and loaded into the Newsbank products. The use of subject headings, five to six per article, allows users to locate appropriate articles quickly, with few false drops (i.e., irrelevant returns from the search engine, often caused by unclear context). "Customized Search" allows advanced searches limited by document type (newspapers, newswires, etc.), search fields (subject, title, author), or date ranges (6/1991–8/1997, 1999, 2/5/2001–4/30/2001, after 10/12/2000). Help screens include assistance on keyword search tips and even a section on "How to Cite Newsbank."

LexisNexis Academic and Newsbank both offer users multiple newspapers at one location. Both database vendors offer full text and both are Internet accessible. The individual U.S. newspaper titles offered in each largely overlap, with variations occurring mostly in sources that are not strictly city newspapers—wire services, transcript providers, business magazines, etc. LexisNexis Academic generally loads most of the newspaper text directly into its database without eliminating duplicative stories, while Newsbank selects items and then loads them. With LexisNexis Academic, much of the search process focuses on how to limit the number of items returned in a search to fewer than 1,000 documents. This problem of volume arose for the parent LexisNexis once the database, which was developed for journalism and legal professionals, was offered to less focused users—in this case, college students, which led the company to spin off LexisNexis Academic for the college market. Newsbank search results default to the largest number of returns per topic. Search terms used in LexisNexis Academic must exactly match wording used in the article or all relevant items will not be retrieved—thus, knowledge of the way that journalists word articles can be of major importance to a search (e.g., "federal law," not "United States law"). Newsbank, on the other hand, applies approximately four or five subject headings and geographic headings to all articles included in the database. Keyword searching is also provided, and while one may limit search results by date, it is not required. Lack of subject headings in LexisNexis Academic results in more hits and lower relevancy than with Newsbank, even though the former provides a number of search tools such as adjacency and multiple word counts in an effort to specifically target more appropriate articles. Newsbank and LexisNexis Academic are both fairly expensive, unless purchased through consortial buying agreements.

Northern Light http://www.northernlight.com

An alternate method of searching the Internet for news sources from a large group of newspapers and other media is Northern Light, a sort of poor man's LexisNexis Academic. Searching is free as it is for Web sites produced by individual newspapers, but, also like those, full text of the articles more than two weeks old is only available for a fee, which ranges from $1.00 to $4.00/article. Using the "Power Search" for older materials is useful. And while it is possible to search specific publications, searchers are limited to words in the titles of articles or (in the case of newspapers) headlines. Northern Light includes over 7,000 publications, 480 of them news sources, a large percentage of which are campus newspapers. Among the newspapers expected but not covered, however, are the *New York Times* and *Los Angeles Times*. Others included duplicate the titles found in LexisNexis Academic and Newsbank. Under these circumstances, users interested only in a specific location will probably find it cheaper to go to the Web sites for specific newspapers, as frequently their search engines allow more detailed search parameters in locating relevant articles.

Other Local News Internet Sources

Newsdirectory.com http://www.newsdirectory.com

Although this Web site does lead to official municipal Web pages, this is not its primary purpose, which becomes evident upon entering the site. The official purpose of this site is to locate local media, including newspapers, city magazines, and local television stations. One may do so by state, region, or telephone area code. The first list to which the Web site defaults includes daily newspapers—for Memphis, this is the *Commercial Appeal*. Weekly newspapers for Memphis include the *Memphis Business Journal* and *Memphis Flyer*. Magazines include *Memphis Magazine*. News stations are also included. Anyone who does not have access to pay-for-use databases like LexisNexis Academic or Newsbank can still have access to these Web sites. Newsdirectory.com allows users unfamiliar with the names of publications specific to a city or town to gain access to them.

ChamberFind.com http://www.chamberfind.com

Local chambers of commerce are longtime providers of information for newcomers, tourists, and city inhabitants. This information is reputable and Chamberfind.com allows users to locate such sites quickly. Other sites leading to chamber of commerce sites are Official City Sites (http://officialcitysites.org) and Munisource.org, at http://www.munisource.org.

NATIONAL AND REGIONAL SOURCES

Regional Library Networks

In moving away from documents and newspapers produced locally, resources become more multifunctional and less news oriented. Sources given in the next sections may list government publications or newspapers and newspaper articles, but also frequently other types of sources, such as research studies on different aspects of local government, comparisons of city managers vs. mayoral councils as a form of city government, how county administrators and city mayors manage relationships in large urban areas, or how to handle security issues after September 11, 2001. Local libraries in smaller towns or cities may not have access to all the materials listed in these sources, and recourse to external locations through interlibrary loan or travel to a more salubrious location may be necessary.

Another inexpensive alternative to use of some of these databases is to access regional groups of libraries through state Web sites. Libraries were moving to online catalogs long before the Internet was available, so most regional libraries are now available through Web site locations. While pay-for-use databases are not always available for outside users, almost every library will allow access to its book collection (frequently including local documents) via catalog, whether in Telnet or Internet formats. Regional libraries like the Tennessee State Library and Archives in Nashville, Tennessee, contain online catalogs that list materials found in all contributing libraries in the state.

Tennessee State Library and Archives (Tennessee Department of State) http://www.state.tn.us/sos/statelib/tslahome.htm

This Web site not only contains a catalog that can be toggled to include the state library holdings only—or those of all libraries—but its "Tennessee History and Genealogy" links various lists of import to local government researchers, including lists of local newspapers held on microfilm in the state archives and county records held in its Nashville location. Although some materials require use on site, others can be borrowed by other Tennessee libraries for the use of their constituents.

For Web sites that allow searches for libraries by various criteria such as keyword, name, or geographic location, see either LibWeb (Library Servers via the World Wide Web), at http://sunsite.berkeley.edu/Libweb, or LibDex (The Library Index), at http://www.libdex.com.

Databases

WorldCat (FirstSearch/Online Computer Library Center [OCLC]) http://www.oclc.org/worldcat

WorldCat is easily the largest and most comprehensive bibliographic database in the world. It functions as a union catalog for the database of OCLC, familiar to most librarians as a cataloging and interlibrary loan network, and is available through OCLC's group of databases, FirstSearch. WorldCat includes records of all OCLC member libraries (some 41,000,000 records at present) for any items cataloged in participating libraries' collections, including books, serials, audiovisual materials, manuscript collections, theses, dissertations—any items that might be added to a local catalog database. Types of records included depend on policies of participating libraries (e.g., some libraries may not include information about manuscript collections, others may not include dissertations and/or theses). FirstSearch provides three levels of search capability: basic, advanced, and expert. Basic search allows searching by author, title, or keywords. Use of author or title functions is limited to keywords in chosen fields only, not to specific phrases. Results may be further limited by checking boxes labeled "Items on the Internet" and/or "Items in My Library." One may rank these items by relevance or date (the top 1,000 items), and may limit the search to format types: books/text, visual materials, computer files, serial publications, sound recordings, archival materials, musical scores, or maps. Basic searches are extremely crude for a database of this size and users should refrain from searching in this format, as the large volume of items returned may become frustrating when looking for a specific one.

Advanced format searching allows the most flexibility with the least effort. While the expert format necessitates that users learn prefixes for various search modes and other aspects of Boolean search mechanisms, advanced format users can identify changes in author, title, publisher, etc., by a mere change of the menu. Exact word phases can be searched as well as keywords. The large variety of labels is categorized by keyword, access method, accession number, publisher, standard number, subject, and date of update. Three dialog boxes allow one to search three different key elements in Boolean fashion while limiting results by format type (including Internet sources), language, date, and library location. WorldCat can be used to identify bibliographies as well as books and other published and unpublished works, including some master's theses, doctoral dissertations, manuscript collections, and other Web sites. Some libraries will catalog these, and others will not, which is part of the problem when using WorldCat. Identifying subject headings is enhanced by the availability of Library of Congress subject headings (LCSHs) or Sears subject headings in most libraries, which are most useful, since WorldCat is a union catalog based on catalogs developed by librarians who use these subject headings to maintain a certain amount of consistency and an ability to locate all books on a topic by using one term rather than trying to remember all terms that might be appropriate, as is true when using a keyword approach.

Public Affairs Information Service (PAIS)

"A little group of special librarians meeting at Kaaterskill in June, 1913, discussed a plan for keeping themselves informed systematically in regard to publications and movements of interest to them in their work. As the result, PAIS was organized on a cooperative basis, with Mr. John A. Lapp, director of the Indiana Bureau of Legislative Information, in charge" (Evans, p. v). PAIS has become one of the most well known and readily available sources of public policy information, including state, local, national, and foreign government publications and articles from a wide variety of periodicals, monographs, and conference proceedings. Covering 150 periodicals and 196 books, the first volume was published in 1915. By 2001, over 1,800 journals, 6,000 books, and thousands of Web sites and electronic documents have been reviewed annually for citations to be added to the PAIS database. Although print volumes remain in publication, an electronic version with citations dating from 1972 is available on CD-ROM (SilverPlatter Information, Inc., and Ovid Technologies) and online through NOTIS (Northwestern Online Total Integrated System), INNOPAC (Innovative Interfaces, Inc.), OCLC, and Cambridge Scientific Abstracts (CSA), as well as part of the OCLC FirstSearch databases, Ovid, the Gale Group, and Dialog. Present-day information is based largely on the holdings of the New York Public Library and materials received directly from publishers.

OCLC Public Affairs Information Service (Public Affairs Information Service) http://www.pais.org

The database contains 7,000 authorized subject headings. The 24 broad topics included in the subject classification system indicate the broad range of concerns included in the PAIS index, ranging from administration of justice to the environment and environmental policy. Other broad areas include government/health conditions and policy and transportation and transportation policy. Subject subdivisions and the complete list of journals indexed are available at this Web site. PAIS is available from other vendors, such as CSA, at http://www.csa.com, and Silver Platter/OVID, at http://www.silverplatter.com/catalog/pais.htm. While search methodology and practices rely on how the database has been designed by the vendors, FirstSearch, the OCLC product and the producer of this PAIS Web site, allows searching by abstract, access method (Internet address), accession number, author, government document number, publications date, publisher, series, source (journal title), special feature (tables, charts), standard number (ISSN or ISBN), subject, title, volume, or Web site special features (news, links, current events). In the advanced search format, one may limit a search by year, by phrase per document type (monograph, periodical article, Web site), by language phrase, government level, government document, electronic document, or local availability. The value of this source lies largely in its ability to identify a large number of different types of sources, particularly when considering local government information. The OCLC Web site listed for the database provides links to each individual vendor.

Internet Resources

State and Local Government on the Net
    http://www.statelocalgov.net/index.cfm

This Web site, produced by Piper Resources, was mentioned earlier as a primary locator to official city Web sites. It is also a resource for locating regional- and national-association Web sites and other sites related to local government information.

State and Local Governments: A Library of Congress Internet Resource Page
    http://lcweb.loc.gov/global/state/stategov.html

Another major Web site for locating information relating to local government information, this link is maintained by the Library of Congress, former publisher of *The Monthly Checklist of State Publications*. Besides the listings for individual states, this site includes sections on "Meta-Indexes for State and Local Government Information" and "State Government Information." The sections relating to other sites are brief in all of these sites, but the effectiveness of their lists is indicated by the frequency with which they are cited by other, lesser Web sites. These other Web sites may come and go, but these, because of the stability of their publishers, will continue to be maintained.

On the one hand, Web sites continue to increase in frantic numerical proportion, while on the other, they are being abandoned in almost due proportion. Site locations change and names frequently change as well. Local government researchers should place as much importance on knowing the means of locating sites of assistance as on familiarity with present sites. While search engines offer the possibility of searching for specific sites and types of information, subject browsing is likewise frequently offered. Yahoo, Ask Jeeves, Lycos, Google, and Netscape work through categories from North America to the United States to regional sections to local government. LookSmart and Overture subject browsers move more quickly toward local government sites but also include sites from the United Kingdom and other foreign nations. Because search engines cover only a fraction of the Web, searchers should use as many search engines as possible.

ACADEMIC AND RESEARCH SOURCES

Sage Urban Studies Abstracts (Sage Publications, quarterly http://www.sagepub.com/

Sage, which publishes several periodicals related to urban studies, including *Urban Affairs Quarterly*, *Urban Life*, *Urban Education*, and *Urban Affairs Annual Reviews*, is an appropriate publisher for an abstracting service in this field. *Urban Studies Abstracts* covers 100 mostly academic periodicals and "books, pamphlets, government publications, significant speeches, legislative research studies, as well as other fugitive material" (verso of title page). In this quarterly individually numbered publication, entries are arranged under 14 broad headings covering such topics as "Trends in Urbanization and Urban Society" and "Social and Public Services." Multiple specific headings (an average of 5 or 6) are assigned to each entry, including geographic headings when applicable. Subject indexes containing these more specific designations are included in the back of each quarterly

and cumulated in the final quarter of each year. Separate author indexes are also included each quarter and cumulatively at the end of the year. The year's final quarterly also includes a list of publications. Coverage is international in scope but appears to include only English-language articles, with an emphasis on American publications. This publication, which began in 1973, is now available online through EBSCo Information Services (Elton B. Stephens Co., Birmingham, Alabama).

Urban Affairs Abstracts (*Urban Affairs Review*) (Sage Publishing, quarterly) http://www.sagepub.com

A publication, now defunct, similar to *Urban Studies Abstracts* was *Urban Affairs Abstracts*. Published from 1972 to 1994 and coproduced by the National League of Cities and the University of Kentucky's Center for Urban and Economic Research, it covered more than 400 periodicals. Despite the similarity of subject matter to *Studies*, the almost indistinguishable overlap between the two abstracting services was only 20 titles. Besides academic journals, this publication, which listed articles only, also referenced government periodicals (federal and state), foundation and association newsletters and periodicals (chambers of commerce, state municipal leagues, the National Association of Towns and Townships). Many of the periodicals are now available online, so that while indexing is historical only, it can help point the way toward associations and publications that can assist in locating information on a specific city. The National League of Cities Web site (http://www.nlc.org/nlc_org/site) can often be helpful in accessing their own publications and those of the state leagues.

ABC Pol Sci (Cambridge Scientific Abstracts) http://www.csa3.com/csa/factsheets/polsci.shtml

The subtitle to this ABC-Clio publication (now produced by CSA) explains its focus and arrangement: *A Bibliography of Contents: Political Science and Government*. Since 1969, this guide to approximately 300 international journals has included such relevant titles as *Urban Affairs Review*, *State and Local Government Review*, and *Journal of Urban History*. Tables of contents from the included journals are arranged alphabetically by the title of the journals in each issue. A brief survey of the subject index by category for the year 2000 indicated 97 articles under local government, 52 under cities, 198 under urban affairs, and many entries under topics often associated with local government, such as housing, police, public schools, and museums. Each issue contains a subject index, and the sixth issue of each volume contains annually cumulated subject, author, and periodical title indexes. Numbers at the end of subject arrays or author's name refer the user back to item numbers in the table of contents section.

Dissertation Abstracts Online http://www.umi.com/ products/pt=product=disabonline/shtml

Dissertations are generally unpublished reports or studies, some of which may prove beneficial to those seeking information on local governments. The number of records written by graduate students in public administration or political science presently exceeds 13,500. A general search using title keywords "(municipal or local or city) and government" garners some 840 documents. "Chicago" and "government" as title words net some 13 items. UMI (University Microfilms, Inc.) provides full text digital access to dissertations from 1997 through Dissertation Abstracts only are available through ProQuest Information and Learning, its parent company, in both CD-ROM and Internet formats and from Dialog DataStar and STN (The Scientific and Technical Network) International in an online format. Subjects/descriptors are extremely broad and relate more to degree types than to specific contents; for instance, public administration, hydrogeology, environment. In many cases, keyword searching includes the abstract as well as the title and other bibliographic elements, but restricting keywords to the title field is an appropriate search strategy, as dissertation titles are generally more explicit of the contents than those of published works. Despite the addition of a European section in 1988, most of the dissertations are North American (United States and Canada).

FEDERAL GOVERNMENT RESOURCES

The federal government has devolved certain responsibilities upon state and local governments. Yet, it spends millions of dollars yearly on urban housing, education, transportation, public safety, and health— all topics that interest or form a part of the concerns of local government. Some of the titles that indicate the wealth and variety of government publications relating to the field of local government are

The Status of Major HUD Funding Awarded to the Memphis Housing Authority Site

Researcher Training and Orientation, Louisville, Kentucky, September 13–15, 1999
Report on the Formative Evaluation Process for School Improvement: A Joint Initiative between AEL, Inc. and the Center for Research in Educational Policy (CREP) at the University of Memphis
Equal Educational Opportunity for Hispanic Students in the Oklahoma City Public Schools
Police Practices and Civil Rights in New York City
Problems of Urban America: Hearings before the Committee on Government Operations, House of Representatives, One Hundred Second Congress, first session, January 25 and March 12, 1991

The databases or indexes previously discussed—the major exception being PAIS—list these government publications, so some recognition of the media that index these materials is pertinent.

GPO Access (U.S. Government Printing Office [GPO], Superintendent of Documents) http://www.access.gpo.gov/su_docs/index.html

As the GPO has turned more and more to Web resources, the *Monthly Catalog of U.S. Government Publications* moved from print to the Web at the GPO Access Web site. This site also provides access to online versions of the *Code of Federal Regulations*, the *Federal Register*, the *Congressional Record*, the *United States Code, Commerce Business Daily*, and several other sources that are listed as actual separate databases on the GPO Access page entry point. These databases can contain information specific to local governments. Multiple access points are searchable, such as Superintendent of Documents (SuDoc) class numbers, but most of the details are unknown to the casual searcher. For those seeking specific topics, three methods are available: keyword search, keyword search of online titles, and title search. For those seeking online titles only, use of the keyword-search-of-online-titles dialog box is necessary. In addition, it is necessary to add "http," "url," or "purl" to the search. Although samples of these are displayed just beneath the dialog boxes, users seeing "endangered species" as one example or PURL and "Dept. of State" as another may not grasp the signals expressed. Clicking on "More Help" gives one information about Boolean search methods and how to do numerical searches, but not about the differences between the keyword and title searches. Searches normally return a default number of 40 records, but 200 is the maximum. To search on more than one element, such as title words and date, move the page down to the section labeled "Multiple Field Search." To obtain the appropriate search form, click on elements you wish to search and submit this request. At this point it is possible to insert words, phrases, or numbers to be searched. The listing of records returned is one of the weakest features of this database. It is supposedly in order of relevance, but often the results are unrelated to the actual topic being researched.

People unfamiliar with the GPO Access site may find it rather daunting. On the first page, one is offered the chance to do a site search that searches topics on the site, but not records within individual databases. On the page devoted to the Catalog of U.S. Government Publications, one is offered the chance to "Search Government" or to "Browse Topics." "Search Government" leads to searching FirstGov, which the user is told may leave GPO Access, but what exactly is being searched or the difference between what "First-Gov" leads to and what "GPO Access" leads to is unclear. "Browse Topics" leads to a University of Central Oklahoma Web site, which contains pathfinders to government publications on some 150 topics listed and searchable by keywords. The lack of explanation of what really constitutes a database lies in the difficulty of generalizability of the concept and the blurring of distinctions that occurs when items are available on the Internet. Books, articles, documents, and Web sites are no longer separate tangible entities but merely different entry points, some of which are longer and others shorter.

MarciveWeb DOCS (Monthly Catalog of Government Printing Office Documents) (Marcive Inc.) http://www.marcive.com/webdocs/webdocs.dll

While GPO Access is a free database dating from 1994, MarciveWeb DOCS is a similar pay-for-use database for documents published since 1976. Published by Marcive for the purposes of developing MARC (Machine Readable Cataloging) records for U.S. government publications to be listed in library catalogs, this database allows general searchers to access records on all U.S. government publications cataloged by the U.S. Government Printing Office—an estimated 10 percent of total federal government publications actually produced between July 1976 and the present. Since MarciveWeb DOCS searches only the records found in the monthly catalog, it is not as confusing as GPO Access. Before listing search terms in

the dialog box, one should choose both a search type (browse or keyword) and search index (title, author, subject). One may also choose a numerical index if one wishes. These include SuDoc number, technical report number, stock number, GPO number, monthly catalog number, or OCLC number. The browse function allows one to search words or phrases *at the beginning* of the title, author's (last) name, or subject—the keyword allows one to locate words or phrases *anywhere* in the title, etc. Keyword is obviously the broader function, so anyone attempting to find the most matches would, in all probability, choose the keyword function.

FirstGov: Local Governments [formerly U.S. State and Local Gateway] (Office of Citizen Services and Communications, U.S. General Services Administration) http://www.firstgov.gov/Agencies/Local.shtml

This FirstGov page is a product of several federal government agencies, such as Housing and Urban Development and Department of Education, that have an interest in state and local government developments. This Web site contains links to a wide variety of information defined either by topic (administrative management, disaster/emergencies, education, families/children, housing, health, etc.), by type (best practices, laws/regulations, contacts, tools, etc.), by "Current Issues" (Brownfields, performance measures, sustainable communities, welfare reform), by "Partners" (national organizations related to state and local government), and by "Hot Links" (federal one-stops, state/local links, federal agencies, reference room, news). Most of the links lead to federal government information, with the exception of "Partners" and the state/local hot links. The "Partners" listings link to the organizational Web sites, while the state/local hot links are three or more outside links—usually including Piper's State and Local Government on the Net (http://www.statelocalgov.net/index.cfm), previously discussed.

FirstGov http://www.firstgov.gov

The portal of the United States Government. This database provides access to federal government information of interest on the local level. Services to citizens include filing address changes, finding government jobs, applying for student loans, locating post offices and schools, applying for passports, obtaining birth and marriage certificates, and finding zip codes and product recall information. Businesses may find out about federal auctions and sales and business and subcontracting opportunities, file taxes, file for patents and trademarks, report wages, and obtain employer ID numbers. Governments and their employees are offered grants, geographic information, an employee locator, and information on government jobs, buying supplies and services, and auctions and sales.

There are always more places to search for information, but those who search must always take into consideration that there is a sort of law of diminishing returns as fewer and fewer highly related sources are searched. Generalists are prone to search Readers Guide to Periodical Literature or Gale's Infotrac or Expanded Academic Index. When the other more specific resources are unavailable, then these might be the most appropriate sources from which the user might profit. Academicians would also search Social Science Abstracts or Social Sciences Citation Index, and while much would be gained in the number of journals covered, most of the information would be repetitive and perhaps disappointing. At other times, subject-specific indexes can be more appropriate. When looking for materials produced by the Memphis City Schools, the Educational Resources Information Center (ERIC) database with its accompanying ERIC documents could very well be the best source, yet to suggest it as a general or all-inclusive database for local government materials would be misleading. For scientific reports, particularly of government-assisted research related to urban technology, the National Technical Information Service (NTIS) database would be of import, but much concerning urban and county government lies outside this area as well. In such cases the more subject-specific chapters included in this work will probably point the way toward databases and indexes that are appropriate.

FOR FURTHER READING

Evans, Orrena Louise. Preface to *Bulletin of the Public Affairs Service: A Cooperative Clearing House of Public Affairs Information: First Annual Cumulation*. White Plains, N.Y.: H. W. Wilson, 1915.

CHAPTER 5
Finding Information on Municipal and County Codes

Mary Martin

MAJOR TOPICS COVERED

MAJOR SOURCES DISCUSSED

INTRODUCTION

Finding a city ordinance or municipal code of ordinances can be a daunting experience. Alternatively, it could be as easy as sitting down at a personal computer. There is a certain strategy, when employed, that can make searching for laws and codes more efficient. The strategy used would depend on what type of information you have. If you have access to a telephone or an Internet-connected computer, the information might be found online. If you can travel to a library, or a city or county office, you may be able to find the codes there in paper. Imagine the following scenario: You have received a ticket for having snow on the sidewalk in front of your house. All the information you have about the law that you have broken is a citation with the number of a municipal code violation. You also know that at some point you did not receive a ticket for leaving snow on a similar sidewalk. You

might ask yourself, "What did the law actually require of me?" You might also ask, "What options for handling the citation may be available to me?" Finally, you might ask, "Where might I be able to find out more about the code I have been accused of violating?" This chapter outlines a search strategy for locating this information. The strategy will describe what to look for, how to look for the information, what you can expect to find, and where to look for it.

First, laws/ordinances and codes will be described, and the differences between them clarified. Second, the subject of jurisdiction will be introduced to better understand where copies of laws/ordinances and codes can be located. A short discussion of the legal structure of local government bodies will be included to help in understanding what one can generally expect to find in local government law. A brief discussion of the relationship between federal, state, and local government jurisdiction will also be included to further clarify issues. Specific resources will then be described and examined in detail.

ORDINANCES AND CODES

It is helpful here to distinguish between the terms *ordinance* and *code* within the context of their application to the law. The terms are sometimes used interchangeably, although they have very different meanings.

The term *ordinance* is formally defined as a rule established by authority, a permanent rule of action, a law, or a statute. It designates a local law of a municipal corporation, duly enacted by the proper authorities, prescribing general, uniform, and permanent rules of conduct relating to the corporate affairs of the municipality. An ordinance is the equivalent of a municipal statute, passed by the city council or equivalent body, and governing matters not already covered by a federal or state law. Ordinances commonly govern zoning, building, safety, and other matters of municipality.

A *code* is a systematic collection, a compendium of revisions of laws, rules, or regulations. It is a private or official compilation of all permanent laws in force consolidated and classified according to subject matter (e.g., United States Code). A code can include laws of all jurisdictions; for example, state and federal laws regarding commerce, such as the Uniform Commercial Code. It can also consist of only local laws, such as the Chicago Code of Ordinances. Most codes are updated irregularly. Some cities or counties might update them annually, and some might publish a new edition when revisions are required. A very common format consists of a loose-leaf volume that can be updated with new pages on a regular basis or whenever new ordinances are passed. An archival volume usually resides in the city or county clerk's office and any other government office that has need of them. Many public libraries keep copies for public use. Many municipalities and county governments are putting copies of their code on the World Wide Web. There are collective sites that point to many of these municipalities from the one site.

The reason both terms (*ordinance* and *code*) are described in detail here is that they are often used interchangeably when referring to local law. They do not necessarily mean the same thing. One can look at an ordinance that is not presented as a part of a code. Codes can pertain to only one particular subject, such as the electrical code. The "Code" can also refer to the collection of all codes that exist for a local government. For example, if you ask a city clerk to see a copy of the city's law against leaving snow unshoveled on your sidewalk, you may be referred to the ordinance itself, or to the (municipal) city code. It is important to know exactly what is being presented to you.

Content of Code Sources

Finding sources for municipal and county codes can be as problematic as the sources are varied, reflecting the diversity of government organizations that create and maintain them. There are not yet publishers of aggregate paper collections of municipal codes such as the state codes published by West's or Deering's. The logistics of such a project have proved too daunting for a single publisher. The amount of updating that would be necessary for all the municipal and county governments in the United States (tens of thousands) is evidently too formidable a task for any one publisher to undertake. Each local government entity is responsible for the compilation and maintenance of its own code. Most have paper loose-leaf versions that can be compiled and updated when necessary. Some use electronic versions published on CD-ROM by companies such as West's Publishing. However, keeping the code updated when there are changes requires replacement of the CD.

Another means of accomplishing dissemination of codes is via the fast-growing popularity of the Internet. There are some companies that offer to convert the city and county codes of a government to an electronic format that can be published and updated on the Web. The company then provides a link on its Web site to the city code. Although this is a relatively efficient way to handle a large number of municipalities, there are only a small number of cities that currently have their codes available through these sites. This same process is occurring on the level of county government. This process requires a high degree of technological capability that many local governments do not yet have. The municipal and county code sites are discussed in more detail in the section on Internet sources of codes. When searching for a local law, there are three important steps. One, it is important to establish the jurisdiction of the law (e.g., federal, state, county, or city). The second step is to determine where copies of the law might be located. The third step is to determine how to best view or obtain a copy of the law.

Local Government Jurisdiction

There are two questions that are important to ask when looking for copies of laws. The first is, "Is it a local, state, or federal law?" There is a second question few people even know to ask, about whether or not the issue is merely an internal agency policy—not the law per se, but a necessary agency rule that is needed to apply the law. The latter usually involves another type of law, called administrative or regulatory law, which will be discussed more thoroughly in the next chapter. Making this distinction before beginning the search can help one avoid searching in the wrong source. It is important to find out what aspect and geographic scope of government has jurisdiction (provenance) over a matter. That factor influences who wrote the law, where it is currently stored, and how it can be accessed.

Once it is known who collected, archived, and/or published the law or related information, the user can then follow a paper (or electronic) trail to its current location. Once the location is determined, then the task becomes one of retrieval. This may involve the use of specialized technology such as a microfilm reader/printer in a library or a personal computer system with Internet capability. It may be necessary to travel to a government office and request the information from a government representative, such as a court clerk. Retrieving documents at these types of service points may also involve a monetary cost such as per-page photocopying charges or, in extreme cases, fees to an online service provider.

When working with local government law and information, it is helpful to know the structure of the government entity. County, city, and township governments have a certain jurisdictional and institutional organization. An initial source of information to consult when an inexperienced searcher is looking for government information is a simple government organization chart. Such government organization charts are sometimes available from a city or county clerk's office. Charts are sometimes available on the Web site, when there is one. Charts can indicate what level of government is responsible for a particular area.

Local governments may have some flexibility in forming a structure subject to higher levels of political subdivision. There are model organizational outlines that are often followed when municipalities are created or modified by legal authority. These written models can be found in several sources. These sources can be found in a library that houses legal materials, such as an academic or county law library. More detailed information on the organization of city and county government is provided in the chapter on structure of local government.

As described in the chapter on local government organization, there are certain prescribed areas in which local government has jurisdiction. In some instances, jurisdiction is shared, or concurrent, with local, state, and/or federal government. In others, jurisdiction is exclusive to local, state, or federal authorities. Regional or joint powers authorities such as the Southern California Association of Governments or the Los Angeles Metropolitan Transit Authority are local government entities that have a mixture of both concurrent and exclusive jurisdictions.

In general, local government authority centers on regulation and administration of permits, licenses, and certificates (inspections and issuance), local contracts, planning and zoning (land use), environment, local roads, and public works. There is also local jurisdiction over various kinds of property, public assistance and housing, schools, fire, police, and animal protection. There are additional laws and rules governing judicial actions and local courts, local elections and referendums, local government employees and officials, local authorities, districts and utilities, public corporations and local finance. Local government law is created and then organized into subject areas, which mirror how the ordinances (laws) are organized into codes.

It is not always practical for an ordinary citizen (or searcher) to locate organizational information about a government. There are simple steps that one can take to find information without establishing government authority. Even if the government authority is not known, locating local government offices through a directory can be the next step to finding more information.

GENERAL GUIDES

Guide to Finding Legal and Regulatory Information on the Internet, by Yvonne J. Chandler (Neal-Schuman Publishers, Inc.)

A good general starting point for Internet sources of government codes available online is this guide. This source, as the title indicates, focuses on legal information to be found on the Web. There is a scarcity of information in this publication, as elsewhere, about municipal and county codes of ordinances. Published in 1998, the *Guide* is organized according to the descriptions of the nature of legal information on the Internet. It identifies guides and meta-indexes (an all-inclusive term describing a Web site that includes indexes, sources, and other Web sites) to legal and government information resources, judicial law resources, and the U.S. Government Printing Office online system (GPO Access). The *Guide* also describes federal and state legislative sources, federal and state administrative law sources, and secondary reference sources for legal and government information. There is a subject and name index as well as a Web site index in the book. Web sites, of course, are often only as permanent as the computer on which they reside—and sometimes less so if the author or another person does not continue to monitor changes in URLs (uniform resource locators, or World Wide Web address). Many sites provide referring links, or forwarding addresses, so to speak, when changing URLs. The *Guide* is nevertheless a good current resource.

State and Local Government on the Net http://www. statelocalgov.net/index.cfm

It naturally follows that meta-indexes develop into meta-sites that are collections of links to and descriptions of Web sites in the area of government. One of the most comprehensive meta-sites, State and Local Government on the Net, is maintained by Piper Resources and has an extensive list of links arranged geographically by state, regional, county, and city place names.

A quick check of the city Web sites available on this resource revealed that about 50 percent of the listings included a city clerk's office or a county recorder's office. This site features a keyword search engine that determines whether a place has a link on the Web site. The first section provides links by state—under California, for example, there are Web links to statewide offices, agencies, regional agencies, county and city governments, and sometimes the chamber of commerce. There are also sections with links to state sites, multistate sites, federal sites (limited) and national-organization sites. There are links to organizations such as the Local Government Institute and the Municipal Code Corporation, as well as to some local nongovernmental organization (NGO) sites. A quick check of a county link, Contra Costa County, California, took me to the county government Web site. The site was loaded with information, including a search engine with capacity for a long list of recorded documents, ranging from an affidavit of title to a zoning permit. There was not an obvious source to an online version of the Contra Costa County Code of Ordinances. The link to the Orange County site did have a link to the Orange County Code of Ordinances. This

Web site has a sensible hierarchy and is easy to use. The simple, straightforward approach is easily followed.

University of Michigan Documents Center: Local Government and Politics http://www.lib.umich.edu/govdocs/pslocal.html

This Web site is comprehensive. The links are eclectic and cover a wide range of resources on local government and politics and city and county directories and Web sites. There are separate sections that provide links and descriptions of categories such as associations of local officials, laws and municipal codes, local government reports, and resources specific to Michigan.

The Web site lists such varied links as an "International Local Government Home Page" and Official City Sites (http://OfficialCitySites.org). At first glance this site appears to be tourist related, but when I linked to the Alameda County, California, Web site, http://www.co.alameda.ca.us, the county ordinances were linked right there on the home page.

DIRECTORIES OF MUNICIPAL AND COUNTY INFORMATION

Directories of municipal information vary considerably in scope and organization but usually have certain features in common, such as indexes by name and geographical jurisdiction. A telephone company servicing a particular area, a commercial publisher such as Donnelly, or a governmental agency such as the county of Los Angeles can publish directories, which can be as comprehensive as a local telephone book or as specialized as a list of contacts for local government throughout the United States. Directories have special features that depend on what the user's purpose might be.

One citizen might be looking for a person to talk to about a problem with her neighbor's animals. Another case could involve a government official who is interested in the structure of the municipal government to determine how to proceed with a zoning matter. A different directory is appropriate for each situation.

If one does not know the jurisdiction of a law, a call to city hall or a township or county office may help find the answer to this question. Simply consult your telephone book, where government listings will usually be on the blue pages. Local telephone books are good resources for local government addresses and telephone numbers. Most telephone directories have a section in the front called Government Offices—City, Government Offices—County, etc. This section lists telephone numbers for federal, state, and local government offices located in the particular area covered by the telephone directory. Telephone books can be limited in scope by the local governmental jurisdiction.

The nearest city or county clerk's office may be able to tell you where to locate the information, or whom to contact if the office cannot help you. It is important to remember that the person who answers the telephone may not be an expert on the subject. Sometimes one must persist in asking to speak to an authoritative source.

There are also directories that list local government offices, officials, and telephone numbers throughout the United States. There are additional specialized directories for municipal or county officials. There are both telephone and specialized municipal directories available online. Some are free and some are fee based.

Database searching of online telephone and other directories can yield additional advantages, such as keyword and name searching. The paper directories are described in the following section, and the Internet sources are described separately.

Government Phone Book USA (11th ed., Omnigraphics, Inc., annual)

This publication is a comprehensive guide to federal, state, county, and local government offices in the United States. It provides access to every key government office—from the municipal to the federal level. There are listings of telephone numbers and mailing addresses for over 165,000 government offices in the United States. There are also fax numbers, e-mail addresses, and addresses of Web sites when available. The volume runs over 2,000 pages.

It is arranged into three sections. The first, the Quick Reference Section, lists key telephone numbers and addresses of federal government. It includes offices such as the Executive Office of the President, cabinet offices such as the State Department, and administrative agencies such as Health and Human Services. There are also listings for the entire U.S. Congress, with contact addresses and phone numbers for all congressional representatives, House and Senate. E-mail addresses and fax numbers are provided when available. The directory lists regional government offices (such as those for congressional representatives), administrative agencies, and regional offices; provides maps; and has a keyword index.

The state section is arranged similarly, beginning with quick references for capitols, governors, and state information offices (including those in Washington, D.C.). The next section lists individual state government offices alphabetically arranged. There are names, addresses, and telephone numbers of every elected state official. There is also a listing of state courts and a keyword index to all entries.

The City and County Offices section begins with a quick reference listing of contact information on sources for county or municipal associations. The second section has county maps by state, followed by a County Offices section, and a complete listing of all county bodies of government. Although it does not have personal contact telephone number information, it does have office contact information, which is valuable in case of changes in employees. City and county sections have organizational listings for cities with populations over 15,000 and for counties with populations over 25,000. This is an excellent resource for any library, particularly public libraries, or government office. A nice feature is that all governmental jurisdictions are in one volume. It is a very complete listing for municipal and county government offices. The price is high but not unreasonable.

Municipal Yellow Book: Who's Who in the Leading City and County Governments and Local Authorities (Leadership Directories, Inc., semi-annual)

There are several sources of municipal directory information located in most libraries. The most current, because it is updated semiannually, is the *Municipal Yellow Book*. Municipal and county officials are listed according to the most recent elections, and the volume lists when elections have not been determined. Also listed is whether or not city and county government is combined, along with the official name of the municipality and general election information. There are also geographic, name, and master indexes. The selection of cities was based on 1990 Census Bureau population data. To represent counties that do not have county government, the largest city in the county is selected and listed in the Cities section. Cities and counties are also included based on a combination of revenue and subscriber interest.

This source is excellent for locating the seat of governmental jurisdiction for a particular area, especially if the local telephone book is not able to do it. The directory is organized alphabetically by city and by

City	State	Type	Service provision	Full-time paid personnel	Full-time uniformed personnel	Duty hours per week	Minimum base salary ($)	Maximum base salary ($)	Longevity pay	Maximum salary with longevity ($)	Years of service for longevity	Total expenditures (A) ($)	Total personnel expenditures (B) ($)	(B) as % of (A)	Salaries and wages (C) ($)	City contribution to retirement and social security (D) ($)	City contribution to insurance (E) ($)	Capital outlay (F) ($)	All other (G) ($)
10,000–24,999 continued																			
SELMA	CA	C	3	21	19	56	27,804	33,804	N	—	—	1,832	1,266	69	1,027	133	105	206	361
SHARON	PA	C	1	139	53	42	19,123	35,464	Y	37,464	4	1,190	223	19	0	118	105	11	235
SHERWOOD	AR	C	—	—	—	—	—	—	—	—	—	—	—	—	—	—	—	—	—
SIDNEY	OH	C	1	37	36	—	32,240	42,440	Y	44,562	5	3,820	2,508	66	1,841	449	218	60	1,252
SIERRA MADRE	CA	C	3	—	—	40	—	—	—	—	—	455	151	33	143	5	3	129	175
SMITHFIELD	RI	T	1	44	38	42	28,763	37,238	Y	—	5	3,914	3,479	89	2,444	535	500	98	337
SNELLVILLE	GA	C	—	—	—	—	—	—	—	—	—	—	—	—	—	—	—	—	—
SNYDER	TX	C	3	9	9	53	24,372	27,588	Y	27,788	1	540	400	74	317	59	23	34	106
SOLANA BEACH	CA	C	1	—	—	56	37,138	45,249	N	—	—	1,956	1,062	54	1,062	0	0	220	186
SOLEDAD	CA	C	3	—	—	40	—	—	N	—	—	246	110	44	90	11	8	29	107
SOMERSWORTH	NH	C	1	12	12	42	24,744	30,095	Y	31,135	—	800	702	88	564	36	102	7	92
SOUTH CHARLESTON	WV	C	3	—	—	40	21,158	30,643	N	—	—	—	—	—	—	—	—	—	—
SOUTH DAYTONA	FL	C	1	14	13	56	22,017	33,026	Y	—	—	1,004	779	78	587	154	38	6	220
SOUTH EL MONTE	CA	C	—	—	—	—	—	—	—	—	—	—	—	—	—	—	—	—	—
SOUTH EUCLID	OH	C	1	32	—	—	35,978	51,703	Y	52,853	6	2,401	2,175	91	1,703	319	153	100	127
SOUTH HADLEY	MA	T	—	—	—	—	—	—	—	—	—	—	—	—	—	—	—	—	—
SOUTH LAKE TAHOE	CA	C	3	36	34	56	34,390	41,802	N	—	—	—	—	—	—	—	—	—	—
SOUTH MIAMI	FL	C	—	—	—	—	—	—	—	—	—	—	—	—	—	—	—	—	—
SOUTH PARK	PA	Tp	2	—	—	—	—	—	—	—	—	151	—	—	—	—	—	—	151
SOUTH SALT LAKE	UT	C	3	36	35	56	29,136	41,556	N	—	—	4,349	2,562	59	1,645	700	217	1,793	390
SOUTH WHITEHALL	PA	Tp	2	—	—	—	—	—	—	—	—	203	—	—	—	—	—	—	200
SPANISH FORK	UT	C	2	—	—	—	—	—	—	—	—	—	—	—	—	—	—	—	—
SPENCER	MA	T	2	—	—	—	—	—	—	—	—	—	—	—	—	—	—	—	67
SPENCER	IA	C	3	5	5	56	27,643	33,218	Y	—	10	256	212	83	179	33	—	22	55
SPRINGFIELD	TN	C	1	23	23	53	23,068	31,471	N	—	—	1,131	934	83	770	76	88	77	119
SPRINGFIELD	OH	Tp	7	16	16	40	—	—	—	—	—	2,627	1,759	67	1,441	245	73	417	451
SPRINGVILLE	UT	C	2	—	—	—	—	—	—	—	—	—	—	—	—	—	—	—	—
ST. ALBANS	WV	C	1	—	—	56	19,211	23,201	Y	—	5	969	758	78	541	76	141	15	196
ST. AUGUSTINE	FL	C	1	27	26	56	25,640	34,615	N	—	—	1,238	1,134	92	913	160	61	2	102
ST. CHARLES	IL	C	3	—	—	—	35,844	55,145	N	—	—	3,780	2,984	79	2,369	349	266	66	729
ST. CLOUD	FL	C	1	35	33	56	26,566	38,242	N	—	—	2,443	2,081	85	1,566	271	244	169	194
STAFFORD	CT	T	2	—	—	—	—	—	—	—	—	220	—	—	—	—	—	—	220
STARKVILLE	MS	C	1	46	45	56	22,996	24,396	—	—	—	1,992	1,672	84	1,340	230	102	49	271
STATESVILLE	NC	C	1	55	54	53	22,935	32,417	N	—	—	—	2,127	—	1,752	219	156	464	353
STAUNTON	VA	C	3	31	30	56	20,588	32,951	N	—	—	1,746	1,346	77	1,058	229	59	266	134
STEPHENVILLE	TX	C	3	—	24	56	26,892	33,300	Y	34,800	1	1,358	1,183	87	930	175	77	22	152
STERLING	CO	C	7	—	16	53	28,680	40,340	N	—	—	1,000	780	78	602	66	112	53	167
STEUBENVILLE	OH	C	1	—	—	56	—	—	—	—	—	—	—	—	—	—	—	—	—
STEVENS POINT	WI	C	1	39	38	56	34,779	40,588	Y	41,248	5	2,985	2,854	96	2,027	827	—	47	131
STILLWATER	MN	C	1	—	—	56	40,212	45,228	Y	48,348	5	—	—	—	—	—	—	—	—
STONEHAM	MA	T	1	41	40	42	34,957	44,332	N	—	—	2,448	2,269	93	2,095	—	174	39	140
STUART	FL	C	1	33	—	—	27,620	41,003	N	—	—	2,912	1,895	65	1,377	378	140	277	740
STURGIS	MI	C	3	13	—	56	31,061	37,561	Y	—	5	968	657	68	637	14	5	—	312
SUDBURY	MA	T	1	36	32	42	35,172	38,523	Y	40,064	6	2,519	1,802	72	1,802	—	—	567	150
SUFFERN	NY	V	2	—	—	—	—	—	—	—	—	—	—	—	—	—	—	—	—
SULPHUR	LA	C	1	59	57	53	23,468	—	Y	43,296	3	2,825	2,076	73	1,787	162	127	318	431
SULPHUR SPRINGS	TX	C	3	22	22	53	26,664	29,640	Y	29,880	1	1,016	896	88	705	131	60	41	79
SUMMIT	NJ	C	3	—	—	42	—	—	—	—	—	—	—	—	—	—	—	—	—
SWEETWATER	TX	C	1	24	24	53	27,888	30,768	Y	—	1	521	144	28	—	71	73	70	24
SYCAMORE	OH	Tp	—	—	—	48	—	—	—	—	—	—	—	—	—	—	—	—	—
SYLACAUGA	AL	C	1	—	—	56	25,043	27,670	N	—	—	841	724	86	602	50	72	—	117
TARBORO	NC	T	3	18	18	—	20,884	61,097	Y	—	5	1,110	832	75	674	105	52	132	146
TARPON SPRINGS	FL	C	1	27	25	56	26,664	39,996	—	—	—	1,543	1,301	84	1,069	163	70	7	235
TAYLOR	TX	C	3	26	—	56	24,290	34,322	Y	35,522	1	1,015	926	91	765	104	57	10	79
TERRELL	TX	C	3	—	—	53	29,828	34,932	Y	—	1	—	—	—	—	—	—	—	—
THE DALLES	OR	C	—	—	—	—	—	—	—	—	—	—	—	—	—	—	—	—	—
THIBODAUX	LA	C	2	—	—	—	—	—	—	—	—	257	—	—	—	—	—	—	223
THOMASVILLE	NC	C	1	50	50	56	20,497	30,746	Y	32,437	1	2,371	1,867	79	1,580	174	112	28	476
TIFFIN	OH	C	1	36	35	—	27,764	34,547	Y	38,002	20	2,458	2,205	90	1,657	382	166	52	200
TINTON FALLS	NJ	B	—	—	—	—	—	—	—	—	—	—	—	—	—	—	—	—	—
TIVERTON	RI	T	1	28	28	42	23,975	35,182	Y	37,293	5	—	1,165	—	1,165	—	—	—	—
TONAWANDA	NY	C	8	28	27	40	29,900	—	Y	43,512	5	2	—	—	—	—	—	—	—
TRAVERSE CITY	MI	C	1	23	23	56	25,101	33,022	Y	35,323	8	1,815	1,281	71	1,053	105	123	—	534
TROY	OH	C	1	42	41	56	32,525	45,028	Y	49,531	5	3,278	2,841	87	2,107	508	226	143	294
TUKWILA	WA	C	1	64	60	56	45,564	57,096	Y	59,796	5	6,781	5,616	83	4,668	217	731	54	1,111
TULLAHOMA	TN	C	3	31	30	—	26,760	26,760	N	—	—	1,535	1,263	82	1,003	122	138	27	244
TWENTYNINE PALMS	CA	C	—	—	—	—	—	—	—	—	—	—	—	—	—	—	—	—	—
TWO RIVERS	WI	C	1	20	19	56	31,865	36,379	Y	37,461	15	1,574	1,468	93	1,028	269	171	1	104
UKIAH	CA	C	1	16	15	56	36,103	43,883	N	—	—	1,819	1,219	67	1,054	94	72	11	589
UNIONTOWN	PA	C	1	—	—	48	—	—	—	—	—	—	—	—	—	—	—	—	—
UNIVERSITY HEIGHTS	OH	C	1	29	29	—	38,459	47,809	Y	48,048	3	2,386	2,186	92	1,659	286	241	103	98
UNIVERSITY PARK	TX	C	1	35	2	—	36,828	46,985	Y	—	1	2,745	2,364	86	1,844	393	126	107	274
UPPER ALLEN	PA	Tp	2	—	—	—	—	—	—	—	—	—	—	—	—	—	—	—	—
UPPER MORELAND	PA	Tp	3	5	5	48	43,905	51,792	Y	—	5	580	340	59	277	26	37	19	221
URBANA	OH	C	3	24	23	56	31,694	42,907	Y	42,907	20	2	—	—	—	—	—	—	—

Table 5.1 Fire Department Personnel, Salaries, and Expenditures for Cities 10,000 and Over: 2001 (Source: *The Municipal Yearbook 2002*)

county or parish (counties are called *parishes* in Louisiana) throughout the United States. Information on over 32,000 officials, such as name, job title, address(es), telephone number(s), and fax and e-mail addresses, is kept updated. Their educational background is included, along with information on whether they were elected or appointed to office. In the front of the book is a list of names of officials newly elected since the last edition. It is an excellent comprehensive source for a user who might have occasion to contact many city or county governments or for a large library or organization in which there might be many users looking for this information in a wide variety of geographic jurisdictions.

This source is very comprehensive in the amount of information provided for each city or county, but it is more selective in terms of the number of cities covered than some directories. Only very basic information is provided for all municipalities. This publication is also available on CD-ROM as part of a pricey subscription to 14 of the company's directories. It is a valuable resource.

Municipal Yearbook (International City Managers' Association, annual)

The International City Managers' Association has published the *Municipal Year Book* since 1934, with a few variations in titles and organization name changes. Data is gathered via the International City Managers' Association questionnaire, which surveys a wide variety of topics. The book provides compilations of the data gathered by responses and also has a section that lists names and telephone numbers for city officials in cities with populations of 2,500 and over, as well as those of officials in all U.S. counties. It lists the type of government, population figures, chief elected official, main telephone number, name of the clerk to the government board, and other top officials. There are chapters of specialized information on state–local relations and actions of Congress and of recent Supreme Court cases affecting local government, which are especially applicable to issues concerning local government law. There are tables of data on salaries of government officials and data concerning police and fire departments. An extensive list of sources of information is arranged alphabetically and topically, and there was a cumulative index in the latest (2002) edition.

The *Municipal Yearbook* is useful for determining the seat of government of a municipality and current telephone numbers and is helpful for historical information on the limited subject areas covered. The publication is organized by topical chapters, followed by data tables, and then the directory information, which is arranged alphabetically first by state, then by municipality, with a separate table arranged similarly for county governments. It is much more comprehensive in terms of the number of municipalities covered than the *Municipal Yellow Book*. The information that the *Yearbook* provides is very limited, and the *Yearbook* is published only once a year, while the *Yellow Book* is semiannual. The *Yearbook* is an excellent purchase for a smaller library and does not require as much shelf space and maintenance as a quarterly publication. It is also recommended for use by government offices and nonprofit organizations.

Cities of the United States (Gale Research Inc., 1998)

For an eclectic approach that includes information on economic, cultural, geographic, and social conditions, *Cities of the United States*, published in 1988, 1993, and 1998 by Gale Research Inc., is an interesting source. This publication, published every four to five years, provides a good snapshot of the nation's cities, although it obviously does not remain the most current source. Most information is factual rather than directional, but limited telephone numbers and addresses are provided. This source takes a predominantly analytical approach, describing management issues and trends, intergovernmental relations, relevant court cases, and staffing and compensation, and includes a directory of 70,000 contacts in U.S. local governments. A reference section lists the latest books and periodicals in 15 functional areas, including basic statistical sources, human resources and services, law enforcement and criminal justice, and public finance and roads. For example, the following statistics are provided for the number of local government entities in the United States.

Local governments	84,955
County	3,043
Municipal	19,279
Town or township	16,656
School districts	14,422
Special districts	31,255

Table 5.2 NUMBER OF LOCAL GOVERNMENT ENTITIES

These figures put the difficulty of providing comprehensive information on all local government entities into perspective. Local governments are also constantly reorganizing. Jurisdictions are changed regularly. *Cities of the United States* actually consists of several volumes, divided by region (South, West, Midwest, and Northeast). Each volume is divided into sections on various subjects such as form of government and type of economy. In an attempt to provide as much information as possible, several lists are provided in the back of this volume. One gives lists of state and local libraries that have collections of municipal codes, and another lists state and local agencies that list municipal codes for their states and cities. A final comprehensive list of agencies by state, city, and county that provide government information is organized by subject category in the back of the book. This is a rather expensive and infrequently published standard library reference book, but most libraries (public and academic) would benefit from having it in their collections. However, it is not current enough for use in government offices.

Infospace http://ypng.infospace.com/_1_IFPUS
  W0498Z7MC__home/redirs_all.htm?pgtarg = ctyi

This Web site is actually an online directory of federal, state, and local government contacts and offices, searchable by state, county, and city. It provides directory-type information such as personal name contacts by department, addresses, fax numbers, Internet addresses, and includes telephone numbers. This is an easy alternative to having to go to a library to use a municipal or county directory.

City and County Directories

A Public Records Primer and Investigator's Handbook (BRB Publications, 1991)

There are general directories published for states that seem to have been created for the use of an investigator. These sources are numerous and are usually locally published. One problem is knowing who publishes these sources and where to locate them. Some local jurisdictions in the United States have similar sources. A California source is described here. When pursuing legal matters, attorneys and investigators must often consult public records and laws. For a popular, simple, hands-on approach, written before the Internet really exploded as a major source of information, see *California: A Public Records Primer and Investigator's Handbook*, by Don Ray, published by ENG Press in 1995. This resource is a practical guide that lists what records are publicly available, such as in city clerk's offices and county recorder's or assessor's offices. It gives their addresses and con-

tacts, and telephone numbers are listed. This directory is comprehensive in its coverage of California municipalities. These offices may not be listed in the standard directories. Commercial telephone directories have a minimal number of listings for government offices. A municipal or county directory can have up to 250 pages for a large county, while a telephone book might have only 10–20 entries for each city or county listed. It is also not clear how many states are covered, but this publisher appears to be limited to the southwest. State and federal offices with possible jurisdictional issues are listed. There is a section that suggests a practical approach to working with municipal and county clerks, as well as other information gatekeepers. In the beginning chapters, there are some very basic rules that are useful when trying to obtain information that is difficult to find or retrieve.

This is a valuable resource for public librarians, law enforcement officers, attorneys, and private investigators.

Los Angeles County Directory (Los Angeles County, California, Internal Services Department, 1999)

A direct source of information is the government itself. Many local government entities publish agency directories. These can sometimes be obtained by calling the city. It may take some legwork or fancy footwork to locate who is responsible for the actual publication. For example, when I attempted to obtain the *Los Angeles County Directory*, it actually took four months to get a physical copy. It is of course a very large metropolitan county with many municipalities. My first step was to call the county general information number to determine who compiles and publishes the directory. My second step would have been to request or purchase a copy, but in this particular case, current copies were exhausted and a new directory was being compiled. A new copy was sent out when it was made available four months later. It is important not to get too frustrated while filtering through various levels of bureaucracy when looking for this type of information. The *Los Angeles County Directory*, for example, is designed for the use of county officials and people doing business with county departments. For a commonsense approach to interacting with local government officials and clerks, see the Don Ray book in the preceding section.

The *Los Angeles County Directory* is a useful collection of information, with a table of contents in alphabetical order that lists agencies as well as useful services by name, such as business licenses, building crafts, the law library, county mail delivery locations, and courts. There is a useful list of names, addresses, and telephone and fax numbers, along with a functional list of addresses and telephone numbers arranged alphabetically by agency and facility. A personal name index is in the back of the volume. These types of directories, when they can be obtained, are invaluable. It is impractical for libraries to collect them for any but the nearest cities or counties.

Using one of these directories should provide a telephone number or address to facilitate a trip to the nearest city hall—to the clerk's office—to request to see a copy of the code or its parallel ordinance. If one has access to a computer, the information might be found by exploring the Internet to see if the city's code can be found online. Many cities and counties have placed their codes online, but not all. Sometimes, this may yield results. Once a copy of the code of ordinances is located, it is helpful to know something about codes to use them effectively. It may be necessary to look further into the subject. Using sources listed in the following sections can do this.

SOURCES OF MUNICIPAL AND COUNTY CODES

Commercial Publishers

Codes are published by commercial publishers such as the Municipal Code Corporation, American Legal Publishing, or perhaps a publisher local to the particular municipality or county. Municipal Code Corporation (MCC) is the nation's leading publisher of local government codes of ordinances. The company has published codes for more than 2,500 cities and counties in 48 states. Most of those cities and counties are still customers. MCC employs 11 attorneys who have on average over 12 years' experience in the specialized field of codification. For example, when the publisher contracts with a city, it sends consultants to the city to review legal issues and organize and compile the codes. A printed edition is created, with a loose-leaf supplement service. Most code compilations should contain features such as a listing of all sections at the front of each chapter and catchlines preceding each section that describe the subject of the section. Also included should be history notes at the end of each section giving the ordinance number from which the section is derived; cross-references, which tie related sections together; and state law references, which cite the applicable state statute. The organizational arrangement usually includes articles and divisions and allows for an alphabet-

ical sequence of chapters by subject matter. Codes are also available in a title arrangement. Each title is a broad array of ordinances, generally grouping provisions applicable to municipal departments. This is usually customized to accommodate a particular organization. The new code is kept up-to-date with the new ordinances passed by the city, and the affected pages of the code are printed or reprinted to remove any repealed or amended provisions and insert the new ones. The index and tables are also updated. MCC has several options for providing the code in electronic media for the purposes of searching and retrieving information and drafting amendatory ordinances.

All cities and counties do not use MCC, but each city or county should have a printed copy of its code of ordinances available in a similar format. Most cities, townships, and counties have an office where copies of public records are kept. This is most often called the city clerk's office or the county recorder's office, which are the best, and surest, sources for a city or county code. City and county libraries also often have copies. It is very difficult to find a centralized course of paper code because of the sheer number available. It is unlikely that a library would collect copies of municipal codes for any other than the city in which it is located or the immediately surrounding area. The steps outlined in the previous sections of this chapter have directed the user to sources of information on what the government authority might be, where government offices might be located, and how to contact the office for further information. There are full-text Internet sources of codes that are a limited but fast-growing resource.

Searching Paper Copies of Codes of Ordinances

To effectively use paper copies of municipal codes, a cursory understanding of the organization of city or county government will be necessary. Understanding what branch of a government is responsible for a particular law makes it easier to find. Codes have subject indexing available, which might be helpful if the indexing is clear and you have an understanding of the terminology. In general, the table of contents is arranged according to the organization of the collection, and the index is the subject or keyword access to the collection.

INTERNET RESOURCES

Specialized Web Sites/Municipal Codes

NACo [National Association of Counties] http:// www.naco.org

The NACo Web site provides links to many of the 3,066 counties in the United States. Forty-eight of the 50 states have operational county governments. Connecticut and Rhode Island are divided into geographic regions called *counties*, but they do not have functioning governments. Alaska calls counties *boroughs* and Louisiana calls them *parishes*. NACo is developing a database of county policies, ordinances, codes, and model programs that can be used as examples for other counties.

The site is divided into several informational categories, and links to actual county sites are provided through the section "About Counties" and then "U.S. Counties." One category provides a search for what county a city is in and who the county officials are and allows searching by name of county, among other choices. There is a section called "County Codes and Ordinances" and it allows searching by county, city, state, or keyword, and an additional category called "County Codes Web site Links." There is also "Search County Codes by Subject," "Search County Codes by State," and "Search County Codes by County." This is an excellent resource for searching for county codes that are available online.

Municipal Codes Online (Seattle Public Library)
   http://www.spl.org/default.asp?pageID=
   collection_municodes

This is the most popular Web site for city and county codes, maintained by the Seattle Public Library. It is one of the most comprehensive and consistently maintained listings of municipal codes on the Internet. There are, however, listings for over 1,600 out of the tens of thousands that exist in the United States, with the state of California being heavily represented. The site links to URLs in each city that has a Web server that makes city municipal codes available. It is searchable by state and city and has an advantage over many city sites in that it connects directly to the code for the city. MCC, the publisher of the paper municipal codes, creates many of the online code sites.

Municipal Code Corporation
   http://www.municode.com

MCC's Web site is very nicely designed. The links on the site are mostly of local government codes of ordinances from around the United States. The state of Florida is heavily represented at this site. The publisher maintains it for the municipal codes in paper described earlier. It provides links to codes of all cities for which this publisher has provided computerized

code services. There are over a hundred cities at the site that are not necessarily the same as the cities listed at the Seattle Public Library site. The search software used is called Folio, which is commonly used for automating state and local government codes but is not very intuitive. The search engine allows for multiple document inquiries but is not too precise. That allows you to search several cities at the same time. This could be useful for ascertaining what laws are in effect in cities of a similar size or a similar area. This Web site is very useful and hopefully will be expanding the list of cities for which services are provided.

Library of Codes of Ordinances (Book Publishing Company)

The Book Publishing Company (BPC), now defunct, was in the same business as MCC and had a Web site, http://www.bpcnet.com/codes.htm. This publisher is included to illustrate the transient nature of some aspects of the publishing industry and certainly of the Internet. Since this Web site was viewed several months ago, it has disappeared. It apparently has been purchased by LexisNexis and incorporated into its product, a review of which follows.

LexisNexis Municipal Codes
   http://www.lexisnexis.com/municipalcodes

This Web site offers local governments an ongoing service that allows them to keep their municipal code available online and to update and change it whenever necessary. LexisNexis provides this service to about 1,400 municipalities, a small fraction of the total. Subscribers can also receive copies of their codes on CD-ROM. One major advantage is LexisNexis' stability in the legal publishing field. All codes published by LexisNexis are made available through Municipal Codes Online for free. There is a geographic listing by state and by city within the state. The software used to view the codes is the Folio product, popular with many municipal and state government publishers. It includes a nice clickable table of contents in a column on the right. The copyright is held by BPC, so apparently LexisNexis purchased that company and now offers the service previously offered by BPC. It is obvious, however, that only a minority of municipal government entities actually make use of online services in the publication of municipal codes.

Searching for information on local government codes of ordinances follows a logical progression for the novice user. The steps can proceed in a different sequence that depends on where you start and what information you have. If you do not have Internet access, then seek out directories that provide information on offices, locations, and telephone numbers where copies of codes might be located. Knowledge of government organization can help you to find information more efficiently. If you do have access to the Internet, the Web is a very convenient way to locate and search codes online. The source is only as reliable as whoever maintains the database, but the same can be said of paper resources. If the codes are not available online, then the searcher can return to the paper directories and pursue the information in a traditional manner. Undoubtedly other methods of providing information about municipal and county codes of ordinances are being developed. There are initiatives under way to promote and even require development of online codification of law. Online provision of municipal law is a growing area and a very useful resource, which should become a premier way to provide access to city and county codes in the future. However, until there is much more widespread access, the paper sources will be the most common and authoritative format for municipal and county codes.

Chapter 6
Finding Local Government Administrative Sources

Denise Johnson

MAJOR TOPICS COVERED

Introduction
General Guides and Resources
  Guides
  Directories
Comprehensive Resources
  Comprehensive Directories
  Comprehensive Web Sites
Specialized Directories
Topical and Specialized Resources
  Topical
  Geographic
Special Information on Finding and Using Local Administrative Resources

MAJOR RESOURCES COVERED

Administrative Law and Regulatory Policy: Problems, Text, and Cases

Rulemaking: How Government Agencies Write Law and Make Policy
2002 Government Phone Book USA
Municipal Yellow Book: Who's Who in the Leading City and County Governments and Local Authorities
State Reference Publications: A Bibliographic Guide to State Blue Books, Legislative Manuals and Other General Reference Sources
StateList: The Electronic Source for State Publication Lists
Municipal Code Corporation
Municipal Codes Online
State and Local Governments (Library of Congress)
About Counties
California Public Sector: The Most Comprehensive Directory of State, Federal, County, Municipal and Special District Governments in California
Local Regulation of Adult Businesses

INTRODUCTION

Finding regulatory (rules, regulations, and licensing) information resources at the local government level is a task requiring some detecting skills on the part of the researcher. States differ in the way they organize and distribute state government publications and in the way they authorize and provide regulatory oversight for municipalities within the state. There are no current, comprehensive compendia listing the access points for local government administrative resources, nor will this chapter provide detailed lists of titles and contact information. Rather, I will try to point you in the direction of likely places to look for local government administrative resources that will be useful, regardless of your location.

Researchers familiar with administrative resources and law at the state and federal level may find research into local administrative resources confusing, since local administrative law is seldom organized in separate

regulatory publications, such as the *Code of Federal Regulations*, the *Federal Register*, and state administrative codes. For researchers seeking administrative information at the local level, it is useful to be aware that in municipal publications there is little difference between regulations and laws or ordinances. The smaller the city or locality, the more likely this is to be true. Larger cities, such as New York, Los Angeles, Chicago, and Washington, D.C., are more likely to have administrative structures and publications similar to state and federal administrative bodies. This is not to say that there are not rules, regulations, and licenses at the local level in smaller localities. Instead, the issuance of licenses and the promulgation of rules and regulations are likely to be spelled out in the municipal code or ordinances, rather than in separate administrative publications.

When researching local government administrative sources, it is useful to begin with an understanding of the administrative structure of the particular municipality or other local governmental unit responsible for promulgating administrative law. For most municipalities, incorporation and powers are granted through the state legislature. In addition to state and federal authority, municipalities must govern within the confines of county or parish governmental authority. Within the United States, only Louisiana has parishes rather than county governmental units. Washington, D.C., has a municipal government with federal oversight rather than state oversight and authority.

A good place to look for administrative information at the municipal level is in the municipal code or code of ordinances for the area in question. Municipal and county codes are systematically arranged sets of the rules, laws, and ordinances promulgated by the legal authority of a place. In a municipality (city, town, or other incorporated place having its own governing body) the legal authority will usually be the city or town council, board of aldermen, board of trustees, board of supervisors, or similar administrative body. In a county or parish, the legal authority will usually be the county commission, county board, parish authority, or police jury. In larger municipalities with more formal administrative publications, it may still be useful to look at the municipal code of ordinances to find the authorizing code for administrative agencies. Once the researcher knows the name of the agency responsible for regulations of a particular type, it is easier to find the appropriate publications.

Most city and town libraries own copies of their local municipal and/or county codes of ordinances. In recent years, many municipal and county codes of ordinances have begun to be made available on the Internet. To find out if the code of ordinances you're seeking is one of them, you could use a Web search engine. One of the best and most popular for locating government publications and/or information (as well as almost anything else on the Internet) is Google.

GENERAL GUIDES AND RESOURCES
Guides

Home Rule in America: A Fifty-State Handbook, by Dale Krane, Platon N. Rigos, and Melvin B. Hill, Jr. (CQ Press, 2001)

This book describes the concept of home rule in general and provides a chapter of descriptive information on state and local governmental organization for each of the 50 states. Each state chapter includes information on the following topics: governmental set-

ting, home rule, functions of local government, fiscal autonomy of local governments, citizen access to local government, state–local relations, and notes. The appendix provides comparative information on home rule across the 50 states. A glossary is included.

American County Government with an Annotated Bibliography, by John C. Bollens in association with John R. Bayes and Kathryn L. Utter (Sage Publications, 1969)

This publication is a general survey and research guide to county government information for the United States and has been an excellent and useful one. Unfortunately, it has not been updated since its 1969 copyright date.

An Introduction to Comparative Administrative Law, by H. B. Jacobini (Oceana, 1991)

This volume provides no direct information on local administrative law, but the section on "American Administrative Law" gives a good overview of the processes inherent in the creation, maintenance, and enforcement of regulations in the United States. The role of the ombudsman is also discussed in this chapter. A later chapter is devoted to the history, development, and usage of the office of ombudsman in various parts of the world, with a section on the United States that includes local/urban information. The opening chapter gives an overview of administrative law.

Administrative Law and Regulatory Policy: Problems, Text, and Cases, by Stephen G. Breyer (5th ed., Aspen Law and Business, 2002)

This is a basic study of the uses and forms of regulatory powers, with illustrative problems and cases concerning various types of administrative regulations and circumstances. Local/municipal regulation is only briefly mentioned. This is a basic text for regulatory information. This publication can be found in many law libraries.

Governing: Issues and Applications from the Front Lines of Government, ed. by Alan Ehrenhald (CQ Press, 2002)

This book is a selection of 40 representative articles from *Governing*, a leading magazine on state and local government issues, as a resource for researchers and investigators.

Municipal Government Reference Sources: Publications and Collections, ed. by Peter Hernon, John V. Richardson, Nancy P. Sanders, and Marjorie Shepley (American Library Association, Government Documents Round Table, 1978)

This book provides state-by-state listings of local government publications available at the time, as well as descriptions of library collections of municipal documents. Most of the information is outdated, but the book is useful to provide researchers with some ideas about where to begin searching. One example is the document *A Report on the State of the City*, generated by the New Orleans Chief Administrative Office, September 4, 1974.

Rulemaking: How Government Agencies Write Law and Make Policy, by Cornelius M. Kerwin (2nd ed., CQ Press, 1998)

Rulemaking is a good introductory text for researchers interested in finding out what administrative law is, the history of administrative law, and how administrative law works. It addresses primarily administrative law at the federal level but is nevertheless useful for an understanding of the history and practices in this area of law.

State-Local Relations: A Partnership Approach, by Joseph F. Zimmerman (2nd ed., Greenwood Publishing Group, 1995)

This is a descriptive text on the relationship between state and local governmental authority. It describes various areas in which various governmental authorities cooperate, such as taxes, financial assistance, and bond issuance. Tables in the appendix give comparisons of levels of local discretion from state to state. A lengthy and useful bibliography is included.

Tools for Decision Making: A Practice Guide for Local Government, by David N. Ammons (CQ Press, 2001)

This book is intended for local government administrators, but may be of use in helping researchers understand local government procedures. It is designed for those responsible for fiscal predictions and reporting and contains mathematical accounting equations.

Directories

2002 Government Phone Book USA (10th ed., Omnigraphics Inc., 2002)

This is a comprehensive directory of federal, state, and local government offices. Local government directory information is provided for all U.S. counties, including county seat, area code, population, address of the county courthouse, and telephone and fax numbers for county offices. Electronic access information is provided for some counties. The amount of information available for each county varies considerably. Two sections of the directory provide information on municipalities. There is a section with fairly detailed listings for cities with populations over 15,000. Very brief information is provided for municipalities with populations under 15,000. While an attempt has been made to be comprehensive, not every municipality is represented within the 2,813 pages in this directory. No publication schedule is indicated, but recent editions have been published annually.

Counties USA: A Directory of United States Counties (Omnigraphics Inc., 1997)

Counties USA provides listings for over 3,000 U.S. counties, including contact information, population estimates, and other descriptive information. Although catalog copy lists this title as an annual publication, I see no evidence that any volumes were printed after the initial 1997 edition. Electronic contact data (e-mail and Web addresses) are provided where available at the time of printing.

Directory of Special Libraries and Information Centers (Gale Research, 2001)

This directory is a frequently updated guide to specialized collections in libraries. It is a two-volume set, with the index in the second volume. Brief descriptions of each of the libraries include the size of the collection, area of specialization, and contact information. More than 40 collections in 24 states were listed as having collections of municipal government materials in the edition I examined.

Municipal Yellow Book: Who's Who in the Leading City and County Governments and Local Authorities (Monitor Publishing Company; Leadership Directories, Inc., semiannual) http://www.leadershipdirectories.com

The *Municipal Yellow Book* provides directory information on over 35,000 officials in city and county governments and local administrative units. It covers primarily larger cities and towns. A detailed description of the semiannual directories, sample entries, and the geographic index are available to download from the publisher's Web page.

COMPREHENSIVE RESOURCES

Comprehensive Directories

State Reference Publications: A Bibliographic Guide to State Blue Books, Legislative Manuals and Other General Reference Sources, by Lynn Hellebust (Government Research Service, 1996)

This source is of use in finding out what reference resources are published about and/or by a state. Many state publications may be useful in finding county and municipal information. For instance, state Blue Books (official reference manuals) often list counties and contact information for county officials. Some states publish guides for the use of municipal officials, such as the *Illinois Municipal Handbook*. Such guides can be very useful in determining the jurisdiction for regulations and licensing.

Comprehensive Web Sites

StateList: The Electronic Source for State Publication Lists http://www.library.uiuc.edu/doc/StateList/check/check.htm

StateList is a Web site developed and maintained by the Government Documents Department and Law Libraries at the University of Illinois at Urbana/Champaign. This site provides links to lists of state documents available from some 32 states, at the time of this writing, that make their state publications catalogs or checklists available on the Internet. (This replaces the Monthly List of State Documents, formerly published by the Library of Congress.) The site also provides a link to the American Association of Law Librarians Web site, where some printed publications listing state documents can be ordered. State documents checklists can be used to find out whether a state publishes documents that might be useful for local regulatory research.

GODORT Handout Exchange: State and Local Governments (Government Documents Round Table of the American Library Association [ALA]) http://www.lib.umich.edu/govdocs/godort/state.htm

The Handout Exchange is a feature of the ALA annual conferences, where librarians from around the United States bring locally produced handouts and links to locally produced Web pages to share with their colleagues. The State and Local Governments Task Force has assembled this list of Web sites of interest to people researching information published in state and local documents.

Local Government and Politics (University of Michigan Documents Center) http://www.lib.umich.edu/govdocs/pslocal.html

This Web site provides links to numerous other Web sites selected by librarians as being useful for researching information published by and for municipal and county governments.

Hastings Law Library, Local Government Clinic (University of California, Hastings, College of Law Library) http://www.uchastings.edu/library/Legal%20Research/Class%20Pages/local-govt.htm

This Web site provides links to numerous other Web sites of interest for finding local government legal information. Listings are also provided for standard reference books on local government law, such as *Antieau on Local Government Law* and *Matthews*. Legal resources on the Web can be useful for finding county and municipal codes of ordinances.

Google Uncle Sam http://www.google.com/unclesam

Google has a special section for searching for government information. The only way to know you are there is that the name "Google" is in a red, white, and blue motif. Otherwise, Google is known for its extremely spare and unbusy home pages.

Municipal Code Corporation http://www.municode.com

From the opening page, if you click on "Online Codes" under "Free Resources," you will be directed to a page of links to codes of ordinances for municipalities that publish their codes through Municipal Code Corporation (MCC), the premier printer of such codes.

Municipal Codes Online (Seattle Public Library)
http://www.spl.org/default.asp?pageID=
Collection_municodes

The Seattle Public Library maintains a Web page with links to municipal codes, as well as links to municipal code publishers such as MCC, General Code Publishers, and Sterling Codifiers. All of the municipal code publisher sites listed provide links to some of the texts of the municipal codes they publish. This is a small number compared with the total municipalities in the United States.

RegInfo (Regulatory Information Service Center)
http://reginfo.gov

The RegInfo Web site is a project of the federal Regulatory Information Service Center, established to assist researchers who want to find information about federal, state, and local regulation. Most links are to federal agencies and sites; there is a link to the Piper Resources State and Local Governments Web site.

State and Local Governments (Library of Congress)
http://lcweb.loc.gov/global/state/stategov.html

This Web site provides links to meta-indexes (Web sites that link to information of interest in many states, such as the Council of State Governments Web page and the FirstGov local and state governments pages) and to the official Web pages of states and municipalities throughout the United States.

About Counties (National Association of Counties
[NACo]) http://www.naco.org/counties/counties/
index.cfm

The About Counties Web site provides brief county information; links to state and county resources; county contact information such as addresses, telephone numbers, and the names of elected county officials (some with links to their own Web sites); and links to county code information for some counties. To see a listing of all the types of information available on the Web site, click on the "Site Index" tab, from the main About Counties page. The site also provides a tab for "Links" and a "Search" tab, which allows you to search the site for relevant information.

State and Local Governments on the Web (Piper Resources) http://www.statelocalgov.net

This Web site provides links to state, county, and city Web sites. Links are also provided to state offices,

libraries in the state, and county, state, and municipal association Web sites. Links are frequently updated. The FAQ (frequently asked questions) section gives the criteria for inclusion in the Web site. The "Comment" link enables searching of the site or the Web, via Google. This is a very comprehensive and useful Web site.

SPECIALIZED DIRECTORIES

Directories of municipalities in individual states may be available in your local library. Most libraries carry such materials only for their own state, although they will sometimes carry materials for neighboring states. Larger research libraries and law libraries are more likely to have materials for multiple states. Most current directories are likely to be reference materials, and unavailable for interlibrary loan. The municipal leagues of the states publish many such directories. Searching for materials with the keywords "municipal" and "league" along with the name of the state in which you are interested is a good way to find useful publications. WorldCat or the local library online catalog are good resources for your search. If you don't find any useful publications, try dropping the word "league" from your search; some states either don't have a municipal league or have another name for their municipal organization. Another useful search is to enter the keywords "municipal," "government," and "directory." If you still don't find anything useful, try exchanging the word "municipal" for synonyms such as "cities," "towns," or "counties." Some examples of state municipal directories are listed below.

Community Profiles, Illinois Directory of Cities, Villages, Towns, Counties, and Public Officials (Infra-Net Publishing, 2001)

This directory provides brief information on the state of Illinois, including government information and community profiles for cities, towns, villages, and counties. Information provided includes comparison tables of population, per capita income, sales tax, among others. Infra-Net also publishes guides for Ohio, New York, and Indiana.

Directory of Official New Jersey (Resource Communication Group, 1997)

This book is a guide to municipal officials; state officials; county and municipal governments; local and county authorities; planning, economic and industrial development boards; and congressional, Assembly, and Senate members.

Directory of Municipal and County Officials in Colorado (Colorado Municipal League, 2001)

The Colorado Municipal League regularly publishes this directory, as well as a number of resources of interest for researching home rule and administrative issues for the state of Colorado. A catalog of their publications is available from the League's Web site, http://www.cml.org.

Iowa League of Cities http://www.iowaleague.org

The Iowa League of Cities provides links to the Web sites of cities in Iowa, particularly to city government Web sites. In addition, the "Other Links" page provides additional municipal and governmental Web sites.

Wyoming Municipal Directory (Wyoming Association of Municipalities, 2000)

This annual publication of the Wyoming Association of Municipalities lists municipalities, municipal officials, and contact information. It takes the place of the *Official Municipal Roster*.

California Public Sector: The Most Comprehensive Directory of State, Federal, County, Municipal and Special District Governments in California (6th ed., Public Sector Publications, 2001)

This publication provides directory information for state, municipal, and special districts (school districts, community college districts, etc.) in California. It is organized by state office, then local government office. There is a topical index for education and a listing of U.S. government offices. Appendices include a state chronology, maps, and statistics. This directory is also published for other states.

Mississippi Municipal Directory (Mississippi Municipal Association, annual)

The Mississippi Municipal Association has published this directory of Mississippi municipalities since 1948, and also provides useful municipal links from its Web site, http://www.mscity.com. Both contain information about cities, schools, and some other interesting information such as radio stations, television stations, online publications, and organizations.

DC Watch, an Online Magazine about Politics and Public Affairs in the District of Columbia (DC Watch) http://www.dcwatch.com

This DC Watch site is a useful source of information about governmental agencies in the District of Columbia. The link for "Government and People" leads to directory information as well as information about municipal government agencies and boards. DC Watch describes itself as a citizen-watchdog group.

Hawai'i Directory of State, County, and Federal Officials (state of Hawaii) http://www.state.hi.us/lrb/dir

The Hawai'i Directory page allows the presentation of files in PDF (portable document file format—usable with Adobe Acrobat) download of a directory including state, county, and federal offices. Web addresses for county sites are included in the directory. County Web sites for Honolulu (http://www.co.honolulu.hi.us/), Hawaii (http://www.hawaii-county.com), Kauai (http://www.kauaigov.org), and Maui (http://www.co.maui.hi.us) include links to departments, boards, commissions, and other municipal offices. This Web site is very useful for locating any information about local government in Hawaii.

TOPICAL AND SPECIALIZED RESOURCES

Some municipal and county regulatory information appears in books on subjects of regulation, such as land use and adult businesses. If you are interested in a wider subject, such as land use regulation, topical resources may be useful for your research. If you are interested only in the regulations on land use in a specific locality, topical resources are likely to be of limited value for you. Topical resources may be found in much the same way as geographic resources. Search in local library online catalogs or WorldCat for key words such as "municipal," "land use," "adult," and "regulation." Following are some examples of topical regulatory resources.

Libraries on the Web: USA Public Libraries http://sunsite.berkeley.edu/Libweb/Public_main.html

Public-library Web sites can be a good place to look for information. This Web site provides links to public-library Web sites organized regionally, then by state. If Connecticut is selected, then the Acton Public Library and the Acton Public Library catalog, proceed with the search even though it asks for a password. Type in "land use," and several citations to books are produced. This can be done with many public-library online catalogs. This is a great way to do research remotely. Following are some examples of topical regulatory resources.

Topical

The resources listed in this section are briefly annotated examples of the types of publications that can be found on a variety of topics concerning local governmental matters. Some are published by governmental agencies, some are by private publishers or nongovernmental organizations. They are as varied as the many cities and counties that inspire them. They can often be found only in the city or county they describe. The best way to locate them is to visit a local chamber of commerce or city hall. More information is being conveyed through the use of Web sites and will increase in the future.

Local Regulation of Adult Businesses, by Jules B. Gerard (West Group, 2002)

Local Regulation of Adult Businesses is an annually updated, multistate handbook covering the various regulatory methods that local governments use to control adult businesses, such as zoning, licensing, and nuisance control.

Sign Regulation for Small and Midsize Communities: A Planner's Guide and a Model Ordinance, by Eric D. Kelly and Gary J. Raso (American Planning Association, 1989)

This brief resource discusses legal issues related to sign regulation and provides a model ordinance. Legal issues might involve size, subject matter, and placement of signs.

Recycling, a Local Solution to the Solid Waste Crisis: Local Government Planning for Recycling in Commercial and Multifamily Buildings, by Judy Corbett and David Manhart (Local Government Commission, 1990)

Includes recycling-planning documents and model ordinances. This resource provides examples of model programs for implementation in large building units.

Dog Law, by Mary Randolph (4th ed., Nolo Press, 2001)

Dog Law includes information on licenses, vaccinations, leash laws, burial restrictions, and much more

concerning keeping a dog as a pet. Nolo Press is known for commonsense legal guides that are accessible to the general reader.

Takings Litigation Handbook: Defending Takings Challenges to Land Use Regulations, by Douglas T. Kendall, Timothy J. Dowling, and Andrew W. Schwartz (American Legal Pub., 2000)

This is a handbook that covers the legal issues of right-of-property, eminent domain, and land use regulations that affect municipal government takings cases.

Geographic

Larger cities and counties may have published regulatory materials, which you are likely to find in major public libraries. Many municipal and county publications are available online, via the World Wide Web. Any such items can be researched through the methods outlined previously in this chapter, using local library online catalogs, WorldCat, and Web search engines, such as Google. Following is a list of examples of local area regulatory materials. Most of the Web sites included were found using the keywords "city" and "regulations" in the government search section of Google Uncle Sam (http://www.google.com/unclesam).

The 2002–2003 Green Book: Official Directory of the City of New York, ed. by Krishna Kirk (City of New York, 2001)

New York's *Green Book* provides directory information for city officials and employees. County, court, state, federal, and international offices are also listed. A section of the *Green Book* is devoted to licenses, referring users to the appropriate officials and providing brief information.

Uniform Mechanical Code, City of Houston Amendments, 1994 ed. (International Association of Plumbing and Mechanical Officials, 1996)

This publication contains regulations about heating, ventilation, and refrigeration regulations for the city of Houston, Texas. A uniform code manual is one that attempts to compile all the laws (federal, state, local) on a particular subject, such as fire safety regulations and electrical construction regulations, and make them available to construction companies, safety inspectors, and others in the industry.

Florida Law Enforcement Handbook: Metropolitan Dade County (Florida, Board of County Commissioners, Metropolitan Dade County, Florida, 1975, annual)

This is an annually updated handbook of criminal procedure, traffic regulations, and municipal ordinances.

Building Code of the City of Atlanta: An Ordinance Providing for Fire Limits, and Regulations Governing the Construction, Alteration, Repair, Equipment, or Removal of Buildings or Structures, by Catherine E. Malicki (Department of Buildings, 1980)

This book comprises the building code ordinances for Atlanta, Georgia.

City and County of San Francisco Municipal Code (American Legal Publishing Co., 1999)

This loose-leaf manual is kept updated with additional and replacement pages and includes regulations pertaining to fire code, health code, municipal elections, parks, police, subdivisions, traffic, public works, and business and taxes. This is a common way to publish code information. The municipal code can also be found at American Legal's Web site, http://www.amlegal.com/sanfran/viewcode.htm

The City Clerk of Chicago http://www.chicityclerk. com/legislation/codes/index.html

This Web site includes links to frequently requested regulatory information. There are links to selected municipal code sections, licensing information, city council information, and various other areas of interest.

New York City Department of Transportation http://nyc.gov/html/dot/html/motorist/scrintro.html

This Web site provides regulatory information for New York City parking, street cleaning, etc. There are links to information about traffic advisories, the road resurfacing schedule, street-cleaning rules suspension calendar, and various safety tips.

@LA http://www.at-la.com/@la-gov/laws.htm

This page includes links to state, county, and city codes for Los Angeles, Orange, San Bernardino, Riverside, and Ventura Counties, California. The city of Los Angeles municipal code is available, and the site provides links to the city charter, the municipal code, and the administrative code. Links to regulatory agencies are arranged by subject, such as licensing, occupational safety, and vector control, then by jurisdiction (state, county, or city). An example of a regulatory agency, the County Agricultural Commission of Weights and Measures, is found at http://acwm.co.la.ca.us.

City of Philadelphia http://www.phila.gov

The City of Philadelphia Web site provides links to numerous city offices, many with administrative publications, such as "Licenses and Inspections," "City Planning Commission," etc. This type of Web site is useful. Many city sites are substituting e-mail addresses for telephone numbers.

San Bernardino County http://www.co.san-bernardino.ca.us/default.asp

This Web site allows county residents (or anyone, really) to ask informational- and administrative-type questions about county services and receive replies via e-mail. Two questions were asked, one regarding voter registration and the other regarding the availability of court records, and both were answered within two hours. Many local governments are using their Web sites to answer simple administrative and directional questions through email.

City of Santa Monica Building Regulations http://santa-monica.org/municode/codemaster/Article_8/index.html

These regulations are on a Web page that is part of a larger Web site for the municipal code of Santa Monica. The regulations are hot-linked but do not appear to be searchable, so it would be necessary to know what code section is needed.

City of Boston Online http://www.cityofboston.gov

Boston, Massachusetts, maintains a Web site and uses it to convey useful information such as the emergency response guide. There are links to e-services and a special place for youth services. The Web site includes links to regulatory information for pets (http://www.cityofboston.gov/animalcontrol/petpeeves. asp), for resident transactions (http://www.cityofboston. gov/transactions), for permits and applications (http:// www.cityofboston.gov/transactions/permitsandapps.asp, and more. This is a nicely designed and useful site.

King County and Seattle Metropolitan Area
  http://www.metrokc.gov

The King County government home page includes regulatory information for both the county and the city of Seattle. A very useful link is to the Department of Development and Environment's Online Search and Report on Permit Applications (http://apps01. metrokc.gov/www6/ddes/scripts/permsearch.cfm), which allows searching for license applications. By selecting a permit type, a search can be conducted to find out how many have been issued, as well as where they were issued. Of special note is a link to a page on Timber Harvest Conversion Options (http://www. metrokc.gov/ddes/forest/index.htm).

Tempe, Arizona: Tempe In Touch (Development Services, city of Tempe) http://www.tempe.gov/tdsi

This Web site provides links to the Building Safety, Code Compliance, and other divisions of government, with links to regulatory information.

SPECIAL INFORMATION ON FINDING AND USING LOCAL ADMINISTRATIVE RESOURCES

Larger public libraries, particularly libraries with municipal reference collections, are undoubtedly among the most useful places for research into local administrative rules and regulations. If your research is not limited to a single locale, you may find more resources in larger academic and academic law libraries. Some academic and law libraries have restrictions on usage of their collections by nonaffiliated people, so it is wise to check with the library prior to visiting. Any library that provides Internet access will be useful, if you don't have access to the Internet personally. For a general Web site that lists links to library Web servers, try Libweb, Library Servers via WWW, at http:// sunsite.berkeley.edu/Libweb. Libraries' links are arranged geographically and by type. Many smaller libraries provide Internet access and access to useful resources such as WorldCat. If your local library does not have access to materials you need, check with the reference librarian to see whether your library is affiliated with a system or consortium that may offer access to resources to member libraries and their patrons.

An increasing number of governmental agencies are providing access to their publications on the Internet, via the World Wide Web. If the materials you seek are not available in a library accessible to you, you may be able to find them using the Internet. If you still experience difficulty in finding materials, don't forget that a call or visit to city or county offices may be all that is necessary to locate needed materials. Most telephone directories have special sections for government agencies.

CHAPTER 7
Finding Information on Local Courts
Mary Martin

MAJOR TOPICS COVERED

MAJOR RESOURCES COVERED

INTRODUCTION

Local court records can comprise a very large, complex body of material. Searching for these documents can be very time-consuming. There are hundreds of types of local court documents, as well as approximately 38,000 cities and more than 3,000 counties for which records could conceivably be available. Records of court cases and accompanying documentation are examples of very important information that cannot be found anywhere else. It is helpful to describe court proceedings as a prelude to actually looking for documents generated during these court proceedings. The type of activity or proceeding is usually the deciding factor in where such a document would be stored. There are three general types of court proceedings—civil, criminal, and equity cases—as well as different levels of jurisdiction (city or township, county, state, national). Even today, few people escape mention in court records at some time in their lives—most people appear in court records an average of three times in their lifetime. Events requiring a court representative or a personal appearance include marriage, sale of property, and probate (inheritance) proceedings. Court records are among the oldest records in the United States, dating to colonial times (early seventeenth century). Many local municipal courts predate county, state, or federal courts. Local courts served as units of government as well as judicial bodies. Local administrative bodies now perform many functions once performed by local courts, each generating accompanying separate records. Court records are quite numerous, and they are difficult to trace and use. There is scant general indexing, and legal terminology is confusing in any time period. Some cities and counties are indexing and digitizing (scanning) lists of court records, but there is no general source of indexing for the majority of local court records.

There are some sources of general legal terminology and organization that are useful to define concepts. Some are mentioned in chapter 3 on Municipal, County, and Regional Government Archives, and some are listed at the end of this chapter. Court procedures, jurisdiction, and records vary from state to state, particularly in the case of the lower jurisdictions. The most valuable pieces of information to have when looking for court records are: Who are you looking for? Where were they at the time? and When were they there? Most local court cases are stored at the local or county level and may require a visit to the area to use the records. There are also record retrievers who will physically obtain records for a fee. Record retrievers are particularly helpful if the searcher lives a significant distance from the records. The resources reviewed here range from very general to extremely detailed. Although a particular resource might cover only one city or county, it serves as an example of the type of resource that may be found at the local level anywhere.

To start a search for court records, the user needs to acquire some basic knowledge of the structure of court systems in an area, particularly the types of local court records (municipal or county) that can be found. It is sometimes necessary to expand the search to a larger geographic level, such as state or federal court records, as the scope of the matter moves to a correspondingly higher jurisdictional level. Local court records are also sometimes physically moved to a central location at the county or state level. It may be necessary to contact the court to determine where certain records are stored.

GENERAL GUIDES AND RESOURCES TO THE COURTS

It is important to know certain information when looking for a court record, but this is not always possible. Certain questions must be answered. What type of record is the searcher looking for? How old is the record? What government agency would have a copy of the record? How can a physical copy be obtained? If the answers to some of these questions are not known, then it may be necessary to locate an organizational manual, such as one of the resources described below. These resources will help indicate what information might be necessary to locate a court record. These general resources will begin to provide answers to these questions.

Guides

The Source: A Guidebook of American Genealogy, ed. by Loretto Dennis Szucs and Sandra Hargreaves Luebking (Ancestry, Inc., 2000)

This publication is written primarily for genealogical researchers; however, the chapter on Research in Court Records is an excellent introduction to the overall importance and scope of court records. The chapter is extensive and helps create an image of how courts have generated historically important evidence for researchers. The book focuses primarily on historical records and presents several tables of information about particular courts, whether the records of the courts are indexed, and where the records can be found. It has an extensive section of notes and a useful bibliography on sources of historical court records. This resource is a very good introduction to finding and using court records. There is detailed information on historical records in particular, as these are of primary interest to genealogical researchers. An example of a court record might consist of a nomination of guardianship petition for a minor child. The publisher does not currently sell this publication by this title, but the information contained in it is sold under several different titles.

Librarian's Guide to Court Records: The Complete State, County and Courthouse Locator (BRB Publications, 2000)

This publication is another good starting point for a public records search. The introduction explains various methods of searching, and a quick summary of state and federal court organization and record-keeping procedures follows. (Local courts are actually part of the state court structure but are usually administrated on the local level.) The guide is organized alphabetically as a state-by-state directory of records

Record	Type	Bound Volume	Filed Papers	Loose Papers	Case File
Indexes (alphabetical):	Plaintiff	•			
	Defendant	•			
	Reverse	•			
	Every name	•			
Dockets: calendar or waiting list of pending cases, in the order they will be considered by the court	Civil	•			
	Criminal	•			
	Equity	•			
	Chancery	•			
	Estate	•			
	Orphans'	•			
	Guardian	•			
	Probate	•			
	Name change	•			
	Claims	•			
	Insolvents'	•			
	Bankruptcy	•			
	Divorce	•			
	Adoption	•			
	Lunacy	•			
	Reference	•			
	Execution	•			
	Appearance	•			
	Appeals	•			
	New actions	•			
Minutes: descriptive entries of all actions taking place in the court process	Journals	•			
	Register of actions	•			
	Appeal briefs		•		•
Orders: official record of all orders of the judge(s)	Journals	•			
	Writs		•		•
	Summons		•		•
	Warrants		•		•
	Subpoenae		•		•
	Actions	•			
	Indictments				•
	Presentments				•
	Executions	•			•
	Stays (demurrers)	•			•
	Injunctions				•
	Foreclosures				•
	Attachments				•
	Distraints		•		
	Jury lists				
Judgements: final decisions, punishments, and awards made by the court	Satisfied	•			
	Short	•			
	Equity	•			
	Decrees	•			
	Fines	•			
	Liens	•			
	Verdicts	•			
	Opinions	•			
	Decisions	•			
	Reports		•		
	Appeals		•		
	Bills of costs		•		

Table 7.1 TYPES OF COURT RECORDS

sources. Each state also has an introductory page with general-help telephone numbers and a listing of major state Internet sites. A list of state agencies with public records and a county-by-county listing of courts and recording offices with addresses, telephone numbers, and office hours are included. A general page entitled "What You Need to Know" includes details of court structure, searching hints, and sources of online access. The book is available under a different imprint from a different publisher, with only slight modifications, as *Find Public Records Fast: The Complete State, County and Courthouse Finder* (Facts on Demand Press, 2000 edition). This directory organizes information on the federal, state, county, and courthouse level at more than 11,500 locations throughout the United States.

Connecticut's Courts (State of Connecticut, 1999)

This publication is a guide to the court system of the state of Connecticut. It is an example of a special pamphlet that is written to describe the state courts. It gives a concise explanation of the system of courts (which is one of the more unusual systems), describing some of its history, and gives the types and numbers of each court, the officers of the court, and the court's jurisdiction. This is the type of pamphlet often made available to visitors to the courthouse or state library and is primarily informational. It does not give addresses or telephone numbers and is not useful for actually contacting the Supreme Court of the State of Connecticut. This type of pamphlet can usually be obtained by calling or writing the appropriate state agency. Contact information can be found at any of the state's Web sites or through a general Web site such as State and Local Government on the Net, at http://www.piperinfo.com/state/index.cfm.

Directories

Sourcebook of County Court Records (BRB Publications, Inc. 1997)

This source has information similar to that found in the *Librarian's Guide to Public Records*, but its entries contain more detailed information on each court. It lists civil, criminal, and probate court records at the county and municipal levels within the state court system. There is a chapter for each state that describes the court system, listing the court of general jurisdiction, and then courts of limited, municipal, and special jurisdiction. Court types with an asterisk are profiled in the book. Physical locations for case records are identified, and when two court classifications are combined but only one entry appears in the profiles, the number of combined courts is noted. There are locations not profiled in the book, and their numbers are estimated.

This source presents charts that describe what kinds of cases particular courts hear and lists information about when there is more than one court having jurisdiction over a particular claim (overlapping jurisdiction). The charts admittedly oversimplify complex sets of state statutes in order to provide the user with a practical starting point in searching for case records. If there is still a question about where to look, the address and telephone number for the administrative office of each court system is listed.

More than 3,139 counties are headlined, in alphabetical order within each state. If a county has more than one court profiled, they appear in order from general to limited jurisdiction. Civil courts are listed before criminal courts. Where more than one court of the same type is located in a county, they are listed alphabetically by the name of the city in which the court is located.

All city/zip code combinations have been verified against the *County and Courthouse Locator* (BRB Publications) for accuracy, although about 10,000 zip codes cross county lines. There are multiple county entries, meaning that addresses within a designated zip code may not be in the county usually associated with that place name. This information can be crucial when searching for public records that are filed by location of the property or residence (court records as well as public records). Also 10,000 zip codes are useless in determining the county of residence, as they are assigned exclusively to post office boxes or rural routes. Nongeographic zip codes should not be used to locate records. In addition to address and telephone number, the time zone is indicated. Fax numbers are given for most courts. Other information available is whether or not the court accepts searches by telephone (1,299 do), whether the records are available for download by modem, the payee for checks, certification fees, and the turnaround time for mailed requests. When there are multiple offices in a county, there is direction on how to determine in what office to begin searching depending on the address of the subject (person). Information is given on the status of online system availability for each state.

It is important not to assume that court structures within states are similar. A reason that *Sourcebook of County Court Records* is so useful is that these structures can vary greatly. Many courts allow in-person searching only, so if you cannot do it yourself, you need to hire a record retriever to do it. Some of these offices will accept requests by mail. This does involve a longer turnaround time. Many courts offer a free computer terminal from which available indexes and documents (but not case documents) that have been scanned can be viewed. Profiles should indicate whether a plaintiff as well as a defendant is indexed by name. Recently (in the last 10 years) many courts have installed computerized indexing systems. The year the index coverage begins is listed in the profile in this volume. Often listed are search requirements (names, dates, date of birth, Social Security number, etc.). Some court records, such as juvenile and adoption, are restricted and require a court order for release. Various fees are listed, as many require prepayment.

Where a court covers only part of a county, the area covered is listed in the profile. If a searcher knows the city but not the county, there is a city/county cross-reference at the end of each state's section. Information is summarized from the *County and Courthouse Locator* (BRB). *Sourcebook of County Court Records* contains 31,000 entries, covering a substantial number of local jurisdictions. However, since there are over 81,000 local government jurisdictions in the United States, obviously many places are not included in this comprehensive source.

Valuable information is provided on how records are kept in courts. Case-numbering methods (used on docket sheets) are described, as docket sheets contain certain pieces of information essential to many court cases. Most courts are now computerized, meaning that the docket information is entered into a computer system. Many court systems are linked within a state or judicial district. Unfortunately, little retrospective indexing has been done, so for precomputerized cases, old-fashioned microfilm, microfiche, or even index cards (!) contain summary case information. Case documents themselves are rarely kept on computer. They are available only from the court where the case records are located.

Information about online sources is provided, but it is estimated that only 15 percent of public records are online. Indexing and location-finding aids are more likely to be automated, and these will be profiled whenever possible. This publication features a time-saving city/county cross-reference index. Many times the name of the county in which a particular city or township resides is not readily known, and the cross-reference index provides that information.

Directory of State Court Clerks and County Courthouses (WANT Publishing, annual)

This publication is similar to the others, organized by state and city or county within the state. It also contains useful charts showing the structure of each state's courts. It does not have a great deal of additional detailed information. The directory lists the names, addresses, and telephone numbers of clerks of appellate and trial courts and indicates the counties in each judicial circuit or district. It also covers county clerks, attorneys general, and state corporation commission offices and includes instructions for obtaining vital statistics and records, deed records, and probate information. The charts of each state's court structure are included here as well. This directory is very reasonably priced and would be useful as a general reference resource.

Lists

Lists of documents are useful in searching for local court documents. Unfortunately, these are usually subject to directives or decisions made on the local government level. In fact, lists of documents are usually kept, if at all, by the individual office responsible for archiving the documents. These lists are usually created and maintained by an individual (or a succession of individuals) who are responsible for filing the documents. This leaves the filing system process open to each individual archivist. Since many of these court systems can exist for literally dozens and even hundreds of years, the archivists are often individuals who create their own system of filing documents. Lists of documents and docket materials often exist at the city or county clerk's office of each place. Some lists of county and city administrative records also exist, including court records that were compiled by the Works Progress Administration (WPA) in the 1930s and 1940s. These projects were definitely conducted locally, and most of the records completed were left in the local jurisdictions. Some materials documenting the projects were distributed to Depository libraries and may be accessible at some of the older federal government depositories.

The goal of the Historical Records Survey of the WPA was to inventory and provide accessible guides to state, county, municipal, and other records. Through its work in the 1930s and 1940s, the project rescued from oblivion tens of thousands of volumes of original records. Because the county was the basic unit of government in many states, the primary objective of the survey was to locate, catalog, describe, and evaluate old county records. A report on the project dated June 30, 1938, stated that this work had been completed in approximately 2,000 of the 3,000-odd then-existing counties in the country. Fifty of these inventories had been published at the time. Inventories of the records of 1,040 towns had also been completed. Innumerable documents such as deeds, wills, vital statistics, and reports of prices were brought to light, and records of county activities in the fields of public works and public services were identified and listed. An example of a list compiled during the project is a record of some historical court records in the state of Illinois.

Inventory of Municipal Archives, 1936–1941 (Illinois Historical Records Survey, 1936–41)

This is a listing consisting of field workers' inventory work sheets on municipal archives that include maps, photographs, unbound records, and volumes. It is really just a list of documents, held in various municipal and county government archives in the state of Illinois, that were eventually deposited at the Illinois

State Archives. Only a small number of these inventories were ever published, but many may be held in the archives of various states. Record keeping on these ventures was actually quite good for the time, and inventories of projects completed were submitted to the federal government.

Information can be found in certain publications of the WPA.

Inventory: An Appraisal of the Results of the Works Progress Administration (Works Progress Administration, Superintendent of Documents, 1938)

This volume contains a short narrative describing various types of projects, in addition to an inventory of the total number of projects completed during the years 1933 through 1937. For example, under "Historical Surveys," we learn that records for 1,040 towns were listed as projects.

Index of Research Projects (1933–1938), 3 volumes (Works Progress Administration, Superintendent of Documents, 1938)

This volume lists individual projects such as *Popular and Legal Tribunals of Tuolumne County, 1849–1867*, which describes the records of "popular tribunals" often formed for the administration of justice in the gold rush encampments, where regular judicial agencies and a standard system of enforcement were lacking. Another is *Survey of Criminal Court Procedure in Georgia* (Georgia Department of Public Welfare, Atlanta, 1937), which described the judicial structure of the state and the numbers of courts and judges and summarized their various jurisdictions. There were extensive tables and charts that actually listed statistics on the disposition of court cases in the state. It is not clear from the description whether the actual court records were listed, which is a consistent problem in trying to determine what is available for research in locations remote from the researcher.

Records, 1909–1939 (Nowata County, Oklahoma)

This list is interesting, as it is in a national database of publications and appears to be a categorical listing of a collection of county government records, including judicial dockets of the Nowata County civil and criminal courts, as well as various tax-exemption applications and documents. The boxes of material described are 50 feet in length.

Many courts are now keeping lists of documents and court records online, available for people who come into local court offices looking for records. They are usually indexed by name of plaintiff and name of defendant. Information about availability of online lists is sometimes available in directories, such as those previously reviewed, or by checking the local government Web sites. Several Web addresses for this type of listing are available under the section on Comprehensive Web Sites.

COMPENDIUMS

Comprehensive Directories

Sourcebook to Public Record Information: The Comprehensive Guide to County, State, and Federal Public Record Sources (BRB Publications, 2004)

This is a compilation of several earlier publications: *Sourcebook of County Court Records*; *Sourcebook of State Public Records, Federal Courts*; and *U.S., District, and Bankruptcy and County Asset/Lien Records*.

This very large, complex volume is more comprehensive in scope than the earlier publications, in some instances to the extent that more is provided than is needed. The volume is physically cumbersome to use, and a smaller, more focused publication—such as the *County Court Records* volume described earlier—may be preferable. This volume combines all public record information covered by the publisher on a state-by-state basis. For example, in the chapter for a particular state, there are sections on state agencies, state licensing boards, federal courts, county courts, and recording offices, and there is a county locator section for each state. If a user were searching for different kinds of public records, then this publication would be a comprehensive and useful resource. Because it is most helpful in searching for administrative records, it will be described in more detail in that section. One last important point is that since *County Court Records* was last published in 1997, the latest information on the courts is only in the *Sourcebook to Public Record Information* or one of the online databases the publisher maintains.

Two other directories are worthy of note, the *National Directory of Courts of Law* (Information Resources Press, 1991) and the *County Courthouse Book* (Genealogical Publishing, 2nd edition, 1995), but they are too dated to be of much current value.

Comprehensive Web Sites

Your Nation's Courts Online (WANT Publishing, Inc.) http://www.courts.com/online.htm

This Web site offers speedy, point-and-click access to federal, state, and county courts, for a fee. The information includes names, addresses, and phone numbers of federal appellate, district, and bankruptcy judges and clerks of court, magistrates, judges, and U.S. attorneys, all updated monthly. Names and biographical information on new federal nominations sent by the president to the Senate for confirmation are included, as is information on federal court vacancies on a court-by-court basis. New federal judge confirmations (or rejections), within days of the Senate's vote on their nominations, are available. Names, addresses, and phone numbers of clerks for each state court, from the state's highest down to the county courthouse level, are listed, as are those of state attorneys general, state court administrators, and secretaries of state. Links to federal and state court Web sites are all listed. The information included on Your Nation's Courts Online complements and updates the material available in the annual print publications *Want's Federal-State Court Directory* and *Directory of State Court Clerks and County Courthouses*, adding many features not available in the print versions and including biographical information on new judicial nominees. Conversely, there is material in the print versions not available online, such as the State Court Organization Charts. The subscription rate is reasonable, considering what many online services cost. There is a rate available that is based on the number of users, which would be a good resource for a government agency handling interstate transfers of court records or a private investigator needing access to as much court information as possible. The amount of information on municipal courts, however, is limited. This database might be useful in a law library or a public library.

Search Systems (Public Information Resources, Inc.)
  http://www.searchsystems.net

This site contains a directory of over 2,376 searchable free public records databases. Federal government, state and local governments, and Canadian government databases are included. Depending on the state, there are licensing records, court records, unclaimed property, sex offender registries, etc., as well as some county-level databases.

For example, under the state of Arizona, there is a link to the Department of Accountancy that in turn links to the Arizona Public Records Reproduction Request Form, Information and Instruction Sheet. This online access to the form can save time that would be required to write or call to request one. Links exist to a wide range of records databases. If the county of Yellowstone in Montana is selected, there is a link to the clerk of the federal district court, but no link to local county or city courts. Although online access to local courts varies considerably in availability, the number of Web sites with online access to at least basic contact information is increasing.

State and Local Government Information on the Net
  http://www.statelocalgov.net/index.cfm

This is a Web site maintained by Piper Resources that provides links to official state Web sites. Under these Web-site links, there are often listings of counties and cities in the state that also have Web sites. Each state Web site is unique and provides different links to categories of information that may be important in that state.

SPECIALIZED DIRECTORIES

The jurisdictional lines between county and municipal courts vary from state to state. These courts are usually a lower level of an overall state court structure. How court structures differ is demonstrated by comparing the state of Delaware to Connecticut. In Delaware, there are three counties: Kent, Sussex, and New Castle. In Kent County are the chancery court, the superior court, the court of common pleas, and the justices of the peace for the communities of Dover, Harrington, and Smyrna. The jurisdiction of each court is described in the introductory paragraph for the state. In contrast, the Connecticut court structure generally consists of one or more superior courts within each county, under which are numbered courts of "geographic" jurisdiction, which can be at the county level (although there are no counties in Connecticut, and courts can have multiple jurisdictions; counties are actually collections of townships, with no county government per se, so they exist geographically, but not politically) or at the single-township level. There are 12 judicial districts, 22 geographic areas, and 14 juvenile districts. It is easy to see that court systems can be very confusing. It may be necessary to use one of the guides mentioned above before knowing the name of the court of jurisdiction for a particular case.

Superior and Municipal Court Records

It is difficult to locate a directory of municipal and superior court locations. First, although there are a huge number of these courts, very few comprehensive listings of their locations exist. A few of the national-level directories, such as the *Librarian's Guide to Court Records: The Complete State, County, and Courthouse Locator* and the *Sourcebook of County Court Records*, have some but not all municipal courts listed. These resources are described in more detail in the section on General Resources.

No single directory claims to be comprehensive. This is in part because many states organize and name their courts differently from each other. It has been too time-consuming for a publisher to collect this information and update it regularly. Most often people are interested in courts close to them, but as the population becomes increasingly mobile (and global), more people may need court and other types of government records from distant locations.

Sourcebook of County Court Records (BRB Publications, Inc., 1997)

From the *Sourcebook*, an example of how a state may list local courts differently follows. In Connecticut, the courts are called *superior courts*, but they could hold the name of the county, such as New London County or Ansonia-Milford Superior Court (New Haven County).

The following listing is found under New London County:

Geographical Court #10, 112 Broad Street, New London, CT, 06320, (860 443-8343. Hours 1pm-2:30 pm, 4pm-5pm (EST). Misdemeanor, eviction, small claims. Civil Records: Access: Mail, in person. Required to search: name, years to search. Cases indexed by defendant. Civil Records on Computer back 2 yrs, on microfiche from early 1985, prior on index cards and docket books. Criminal records: Access: same as civil. Required to search: name, years to search; also helpful-DOB, SSN. Criminal records on computer for 2 years; prior records on microfiche. Only court conducts searches. General information: No search fee. No sealed, dismissed, youth or program records released. SASE required. Turnaround time: up to 1 month. No certification. Certification available from the State Records Center. Personal checks accepted.

It is easy to become confused. An index such as this one, organized geographically and alphabetically by state, then alphabetically by county, with the names of local courts listed under the county, is invaluable. It is especially useful to have these court directories in one volume. Most local telephone directories list all government offices in the front of the volume, but very few libraries carry more than their own local telephone directories. There are some national-level directory services, but not many free ones.

New York Judge Reviews and Court Directory (James Publishing Co.)

This resource comes in loose-leaf form with annual supplements. We include it as an example of a court directory for a particular state. This large volume (620 pages) provides thorough coverage of courts in the state of New York. Also included are reviews of judges (similar to those found in the volume on Southern California Courts, to be described subsequently). Although difficult to ascertain, it is likely that similar jurisdiction-specific directories exist that are available only in that area. This volume is published irregularly. Usually only libraries or law firms that practice in the area of jurisdiction covered own directories such as these. James Publishing has produced several such directories (about 30) for differing jurisdictions. This is a very small number compared with all possible jurisdictions.

Superior Court of Arizona in Maricopa County
http://www.superiorcourt.maricopa.gov/index.asp

This is a Web site for a regional court that provides information about public access to court records, as well as case histories, court calendars, and an attorney court calendar. News releases and information concerning court rulings are also provided. A page exists from which forms can be downloaded (http://www.superiorcourt.maricopa.gov/ssc/info/gen_info.asp). This Web site was found by using the Piper State and Local Government Information on the Net Web site (http://www.piperinfo.com/state/az.htm), then finding the state Web site and looking for links to counties, and then courts listed there. It does require moving through several levels to find the actual Web site of the court. Each site also does this somewhat differently. It is always possible to do a more general Web search on Google (http://www.google.com), using the name of the county, and then searching through the many retrievals to find the right one. These searches can easily be performed on any Web search engine (e.g., Yahoo [http://www.yahoo.com], AltaVista [http://www.

altavista.com]), but Google is usually very accurate in retrieving the right Web site within the first several hits. These Web search engines all have different protocols for searching, so it is not necessarily safe to assume that if one of them does not retrieve a Web site, it does not exist. It is better to try several search engines in succession, if necessary.

County Court Records

County court records encompass a wide variety of types of records and documents. There are a number of ways to search for them, including through indexes of court files, which are not consistent, and dockets and lists of court record files in state, county, and local courthouses. There are a few national-level court record locator publications and databases, but most local court records are stored locally for a certain period of time and then often transferred to a county or state archive.

In most cases, it is difficult to distinguish between county and municipal court record files, if only because municipal court records are often transferred to a central location, which is most often the county clerk's office. The resources described earlier in the section are perhaps the most comprehensive way to address this problem. There are a couple of other county court directories that are not updated as frequently as the BRB publications, which, however, can be expensive. For a smaller library or office, a few other county court directories may be more suitable.

Tyson Guide to Southern California Courts (Judicial Publications)

This court guide, updated irregularly, is useful in a different way than the previous guides that simply list court contact information. It is an explanatory guide to the courts in the Southern California region, in a loose-leaf volume, divided by county. Each county section carries a judicial profile that describes the structure of the courts in that county, as well as more detailed information about judges and the rules certain judges favor in their courts. This is useful for someone who will be appearing in a court outside of their home area and will familiarize them with hours and rules specific to each judge's courtroom. An example of the type of information found in this book is that provided for Judge Fredrick N. Wapner, Los Angeles Superior Court. Current assignment, previous appointments, education, practice history, professional activities, and personal history are listed. Specific information is provided, such as the answers to

the following questions: During trial, what time of day do you start and finish for the day? Under what circumstances, if any, would you impose sanctions on an attorney?

This publication is fairly large and detailed, as the Los Angeles area court system, like that of any major metropolitan county, is quite large, and even attorneys working in the county may be unfamiliar with a particular court. It is found primarily at law libraries and law firms.

Such a publication may be available to local law practitioners in many other large metropolitan areas. The best way to determine whether one is available is to use one of the county government directories available online or at a large local public or university library, if one is located nearby, or calling or writing the county law library or county clerk's office for further information. If one has access to a BRB publication, such as the *Sourcebook to Public Record Information*, further searching might not be necessary. However, most small-town and county libraries will not have this publication. Very small towns are not likely to be listed, even in this comprehensive directory. A telephone directory is the only likely way to locate contact information for these very small local areas. There may be some Internet telephone directories that may be helpful, such as 555-1212.com, at http://www.555-1212.com/mindex.jsp, and AnyWho, at http://www.anywho.com.

Texas Courthouse Guide (Texas Lawyer, annual)

This very specialized resource is an example of another comprehensive directory for judges and courts in a particular state. The latest *Texas Courthouse Guide* contains vital, up-to-date information about the courts, administrative agencies, associations, and other institutions that compose the legal landscape. The directory lists such contact information as phone, mail, and fax and e-mail addresses for elected officials and staff employees throughout the Texas public legal scene, including judges, district and county clerks, prosecutors, court reporters, court coordinators, and others. The guide also contains filing fee information for the largest counties. This is a good choice if the state's court information is all that is needed. It covers details on courts throughout the county system, which, like most local court systems, has its own organization. Such a directory is probably necessary to determine which court is the appropriate one to contact.

Sourcebook of County Court Records (BRB Publications, Inc. 1997)

This resource is described in detail in the section on directories, and it is mentioned here to reiterate the fact that it is a major source of county court information. This source has information similar to that found in the *Librarian's Guide to Public Records* (BRB Publications, 2000), but more detailed information is included in the entries. The *Sourcebook of County Court Records* is also updated by the more comprehensive *Sourcebook to Public Record Information* (BRB Publications, 2004).

State and Federal Court Records

Sourcebook to Public Record Information: The Comprehensive Guide to County, State, and Federal Public Record Sources (BRB Publications, 1999)

As previously mentioned, this publication is a compilation of several earlier ones: *Sourcebook of County Court Records*; *Sourcebook of State Public Records, Federal Courts*; and *U.S., District, and Bankruptcy and County Asset/Lien Records*. This volume combines all public record information covered by the publication for each state on a state-by-state basis. The federal courts are outlined and listed first, in each chapter, by state. For example, in the chapter for a particular state, there are sections on federal courts as well as state and county agencies. This publication has the same information as *County Court Records*, such as names, addresses, telephone numbers, access policies, and requirements for searches, costs, and methods of payment. It is definitely more cumbersome to use if the user is looking for only federal court information. A more specialized directory containing only information about federal courts may be more efficient to search. If the searcher is looking for public records on many jurisdictional levels, then this directory is the most comprehensive and useful.

Judicial Staff Directory: Federal and State Courts, Judges, Staffs, Biographies (Congressional Quarterly, annual)

This publication is organized primarily around federal and state courts but has information about appeals, bankruptcy, and other specialized courts. It also has a very useful listing of counties and cities by state that indicates which judicial district the county is in as well as which federal circuit the county or city resides in, with the name of the circuit judge (Supreme Court justice) for that jurisdiction. This information is not useful for locating a city or county court, but it is useful in determining which judicial district constitutes

the larger jurisdiction. This index is unique to this source. It is reasonably priced for almost any library and is a good general resource.

TOPICAL AND SPECIALIZED RESOURCES

General Court Documents

There are many types of documents and records processed and filed by courts that yield useful information. While such records might not be actually court-generated documents, they may have been submitted as evidence in a case, and are therefore part of the court record files. They include state and federal court records of local research value such as those from appeals courts, bankruptcy courts, the court of claims, the court of patent appeals, the court of military appeals, criminal courts, chancery courts, and tax courts. These records can all contain information of local governmental interest. A sample listing of the types of court documents and records that exist is extensive and provides an idea of how much information may actually be available.

Bankruptcy Courts

Bankruptcy Courts and Procedures (James Publishing Company)

This resource, updated semiannually, is a comprehensive guide to the entire bankruptcy process, including involuntary, creditor, and adversary proceedings. The book also lists fees, filing requirements, names, addresses, and telephone numbers for every bankruptcy court in the nation.

In addition to containing filing guidelines, the book is a comprehensive source for bankruptcy proceedings, offering a thorough overview of bankruptcy, including all types of bankruptcy cases, adversary proceedings, conversion and dismissal, role of the trustee, debtor's estate and appeals, and the Bankruptcy Reform Act of 1994. It is reasonably priced and is available from the publisher.

Sourcebook to Public Record Information: The Comprehensive Guide to County, State, and Federal Public Record Sources (BRB Publications, 2004)

Although this publication is described in detail in an earlier section of this chapter, it is listed here as a source of information about bankruptcy courts.

FindLaw: Federal Resources—Judicial Branch— Bankruptcy Courts http://www.findlaw.com/10fedgov/judicial/bankruptcy_courts.html

FindLaw is a Web site that has links to many law resources. It has been free up to this point, but has recently been purchased by the West Group. It is a nicely organized Web site, with links to legal resources on a variety of subjects from many sources. There are geographic jurisdictional arrangements as well as topical arrangements. This particular link lists bankruptcy courts by state and district and names of judges, trustees, clerks, addresses, telephone numbers, dockets, calendars, and required filing forms. It's quite useful for locating information about a bankruptcy court from a distance.

Bankruptcy Courts (FedLaw)
http://www.thecre.com/fedlaw/legal33.htm

This Web site was meant to be similar to the FindLaw—Bankruptcy Courts Web site. When tested, however, many of the links functioned poorly or were not found at all, although some did provide referrals to other Web sites. This Web site is described for the sake of contrast to a well-regulated and maintained Web site. The first page of the Web site does state, however, that there is a "major link restoration" under way.

BankruptcyData.com (New Generation Research, Inc.) http://bankruptcydata.com

This is a Web site that claims to be "the premier site for bankruptcy information on the Web." The site includes searchable links to opinions of the bankruptcy courts and a directory of judges, clerks, and courts with Web sites. There is a directory of U.S. bankruptcy court clerk's offices, trustee Web sites, and other miscellaneous information.

A link to the "Bankruptcy Library" exists with references and links to current articles about bankruptcy issues. The searchable index allows one to search for bankruptcy cases in the bankruptcy courts files. An interesting link gives current statistics for bankruptcy filings. This is a useful, easy to use Web site.

Land Records

Many land documents are included in records produced by regional and local courts. With the exception of some federal or state land cases, most land records are deeds recorded, transferred, or sold. Many times these filings occur as a result of a death requiring probate, or some other official court-sanctioned action that requires a decision or an official transfer of property. Many times controversies arise over title to land, and the issue must be settled in court. The United States Bureau of Land Management has millions of land records, due to the huge amount of land claimed by the federal government and later homesteaded. The comprehensive directories for these records are created primarily for investigators, title searchers, etc., and are similar to those sourcebooks published by BRB Publications. Most of the other resources are compiled primarily by a specialized researcher and often cover a small geographic area and a narrow time period. Some examples are described below.

New Castle County, Delaware, Land Records, 1715–1728 (Willow Bend Books, 2000)

This publication is a description of records concerning land tenure and ownership in a small county during the pre–Revolutionary War period. A researcher who kept records of the structure of the files and indexed the records for future research probably compiled this book. There are probably many of these types of indexes, and most will be located at each local library or historical society. A few are cataloged on a large bibliographical database such as Online Computer Library Center's (OCLC) WorldCat (a very large for-fee bibliographic database available in most large research libraries). Most often, only those who do work with the actual records will know guides or indexes such as this. Contacting a local library or historical society or the county or city clerk's office would be a good way to find out whether one exists.

The Official Federal Land Patent Records Site (U.S. Bureau of Land Management)
http://www.glorecords.blm.gov

This Web site contains 260,000 land patents dated before 1908 from the Bureau of Land Management Eastern States Repository. Documents may be searched by patentee name, document number, document authority, land office, or legal description. Records are currently available for Alabama, Arkansas, Florida, Louisiana, Michigan, Minnesota, Mississippi, Ohio, and Wisconsin.

Land Patent Search (U.S. Bureau of Land Management) http://www.glorecords.blm.gov/PatentSearch/Default.asp?

This is the actual Web site that allows access to the General Land Office (GLO) records, which are the first land records for all public-land states. The agency is digitizing these records to provide online database access to federal land conveyance records for these states. Image access is provided to more than 2 million federal land title records for 31 public-land states issued between 1820 and 1908. Images of serial patents issued between 1908 and the mid-1960s are currently being added to this Web site. Due to organization of documents in the GLO collection, this Web site does not currently contain every federal land title record issued for the listed states, but that is a goal of the project. Land ownership records subsequent to the first patent are kept at the local county recorder's office for that state. This is a great resource for original title information, which can be searched from any Internet-connected computer. The typical record accessed will include an index listing of the patent, a legal land description, a document image, and an order form for ordering a certified copy online. The Web site is easy to use and very useful, although busy and hard to get into sometimes.

General Land Office Automated Records Project
(CD-ROM, U.S. Government Printing Office)

For those who do not have access to the Internet, the databases produced for the GLO have also been put on CD-ROM and can be used at Depository libraries or purchased from the U.S. Government Printing Office. The CD-ROM is not as easy to use as the online version, but it has advantages of allowing unlimited use as long as there is a computer with a CD-ROM drive available. CD-ROMs have not yet been produced for all available states.

Land records issued after 1908 are located at the county recorder's office. As outlined elsewhere in this book, there are a number of ways to locate county offices.

State and Local Government on the Net
http://www.piperinfo.com/state/index.cfm

This is a very good site for locating local geographic jurisdictions. First, select a state, then a county, and search for the county recorder's office. This may lead to land parcel information by county. For example, a random search of "North Carolina" and "Cabarrus County" led to a link to "GIS." This link, interestingly enough, although connecting to a "Geographic Information Systems Page," actually provides links to parcel maps that can be used to request land title information from the county. Some places are providing these services, and some are not yet that technologically advanced. Expect to find more of these Web sites in the future.

Probate Records

Probate records are the records of the transfer of the legal responsibility for the payment of taxes, care and custody of dependent family members, liquidation of debts, and transfer of property title to heirs from the deceased to an executor/executrix (where there is a will), to an administrator/administratrix (if the person dies intestate, without a will), or to a guardian/conservator if there are heirs under the age of 21 years or the estate holder has become incompetent through disease or disability (see pp. 202–211 in the *Sourcebook: A Guidebook of American Genealogy*).

In contrast to most other court records, file indexes and lists of probate courts have been compiled and often cataloged for many small towns and counties. There are thousands of them on WorldCat, which contains records for publications from all over the United States and the world. For example, one of the indexes is *Heirs and Orphans: Anne Arundel County, Maryland Distributions, 1788–1838*, containing abstracts of volumes of the distributions of personal estates of Anne Arundel County intestates. Another example is entitled simply *Papers, 1880–1985*, but in spite of its generic name, it is an index to photocopies of field notes compiled by a researcher during his studies of Cheyenne and Arapaho Indian kinship; census coding sheets, Indian censuses, Indian allotments, and copies of probate and land grant–related records are among the records indexed in this volume.

There are thousands of these types of indexes, and the key to finding them is to use an online union (multilibrary) catalog like OCLC WorldCat or contact the local public library or historical or genealogical society.

SPECIAL INFORMATION ON FINDING AND USING COURT RECORDS

Sourcebook of Local Court and County Record Retrievers (BRB Publications, 1999)

This specialized source lists services and people who will retrieve records for a fee, useful primarily in geographic areas distant from the researcher. This can be more economical than traveling there to get court records. There are services that will do it for you, and they are listed in this *Sourcebook* alphabetically by state. A listing includes the state, the name of the county, record retrievers for/in the county, and telephone numbers. There is a court code for all of the courts within that jurisdiction, and a black dot indicates from which courts the retrievers will get records. The types of courts from which records are retrieved are U.S. district courts, bankruptcy courts, civil courts, criminal courts, and probate courts. There is also a listing for public records and which ones the services will retrieve. Those types of records will be described in more detail in the chapter on administrative government agency records. A section called "Retriever Profiles" lists more detailed information about the retriever, such as address, telephone number, fax number, where they will retrieve records, what records they will retrieve, normal turnaround time, and correspondence relationships (basically, their clientele). This publication is useful for learning about not only a particular court, but the judge and rules of that court. An important note here is that there is a free online news service available from the publisher that releases information such as the fact that a court in Maryland has restricted the types of so-called public records that can be retrieved by the public.

National Directory of Public Record Vendors (BRB Publications, 2001)

This news service can be subscribed to through the publisher's Web site, http://www.brbpub.com. The special local court guides and directories mentioned in this section are probably similar in each state or county court system. The best place to obtain information such as that in these guides is to contact the local county library or law library in that county. If the research is actually in the local area, a library is always a good place to begin searching for information. This can be done by using a county directory such as State and Local Government on the Net, http://www.piper info.com/state/index.cfm.

A more unusual finding aid is *Death Records, Obituaries, and Probate Files—What the Dead Can Tell You*, by Sheila Benedict (Federation of Genealogical Societies, 1999). This is a sound recording (on cassette or CD) of a presentation made at a conference of the Federation of Genealogical Societies.

One final example of a resource for using specialized court records is *Native American Wills and Probate Records, 1911–1920* (Mountain Press, 1997). This resource addresses the use of a specific set of documents from a short time period. A number of libraries own this resource, so it is always important to contact a local library or historical society for indexes and general finding aids before beginning a document-by-document search.

The resources described in this chapter represent just a few of the many local, individually produced indexes, directories, finding aids, Web sites, and various useful tools that are available for doing research in local court records. Although there are few general comprehensive directories, the more focused the search becomes, the more likely that something may be found that will be helpful to the researcher at the local level. There are lists of libraries, archives, and historical and genealogical societies in the chapter on general resources that are useful to find further information.

CHAPTER 8
Finding Local Census Information

Mary Martin

MAJOR TOPICS COVERED

MAJOR RESOURCES COVERED

INTRODUCTION

Data collected by the United States Bureau of the Census are some of the most important information available to users of local government information, as it is applicable to a wide range of purposes. The original purpose of the Census was mandated in the Constitution for the purpose of apportionment of seats in Congress (the determination of congressional representation of various state and local areas). Therefore, by its very definition, the Census is taken in local geographic areas. The Census of Population is conducted only every 10 years (the Decennial Census). By contrast, the current Economic Census is conducted every five years. As population figures can be out of date after five years, surveys are conducted to keep the information up-to-date. There are other demographic and economic data surveys that are conducted between the Censuses, but none are anywhere near as comprehensive as the Decennial or Economic Cen-

suses. The Decennial Census, taken since 1790, is the most comprehensive and reliable set of data available for any geographic jurisdiction in the United States. Originally, the Population and Economic Censuses were published together. They have been published separately for some time. The Census is not perfect, but it is considered to be very reliable, particularly for 100 percent counts (i.e., replies to questions that were asked of all households). There are various criticisms leveled at the Census, some with validity, but it is the best measurement tool of its kind that exists.

This chapter will provide an overview of some concepts and publications helpful to users of sources of Census data for local government jurisdictions and places. One basic concept is that Census data collection consists of the tabulation of answers to questions (and only those questions) asked on the Census questionnaire. For example, the Census has a question about telephone ownership, but not television ownership. The second basic concept is that of geographic jurisdiction.

Data are collected on a form that is mailed to each housing unit. Questions are asked about individual family members and family units, then aggregated according to various geographic areas such as county, city, Census tract, or block numbering area. For example, population is a simple value to display, but tabulation of population by race, income, and age is more complex. This multidimensional feature is what makes Census data so valuable. Because data are collected at the smallest level, it has been enumerated at that level, but not always *tabulated or published at that level*. A summary list of data elements counted and geographic jurisdictions for which data are commonly tabulated are summarized in this chapter. This information is also available in the Appendices of most Census volumes and can be located at Depository libraries (libraries that receive and house publications for the U.S. government) and certain other libraries. Most congressional districts have at least one Depository library. For a list of Depository libraries, see the GPO Access Web site, at http://www.access.gpo.gov/su_docs/locators/findlibs/index.html.

Most 1990 Census data is available in multiple formats, paper, CD-ROM, tape, and electronic (Internet). Census 2000 data is available in limited paper and CD-ROM format. The principal means of access is electronic from the Census Bureau Web site. Data that have not been released or published may still be available from the Census Bureau or a private source. There are also libraries and public agencies that purchase Census Bureau data. Some of these agencies sell specially tabulated reports. Also, State Data Centers, which were created in 1978, are combinations of state agencies, state universities, and affiliates such as public libraries, university research centers, and regional planning agencies throughout the state that are experts in using Census data. There is also a Business and Industry Data Center (BIDC) program and the Census Information Centers program. A list of these centers is available at the State Data Center program Web site, http://www.census.gov/sdc/www. The Census Bureau Web site has a page on Census 2000 that will be updated to reflect current information regarding the Census (http://www.census.gov/dmd/www/2khome.htm). Information will continue to be released and disseminated well into the early twenty-first century. It is necessary to have knowledge of how the Census was conducted in the past to understand historical statistics and comparability of data. One of the most important uses of Census data is for regression analysis, or the measurement of change over time.

Historical Data

Census data are available back to 1790. The summary data are available in paper volumes, held by mostly older, larger academic and public libraries. The reports have also been reproduced in paper and are available from Hein, Inc. (Buffalo, New York). They are very expensive. Some libraries and data centers have purchased the older volumes on microfilm. It is important to check with the library to find out whether the volumes are held in the collection. Often Census volumes, because of their age, are not included in the online catalog. The best strategy is to ask the reference librarian. If a local library does not have the volumes, another library in the state might. It is important to distinguish here between summary data sets and Census schedules, which are microfilm copies of the original Census documents, as recorded by the Census taker. These Census schedules are used by genealogical and other researchers and are explained in more detail in chapter 9 on genealogical resources. Technically, the Census schedules provide a street-by-street or farm-by-farm enumeration of the inhabitants of the United States during each particular Decennial Census year. They are formidable to use, as most are handwritten, faded, and old microfilm copies. These are extremely useful historical records, and all the branches of the National Archives have copies. The genealogy page of the National Archives Web site, http://www.nara.gov/genealogy, has more detailed information about research using these resources. Some libraries also have archives of this material, particularly large city libraries and the libraries of the Church of Jesus Christ of Latter-day Saints.

An additional concept that has implications for data users is that of *confidentiality*, or an individual's right to privacy in relation to data gathered by the Census Bureau. Since 1910, because of confidentiality issues, a presidential proclamation has decreed that the replies to Census questions be used only to compile statistical information, and the answers are protected from divulgence by law. If it is determined that the publishing of a particular data item might reveal personal information about residents in a particular area, the data are suppressed. For example, if there were only one Native American in a Census tract and publishing the income data for that race group in that tract would reveal the income of this one Native American, all of the data would be suppressed. There is a 72-year limit on the confidentiality of data, so Census schedules are made available after 72 years and are used primarily by genealogical researchers. As of this date, Census records from 1790 to 1930 are available for public use. The chapter on genealogy in this book has additional information on the Census schedules.

Data Comparability

It is important here to remind users about data comparability. Data definitions sometimes change during the 10 years between Decennial Censuses. It is important to check the definitions of data items in each Census. There are appendices provided in the back of each Census volume, as well as separate publications that define data items and geography. A resource that is very helpful in defining concepts, at least for the 1990 Census, is *Census of Population and Housing Guide* (Parts 1A and 1B), published by the Census Bureau in 1992, which provides explanatory text and an extensive glossary of terminology. There are similar publications for many of the Decennial Census years. The titles are usually *Guide to the 1970* [etc.] *Census.*

There are not yet many publications on Census 2000. The help screens and explanations at the Census Bureau Web site are the main resources for questions. As an example of why this knowledge is important, a user once wanted data on church membership but was told by the staff consulted that church membership was not a Census item, on the assumption that since it *currently* is not a Census item, it never had been. In fact, it actually had been a data item for many years before legal decisions affecting the separation of church and state made such data collection by the government illegal. It can be very important to check to see what data were collected in a particular year. The definitions can get very complicated; for example, as recently as 1940, racial data were collected and reported for only major racial categories (native-born white, foreign-born white, Negro, other races). In 1950 and 1960 the available racial categories were white, Negro, Indian, Japanese, Chinese, Filipino, and other race—however, most tables reported only native-white, nonnative white, Negro, and other race. Although statistics were collected for other racial categories in 1970, most tables still reported only white, Negro, and other race. In 1980, racial categories reported expanded to include American Indian, Aleut and Eskimo, Asian and Pacific Islander, and Spanish origin (Mexican, Puerto Rican, Cuban, and other Spanish).

By 1990, categories reported included all of the above in addition to detailed breakdowns within Asian and Hispanic-origin categories. It is important to understand the categories of data presented in the 1990 Census in order to fully utilize the data presented in Census 2000. For Census 2000, the racial categories will be even more complicated, as a direct reflection of multiculturalism in the United States. Racial categorizations are used for a multitude of purposes, from educational planning to congressional reapportionment and federal and state block-grant allocation for neighborhood services. Limited paper volumes for Census 2000 are being published, and it is not possible to understand the structure of the data collected without seeing the scope of the tables published in the 1990 Census. Census 2000 on its Web site is presented differently from the paper version, with a menu approach—in other words, if the data element sought is located, it can be retrieved, but not all data elements collected are available. The section on Census 2000 will show further details and examples of actual searches.

Geographic jurisdictions are very important, as they certainly change over time. The greatest example of this is the migration from country to city earlier in the twenty-first century, and the move from city to suburbs in the past few decades. The population is generally also moving south and west. Census data can be used to substantiate these facts. When using Census data for a geographic jurisdiction, it must be one that is recognized and for which statistics are tabulated and published. Otherwise, the statistics will have to be calculated. It does tend to get confusing when boundaries change, which happens when metropolitan areas are growing. There are other details that can be consulted in chapter 12 on maps and geographic concepts, as well as information provided in the appendix of most Census publications.

Census 2000/American FactFinder http://factfinder.
    census.gov/java_prod/dads.ui.homePage.
    HomePage

The U.S. Census Bureau is developing a new product for use with the 1997 Economic Census and Census 2000, called American FactFinder. It was released in its first form in 1999. In 1996, the U.S. Census Bureau undertook a comprehensive, multiyear development effort to build a data dissemination system. In order to expand public access to demographic and economic information, the Bureau wanted to provide access to its data through the Internet. American

FactFinder uses supercomputers, Oracle database capabilities, and ESRI (Environmental Systems Research Institute) geography software to provide users with the capability to browse, search, and map data from many Census Bureau sources: the 1990 Census, the 1997 Economic Census, the American Community Survey, and Census 2000.

Beginning in 2001, the data from Census 2000 became available at American FactFinder. You can use American FactFinder to select data tabulations and maps from the data sets available in the system. The choices are subject to the data available in the system and the strict confidentiality standards of the Census Bureau. American FactFinder will continue to expand and improve functionality and add data in the future. These summary data products are derived from data sets with preaggregated, or summarized, data records. One drawback is that an unfamiliar user will find only data elements that the Census Bureau tabulates. It is necessary to have knowledge of the kind of information available to know to look for it. Examination of past Census reports is one way to know about the additional data items not available from American FactFinder.

American FactFinder lets you search, browse, retrieve, view, print, save, and download the data. There is a feature that allows you to enter an address and obtain pertinent data for the location. Another feature provides geographic comparison charts, which are tables with sets of data for the United States and all states and local areas. You may request tabulations online or you can obtain an extract of the data set (tables) and use your own software to analyze them.

Tables and maps that can be requested include quick tables, geographic comparison tables, detailed tables, reference maps, and thematic maps.

Microdata products are derived from data sets that contain individual data records. Public Use Microdata Samples (PUMS) from the 1990 Census of Population and Housing, the American Community Survey, and Census 2000 will be available. You can request extractions from the PUMS files and carry out any statistical analysis you wish on your own computer or request custom tabulations from the data sets with American FactFinder. There are hundreds of Census Bureau data products available on the Internet, including press releases, statistical abstracts, Census briefs, and information bulletins. (These are predefined, static data products, so you cannot manipulate any of the data or information they contain.) For additional information about these products, see the Census Bureau Web site, http://www.census.gov.

GENERAL RESOURCES

U.S. Census Bureau http://www.census.gov

Census data are extremely important to local government, as it is used to determine matters such as congressional representation and money allocations by the federal government to education and other social programs. Census data are used to determine information about a geographic area, from population totals to income levels, educational attainment, and racial characteristics. The amount of information available is phenomenal, and in fact the Census Bureau Web site is one of the only sources of detailed social and economic data available for local areas. Census questionnaires are available for 1980 and 1990 as well as for Census 2000. For a listing of data items asked and a table listing their corresponding possible use for funding, visit http://www.census.gov/dmd/www/2000quest.html. We recommend the examples provided in the sections "How We Ask It" and "What It Means for Everyone."

Also available on the Census Bureau Web site is access to an electronic products catalog (under "Product Catalog" on the home page) and a list of expert contacts (under "Contacts," at http://www.census.gov/contacts/www/contacts.html).

Census Bureau News http://www.census.gov/pubinfo/www/news.html

This is a great place to find updates on all the latest Census Bureau products being released. This is important during the years when Census data are being released. This Web site is also informative about future products and tips on how to use data. There are links to news releases, videos, help sheets, statistics, and major products. Information on Census 2000 product releases are provided at the "Census 2000 Data Products at a Glance" page on the Web site, at http://www.census.gov/population/www/censusdata/c2kproducts.html. This information is not really meaningful to the novice and requires the interpretation of an intermediary who is knowledgeable about Census data; however, it is there for the brave.

Guides

Census 1980, Continuing the Factfinder Tradition, by Charles P. Kaplan (U.S. Census Bureau, 1980)

For a thorough explanation of the concept of the Census, see this volume, which explores the historical tradition of the Census, as well as how the concepts have evolved in recent times. Of particular interest is the chapter on "Geography for a Changing Society," which explains how Census geography has changed over time and why. The book also explains race and ethnicity categories, such as the difference between Asian and Hispanic origin. Another interesting chapter is "Census Applications in Urban and Regional Planning." There are explanations of what variables are used and what possible inferences can be made from studying them. Although published in the 1980s, this volume is a timeless reference for understanding Census concepts and data. The book may be out of print and not available for sale, but most Depository libraries should have it.

Understanding the Census, by Michael R. Lavin (Epoch Books, 1996)

This book is useful for an extensive and in-depth approach to electronic tabulation and the concepts, uses, and dissemination of Census data. The library edition of this book is distributed by Oryx Press (Phoenix, Arizona).

Intended primarily for marketers, planners, grant writers, and other data users, *Understanding the Census* takes an in-depth look at the 1990 Census, when electronic data dissemination really began to expand. Of particular interest are the detailed examinations of differences in questions from year to year and the explanation of changes. The explanations are formatted as question-and-answer boxes on various pages and take up potentially confusing points. "Rules Affecting Metropolitan and Urbanized Areas" explains demographic and geographic changes over time. Another chapter teaches one how to use Extract, which is the name of a software program developed by the Census Bureau to access Economic Census data. A unique feature of this software is that it allows selection of multiple items for multiple geographic areas and extracts them to a table for downloading. Tables in paper volumes, as well as CD-ROM tables, are limited in the number of variables that are displayed at any one time. Extract allows further multiplicity of values displayed. For example, this program is helpful in extracting information for many cities in a county. The volume also has an extensive listing of data items available from the Census and an index to subjects and titles. The importance of these explanatory resources will extend to Census 2000, as comparability of historical data is essential. Although Census 2000 promises to

have such a data manipulation tool, Extract will still be helpful for older data such as the 1990 Census of Population and Housing and the 1992 and 1997 Economic Censuses. As data change over time, it is often necessary to understand what a concept meant 10 or 20 or even 50 years ago. Demographers often want to track changes over time to predict growth, population shifts, land use, and other variables. When looking at historical data, it often requires the assistance of an expert such as a librarian or Census Data Center specialist.

Directories

Census Catalog and Guide (U.S. Census Bureau, annual) http://www.census.gov/prod/www/abs/gen-ref.html

The *Catalog* is a current and useful source for keeping abreast of Census Bureau publications. It can be purchased from the U.S. Government Printing Office (GPO), the Census Bureau, or a U.S. Government Bookstore. Most Depository libraries not only have copies of the *Catalog*, but also many of the products listed in it. This publication is substantial and describes all Census Bureau publications, reports, computer tapes, CD-ROMs, online data products, floppy disks, and maps available for sale from the Census Bureau. Many products supersede previous editions, and it is important to have the most up-to-date *Catalog*. A list of all of the Census Data Centers can be found in Appendix B. For latest information releases, the newsletter *Monthly Product Announcement*, once found in Depository libraries, has been replaced by the *Census Product Update*, at http://www.census.gov/mp/www/cpu.html.

COMPILATIONS

State and Metropolitan Area Data Book (U.S. Census Bureau) http://www.census.gov/statab/www/smadb.html

This resource is an intermittent supplement to the *Statistical Abstract of the United States* (also published by the Census Bureau). Volumes are published every three or four years. It is a good statistical reference source for information on state and local areas. More importantly, in many instances, some Decennial Census data are updated for intervals shorter than 10 years. The statistics are a summary of social, political, and economic organization of the states and metropolitan areas (over 25,000 population) of the United

States. Data are derived from the Census Bureau as well as other governmental and private sources. There are citations to sources that provide further detail and explanations of data. Source notes at the bottom of tables provide further references. Some sources are published; some are unpublished and refer to the source of the data. The volume is arranged in geographic order by state, metropolitan area, metropolitan county, and central city. There are helpful guides to tables, definitions of symbols and terms, and a list of telephone contacts for further information, along with maps of the major U.S. metropolitan areas. Tables for states and metropolitan areas include demographic statistics such as area and population, population projections and characteristics, households, births and deaths, infant deaths, physicians, hospitals, education, and social programs and crime. There are also tables with statistics on building permits, cost of living and crime, private nonfarm business establishments and personal income, personal income projections and civilian labor force, nonfarm employment and average annual pay, export sales, banking, and federal funds and grants for metro areas. For metro counties, there are breakouts for population by race, poverty, building permits, labor force, private nonfarm business, and personal income of primary statistical metropolitan areas (PSMAs) with consolidated metropolitan statistical areas (CMSAs). For central cities, only population is provided.

The appendices include source notes and explanations, geographic concepts and codes (important for data management), an alphabetic listing of PSMAs with CMSAs, component counties of metropolitan counties by state, and central cities of metropolitan areas by state. There is also a subject index. There are extensive descriptions of data for tables and an additional description of geographic concepts and codes. Statistics contained in a particular table such as that on poverty actually contain data items such as new private housing units authorized by building permits for various years and cost-of-living index composites broken down by sectors, persons below poverty level, and age groups. There is a subject index to tables for each geographic jurisdiction. The *State and Metropolitan Area Data Book* is a very valuable source for updated Census data for local areas. This publication is excellent for finding a broad range of data of interest to researchers, social workers, city planners, market analysts, and other varied users. It contains a broader range of data than is available from Decennial Census publications.

It is available in most Depository and public libraries and is relatively inexpensive to purchase. It is available in paper from the GPO. It is also available online, in PDF, from the Census Bureau Web site on "Uncle Sam's Reference Shelf," http://www.census.gov/prod/3/98pubs/smadb-97.pdf.

County and City Data Book (U.S. Census Bureau)

These products are listed together because they are very similar, with only small differences. The *County and City Data Book* was published by the Census Bureau and the GPO approximately every four to six years from 1952 to 1994. The data are very similar to those found in the *State and Metropolitan Area Data Book*, but the geographic designations are slightly different. For example, data are provided for only metropolitan counties (that contain a major city), not for all counties. For states and counties, tables provide statistics for area and population, group quarters (i.e., those living in military barracks, group homes, institutions, college dorms, and other facilities not deemed as households), vital statistics, health care, social programs and crime, education and income, poverty and housing, building permits, and journey to work. Also included are data for labor force, agriculture and manufactures, wholesale and retail trade, service industries, banking, federal government employment, veterans, state and local government, and elections. For cities of 25,000 or more, statistics are listed for area and population, population characteristics, group quarters, population and households, vital statistics, hospitals, crime, education and income, poverty and housing, building permits, journey to work, labor force and manufactures, wholesale and retail trade, service industries, city government employment and finances, and climate are also listed. For places with populations of 2,500 or less, breakouts for population and money income only are provided. The *County and City Data Book* is not available online but is available for sale from the Census Bureau at Uncle Sam's Reference Shelf, http://www.census.gov/statab/www/ccdb.html.

The *County and City Data Book* is published only every four years, and one source for updating the information in it is a companion Census Bureau publication, *USA Counties 1998*, profiled below.

County and City Extra: Annual Metro City and County Data Book (Bernan, annual)

This publication is another source for updating the data in the quadrennial *County and City Data Book*.

Some of the data in the *Extra* has NOT been updated, however, and is still from the 1990 Census. The volume has a table of contents, table outlines, indexes, and appendices that provide information on geographic concepts and codes and definitions of data items. Various important characteristics such as occupation by educational attainment and detailed occupation by race and income level are tabulated. Most statistics are provided for states, counties, metropolitan areas, cities, and congressional districts. The only statistics not provided for cities and congressional districts are vital statistics, such as births and deaths, and crime statistics. Statistics provided for states and counties include age distribution, 1990 and 1996; percentage female; race and Hispanic origin, 1990 and 1996; population change, 1990–1996; population change, 1980–1990; components of population change; projections to 2025; and immigrants and foreign-born population. Additional important statistics listed include number of households in 1990 and 1996, age of householder, female–family householder, one-person householder, births and birth rates, deaths and death rates, and infant deaths and infant death rates. Statistics on crime (serious, violent, property), physicians and hospitals, persons in mental hospitals, persons in nursing homes, persons without health insurance, and percentage of children lacking health insurance are also included. Information on housing, building permits, journey to work and labor force, cost of living, poverty, personal income projections, and average annual pay is tabulated. Also included are business statistics such as building permits issued, private nonfarm business establishments, civilian labor force, nonfarm employment, export sales, banking, and federal funds and grants. It is important to note here that the *County and City Data Book* uses areas defined by the 1990 Census, and the *State and Metropolitan Area Data Book* uses geographic boundaries determined by the office of Management and Budget in 1996. This is an important distinction, for if geographic boundaries change, then statistics might not be comparable.

USA Counties (U.S. Census Bureau, periodically)
  http://censtats.census.gov/usa/usa.shtml

This source contains the latest updates to data for counties contained in the *County and City Data Book*. Available on CD-ROM, in paper, and online, *USA Counties* has over 5,000 data items covering all 3,142 counties in the United States. Not only do you get updated data, you get many data in time series. These data are also similar to those published in the *State and Metropolitan Area Data Book*. Tables include data on population by criteria of age and sex; race, ancestry, and Hispanic origin; personal income and earnings; crime; education; health; poverty; social programs (Social Security, Supplemental Security Income, Assistance to Families with Dependent Children, veterans affairs); and vital statistics (births/deaths, marriages/divorces). Business statistics are included for agriculture (Bureau of Economic Analysis), labor force (Bureau of Labor Statistics), journey to work (Census Bureau), banking, land area, building permits, manufactures, business total and selected industries, elections, government earnings and employment, retail trade, wholesale trade, and service industries. A useful feature is the ability to save your results as plain text, HTML, database files, or other popular file formats. Results can be graphically portrayed using the fully integrated ESRI MapObjects LT mapping and GIS (Geographic Information System) software.

The file format is dBase III+ and includes specially written Windows software that will permit users to view, print, copy, and map the data. Ordering information can be obtained at http://www.census.gov/statab/www/county.html. An extensive guide to technical information is provided in the *Guide to the USA Counties*, which is available on CD-ROM in PDF format. To view the file, you will need the Acrobat Reader, available for free from Adobe.

STATE, COUNTY, AND LOCAL CENSUS DATA REPORTS

There are many different geographic jurisdictions for which data are compiled and published, most of them referring to local jurisdictions. In general, the geographic areas of most interest to local researchers are (in Bureau jargon) counties, metropolitan areas, cities/places, Census designated places, congressional districts, Census tracts, blocks, and zip code areas. These jurisdictions are briefly described in chapter 12 on maps and geography, and are described in detail in the appendices of the Census volumes, as well as in the user manuals and explanatory texts described earlier in this chapter. Census 2000 has been released for selected statistics at the county and city level, as well as for Census tract and block level. Statistics for many data elements have not been released. An examination of the 1990 Census data series of publications is helpful to understand what is available from the American FactFinder Web site (Census 2000) and what is not yet available. Extensive summary statistics are provided for the United States in the *1990 Census of Population and Housing* volume series. Updates are provided in the *Statistical Abstract of the United States* (although statistics are usually provided for the nation and the states, they are rarely provided for local areas). Special compendiums, such as the *County and City Data Book* and the *State and Metropolitan Area Data Book*, can be consulted for data at the local level.

1990 Census of Population and Housing, Census 2000 [state]*(Decennial Census)* (U.S. Census Bureau)

Although Census 2000 is currently being tabulated and edited, an examination of the *1990 Census of Population and Housing* is still relevant, as Census 2000 is not being released in the same way that any of the previous Censuses had been. Data are being released with geography as the defining characteristic, and selected items are being tabulated and released for these geographic areas. The 1980 Census was the most extensive release of data in paper ever. In essence, almost all data items were tabulated but not published. The 1990 Census was extensive, but not all data were released to the public. The Decennial Census provides extensive sources of data for cities with populations of less than 25,000 and smaller geographic divisions, but many data items were never widely released. The *1990 Census* volumes were issued as paper publications beginning in 1991. There were several series issued. A few of the more popular series are described here, with examples of the kinds of data they contain. The data were also issued in multiple formats, such as magnetic tape, CD-ROM, and via the Internet. More information about the availability of data electronically is detailed later in this section.

General Population Characteristics [state] (U.S. Census Bureau, 1991)

The series *General Population Characteristics* actually has very detailed data on age, race, ancestry, and ethnicity. It is one of the only places, for example, where detailed ethnicity of Japanese, Chinese, Korean, Vietnamese, etc., is enumerated. These data are not available anywhere else in such detail and for the geographic breakdown as in the Decennial Census.

There are some data available from the U.S. Department of Education, but they rarely cover local geographic areas. The data available on *American FactFinder* from Census 2000 as of December 2002 corresponds to the *General Population Characteristics* series.

2000 Census Report: Population, Race, Ethnicity (Minneapolis Planning Department, 2001) http://www.ci.minneapolis.mn.us/citywork/planning/Census2000/docs/2000-Census-Rpt-One-1.pdf

This is an example of the kind of document that can be produced by a local government agency using data derived from the Census and applied to a particular local entity. The data in the report correspond to data released in American FactFinder from the *1990 General Population Characteristics*. There are also maps created from the software available on the Census Bureau Web site, augmented by software owned by the City of Minneapolis Planning Department. The map of Minneapolis, Minnesota, with Census tract outline is an excellent example of how a city uses Census information.

Social and Economic Characteristics [state] (U.S. Census Bureau, 1992)

One of the most popular series, *Social and Economic Characteristics*, is a very useful source, with much of the data pertaining to these subject areas tabulated for places with populations as small as 2,500. Places smaller than 2,500 in population are enumerated by "Rest of County" and Census tracts. Tabulated data match many of the series listed in the *County and City Data Book* and *State and Metropolitan Area Data Book*. Data items include population, race, family type, labor force status, means of commuting to work, poverty status, income, industry, occupation, educational attainment, ancestry, language spoken at home, and many others. Most information is available from this series, also known as *Summary Tape File* (STF) *3A*—four "Tape File" products were produced by the Census Bureau in its data compilation activities; two of them, *STF 3A* and *STF 4*, are mentioned here. Many times, data items such as median figures for age and income, for example, are provided in the paper volumes but not on the CD-ROM or Internet version. Selected data such as those made available in this series are currently available for Census 2000. The full data sets are all now available.

Detailed Population Characteristics [state] (1980 and 1990) (U.S. Census Bureau, 1984 and 1994)

Detailed Population Characteristics tabulated some very important data elements, such as educational attainment by occupation and race, but these volumes were not published for 1990. The Census Bureau exhausted its funds and was not able to widely distribute these data. They were made available as part of *STF 4*, and copies were made available for sale or sent for free to State Data Centers. One product produced from this tape, the *Equal Employment Opportunity File*, was made available on CD-ROM only. It provides data only on the national level. *Detailed Population Characteristics* has detailed information such as 512 detailed Census occupations by race, age, and Hispanic origin, as well as educational attainment by the same categories for the nation, states, District of Columbia, each county, and cities with populations greater than 50,000 only. The rest of the data on this tape is available only by special tabulation and purchase from the Census Bureau. *Detailed Population Characteristics* was published in earlier Decennial Census years, but not in 1990 when only *Detailed Housing Characteristics* was published. A similar data product has not been released for Census 2000.

Population and Housing Characteristics for Census Tracts and Block Numbering Areas [area] *(Census Tract Reports)* (U.S. Census Bureau, 1992)

A report that provides statistics tabulated down to the smallest geographic areas is this series. Data in Census tract volumes are very limited, as the smaller the geographic area, the fewer data elements tabulated and published for it. The following data elements are among those available for Census tracts: population; race; Hispanic origin; occupancy, utilization, and financial characteristics of housing units; labor force and disability status; income and poverty status; and selected structural characteristics. For block numbering areas, data items tabulated include population, race (white, black, Asian, or Spanish origin), age (under 18, over 65), and housing parameters (number of housing units, number of rooms, owner or renter occupied, number of persons per room, mean rent, plumbing facilities, one-person households, family householder, no spouse present, occupants under 18). Statistics for the smallest geographic area, the block, include data that are even more limited. The data were enumerated but simply not compiled, tabulated, and published. The statistics do exist, on magnetic tape. The problem is that the cost is about $150 per tape, and

there is often a tape for each state, and even multiple tapes for certain states. It was possible at one time to purchase a custom-tabulated report from the Census Bureau for $25. It is necessary to consult a specialist such as those at the State Data Centers, or possibly the Census Bureau itself, to obtain these data. It is now available from Census 2000, but not for all data items, and only for one geographic area at a time.

Census Tract and Block Maps—TIGER or LAND-VIEW CD-ROMs (U.S. Census Bureau)
http://www.census.gov/geo/www/tiger

It is usually necessary to have access to Census tract and block maps in order to use the data. Prior to 1990, tract maps were printed and distributed with the Census volumes, but the maps did not provide details beyond large physical landmarks and major roads. It was a guessing game as to what streets were included in a tract. This information was available only on the block maps. With 1990, matters got better and worse. The entire country was mapped, and the data entered into a database called TIGER (Topologically Integrated Geographic Encoding and Referencing). This system is used to produce maps of the Census geographic areas. Maps for each state were produced and distributed to Depository libraries and State Data Centers only within that state. They could be purchased for $5 each, but Los Angeles, for example, has almost 300 Census tracts! However, all geographic data were digitized and made available to those who had access to the *TIGER* or *LANDVIEW* CD-ROMs.

These two CD-ROMs were published for the use of the Environmental Protection Agency for specialized purposes. Depository libraries and State Data Centers received them as well. It is not easy to create these maps, and sophisticated equipment and expertise are required in the use of the CD-ROMs. Many Depository librarians or Census Bureau employees can be of assistance in this task. For Census 2000, many maps (although not highly detailed) will be able to be created online from the Census Bureau Web site. Specialized resources and expertise are required to produce more detailed maps.

1990 Census of Population and Housing, Summary Population and Housing Characteristics, Congressional Districts [state] (U.S. Census Bureau, 1991)

This Census provides a variety of social and economic population and housing statistics provided for congressional districts. Statistics tabulated include age, persons of voting age, ancestry, citizenship, educational attainment, family type, industry, labor force status, language spoken at home, means of transportation to work, nativity, occupation, age, poverty status, sex, and veteran status. This information is very important to political candidates running for election in a congressional district. Many of the more commonly used tables from the Decennial Census volumes are reproduced and even updated in the *State and Metropolitan Area Data Book* and the *County and City Data Book*. Most *1990 Census of Population and Housing* data are available in electronic format in CD-ROM and on the Census Bureau Web Site. Census 2000 data are available for these areas at http://www.census.gov/Press-Release/www/2001/demoprofile.htm.

Public-Use Microdata Samples [PUMS] (U.S. Census Bureau, 1993)
    http://www.census.gov/main/www/pums.html

These data have been compiled by geographic jurisdiction, such as county or city. There are additional data available in PUMS files on the Web site. These files are subsamples of the full Census sample that received the long-form questionnaire. They are essentially full records, with all identifying information excluded. PUMS is useful to users who want to prepare cross-tabulations of population and/or housing characteristics that are not available in summary reports and files. Different PUMS files are available on magnetic tape, diskette, and CD-ROM. There are PUMS data available online, at the University of Minnesota Integrated Public Use Microdata Series (IPUMS) Web site, http://www.ipums.umn.edu (note the similarity in acronyms between PUMS and IPUMS). A similar product called the Advanced Query Function will be available to access these data from the Census Bureau.

Lookup/Census Data (U.S. Census Bureau, 1990)
    http://venus.census.gov/cdrom/lookup

There is now a large amount of detailed Census data available on the Internet through the Census Bureau Web site. The Census/Lookup application was developed at the University of California, Berkeley, for use with the 1990 Census CDs. The first population data on CD-ROM began to arrive in 1991. It actually began with the 1987 Economic Census but quickly began to be used with all Census data. The first technology in this area was primitive and required many CDs to encompass all the data. For example, the CD-ROMs from STF 3A, corresponding to Social and Economic Characteristics, took up about 60 CD-ROM discs. A personal computer with certain capabilities was needed to access the data on the CDs. Many Depository libraries purchased this technology and continue to provide access for these products. Census Lookup provides a free, easy way to access data from these CD-ROMs. The great thing about the search engine is that it allows one to pull custom-selected multiple items for a geographic area into a table. These tables can be produced in ASCII or HTML formats and can be downloaded into spreadsheets or printed. This is very helpful for data users.

To retrieve multiple items for multiple geographic areas at one time, there are still only two ways to do it. One is to photocopy multiple tables from paper volumes, and the other is to use the computer program called Extract, developed by the Census Bureau for use with the 1992 Economic Census. This program is very specialized and requires expertise and a sophisticated computer for its use. The best place to consult for this type of assistance is a Depository library, although there are sometimes experts in city or county government who know how to access and use the data. An example of this type of need for data would be the statistic on educational attainment by race for all the cities in Los Angeles County. Even using Extract, this would require several searches, as Extract only allows searches of 13 geographic areas at a time. Extract also requires that the software be installed on the PC being used for searching, or on a mainframe that allows access to the CDs, but the software is not available over the Internet.

Census Lookup is still the premier way to access 1990 Census data in electronic format. There is no other online database for access to the 1990 Census data, except for the for-fee services such as Population Demographics (expensive) from Dialog, and the Census CD+Maps by GeoLytics Inc. (difficult to use). Because of improved technology and data compression techniques, by 1997 GeoLytics was able to produce one CD-ROM that contained most of the data on all of the original CDs. The software, however, takes some guidance and practice to use. Some Depository libraries also have this product. One strong point for this company is that it has digitized and produced data on CD for the 1970 and 1980 Census. GeoLytics has also produced *CensusCD 40 Years*, which has 40 years of data (this product is described in a later section)—the only commercial publisher to have done so. Census 2000 does not have the capacity to allow multiple geography or multiple data-element search and retrieval. Each geographic jurisdiction must be run separately. This problem has not yet been solved for Census 2000.

For updates to Decennial and Economic Census data, see the *State and Metropolitan Area Data Book* and the *County and City Data Book*, which provide additional data elements. Not all of the items listed for the Decennial Census are tabulated in the above-mentioned volumes, and sometimes data provided are from the Decennial Census, even in recent volumes.

SPECIALIZED TOPICAL CENSUS DATA RESOURCES

Economic Census (U.S. Census Bureau, 1997)
   http://www.census.gov/epcd/www/econ97.html

Census data are for five-year intervals (latest complete data available is from 1997, with some summary data from 2002), and this product is available in paper, on CD-ROM, and on the Internet. The Economic Census is another major source of data available to users that collects industry and establishment statistics on the local and regional level. The Economic Census has been called many things over the years, from the Census of Trade to the Census of Business. In recent years, the Economic Census has been conducted every five years, with data from 1957 beginning the so-called modern cycle of post–World War II collection of economic or business statistics. The Economic Census collects statistics about businesses that are construed as establishments, defined as "physical place[s] engaged in business." Information about individual companies is not released in the Census. The data, aggregated into totals for a category, are collected from individual establishments and tabulated for industries in certain geographic areas. There are several series that are of interest to local area statistics users. The 1997 Economic Census data are almost completely released and available on CD-ROM and on the Census Bureau Web site. The subsequent series are published currently, and most provide statistics for the following Census designated geographic areas: states, various Metropolitan Statistical Area (MSA) configurations, counties, and places and areas not in any of the previous areas. In publications with statistics for Census designated places, most tables include statistics only for places with 350 or more establish-

ments, whereas electronic data have no such restrictions.

North American Industry Classification System (U.S. Office of Management and Budget, 1998)
   http://www.census.gov/epcd/www/naics.html

One important concept of Economic Census data is that industries are classified by Standard Industrial Classification (SIC) and the North American Industrial Classification System (NAICS). The SIC, created in 1987, was demonstrated to be inadequate by the late 1990s. Many new industries had been identified, and many users wished to look at more detailed categories of business operations. Thus, NAICS was created in a joint effort by the United States, Canada, and Mexico to meet these increasing demands. Both systems are published in paper and on the Census Bureau Web site, along with a bridge between the two so that the latest data can be compared with earlier years.

Census of Retail Trade, Census of Wholesale Trade, and *Census of Service Industries* (1997 U.S. Economic Census, 2001) http://www.census.gov/epcd/www/97EC44.HTM

One of the series available from the Economic Census, these data are at five-year intervals, with the latest available complete data from 1997, and the products are available in paper, on CD-ROM, and on the Internet. There are different series compiled and published for each of these economic segments. Statistics reported are fairly uniform, with some small differences because of the nature of the business. For example, in the *Census of Retail Trade* and the *Census of Wholesale Trade*, "Sales" are reported. In the *Census of Service Industries*, "Receipts" are reported. Receipts are so varied that there is an additional volume of information published of just information about "Sources of Receipts or Revenue." Statistics tabulated for sporting and recreational camps include such sources of revenue or receipts as guestroom or unit rentals, sales of meals and nonalcoholic beverages, camp fees, and membership dues. There is also information on the number of establishments, receipts, and certain percentages of receipts down to the city level for selected MSAs. There is a separate publication just on hotels, motels, and other lodging places. Geographic area statistics found in the *Census of Retail Trade* are for establishments (number), sales, payroll, number of employees, and sales per establishment. Additional comparative statistics (for the current and previous Census years) can be found in these publications for industries having an SIC change, counties ranked by volume of sales, and places ranked by volume of sales. The *Census of Retail Trade* under the heading of "Miscellaneous Subjects" lists such statistics for selected MSAs as gallon sales of automotive fuels and numbers of automotive fuel pumps and self-service operators. Also listed are MSA statistics for eating establishments, seating capacity, average cost per meal, and prescriptions and pharmacists for drug stores. The *Census of Wholesale Trade* lists similar statistics, but with some differences. For example, *Wholesale Trade* lists commodity line sales and inventories, which *Retail Trade* does not. These subtleties will be discernible to only the very determined user who needs specific statistics. It is best to consult a librarian or Census Bureau specialist before spending too much time looking for such information.

For each of the Economic Census major series (*Retail Trade*, *Wholesale Trade*, and *Service Industries*), there is a publication subtitled *Subject Series, Establishment and Firm Size*. For instance, the *Census of Wholesale Trade, Subject Series, Establishment and Firm Size* can be found at http://www.census.gov/epcd/www/97EC42.HTM. These series have details on the numbers of establishments and sales by type of operation, number of employees per establishment, and volume of sales. The series also have information about numbers of branches and offices as well as numbers of agents and brokers. This information can be very important when trying to determine the number of large and small businesses operating in a particular service or industry in a certain metropolitan area.

U.S. Subject Series reports on *Transportation*; *Information*; *Utilities*; *Finance and Insurance*; *Real Estate and Rental and Leasing*; *Mining*; *Construction*; etc. (1997 Economic Census, 2001) http://www.census.gov/epcd/www/ec97stat.htm

Like all aspects of the 1997 Economic Census, these reports include data taken at five-year intervals and are available in paper, on CD-ROM, and on the Internet. They have limited statistics for local metropolitan areas, but they do have standard statistics listed in the *Census of Retail Trade, Wholesale Trade*, and *Service Industries*, as well as special reports on *Establishment and Firm Size*. There are additional series that have information appropriate to the industry that is covered. An interesting feature of

statistics from these industries is that they are broken down into types of service, such as the tabulations for real estate; listed are data for real estate operators, operators of nonresidential buildings, operators of apartment buildings, other real estate operators and licensors, real estate agents and managers, title abstract offices, land subdividers and developers, and real estate appraisers, as are similar appropriate categories for the other series.

Data from the Economic Census taken in 2002 have begun to be made available on the Web site. Not all files are available, but at the Census 2002 Web page, http://www.census.gov/econ/census02/, advance reports, summary statistics, and comparative statistics for the United States are available. There are additional reports on advance non-employer statistics, 357 of the 651 Industry Series reports, and some interesting information for data users as well as a schedule for future 2002 Economic Census reports: http://www.census.gov/econ/census02/guide/g02sched.htm. This is a Web site that really needs to be checked weekly or even daily for new additions to the information already available.

Census of Manufacturing (1997 Economic Census, 2001) http://www.census.gov/prod/www/abs/97ecmani.html

The *Census of Manufacturing* publishes limited statistics at the county and metropolitan levels. Statistics for selected MSAs include number of establishments, employees, payroll, production workers, hours, wages, value added by manufacture, costs of materials, value of shipments, and new capital expenditures. These are aggregate figures for the total manufacturing industries. The *Census of Manufacturing*, published every five years, is updated by the *Annual Survey of Manufacturers* (ASM), another Census Bureau publication, published in paper through 1996. It is now available on the Internet for 1998 and 1999 at http://www.census.gov/econ/www/ma0300.html. The ASM provides the following data items by three-digit SIC for state, by year: number of employees, payroll, number of production workers, total hours worked by production workers, and total wages of production workers. Also included are value added by manufacture, cost of materials, value of industry shipments, new capital expenditures, and end-of-year inventories. The ASM, however, publishes data only down to the state level.

Survey of Minority- and Women-Owned Business Enterprises (U.S. 1997 Economic Census, 2001) http://www.census.gov/csd/mwb

This was formerly the *Survey of Minority-Owned Businesses and Characteristics of Business Owners.* Special reports such as these (available in paper, on CD-ROM, and on the Internet) are useful in providing demographic information about diverse types of business owners. It might be important to know whether so-called small and minority-owned businesses do well in a certain city when thinking about applying for or financing a loan for that type of business owner in a particular area. There are separate reports published for black, Hispanic, Asian American, Native American, and Alaskan Native minority-owned businesses, as well as women-owned businesses. Statistics are published by industry for MSAs with 100 or more establishments, and in some cases places with 350 or more establishments. Statistics are represented geographically by state, county, and metropolitan area and include such data items as industry, size of firm, form of legal organization, number of firms, gross receipts, number of paid employees, and annual payroll.

The Economic Census is a rich source of information about businesses in the economy of certain geographic areas. It is safe to say that not many people even know about the collection of this data. The business world, however, most certainly does. There is much more information available than is summarized here, much of it is widely available on the Internet. There will be more released in the coming years. Because of the complexity and richness of the information presented, it may still be necessary to consult a specialist in government information.

Census of Governments (U.S. Census Bureau, 1997) http://www.census.gov/govs/www/index.html

The *Census of Governments* has relevant information for users of local government information. Taken at five-year intervals, with the 1997 data available in paper, on CD-ROM, and on the Internet, it collects statistics on "Government Organization" and "Popularly Elected Officials of County and Municipal Governments" by selected characteristics (number of officials, governing bodies, and elected boards). Taxable property values and general property taxation are listed under various aspects of taxable property by county. "Employees of Major Local Governments" includes such data items as employment, payrolls, average earnings by function, number of employees covered by labor-management contracts, number in bargaining units, and costs for providing selected employee benefits.

There are also surveys in the area of government that are taken quarterly and annually that provide data. *Public Education Finances* provides statistics on revenue, expenditures, debt, and financial assets of public school systems. This can provide crucial information for public officials. In the volume entitled *Finances of Municipal and Township Governments*, however, most of the statistics are aggregates for all municipal governments in the state. *Finances of County Governments* is available and lists statistics such as revenue, general and intergovernmental; taxes; and expenditures for counties. *Consolidated Federal Funds Report* is an annual publication that lists data items for grants, salaries and wages, procurement contracts, direct payments to individuals, selected major programs such as agricultural stabilization, and per capita and percentage distribution of expenditures. Many of these reports for 1997 are available in paper from the Census Bureau Web site (http://www.census.gov/prod/www/abs/govern.html).

Census of Agriculture (U.S. Census Bureau)

The *Census of Agriculture* is not often used in urban areas but is very important to a certain segment of American society. The *Census of Agriculture* has statistics on a great variety of topics of interest to non–urban dwellers. It includes statistics for estimated market value of products sold, average size of farm, number of farms by value group, size of farm, crops for sale, livestock inventory and sales, irrigation, machinery and equipment in place, land in orchards, berries harvested for sale, fish sales, etc. This information is of enormous value to farm owners, investors, land use planners, and retailers of farm equipment. It would be useful to know what crops grow well in certain areas and what the market might be for crops in a particular county. The *Census of Agriculture* from 1992, 1997, and 2002 is available for viewing at the National Agricultural Statistics Services Web site, http://www.nass.usda.gov/census.

Census of Manufactures (1997 Economic Census, 2001 U.S. Census Bureau) http://www.census. gov/econ/overview/ma0100.html

The *Census of Manufactures* publishes limited statistics at the county and metropolitan levels. Statistics for selected MSAs include number of establishments, payroll, production workers, hours, wages, value added by manufacture, costs of materials, value of shipments, and new capital expenditures. These are aggregate figures for the total manufacturing industries. The *Census of Manufactures*, published every five years, is updated by the *Annual Survey of Manufactures* (ASM), another Census Bureau publication, published in paper through 1996. It is now available on the Internet for 1998 and 1999 at http://www.census.gov/mcd/asm-as1.html. The ASM provides the following data items by three-digit SIC for state, by year: number of employees, payroll, number of production workers, total hours worked by production workers, and total wages of production workers. Also included are value added by manufacture, cost of materials, value of industry shipments, new capital expenditures, and end-of-year inventories. The ASM, however, publishes data only down to the state level.

County Business Patterns (U.S. Census Bureau)
http://www.census.gov/epcd/cbp/view/cbpview.html

County Business Patterns and, from 1998, *USA Counties* are publications that provide updated data on counties. Data are provided by two-, three-, and four-digit SIC code for total number of establishments, mid-March employment, first quarter and annual payroll, and number of establishments by employment-size classes. Whereas data in the corresponding printed reports are not shown for SICs with fewer than 100 employees in a given area, there is no such restriction on the data files. This series excludes governmental establishments classified in the covered industries except for liquor stores and wholesale liquor establishments operated by state and local governments. All government hospitals are included beginning with 1989 data. Electronic files are available back to 1988. Various tables are available for downloading at http://www.census.gov/epcd/cbp/view/cbpview.html.

Zip CodeBusiness Patterns (U.S. Census Bureau, 2002) http://www.census.gov/epcd/www/zipstats.html http://www.census.gov/epcd/www/zbp_base.html

Although zip codes are U.S. Postal Service (not Census Bureau) geographic designations, information by ZIP Code is in great demand, mostly by direct-mail advertisers. *zip code Business Patterns*, available on CD-ROM and the Internet, has been compiled for the use of business researchers. This file was released on September 16, 1999, and covers 1996 data. The geography covered comprises five-digit zip codes. The file structure is dBase III+ files. The subjects covered include business data summarized for nine employment-size classes by hundreds of SIC codes and about 30,000 zip codes nationwide. A second data set includes summary data by zip code (no SIC breakdown) for number of employees, first-quarter payroll, annual payroll, total number of establishments, and nine employment-size classes. Those employment classes are 1–4, 5–9, 10–19, 20–49, 50–99, 100–249, 250–499, 500–999, and 1,000 or more. Electronic data are available back to 1994. For updates, see *USA Counties*, available only in electronic format.

American Housing Survey (U.S. Census Bureau, annual) http://www.census.gov/hhes/www/ahs.html

Available in paper and on the Internet for selected areas, the *American Housing Survey* is an excellent source for statistics on the housing industry and the state of housing in general in a region, state, or (probably large) MSA. Although each MSA is not surveyed every year, this source does provide an option for finding data in between the Decennial Census years. The *Survey* includes data on housing patterns, housing conditions, costs, year the structure was built, type and number of living quarters, occupancy status, presence of commercial or medical establishments on the property, property value, kitchen and plumbing facilities, and source of water and sewage disposal. Of additional interest could be the condition of the walls and floors and the adequacy of heat in winter, exterminator service for mice/rats/insects, mortgage or monthly rent payments, utility costs, fuel costs, property insurance costs, real estate taxes, and garbage collection fees.

Respondents who have moved recently provide information on the characteristics and sales value of the previous residence and reasons for moving. Residents indicate the presence of and objection to neighborhood conditions such as street noise, poor roads, crime, trash and litter, abandoned structures, commercial or industrial activity, odors or smoke, and the adequacy of services such as public transportation, schools, shopping facilities, police protection, outdoor recreation facilities, and hospitals/health clinics. Information on condominiums covers number of units in the development, amount and frequency of mortgage payment, amount of property insurance, real estate tax, utility costs, and condominium fee (with identification of selected items included therein). In addition to housing characteristics, data for selected demographic groups are included, such as each household member's age, sex, race, marital status, income, and relationship to the householder. Provided for the householder are data on years of school completed, Hispanic origin, length of residence, and tenure. Income sources identified in the file include wages, farm self-employment, nonfarm self-employment, rent, dividends, Social Security, unemployment and workmen's compensation, government and private pensions, veterans payments, and alimony and child support. The amount from each source also is given. These statistics are valuable for a business planning to provide service to an area, for a company planning to relocate to an area, or for an individual or family seeking to relocate to an area. The American Housing Survey will most likely be combined with other surveys to form the American Community Survey, which is described in more detail below. Data files for 1993, 1995, and 1997 are available at the Census Bureau Web site.

ADVANCED CENSUS DATA RESOURCES

Data Access Tools (U.S. Census Bureau)
http://www.census.gov/main/www/access.html

As many of the previous examples have demonstrated, there is a huge amount of information available through the Census Bureau Web Site. Much of it, actually, is available from the Census Bureau Web servers, and some information is available through links to other sites such as the Oregon State Government Information Sharing Project. Links to specialized tools are provided at this Census Bureau Web page, such as CenStats, MapStats, TIGER|TIGER Map Service Info, US Gazetteer, 1990 Decennial Census Lookup, Data Extraction System (which allows creation of custom data extracts from Current Population Survey, 1990 Census Public Use Microdata Files, and more), DataFerrett extraction and review tool (in collaboration with the Bureau of Labor Statistics and other statistical agencies), and MABLE/GeoCorr, a geographic correspondence engine (mirrored at Columbia University and the University of Missouri). Details are provided for some of these databases. Links to sites such as the Bureau of Labor Statistics, http://www.bls.gov, provide statistics on employment and unemployment, consumer prices (cost of living) and living conditions, wages and compensation, and productivity and technology. Many of these statistics are available down to the local area.

USA Counties (CD-ROM, U.S. Census Bureau, 1998)
http://censtats.census.gov/usa/usa.shtml

USA Counties 1998 features over 5,000 data items for the United States, states, counties, and equivalent areas from a variety of sources. Files include data published for 1997 population estimates and over 500 items from the 1990 Census of Population and Housing, the 1980 Census, and the 1992, 1987, 1982, and 1977 Economic Censuses. Information in *USA Counties* is derived from the following general topics: age, agriculture, ancestry, banking, building permits, business patterns, crime, earnings, education, elections, government, health, households, housing, income, labor force and employment, manufacturers, population, poverty, retail trade, services industries, social programs, veterans, vital statistics, and wholesale trade. Files contain a collection of data from the Census Bureau and other federal agencies, such as the Bureau of Economic Analysis, the Bureau of Labor Statistics, the Federal Bureau of Investigation, and the Social Security Administration. Data can be retrieved for only one county at a time.

Regional Economic Information System, 1969–1997 (U.S. Bureau of Economic Analysis, annual, 2002)
http://www.bea.gov/bea/regional/data.htm

This is another interesting electronic database available from the Bureau of Economic Analysis. This database is very user friendly and allows selection of a tabulated report for a regional area, including states, counties, and MSAs. Subjects covered include personal income by major source and earnings by industry, full-time and part-time employees by industry, regional economic profiles, transfer payments by type of payment, and farm income and expenses. There are numerous data items in each table. For example, under "Personal Income" there is the further subdivision "Derivation of Total Personal Income," consisting of several data items that are used to compute each total. Data is provided for 1969–1997 where available.

Current Population Survey (U.S. Census Bureau and Bureau of Labor Statistics) http://www.bls.census.gov/cps/cpsmain.htm

For annual updates to Decennial Census population data, the *Current Population Survey* is an interesting resource. This survey is conducted throughout the country, and data are collected for selected MSAs. The files are publicly available for data as recent as

1998. The Census Bureau has developed a data extraction tool called DataFerrett for use in accessing files from government agencies such as the Census Bureau and the Bureau of Labor Statistics. DataFerrett is relatively easy to access (at http://dataferrett.census. gov/TheDataWeb/index.html) but difficult to decipher, depending on the complexity of the search and number of data items being requested. The data are in the form of flat-coded files, and codebooks are available for downloading so that data can be interpreted. This is not a system for the casual user. This program is for determined researchers or for extracting a particular piece of information repeatedly over time. For those without Internet access, the data are available on CD-ROM in Depository libraries. There are numerous surveys available in a wide array of subjects such as race and ethnicity, Internet and computer use, school enrollment, work schedules, voting and registration, and housing. The Web site asks for registration, but no fees are charged. These data will likely become part of the American Community Survey.

CenStats (U.S. Census Bureau) http://censtats. census.gov

This database offers free online access to tabulated reports via the Internet. Tabulations are from the following reports: ASM (for states), *Building Permits* (for cities), *Census Tract Street Locator* (all-inclusive), *Consolidated Federal Funds* (states, counties, municipalities, and townships), *County Business Patterns*, *International Trade Data*, *Occupation by Race and Sex* (states, counties, and cities), *USA Counties*, and *ZIP Code Business Patterns* (five-digit zip codes). It allows you to choose data items by geographic jurisdiction and tabulates them for you. These products are of interest to primarily business users.

American Community Survey (U.S. Census Bureau, annual, 1999–2001) http://www.census.gov/ acs/www

The *American Community Survey* is a product under recent development for a number of purposes. The Decennial Census has two functions: (1) it counts the population and (2) it obtains demographic, housing, social, and economic information by asking a 1-in-6 sample of households to fill out a "long form." The information is used for the administration of federal programs and the distribution of billions of federal dollars. Since this is done only once every 10 years, long-form information becomes out of date. Planners and other data users are reluctant to rely on it for deci-

sions that are expensive and affect the quality of life of thousands of people. The *American Community Survey* is a way to provide the data that communities need every year instead of once in 10 years. It is an ongoing survey that the Census Bureau plans to have replace the long form in the 2010 Census. The American Community Survey, as part of the Decennial Census program, is a new approach for collecting accurate, timely information needed for critical government functions. This new approach provides yearly, accurate, up-to-date profiles of America's communities. Community leaders and other data users will have timely information for planning and evaluating public programs for everyone from newborns to the elderly. Full implementation of the survey would begin in 2003 in every county of the United States. The survey would include 3 million households. Data will be collected by mail, and Census Bureau staff will follow up with those who do not respond. The *American Community Survey* will provide estimates of demographic, housing, social, and economic characteristics every year for all states, as well as for all cities, counties, metropolitan areas, and population groups of 65,000 people or more.

For smaller areas, it will take two to five years to accumulate a sufficient sample to produce data for areas as small as Census tracts. For example, areas of 20,000 to 30,000 population can use data averaged over three years. For rural areas and city neighborhoods or population groups of less than 15,000, it will take five years to accumulate a sample that is similar to that of the Decennial Census. These averages can be updated every year, so that eventually we will be able to measure changes over time for small areas and population groups.

An *American Community Survey* goal is to provide data to the users within six months of the end of a collection or calendar year. For states, populous counties and other governmental units, or population groups of 65,000 or more, the *American Community Survey* can provide direct estimates for each year. For smaller governmental units or population groups (those of less than 65,000), estimates can be provided each year through refreshed multiyear accumulations of data.

Plans include the release of a microdata file each year patterned after the 5 percent PUMS file of the 1990 Decennial Census records. The microdata file allows for two different units of analysis: housing unit and person. It includes as many records as possible and shows the lowest level of geography within confidentiality constraints. Users of the survey data can customize tabulations to examine the information in the way that best serves their needs. In addition, it will provide summarized data for population and housing estimates, cross-tabulated by various characteristics down to the block-group (i.e., neighborhood) level. The summarized data will be similar to the STF (Summary Tape Files) of the 1990 Decennial Census records and are designed to provide statistics with greater subject and geographic detail than is feasible or desirable to provide in printed reports. The microdata files, tabulated files, and associated documentation will be available on CD-ROM, as well as on the Census Bureau Web site. These files will allow detailed data from national household surveys (whose samples are too small to provide reliable estimates for states or localities) and can be combined with data from the *American Community Survey* to create reliable estimates for small geographic areas.

Commercial Census Resources

CensusCD + Maps (GeoLytics, irregularly published) http://www.censuscd.com

This is a database product with a unique software package that combines an enormous amount of valuable demographic statistics with the power to easily select, map, and export the data. This one CD-ROM is a good source for detailed information about the people, housing, and economy of the United States.

Census data reports and thematically shaded color maps are created on the fly from the one CD. You don't have to open multiple programs, import boundaries, or edit files and tables, and you don't have to be an expert in statistics or mapping to use *CensusCD+Maps*, although there is a learning curve for this product. The data on *CensusCD+Maps* provides details about the population and housing of the United States. It has demographic information down to the neighborhood level (block groups) from the most recent 1990 Census (STF 3A, B, C, and D), along with more current estimates (1998, 2003) and projections, including estimates and projections of consumer spending. *CensusCD+Maps* combines this rich set of demographic data with statistics going back to 1969 on agriculture, banking, births and deaths, marriages and divorces, building/construction, crime, employment, federal spending, industry earnings, local government, payrolls, personal income, retail businesses, and service businesses for every county in the United States. GeoLytics has even added the historical population counts by county back to 1790, and it has a product that contains the only commercially available electronic data for 1980.

The software on *CensusCD+Maps* makes it simple to search and select the data you're interested in. You can custom-tailor reports down to the neighborhood level, around a central point, or for several areas at once. You can view, export, or print results as maps, text, or data reports. *CensusCD+Maps* lets you create your own computed fields from the data and maps these on the fly. You can even export any of the geographic boundaries to other mapping packages. *CensusCD+Maps* lets you concentrate on results. There is a new CD called *CensusCD: Neighborhood Change Database, 1970–2000 Tract Data*, which provides selected statistics for four different Decennial Census years, 1970–2000.

Population Demographics (Dialog)

This database file, available by subscription from Dialog, provides online access to statistical data on many topics covered by Census data. Included are population statistics for population, households, income, education, and occupations. Data items on household information are tabulated by number of households, household size, age of householder, and households with children. There are statistics on household income and age of householder by income. There are data on educational attainment, occupational data on categories such as white- and blue-collar workers, marketing and sales workers, engineers, computer operators, physicians, teachers, clerical workers, and managerial/administrative workers.

These data come from Census Bureau information and have updated demographic statistics, including buying power indices, standard industrial classification counts, and standard occupation classification totals of employees and key occupations. Some of the updates are to 1995, with projections to 2000. This source does provide the only updates that pull together these particular data items, and its projections are the only current estimates for much of these data. Although 1995 totals are dated, they are still preferable to 1990 data. The data are very helpful to companies and individuals considering moving or relocating businesses or headquarters. It gives a nice snapshot of a geographic area. But, since it is by subscription only, retrieving reports for multiple geographic areas makes costs mount. It is a convenient source for users of Dialog.

FOR FURTHER READING

Barrett, Richard E. *Using the 1990 U.S. Census for Research*. Thousand Oaks, CA: Sage Publications, 1994.

Farrington, Polly-Alida. *Subject Index to the 1980 Census of Population and Housing*. Clifton Park, NY: Specialized Information Products, 1985.

Lavin, Michael R., Jane Winthrop, and Cynthia Cornelius. *Subject Index to the 1990 Census of Population and Housing*. Kenmore, NY: Epoch Books, Inc., 1997.

United States Bureau of the Census. *A Century of Population Growth: From the First Census of the United States to the Twelfth, 1790–1900*. Washington, DC: Government Printing Office, 1909.

CHAPTER 9
Local Government Resources on Genealogy

Mary Martin

MAJOR TOPICS COVERED

MAJOR RESOURCES COVERED

INTRODUCTION

The process by which local governmental records are used to document family genealogy is a long and tortuous one. Finding out about family genealogy, or tracing family roots, is a process that involves many steps. The first step, of course, is to find out how much information family members know or have. A reference guide that helps to map out the procedure is useful at this point. The guide can outline a procedure, beginning with specialized guides that direct one to reference sources, published records, original records, and statistical sources. Reference sources, of which several are described, can direct the researcher to published records such as newsletters, newspapers, and bibliographies. The next step is to begin tracing official records such as birth certificates, death certificates, wills (probate documents, etc.), marriage certificates, and similar records.

There is a great deal of work ahead before the tracing of local governmental records can be done with any efficient results. It is the local records, however, that are considered to be the most reliable by genealogical researchers, even above published genealogies and Census records. If one has good information about where family members may have been in previous decades (and centuries), the search may not be as laborious. If certain valuable information about names and specific locations is not available, there may be some national databases that can help one locate possible ancestors by allowing electronic searching of vast electronic databases such as the Social Security Index, military records, and Immigration and Naturalization Service (INS) records. Social Security records, of course, do not exist prior to the 1930s. INS records go back into the last century, and military records go back further. Census Bureau records go back to 1790 and can be very valuable provided you have certain necessary information. Most other records have been kept at the local governmental level. Many of the resources described here will be helpful in searching for these records.

There are Web sites accessible through the Internet that provide assistance in a wide range of possible areas of research in genealogy. There are very general Web sites, which provide very complete guidance in genealogical research, and there are Web sites that provide a more focused approach and access to a certain type of information. Finally, there are links to research Web sites for worldwide genealogical resources. This assists the researcher who is moving back in time to various countries that are sources of immigrants to the United States.

GENERAL RESOURCES

Guides and directories provide overall assistance in planning research, choosing sources, and selecting research tools and databases. There are also additional references to resources beyond the scope of this chapter. They provide a good introduction to genealogical resources and serve as a resource that can be used repeatedly as research progresses.

Guides

The Genealogist's Handbook: Modern Methods for Researching Family History, by Raymond Wright III (American Library Association, 1995)

This volume is useful, first, because it is concise (189 pages); second, it is written by a person very familiar with genealogical research. The author worked for 20 years at the Family History Library in Salt Lake City, Utah, and teaches family history and genealogy at Brigham Young University.

The book has a summary of the types of records that are valuable for genealogical research and serves as a model for the types of records that are outlined in this chapter. It not only describes public and private family records, but suggests methods of evaluating sources. There is a description of how to create a family record and how to organize the records on a family computer. The book then describes how to find the records you need, breaking the types of records into federal-level records, and how to trace origins through local, state, and national records. There is a special section on "Immigrants in Foreign Records," which describes how to begin research for foreign records in the United States. The research methods described are directed primarily for use at the Family History Library (the major research library of the Church of Jesus Christ of Latter-day Saints [LDS] in Salt Lake City). There is a brief description of research abroad, an adequate bibliography of resources, a listing of genealogical research centers and ethnic and immigration research centers, and an index by subject and name of resource. This source is very useful and easy to use. Most large or special genealogical research libraries should have this volume. It is available for sale from the American Library Association, at the *ALA Online Bookstore*, http://alastore.ala.org

How to Find Your Family Roots, by Timothy F. Beard with Denise Demong (McGraw-Hill Book Company, 1977)

Although this volume was published over 20 years ago, it still serves as a comprehensive guide in constructing a strategy for research. Since almost all records over 10 years old, with the exception of some indexes, are not available online, the strategies outlined in this source remain useful. It is divided into sections called "How to Find Your Ancestors," "Books to Help You Search," "Tracing Your Family's History in America," and "Tracing Your Family's History Abroad." There is a section on local records that includes information on birth, marriage, and death records, church records, wills, deeds, school records, records of clubs and organizations, Census records, the Soundex Index, mortality schedules, additional censuses, and published Census guides. There are extensive lists of resources, although the addresses could be seriously out of date by now. Of particular interest is a large section on where to write for vital records *overseas*. These addresses may not change as quickly as those in the United States. There are further details on these types of references below. This resource has a folksy, anecdotal approach that makes it appealing to read. The book is out of print, but may be owned by genealogical libraries and research centers.

Ancestry's Guide to Research: Case Studies in American Genealogy, by John Cerney and Arlene Eakle (Ancestry Incorporated, 1985)

This volume has good, detailed descriptions of some of the reference tools used for genealogical research. There is apparently a set of codes that deals with certain types of records in government archives as well as those listed in the Family Group Records Collection published by the LDS Library. The coding is related mostly to how the LDS Temple records have been coded in the LDS Library and records groups. LDS is a major source of genealogical records. The LDS Library has created and maintains an invaluable service to genealogical researchers. There are collections of all kinds of records in the LDS Temple archives, as well as research tools in the library, and many are also published and sold.

The records that are reviewed vary from Census Bureau records to the "Marriage Extraction Project" and the "Vermont/Connecticut Extraction Project." There are descriptions of the projects and other larger finding tools such as the Accelerated Indexing Systems Index and the International Genealogical Index (IGI), which can be found on the *FamilySearch* Web site of the Church of Jesus Christ of Latter-day Saints, http://www.familysearch.org/Eng/default.asp. This database, when searched, for example, lists the name, sex, name of parents, locality, type of event referenced, date of the event, date of the edition of IGI, and additional information special to the LDS. An interesting portion of this book is a section that is helpful in tracing American Indian, Hispanic, and Asian ancestors. The American Indian section is extensive and includes maps that show Indian occupation of certain territories during certain time periods. There is an extensive index and table of contents. Unfortunately, it is also out of print and must be used at a library that owns a copy or can borrow one on interlibrary loan from a lending library.

Researcher's Guide to American Genealogy, by Val D. Greenwood (2nd ed., Genealogical Publishing Co., 1990)

This book provides an overview of the field of genealogical research and an extensive section on types of records and their use, and ends with a small section that suggests new ideas and approaches, such as the use of computers for research.

One useful feature of the book arrangement is that the researcher is introduced to the library and research tools in the beginning of the book, as a part of the research process. This section is followed by another that identifies types of records and their uses. There is a chapter that identifies specific state and regional resources, under the umbrella "Guides to Original Resources." There are extensive illustrations and charts, and a nice index, as well as numerous bibliographical references, many to state and local resources. For example, *Handy Genealogical Guide to New Mexico*, by Joyce V. Hawley Spiros, is one of the resources mentioned. The organization of this book makes sense to the library researcher. Although dated, it would certainly still be relevant, as genealogical research is historical.

Directories

Compendium of Historical Sources: The How and Where of American Genealogy, by Ronald A. Bremer (Butterfly Publishing, 1998)

This is a comprehensive source of all types of family records available for genealogical research. It has an extensive overview of types and samples of records, good details, and lists of resources. The book is divided into sections dealing with research, repositories, resources, sources, maps, and forms, and has a glossary. There are descriptions of books, databases, and actual records, and evaluation of the resources. One analysis is of the most reliable and least reliable sources. Among the most reliable sources, according to the book, are property records, deeds and mortgages, place maps, tax lists, probate records, vital records (such as birth, death, etc.), and church records. Among the most unreliable are family tradition, printed histories and lineage books, death certificates, the federal Census, and the LDS archives in Salt Lake City. An extensive bibliography of sources is included. There are descriptions of court systems as well as the records of those courts. The author makes a statement that the average person appears in court three times in 20 years for various reasons, which include contract or property disputes, probate hearings, heirs, and liens, among a multitude of others. Further details on the courts are provided in that chapter. The author speculates further as to certain other governmental and nongovernmental records. Land records are very important in establishing residency as well as ownership. This source tells in detail how land was described and provides examples of maps throughout different time periods as well as map sources. There are full descriptions of county jurisdictions and a list of townships and place names, along with examples of maps showing old emigrant trails and routes.

The book has a section on immigrant arrivals, and as published sources are identified as lacking, the researcher is referred to records held in the National Archives, with a description of record groups there, as well as local archives. The book has a section on libraries and research centers, with extensive descriptions of some of them. Some unusual record sources and repositories are listed, such as those for adoptives and ethnic groups like Acadians. Finally there are excellent examples of how-to letters for requesting information from records of various agencies such as the Social Security and Veterans Administrations.

This is a useful and extensive resource. It could be a little expensive for the individual to purchase, but it would be a good asset for a library or genealogical society. The latest edition is available from the publisher.

The Source: A Guidebook of American Genealogy,
  ed. by Loretto Dennis Szucs and Sandra Hargeaves
  Luebking (Ancestry, Inc., 1997 and 2002)

This volume is a very substantial resource. It lists foundations of family research, databases, indexes and finding aids, and methods of research in various kinds of records, such as those of birth, death, cemetery, marriage, divorce, Census, church, court, land and tax, military, business, employment, institutional, directory, and newspapers. Large sections discuss tracing ethnic origins, including Native American, African American, Hispanic, and Jewish American family history. A separate section includes a consideration of time and place, useful when searching through large amounts of information. There are seven appendices on libraries and research centers as well as helpful information on how to write to request vital records, explanations of selected acronyms and abbreviations, and an extensive subject and title index.

One example of the book's treatment of a subject is a chapter on research in marriage and divorce records.

The registering of marriages and granting of divorces have been a mixture of religious, legal, and social functions from colonial times. While these are some of the most persistent vital records available, the variety of jurisdictions responsible and the formats and the varying amounts of information included or not included make using these records a challenge. Churches, ministers, justices of the peace, state boards of health, colonial governors, military personnel, and local (county and town) governments have kept these records, to varying extents. This resource describes the structure of this vital record keeping from the state down to the local level. Few states had such record-keeping agencies until after 1850. Even though the documents were required by law to be registered, they often were not. Finding these records can be a very labor-intensive search, but the records are usually somewhere. Residents of highly populated cities were often not mentioned in local histories and can be found only by using major record sources.

This volume is arranged in a practical manner, and its size is mitigated by a substantial index. It is reasonably priced and available for purchase.

ONLINE DATABASES

Online databases are of increasing importance in the field of genealogical research. As records and record groups are being digitized and put online, the task of searching through them is becoming a substantial burden. Databases that index such records simplify the task of searching through individual paper copies by allowing the researcher to search many records for a certain piece of information and discard the irrelevant records. This process is not foolproof, of course, but it does eliminate some unnecessary examination of material. The databases reviewed here are growing and changing on a daily basis, and more information is being added daily. Databases can both expand and shrink our workload, depending on the viewpoint. One might find information in them, previously unknown, that has to be further researched, or find that certain information is irrelevant or not helpful. In general, databases make research more exacting.

General

General Web sites encompass a wide range of information and can be used as a starting point. There are usually search engines and indexes to the contents of the Web site, and many links to additional, more specialized Web sites.

WorldConnect (RootsWeb)
http://worldconnect.rootsweb.com

This Web site is an excellent place to start genealogical research. It is, however, dependent on what information the research already possesses. There are links to guides to getting started, search engines, family trees, Web sites, other tools and resources such as the Soundex Converter, volunteer projects, message boards, mailing lists, and research templates. It provides links to free, searchable databases such as the Social Security Death Index (SSDI). One interesting feature is that research results can be submitted to the Web site. There is a search engine for RootsWeb.com and for SearchAncestry.com.

Genealogy.com
http://www.genealogy.com/index_n.html

This is a leading resource for family history research. The site appears as somewhat commercial, but there are many resources that are referenced or linked from this page. There are tabs across the top of the Web page that access categories such as "New Start Here," "Online Data Library," and "Helpful Web Sites." Information for new users includes "Create and Learn with Family Explorer," which suggests software to track research (some of it is free). There is also a link to Find Family Online, at http://www.genealogy.com/ifftop.html, which allows one to search for genealogies done by others. There are links to information about research tools and links to other Web sites, most of which are nongovernmental, but provide information about the kinds of records that will need to be consulted. For example, under "Helpful Web Sites," "Media: Microfilm/ Microform/ Microfiche," there is a link to the "Federal Population Schedules" that is actually the online version of the *National Archives and Records Administration* (NARA) Catalog of Microfilm Holdings Available for Research. Each of these Census population schedules covers a local geographic area, commonly a county. NARA has a lending program, and the microfilm is also available for purchase. More details are provided in the section below on Research Centers and Libraries. Some of the links, such as that for "Ancestor Publishers," were dead. There is really no way to determine when the links in the page were last checked, as the copyright states 1996–2000 (a fairly large window—although it does suggest that the links are updated regularly). This is a comprehensive site with a wide variety of connections to resources. Its primary strength is in links to types of records available online. It should be considered one of the major Web sites for genealogical research.

Cyndi's List of Genealogy Sites on the Internet
http://cyndislist.com

This Web site is a well-known, very extensive list of Internet sites. There were over 184,600 links as of May 2003. The Web site is hosted by RootsWeb.com and Ancestry.com. It offers a free surname search to get the researcher started, and one can use any of six search engines to search by automated surname, automated keyword, SSDI, RootsWeb, GenSeeker, and WorldConnect Project. Each of the search engines can search many databases at one time. There are sections on getting started, examples of research templates, search engines and additional databases, mailing lists, messages, Web sites, and several other more esoteric categories. Several categories on this Web site, such as libraries, archives, museums, magazines, journals, columns, and newsletters, are so extensive that they are profiled in other sections of this chapter. This Web site is a good place to examine a large collection of resources and begin to narrow them down to the more relevant resources for a particular stage of research.

Ancestry.com http://www.ancestry.com/main.aspx

This Web site is not as comprehensive as Genealogy.com, but it begins with a more unique approach. The first thing suggested is to do a search for ancestors by family name. Selecting a state can narrow the search. Records searched include the SSDI, Census records, newspapers and periodicals, and military records. Results of the search are described by how many hits are retrieved and in what index the results were found. For example, records retrieved from a search for "Omohundro" (an unusual family name) included Census records from Missouri, Ohio, Tennessee, and Virginia. To look further into the online Census records requires membership in Ancestry.com. Vital and church records retrieved include an abstract of a tombstone on a grave of a Revolutionary War patriot and death and marriage records. There are also entries in each of the remaining categories such as biography and history, compiled genealogy, military records, reference, periodicals and newspapers (primarily obituaries), and directories. The site provides an interesting start to research, and although access to most of the online databases requires subscription or membership, there are still many hints provided concerning what records contain relevant information.

Specialized

Specialized resources are those that have a particular focus for research. The focus can be geographic or subjective, historical or contemporary. They are usually used after initial research has been completed, or when the search is for a certain type of information that is known. For example, someone doing research for a land title claim may need to find information from only one area or time period.

US County Resources at RootsWeb
  http://resources.rootsweb.com/USA

This resource is of particular interest for finding local government information. This search engine will connect you to the county Web site for a particular city. For example, for Tonawanda, New York, the connection is to resources of Erie County, New York, that are of interest to genealogical researchers. The page for these resources is extensive and allows different search engines to be used for various resources. For example, a search of the name "Cone" retrieved records from sources ranging from tombstones in cemeteries to digitized Census records for Genesee and Ontario counties in 1860. There is an index to all Cones listed in the Census for 1810–1840. An example of oddities that such research can reveal includes the fact that the Cones appear in 1810 and 1830, but not 1820 or 1840. Some of these resources can really help one focus research. This index would indicate that the Cones were probably in another location during the 1820 and 1840 Censuses. One of the records retrieved is a reference to a land purchase by Ebenezer Cone in 1806, in the area township 12, range 7. Each one of these references is to some type of official notice that was kept on the local governmental level. This was just one name search, which actually did not explore all the options available. The researcher should plan on spending a lot of time with these resources, as one discovery leads to another, perhaps far down a particular road. The search demonstrated here is really only the beginning of the many resources available from all of the Web sites.

GenealogyDatabase.com
  http://genealogydatabase.com

This database is still under development and, similar to other leading genealogy Web sites, will be subscription based. It will also be accessible through HeritageQuest.com and SierraHome Network. GenealogyDatabase.com is expected to host 10 million images of Census pages at launch, and its parent, Heritage Quest, is committed to indexing new names at the astounding rate of 500,000 per week! Another interesting feature of this database is that GenealogyDatabase.com will be a living Web community that includes a "sticky note" technology whereby members can leave messages behind for others looking at the same page of the Census. Many genealogists believe that it is essential to research in clusters, since people simply didn't move as often or as far during the eighteenth and nineteenth centuries. GenealogyDatabase. com members can leave behind messages requesting information or photos, or even to correct errors that they know to exist on a Census page. Having spent years reviewing this vast set of images, the professional genealogists at Heritage Quest will add the first notes, highlighting specific errors and problems. This resource became available in Fall 2000.

However, as of 2003, the plan to fully digitize the entire 1790–1920 U.S. Census population schedules appeared to have been postponed indefinitely. This digitized Census data alone would have been the equivalent of 12,555 rolls of microfilm that sell at retail for $250,000.

TOWN, COUNTY, AND STATE RECORDS

General

General town, county, and state record volumes are collections of resources organized by a certain geographic jurisdiction. A wide range of resources is included and described. These are useful for quick referral.

Ancestry's Red Book: American State, County, and Town Sources, ed. Alice Eichholz, maps by William Dollarhide (Ancestry, Inc., 1991)

This resource is organized by state. It gives a summary of how to locate records for various types within each state. The types of records mentioned include vital records, Census records, maps, land records, probate records, court records, tax records, cemetery records, church records, military records, periodicals, newspapers and manuscript collections, archives, libraries and societies, special focus categories, and county resources. The county resources section includes a current map of counties and a table that lists the map position, county address, date formed, and parent county or counties. Also listed is the date when records of birth, marriage, death, land transactions, probate, and district court proceedings began to be kept by the county. County addresses are included.

For example, under the listing for vital records for the state of New York, you can learn that the earliest items that may be classified as civil vital records in New York were marriage bonds issued from 1639 to 1783. This is a source that may have limited availability but is available in the Library of Congress Local History and Genealogy Reading Room.

Ancestry's Red Book is an example of a resource in which detailed information is provided on the history of each type of record, with information on how or where to obtain the records for a particular geographic location. An additional category of interest is the "Special Focus," which includes information on special subjects such as immigration, black American, and Native American resources. It includes published guides and resources as well as the names and locations of special collections. This is a truly rich and comprehensive source and is probably the most complete in tracing the history and disposition of local civil and church records. It is available for sale from the publisher.

Where to Write for Vital Records—Births, Deaths, Marriages, and Divorces (U.S. Government Printing Office, annual)

This is a U.S. government Depository document available through most Depository libraries. In addition, it is available for sale from the U.S. Government Printing Office. For sales information, see the U.S. Government Online Bookstore, http://bookstore.gpo. gov/index.html. The latest edition is available for $4.25. There is also a Web site, http://www.cdc.gov/ nchs/howto/w2w/w2welcom.htm, at the National Center for Health Statistics, which provides an alphabetical directory by state for those users who want direct access to individual state and territory information. The directions are simple and straightforward. First determine the state or area where the event occurred and then select the first letter in the state name from the alphabet. There are instructions to follow the provided guidelines to ensure an accurate response to your request. The federal government does not distribute certificates, files, or indexes with identifying information for vital records. That is a good reason for using the resources identified here.

State

State Census Records, by Ann S. Lainhart (Genealogical Publishing Co., 1992)

Certain states conduct or have conducted a state census. These are useful, as they complement and sometimes substitute for lost federal Census records. Most of the 1890 Census records were burned in a fire, and the state censuses can fill in the gaps left by the loss of this information. Although not as comprehensive as federal censuses, state censuses help provide vital information. Some states that have census records for the gap (1880–1900) in federal Census records are Colorado, Florida, Rhode Island, and Iowa. State census records can not only fill in gaps, but also provide different information than the federal records. For example, the 1925 Iowa census asked for the mother's maiden name. State census records can be useful in patching together information. They sometimes have interesting comments, such as in Hanson, Massachusetts, which lists the birthplace of a child as: "In the Gulf of Siam in a Peruvian ship under a Spanish captain, three hours after the loss of the vessel in which the mother sailed from the U.S." Another feature of state census records can be the spelling out of complete middle names, rather than giving just initials. The book lists where original copies are located, but not all microfilm copies. Much of this material is also available from the LDS Library in Salt Lake City. Those not available at that library are so indicated. This volume may be available at a library or from the publisher.

Guide to Records in the New York State Archives (State University of New York, State Education Department, and State Archives and Records Administration, 1983)

This publication is a guide to the archives of a particular state. Many local government archives for towns, townships, and counties have been transferred to the state archives. For example, a birth certificate from Erie County, New York, dated from the 1950s must be obtained from the state archive of New York. The state of New York has had a long and turbulent history, and this guide is invaluable to anyone doing research in the State Archives and Records Administration (SARA). Its main purpose is to provide guidance to the development and current functions of state agencies that create records. The resources cover the entire range of New York history from the colonial to the current period. The *Guide* begins with an introduction to SARA and is arranged by branch of government and agency within the branch. In the executive branch there are agencies such as the Office for the Aging, the State Education Department, and the Department of Health. The legislative branch has no other agencies under it, but the judicial branch has a description of the unified court system as well as special courts like the state supreme court. There are appendices that contain lists of types of local government records, local government records on microfilm in the state archives, and information on the Research Libraries Information Network (RLIN) archives, manuscripts, and special collections in the state. There is an index to agency functions and office names. As explained in chapter 2 of this book, it helps to have some familiarity with the structure of any government before attempting to find information produced by that government. This resource is helpful and provides needed guidance to these specialized resources. Although this publication describes itself as a directory to the New York State archives, it is important to remember that many local government archives have been transferred to the state. It is not as easy to locate local government agency directories.

Connecticut State Library: Information Services Division: History and Genealogy
    http://www.cslib.org/handg.htm

This Web site is specific to genealogical materials in the state of Connecticut. Since Connecticut predates both statehood and the formation of the federal government, the state archives have many documents relevant to genealogical research on the local governmental level. There are published guides and pamphlets that can be used in the library, and this Web site provides much interesting information for the researcher.

The History and Genealogy Unit maintains and provides access to an extensive collection of materials on the history of Connecticut and its people. Its genealogical resources include Connecticut town vital records (to about 1900), church records, family Bible records, cemetery inscriptions, newspaper notices of marriages and deaths, census records, land records, probate records, and military records. These are technically local government records.

The library maintains a collection of genealogies, histories, and other related materials including comprehensive and retrospective collections of Connecticut maps, city directories, and newspapers. Detailed finding aids are available on a number of topics including the aerial photograph collection; Connecticut land records; naturalization; Revolutionary War, Civil War, and World War II resources; African American and Native American materials; and women's history. This Web site provides good information that can be consulted prior to visiting the library.

Census Records in the University of Virginia Library
    http://www.lib.virginia.edu/govdocs/fact/
    censusrec.html

This Web site is an example of a focused effort by a particular state to provide Census information to users from that state. The Web site provides some historical background and explanation of the project, particularly that it is not comprehensive. There is then a description of what files are available. Some Census population schedules are available and can be used at the library. This is an excellent guide to the Census overall, with particular attention given to Virginia census records.

Counties and Towns

Historical Data Relating to Counties, Cities, and Towns in Massachusetts, by William Frances Galvin (New England Historic Genealogical Society, 1997)

Volumes such as this are very helpful in distinguishing this type of information. Written by a former secretary of the Commonwealth of Massachusetts, this is the fifth edition of a volume that lists when a particular town was legislated into existence, a necessary factor in tracing the disposition of vital records Massachusetts towns have kept since the 1630s. This edition includes county and town maps as well as a comprehensive index that refers to data and survey maps held by the Massachusetts archives. For example, a record lists the town, such as Amesbury, Essex County, with a chronology listing the history from establishment to the latest town charter. It lists archaic names of the municipality and section and village names, which alleviates some of the tedious work involved in looking for old geographic boundary maps. This publication is available from the New England Historic Genealogy Society. For further information, consult the Society's Web site, at http://www.newenglandancestors.org.

The Sourcebook to Public Records (Public Record Research Library, BRB Publications, 1999)

This resource provides information to assist in searching for state public records, county court records, county asset/lien records, and federal court records. There is some practical information on how to search for the records provided, but the main problem addressed is that of finding the court of jurisdiction and the proper addresses, telephone numbers, and information about whether business can be conducted by mail or telephone. The volume is written mainly for paralegals, investigators, and lawyers. These searches can become really problematic if business can be done only in person. E-mail is being used more often and is a very inexpensive way to begin (and hopefully complete) the obtaining of copies of local governmental records. The volume is organized by state and county, with a cross-referenced index by town. This is an excellent resource. It is available from the publisher's Web site, at http://www.brbpub.com/books, and is available in CD-ROM. The Web site has links to related kinds of information.

NATIONAL RECORDS OF LOCAL SIGNIFICANCE

Certain local governmental records are often transferred or kept by a national governmental agency such as NARA: records of court proceedings, property deeds, military service, and local branches of federal government agencies.

National Archives Record Sources

Guide to Genealogical Research in the National Archives (NARA, National Archives Trust Board, 2000)

This book is an excellent resource, divided into sections that describe types of records such as U.S. Census population schedules; immigration records; military records; records relating to particular groups; and land records, claims, and maps. There is also information concerning guides and finding aids available for research. The regional branches of the National Archives are listed, with appropriate contact information. An example of a record described in the attractive and informative volume is found on page 118, an oath of enlistment and allegiance of a Massachusetts man who was a Revolutionary War soldier. Although this is technically a federal record, it is actually information from a then-local governmental resource. This book is recommended reading for anyone who would like to use National Archives records for genealogical or other research.

The Archives: A Guide to the National Archives Field Branches, by Loretto Dennis Szucs and Sandra Hargreaves Luebking (Ancestry Publishing, 1988)

This resource is a comprehensive guide to textual and microfilm holdings in the National Archives Field Branches that are valuable for genealogical research. Although these are primarily national government records, they contain information organized by local geographic jurisdiction. There is a table of contents that lists record groups by government agency, such as the Agricultural Research Service, Census Bureau, courts of appeals, Internal Revenue Service, or the Public Land Review Commission.

This resource is useful in determining what and where records may be found. Records in the National Archives are organized into more than 450 record groups that contain billions of pages, millions of photographs, maps and charts, thousands of audio and video recordings, drawings, and machine-readable tapes. Each regional branch processes records from the geographically adjacent region. For example, the Fort Worth branch has more Bureau of Indian Affairs (BIA) records than the Washington, D.C., branch. The volume contains an introduction on how to use the guide, a bibliography of sources consulted, and descriptions of each branch with contact information and hours of operation. There are listings of major holdings of each branch and of textual and microfilm holdings that each has or that several branches have in common, along with the relevant record group, and a complete description of each agency with records in the archives, with its relevant record group. When records are organized by state or district, further description is provided. Of particular interest to genealogical researchers are the Census record groups and records from district courts, BIA, INS, the Land Management Bureau, Naval Office, Patent Office, and Railroad Retirement Board. There is an alphabetical name and subject index, and an index by record group. This volume will certainly save users time if they consult it before attempting to use National Archives records. The records in the archives are described in more detail in publications such as the *National Archives Microfilm Publications in the Regional Archives System*.

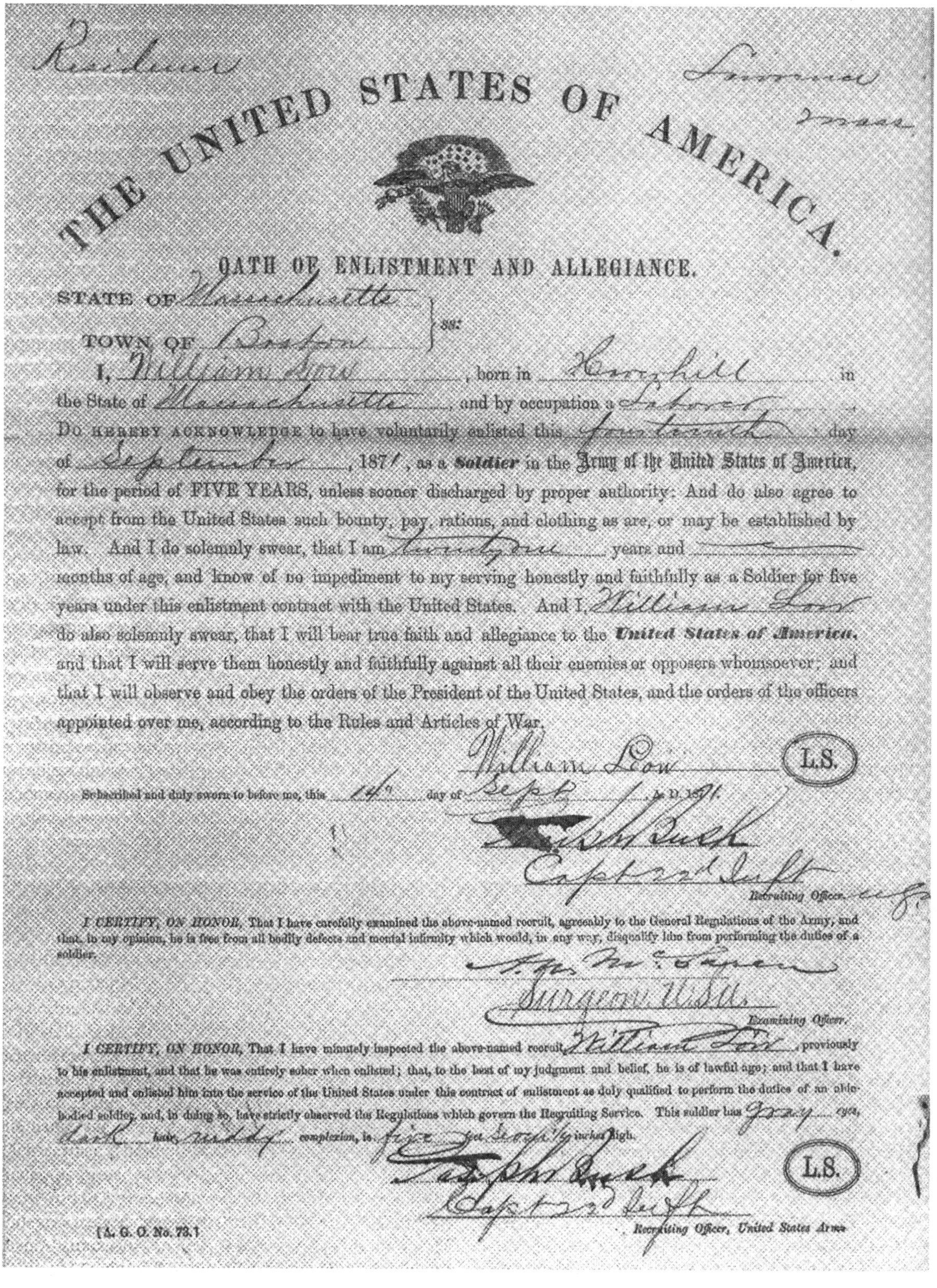

Figure 9.1 Sample "Oath of Enlistment and Allegiance."

*Microfilm Resources for Research: A Comprehensive
Catalog* (NARA, annual)

The *Catalog* is a specialized resource used primarily for ordering copies of microfilm when the reel number is known.

*The Federal Population Censuses, 1790–1890: A
Catalog of Microfilm Copies of the Schedules* (National Archives Trust Fund Board, 1979)

This source is a specific index of reel numbers by county for the various states for each Census.

1900 Federal Population Census: A Catalog of Microfilm Copies of the Schedules (National Archives Trust Fund Board, 1978)

This resource arranges the 1900 Census population schedules and the 1900 Soundex system, which is reproduced as a separate microfilm publication for each state and territory. The Soundex system can be used if searching by name. If the name spelling is too variant, then one can search by enumeration district or geography. This publication describes which states and enumeration districts are on particular rolls of microfilm. If there is no NARA branch nearby, microfilm can be purchased or borrowed from the National Archives. You must have the enumeration district number assigned to a place to order a microfilm copy. This information can be readily obtained from the NARA Web site, http://www.nara.gov, or the *National Archives Microfilm Resources for Research: A Comprehensive Catalog* (NARA, 1996, revised).

*Guide to Federal Records in the National Archives of
the United States, Volume III, Index* (NARA, 1995)

This appears to be a multientry index consisting of agencies, subjects, and names, with an index to entries in the previous volumes that describe the collection more completely.

Indexes

Indexes actually cover a wide range of possible material, from indexing publications, to groups of records, or names in records. The most useful for the purposes of genealogical research are indexes to groups of records or names contained in the records.

The Soundex Reference Guide, ed. by Bradley W.
Steuart (Precision Indexing, 1990)

The *Soundex Reference Guide* is a volume that describes a coding system used by census researchers to group like-sounding names together, and provides an index entry for all names and approximations thereof. This is very helpful in tracing names that have changed spelling for various reasons over the years. The coding system was created for indexing the 1880, 1900, and 1910 Censuses. Names were extracted, coded, and placed on index cards as part of a Works Project Administration project during the Depression. After coding, the cards were hand-sorted according to Soundex rules. The names listed in indexes were therefore grouped together by sound. The cards were then microfilmed, and a master indexing system was derived from the cards. The "Soundex" system is the result of this project. An example of names that are grouped together are Stewart, Stuart, Steuart, Stuert, Steward, Steuard, and Stuard. The names all have the code S363. The index lists the name and counties in which people bearing the name are located. It also lists the volume number and enumeration district number, but the county is the best way to locate the record. This is invaluable in focusing research on relevant local geographic areas. The *Soundex Reference Guide* is usually available in genealogical research libraries and centers, and a description of it exists at the NARA Web site, at http://www.archives.gov/research_room/genealogy/census/soundex.html. An online version of the Soundex system is available from RootsWeb.com, at http://resources.rootsweb.com/cgi-bin/soundexconverter. Just type in the name and it gives you the Soundex code.

City, County, Town, and Township Index to the [1850]
Federal Census Schedules, by J. Carlyle Parker
(Gale Research Company Genealogy and Local
History Series, volume 6, 1979)

An index such as this is invaluable in locating family records on federal Census population schedules. Geography changes over time, and the growth of many towns, townships, and cities has caused census boundaries to change. A more detailed explanation of map sources occurs in a chapter of the book, but indexes such as this one are very helpful in determining on which Census microfilm roll a particular town was located. The lack of an index prior to this one forced researchers to go to maps, atlases, gazetteers, or place-name literature to determine in which county a town was located. Towns and townships are arranged by county on the Census schedules rather than in alphabetical order. Names of towns were recorded as the Census recorder traveled and have not been alphabetized. Since these documents were handwritten, they could not be reordered unless they were copied over and rearranged.

This index is an alphabetical listing by town and township, with the county, state, NARA microfilm reel number, the number assigned by the genealogical department of the LDS Library in Salt Lake City, and the pages on which the data can be located. Pagination is confusing and often renumbered, so the latest hand repagination is provided. The pagination index does not correspond to the bound volumes, but to the microfilm copies that most researchers use. In addition to a listing of cities, towns, and townships, the index also lists boroughs, named "Census beats"; districts; divisions, named "election districts"; grants; hundreds; parishes; plantations, named "precincts"; settlements; and villages. In later years, all of these geographic jurisdictions took the common name "place."

Geographical Subdivisions in the Federal Population Census Schedules of 1830, 1850, and 1860 (National Archives and Records Service, 1963)

This publication is an index to the Census schedules but is not adequate for use with the microfilm copies of the schedules, as many communities were not included in the bound volumes index and many place names were misspelled. But this compact volume is very useful for using the bound volumes of the Census. Though out of print, it is available in research libraries and centers.

A Bibliography of Military Name Lists from Pre-1675 to 1900: A Guide to Genealogical Sources, by Lois Horowitz (Scarecrow Press, 1990)

This resource is very specialized and provides indexing to lists of military records organized by date. Many abbreviations are used and a helpful key is provided. The list of names is taken from payroll lists, muster lists, honor rolls, account books, obituaries, pension lists, and bounty land records held privately as well as by libraries and research centers. One important omission comprises city and county histories. The lists are arranged by war and geographic area, in proper bibliographic format. An example is

Zimmerman, Margaretta. "Clark County Civil War Veteran, Census of 1890." TB, V. 11, no. 4: p. 3–4 (Sum. 1985). Ca. 300 names.

This resource can be very helpful in trying to locate military records that have been scattered throughout the country and not well organized. The volume is available from the publisher at its Web site, http://www.scarecrowpress.com/Catalog/Index.shtml.

SPECIALIZED TOPICAL RESOURCES

Specialized topical resources focus on a particular subject of study, such as a certain type of record, records created by certain agencies, or records that have been documented by an interested group for special purposes such as ethnic identification, adoption records, or something similar.

Requesting and Evaluating Records

Handbook of Genealogical Correspondence (Cache Genealogical Library/Everton Publishers, 1974)

This volume is a very good how-to manual on writing various agencies (governmental and nongovernmental) for copies of records. Most vital records are public but still require a written request, and private records such as those of a historical society or a church certainly require a written request. This resource provides the basics necessary for such correspondence, as well as descriptive information on the types of material that might be requested. There are descriptions of maps as well as how to write to libraries, public archives, and historical societies, and samples of letters to church record keepers and public officials. A chapter describes how to research variant spellings of a surname through correspondence. There is also information on how to advertise in newspapers and genealogical magazines for information—an update on how to do this on the Internet would have been useful. Finally, there is a chapter on how to refer to a specialist such as a trained genealogist and how to organize the correspondence received.

Appendices include a substantial section on maps, atlases, and gazetteers as well as genealogical reference books. There is a nice subject and title index, and tables of examples are throughout the volume. This book is probably out of print, but most genealogical collections should have it. It may be available through interlibrary loan.

Genealogical Evidence: A Guide to the Standard of Proof Relating to Pedigrees, Ancestry, Heirship and Family History, by Noel C. Stevenson (Aegean Park Press, 1979)

This small volume is really a classic in the field of legal evidence pertaining to genealogy. Not only people searching for ancestors do genealogical research. Many times proof is needed for legal claims such as probate hearings for wills, property disputes, paternity suits, adoption proceedings, and all kinds of other legal matters. This volume establishes, at least for the state of California, a "body of rules that judge the reliability of facts relevant to genealogy, history and biography." The volume is divided into sections entitled "Genealogical Hazards, Risks and Remedies," "Right of Access to Official and Public Records," "Principal Unofficial Records," and "Simplified Rules of Evidence." There is also a glossary of legal terminology relating to genealogy. Of particular interest to this study is the description of "Official Records—Public Records," as most of these are registered and kept at the local governmental level. The primary public records identified are the same as those identified elsewhere in this chapter: vital records, court records, land records, and Census records. There is a chart that lists types of evidence and their rating: for example, "Newspaper files: Contemporary accounts of births, marriages, and deaths. Type of evidence: Hearsay. Rating of Evidence: Generally reliable." The hazards here are informant and printer errors. This book is probably out of print, but most genealogical collections should have it. It may be available through interlibrary loan.

Colonial Records

The Great Migration Begins: Immigrants to New England, 1620–1633, Volume I A-F, by Robert Charles Anderson (Great Migration Study Project, New England Historic Genealogy Society, 1995)

This publication is the first of three volumes that are interesting in that they list all types of public and private records dating from colonial times that can be checked to trace ancestry. There are examples of sources such as passenger lists, lists of freedmen, colony and court records, notarial records, town records, vital records, land records, church records, journals and letters, and miscellaneous records, with helpful descriptions. Volume 1 is a detailed analysis of migration and provides examples of certain settlers, with genealogical sketches of them. Maps are also a large part of these records and are often essential in determining what an area may have looked like or what certain places were named at a certain time in history. This is an extensive set of volumes, still available for sale from the publisher, the New England His-

toric Genealogy Society. For further information on this publication as well as its availability in CD-ROM format, consult the Society's Web site, http://www.nehgs.org.

Passenger and Immigration Lists Index: A Guide to Published Arrival Records of More Than 1,775,000 Passengers Who Came to the New World between the 16th and the Early 20th Centuries (Gale Research Inc., 1981)

This index, also in three volumes, is useful when using National Archives materials. Passenger arrivals are listed according to various sources such as newsletters and official lists.

Index of Revolutionary War Pension Applications in the National Archives, Bicentennial Edition (National Genealogical Society, 1976).

This index provides a link to records in the National Archives by name. For details, see the National Genealogical Society Web site, http://ngsgenealogy.org.

A Guide to Pre-Federal Records in the National Archives, compiled by Howard H. Wehmann, revised by Benjamin L. DeWhitt (National Archives and Records Administration, 1989)

This publication is very interesting in its subject matter. These prefederal records are important because of the time period and governmental structure and are actually local governmental records. For example, there are miscellaneous court records, 1777–89; the naval records collection of the Office of Naval Records and Library (containing some Revolutionary War naval records); and miscellaneous manuscripts, 1756–88, from the Department of State's Bureau of Rolls and Library. These records are true copies made by the clerk of a Connecticut court. There are also records pertaining to territorial disputes between or involving states. This resource can be helpful if searching for ancestors. Names can be mentioned in court or other documents. This publication is available from the NARA Web site.

Tracing Ethnic Records

Ethnic Genealogy: A Research Guide, ed. by Jessie Carney Smith (Greenwood Press, 1983)

This publication is extremely impressive. It begins by listing general information on basic sources, including librarians and family records. It then describes major repositories. The final section is specifically devoted to resources for major ethnic groups, such as American Indian, Asian American, African American, and Hispanic American. There are many fine examples of various types of records such as the register of Indian families and the manumission papers of former slaves. The volume begins with a brief and succinct explanation of why librarians once dreaded genealogical research and proceeds to organize the available information in an easy, usable way. There are, of course, documents unique to each ethnic group, and this volume is a good start for beginning that research. The book is available at the Library of Congress and for sale from the publisher, at http://info.greenwood.com.

ADDITIONAL RESOURCES

It is almost certain that after beginning genealogical research, there is a desire to pursue it further. The task is difficult, and one question leads to another. The researcher can now utilize additional resources available for genealogical research.

Research Centers and Libraries

Directory of Genealogical and Historical Societies in the US and Canada (Iron Gate, 2000)

This is a newly published index that, in spite of its long name, is a concise (174-page) directory to genealogical libraries, research centers, and periodicals. It is nice to have a directory that can be used independently of the Internet, and this is a compact and reasonably priced resource. It is available from the publisher, Iron Gate, at http://www.irongate.com.

The Genealogist's Handbook: Modern Methods for Researching Family History, by Raymond Wright III (American Library Association, 1995)

This resource has a list of genealogical research centers that is arranged geographically by state. The resources listed are primarily of major research caliber and limited in number. Judging by the number of resources for this book named in Cyndi's List (profiled below), the list is less than comprehensive. It was written before the number of online resources really began to multiply. It has a nice index to ethnic and immigration research centers in appendix B.

Cyndi's List: Libraries, Archives and Museums
  http://www.CyndisList.com

This site has a section that lists over 1,500 libraries, archives, and museums, at http://www.Cyndis List.com/libes.htm. It also has an alphabetical index, with an overall category of general library resources, as well as an alphabetical listing of particular libraries. For example, under general library resources there is a link to genealogy lending libraries and archives, http://www.cyndislist.com/lib-lending.htm. There are full addresses and contact information, and some libraries are hot-linked. There are also links to specialized libraries by name, such as the Eastern Shore of Virginia Public Library (http://www.espl.org), which has its own special section for genealogy links. The links on Cyndi's List provide information about all sorts of local resources, governmental and nongovernmental. There is an index organized geographically by state. This site is comprehensive and easy to use.

Periodicals

Bibliography of Genealogy and Local History Periodicals with Union List of Major U.S. Collections, ed. by Michael Barren Clegg (Allen County Public Library Foundation, 1990)

This publication, which hasn't been updated since 1990, is a collaboration of eight major research libraries in the area of genealogy. Participating libraries included the Dallas Public Library, Los Angeles Public Library, New York Public Library, and the Wisconsin State Historical Society Library. The bibliography includes many periodicals that were often published for only a short time but may have information of local interest to genealogical researchers. It has a subject and name index. The book can probably be located at the major research libraries, and it was at the Library of Congress.

New England Ancestors: Newsmagazine of the New England Historic Genealogical Society

This publication is published bimonthly by the Society but recently changed its title from *The Computer Genealogist: A Publication of the New England Historic Genealogical Society*. The September/October 1999 issue, for example, published under the former title, contained such useful articles as "Evaluating Web Resources: Part II: Genealogy Research Specifics," with the subtitle "A Given: Anyone Can and Will Upload Anything to the Internet." This particular issue evaluated both paper and Internet resources, governmental and nongovernmental. What was particularly helpful was that the various tools of the process used in Internet searching were evaluated, beginning with search engines. It then evaluated Web sites, Mega-Sites, and tools available on CD-ROM. The current publication includes reports from recent conferences and advertising for new products and is available for sale from the Society. A sample table of contents is available on the Web site, http://www.new englandancestors.org, where further information can also be obtained.

Ancestor Detective http://www.ancestordetective.com

A public service is offered at this Web site. The site is described as maintained by six reputable genealogists who are active in identifying and exposing scams, misleading claims, and outright fraudulent Web sites, and invites public participation in these activities. This e-newsletter is timely and full of valuable information. Further information on membership is available on the Web site.

Cyndi's List: Print and Electronic Publications for Genealogy http://www.CyndisList.com

This Web site has a category devoted to magazines, journals, columns and columnists, and newsletters, with links to them as well as to e-mail newsletters, e-zines, and print periodicals. The list is extensive and where links are not available, addresses and telephone numbers are provided. For example, there is a link to the Ancestry.com columns "Ancestry Family History Columns" and "Ancestry Daily News" (http://www. ancestry.com/learn/library/columnists/main.htm).

Tracing Local Records Internationally

World-Wide Genealogical Research Sources
http://www.genhomepage.com/world.html

This site, although not focused on local government information resources in the United States, has an extensive list of genealogical research resources on an inter-national scale. These resources are organized by geographic area, such as Africa, the British Isles, the Caribbean, etc. There is also an alphabetical listing by country. For example, under Germany, there are links to German genealogical information, the German Migration Resource Center, and *Finding Passenger Lists, 1820–1940*, a basic tutorial for German Americans. This site is very comprehensive and a virtual world reference tour of genealogical libraries and resource centers.

Public Records Office—National Archives (UK)
http://www.pro.gov.uk

Although we tend to think of local government records as being local only to the United States, there are of course Public Records Offices in other countries. Each country has local governmental records of its own. The Public Records Office in Great Britain, for example, has an extensive Web site and publications concerning the records available for research. At the Web site there are links to categories on genealogy, archives, and record copying, and even a link concerning the 1901 British Census. There are finding aids and plenty of information to guide users. Paper publications from the Public Records Office are also available on such topics as copyright, maps in the Public Records Office, and more specifically, *The American Revolution: Guides and Lists to Documents in the Public Record Office*. All of this hints at a rich source of research in countries overseas.

FOR FURTHER READING

Hawley Spiros, Joyce V. *Handy Genealogical Guide to New Mexico*. Gallup, N.M.: Verlene Publishing, 1981.

Names of Persons for Whom Marriage Licenses Were Issued by the Secretary of the Province of New York, previous to 1784. Genealogical Publishing Company, 1860, reprint, 1984.

CHAPTER 10
Finding Information on Local Health Services

Maria Carpenter and Marie-Lise Shams

MAJOR TOPICS COVERED

Introduction
General
 General Web Sites
 Print Publications in Electronic Format
 Guides
 Directories
 Specialized Resources
Compendiums
 Local Government Health Resources
Specialized/Topical Resources
 Specialized Web Sites
 Resources on Special Health Topics
 Resources on Consumer Health
 Resources on Injuries and Safety
 Resources for Special Populations
 Statistical Resources
Conclusion

MAJOR RESOURCES COVERED

U.S. Department of Health and Human Resources
National Center for Health Statistics
Healthy People 2010
Health Data Sourcebook: A Guide to Finding, Evaluating and Accessing Sources of Health Data
CDC Wonder
MedlinePlus
Health and Healthcare in the United States: County and Metro Area Data
Reportable Diseases and Conditions in Michigan
Centers for Disease Control and Prevention
2000 Epidemiologic Profiles of HIV/AIDS in Michigan
Youth Risk Behavior Surveillance—United States, 2003
Kids Count in Michigan 2000 Data Book: County Profiles of Child and Family Well-Being
Women of Color Health Data Book: Adolescents to Seniors
Resource Directory for Older People in Maine
Know Your Rights: Your Medicaid Care and Coverage in a Nursing Home
Statistical Information on Older Persons
HCUPnet
MEPSnet/IC
Substance Abuse and Mental Health Statistics
Directory of Health and Human Services Data Resources

INTRODUCTION

The World Health Organization defines health as "a state of complete physical, mental, and social well-being and not merely the absence of disease or infirmity." Health information resources, therefore, span a wide range of specialized and general topics, services and programs, aimed not only at the treatment of medical conditions, but also at prevention, consumer awareness, improvement of quality of life, and safe environment. All ages and all ethnic groups are represented.

At the national level, health resources are produced and distributed by federal government bodies such as the centers, institutes, and offices of the U.S. Department of Health and Human Services and the Occupational Safety and Health Administration of the U.S. Department of Labor and by professional and health-related organizations and associations. Local government resources are disseminated by state, county, and city departments of health. Federal agencies work closely with local health departments and local surveillance systems. Through this partnership they collect and disseminate local data. Some agencies such as the Centers for Disease Control and Prevention or the Health Resources and Services Administration present analyzed local data in state profiles.

Three major types of resources are encountered: professional, consumer-oriented, and a combination of both. Professional resources include reports, manuals, statistical publications, professional journals, software, CD-ROMs, and databases. Consumer-oriented publications are composed primarily of fact sheets, brochures, booklets, directories, guides, and newsletters. Annual reports of county and city health departments should not be ignored. They provide an overview of the local health status and of the various services and programs offered to citizens, with contact information.

The increasing popularity and availability of the Internet have prompted all federal agencies and most local health departments to provide electronic access to updated resources on their Web sites. For those with Internet access, this is the best starting point for locating health information and available services.

Such a wealth of resources makes it hard to identify those relevant to individual needs. This chapter presents descriptions and availabilities of various health publications, databases, and Web sites with emphasis on local government resources. The goal is to help readers make informed choices and locate the best sources available in their geographic areas. Selected states' resources are described as examples. Readers from other states may contact their respective state departments to request similar publications.

GENERAL

General Web Sites

U.S. Department of Health and Human Resources [HHS] http://www.os.dhhs.gov

HHS comprises over 300 programs and 11 divisions and agencies dedicated to providing essential health and human services. Services such as Medicare, Medicaid, mental health assistance, substance abuse treatment and prevention, maternal/child health, and health services to the elderly and to Native Americans are all administered from the umbrella of this agency. A summary of HHS's activities is found on its Web site, along with a map of its 10 regions. A description of the agencies with a direct link to their respective Web sites is found under "Agencies" on the Web site. By working closely with local governments, HHS-

funded services are provided at the state, county, and tribal level.

National Center for Health Statistics [NCHS]. http://www.cdc.gov/nchs

NCHS develops and disseminates publications and electronic products related to the nation's health statistics. The entire catalog is available through the NCHS Web site with descriptions and availability or purchasing instructions. Most publications are found at local Depository libraries, for a list of which, see http://www.access.gpo.gov/su_docs/locators/findlibs. Several reports, surveys, and tabulated state data are readily accessible online to be viewed or printed. "State Health Statistics by Sex and Race/Ethnicity," available through the "Data Warehouse" link on the left navigational bar, provides tables describing the health of people in each state by sex, race, and age. The "Faststats A to Z" on the same bar links to an alphabetical listing of health topics and state names, which in turn link to related statistical documents or Web sites. This is a great tool for obtaining local statistical data.

Print Publications in Electronic Format

The following publications are found in print at most federal Depository libraries and also on the Internet in various electronic formats. The Web site address of each publication is indicated after the title, and associated details are included in the description. The publications are available as PDF files that require downloading by Adobe Acrobat Reader, which is available for free at http://www.acrobat.com.

Healthy People 2010 (Department of Health and Human Services) http://www.healthypeople.gov/document

The goal of Healthy People 2010, like that of the previous decade's Healthy People 2000, is to provide a comprehensive, nationwide health promotion and disease prevention agenda to increase the quality of healthy life and eliminate health disparities. Healthy People 2010 covers 467 objectives organized in 28 focus areas: access to quality health services, arthritis, osteoporosis and chronic back conditions, cancer, chronic kidney disease, diabetes, disability, and secondary conditions. Measures include educational and community-based programs, environmental health, family planning and sexual health, food safety, health communication, heart disease and stroke, HIV, immunizations and infectious diseases, injury and violence prevention, maternal/infant/child health, medical product safety, and mental health/disorders. Also included are nutrition, occupational safety and health, oral health, physical activity and fitness, public health infrastructure, respiratory diseases, sexually transmitted diseases, substance abuse, tobacco use, vision, and hearing. Publications and toolkits are available online for both Healthy People 2010 and Healthy People 2000, which provide data by state such as health status indicators, priority area data needs, selected mortality, and natality objectives.

Public Health Reports (U.S. Public Health Service, bimonthly) http://phr.oupjournals.org

This journal is a valuable source of information for those concerned with current public health issues. It offers research articles, reports, news, and book reviews, in addition to editorials, letters, and commentaries. Topics covered in a recent volume include hazardous air pollutants, asthma prevalence in American Indian and Alaska Native children, and biological and chemical terrorism in food and water supplies. The table of contents of each issue is available at the journal's Web site. Readers may read the abstracts free or subscribe to view the articles in PDF format. It is available at depository libraries. An advantage of the online version is the capability of searching either an individual issue or all issues to retrieve articles containing desired keywords.

Reports of the Surgeon General (U.S. Office of the Surgeon General, annual) http://www.surgeon general.gov/library/reports.htm

The Surgeon General has issued every year since 1964 reports on current national health issues. In 2001 five reports were published, on youth violence; women and smoking; suicide prevention; sexual health; and cultural, racial, and ethnic aspects of mental health. Previous reports focused on topics such as oral health, tobacco use among various age and ethnic groups, HIV/AIDS, and nutrition. These reports are available in PDF format at the Surgeon General's Web site, which also provides availability and purchasing information.

Guides

Health Data Sourcebook: A Guide to Finding, Evaluating and Accessing Sources of Health Data (Nationshealth Corp., 1999)

This guide is helpful for health care managers and decision makers. The focus is on locating the best sources for government and commercial health-related data. The reader is introduced to various dimensions of health data and data-generation methods. Individual chapters discuss, describe, and evaluate data sources for specific topics such as vital statistics, health facilities, health professionals, health services demand, and insurance/managed care. The appendices include Internet access to health data and a glossary of terms. Order this and other publications from Nations healthdata.com, http://www.nationshealthdata.com.

Directories

Federal Health Information Centers and Clearinghouse (National Health Information Center) http://www.health.gov/nhic/Pubs/clearinghouses.htm

This public-domain online directory provides the public with a concise listing of over 60 national health information centers and clearinghouses. The purpose of these centers and clearinghouses is to provide referrals, answer questions, and distribute information to the public. Information provided focuses on a wide range of issues, including adoption, diabetes, injury, air quality, lead, osteoporosis, and sudden infant death syndrome. Some of the centers include the U.S. Consumer Product Safety Commission Hotline, the Rural Information Center Health Service, the National Resource Center on Homelessness and Mental Illness, and the Alzheimer's Disease Education and Referral Center. Information includes addresses, telephone numbers, and e-mail and Web site addresses. This resource is an excellent starting point for people who have general information questions or are in the beginning stages of gathering information on their health topic. It is a useful source for the general public and for high school and university students. The first section of the directory is organized topically in alphabetical order. Each entry includes a description of the center, addresses, telephone numbers, fax numbers, and links to e-mail and Web sites. Many of the listings include TTY (text telephone for the hearing impaired), also known as TDD (telecommunications device for the deaf), and toll-free phone numbers. The second section is an alphabetical listing by title of these same federal health information centers and clearinghouses. Telephone, fax, e-mail, and Web site information is included. No descriptions are given in this section. This online resource is also available in print format and can be ordered through the National Health Information Center: NHIC, P.O. Box 1133, Washington, DC 20013-1133, 1-800-336-4797.

Traveler's Health Reference Materials (Centers for Disease Control and Prevention [CDC]) http://www.cdc.gov/travel/reference.htm

This site is an information portal to health resources for international travelers and for those who advise international travelers of health risks. There are links to vaccination information including recommended immunizations for children, as well as to the CDC's *The Yellow Book: Health Information for International Travel, 2001–2002, The Blue Sheet: Summary of Health Information for International Travel*, and *The Green Sheet*, a page reporting the results of sanitation inspections of cruise ships. These reports are all available for download.

The Yellow Book (Division of Quarantine, National Center for Infectious Diseases) http://www.cdc.gov/travel/yb/index.htm

The Yellow Book is a comprehensive book published by the Division of Quarantine, National Center for Infectious Diseases, and CDC that provides information on vaccinations, disease prevention (e.g., yellow fever or AIDS), health travel hints (snakebites, environmental effects, motion sickness), geographic distribution of potential health hazards (by continent, then country), and tips for travelers with special needs (HIV-positive travelers, pregnant travelers). The section on specific diseases describes the particular disease, explains its risk for travelers, and discusses prevention and/or treatment options. This book is intended for health care providers and for those who advise international travelers. The PDF version offers hyperlinks to other resources for the latest information available. The book has an index arranged alphabetically by subject.

The Blue Sheet (National Center for Infectious Diseases) http://www.cdc.gov/travel/blusheet.htm

The Blue Sheet was discontinued after March 1, 2004. It provided a summary list of countries infected with quarantinable diseases according to the World Health Organization. Its tables specified a particular disease and listed the affected geographic area by continent and then by country. There are also links to disease outbreak notices. The most current information on yellow-fever-vaccination recommendations by country can be found at http://www.cdc.gov/travel/yb/outline.htm#2.

The Green Sheet (National Center for Environmental Health) http://www.cdc.gov/nceh/vsp/scores/legend.htm

The Green Sheet provides ranking information on CDC sanitation inspections of international cruise ships. There are also links to data pages for ships inspected in the past two months and for ships with unsatisfactory scores. A copy of the most recent sanitation inspection report on an individual vessel may be obtained by writing to Vessel Sanitation Program, National Center for Environmental Health, 4770 Buford Hwy., NE, Mailstop F-16, Atlanta, GA 30341-3724.

The following health databases are available free on the Internet. They are designed primarily for health professionals, public health officials, policymakers, and researchers. Consumers who wish to search them may want to request a librarian's assistance.

Specialized Resources

CDC Wonder (Centers for Disease Control and Prevention) http://wonder.cdc.gov

This system, developed by the CDC, is set up to handle queries to access electronic versions of reports, statistical data, guidelines, and various articles, including those published in the agency's medical journal *Morbidity and Mortality Weekly Report* (MMWR). Occasional visitors may use the anonymous user feature, while frequent users are recommended to set up an ID and password at no cost. An example of a health alert posted on the Web site is an article entitled "Outbreak of Severe Acute Respiratory Syndrome—Worldwide, 2003," at http://www.cdc.gov/mmwr/preview/mmwrhtml/mm5212a1.htm.

HazDat (Agency for Toxic Substances and Disease Registry [ATSDR]) http://www.atsdr.cdc.gov/hazdat.html

This database on hazardous substance release and health effects contains information for specific contaminants, including health effects by route and duration of exposure, interactions of substances, susceptible populations, impact on population, community health concerns, and ATSDR public health threat categorization and recommendations.

WISQARS [Web-based Injury Statistics Query and Reporting System] (National Center for Injury Prevention and Control) http://www.cdc.gov/ncipc/wisqars

This interactive database provides access to statistical reports for fatal and nonfatal injuries, leading causes of death, and leading causes of nonfatal injuries. It includes data concerning death by noninjury causes such as disease, and injury causes such as violence, fire, motor vehicle accident, and poisoning. Data are available by year from 1981 to 2000, by age, race, sex, Hispanic origin, and state.

PubMed (National Library of Medicine [NLM])
http://pubmed.gov

This is a Web-based interface for searching the NLM's Medline, a bibliographic database that constitutes the most authoritative index of worldwide biomedical literature. Each retrieved record on PubMed features the article's title, author(s), primary author's institutional affiliation, selected abstracts, a link to related articles, and a link to the electronic version, if available. The primary audience is health care professionals and researchers.

MedlinePlus (National Library of Medicine)
http://medlineplus.gov

This consumer-oriented resource contains a collection of over 400 health topics, and a medical encyclopedia can be accessed through "Health Topics," which contains links to carefully selected and evaluated health resources. They are organized by categories that vary according to the health topic: general/overviews, anatomy/physiology, clinical trials, diagnosis/symptoms, prevention/screening, specific conditions/aspects, treatment, directories, and organizations, as well as age groups, ethnic groups, and gender. Other MedlinePlus features are drug information for generic and brand-name drugs; dictionaries; directories to locate health professionals and hospitals; and "Other Resources" to access organizations, consumer health libraries, databases, publications, and international sites. A link allows a search for a medical library by state.

COMPENDIUMS

Health and Healthcare in the United States: County and Metro Area Data (2nd ed., Nationshealth Corp., 2001)

This annual compendium of health-related statistics for each county and metropolitan area in the United States is intended as a quick reference source. The body is composed primarily of two tables. In Table A, State and County Data presents data in an alphabetical listing of each state with its respective counties. Table B, Metropolitan Area Data, presents data in an alpha-

betical listing of metropolitan areas. Statistical variables are similar for both tables and are grouped in four categories: population characteristics, vital statistics, health care resources, and Medicare. The latter two categories give useful data difficult to find elsewhere, such as type and number of health care facilities, various ratios of health care providers to persons, and numbers in several categories of Medicare recipients. A section follows that includes reference maps of counties and metro areas for each state. An accompanying CD facilitates data retrieval and manipulation.

Local Government Health Resources

State Resources

Michigan Hospital Report, May 1999 (Michigan Health and Hospital Association)

Consumers of health services will find hospital and health systems performance data and public health data at the county level. The report covers length of stay, mortality rates, and three-year trends for selected medical, surgical, and obstetrical cases. Medical cases include rates by county for cancer, diabetes, and stroke, which in Michigan are higher than the national averages.

Reportable Diseases and Conditions in Michigan
http://www.mappp.org/epi

Michigan local health departments submit electronically communicable diseases reports into a statewide reporting system. The reports are available online at this Web site, maintained by the Michigan Association of Public and Preventive Medicine Physicians and the Bureau of Epidemiology of the Michigan Department of Community Health. Statistical tables of reportable diseases and conditions by county or health department or statewide can be generated. Interactive maps by county are also provided.

County Resources

Oakland County [Michigan] Health Division Materials Center http://www.co.oakland.mi.us/health/program_service/mat_center.html

This is an example of a county information resource. Pamphlets, fact sheets, and audiovisual materials are available to the county residents on a variety of health topics and community resources. The latter include child health clinics, children's special health care services, health education and nutrition services, and women and children's services. Videotapes, cassette tapes, and slides may be borrowed for one week and must be requested either by phone or on a materials center request form at least two weeks in advance.

Public Health Alerts (Oakland County Health Division) West Nile Virus
http://detnews.com/2004/oakland/0408/12/004-239022.htm

The Oakland County, Michigan, Health Division issues these alerts to provide residents with an overview of imminent health threats, such as West Nile Virus, and measures of control and prevention against them.

Your Connection to Good Health: Healthy People ... Healthy Communities (Wayne County, Michigan, Department of Public Health, 2000)

This annual report contains very useful information on the various health services and programs available to county residents. These include dental services, vision and hearing screening, immunizations, a sexually transmitted disease clinic, maternal/infant support services, food programs of WIC (the Special Supplemental Nutrition Program for Women, Infants, and Children), HIV counseling and testing, and several health promotion and environmental health services.

City Resources

Community Information Database (Minuteman Library Network) http://library.minlib.net:81

This database was developed by the Minuteman Library Network, a consortium of libraries in Middlesex and Norfolk Counties, Massachusetts, and provides community members with local program, organization, and agency information via their public library Web site. Users can enter a keyword term (e.g., "mental health resources") and generate a list of related local resources. Each entry provides the organization's Web site, name, address, contact information, description, hours, areas served, and subject terms useful for cross-referencing.

Data Book (Detroit Department of Health, 1998)

This data book presents a picture of the health of the people of the city. Separate sections of the book address prominent health concerns and health problems such as heart diseases, cancer, communicable diseases, and teenage pregnancy. This publication is a good source for local statistical data.

SPECIALIZED/TOPICAL RESOURCES

Specialized Web Sites

Agency for Healthcare Research and Quality [AHRQ] http://www.ahcpr.gov

This Web site contains resources pertinent to both professionals and consumers and focuses primarily on access, quality, cost, and use of health care. Professional resources include research results data, surveys, tools, and evidence-based guidelines to improve the quality and safety of patient care, decrease ethnic and racial disparities, and expand knowledge of medical expenditures and health care cost and utilization. The Consumers and Patients Web site, http://www.ahcpr.gov/consumer, contains useful information for making informed decisions in areas such as prevention and treatment of various medical conditions, prescription medicines, health insurance, and health plans. AHRQ clinical practice guidelines for specific conditions are composed for two publications: one for professionals and one for consumers. They are available free from the National Guideline Clearinghouse, or online at http://www.guideline.gov.

Centers for Disease Control and Prevention http://www.cdc.gov

The CDC Web site provides access to statistical data, full-text reports, publications, downloadable software, and information on a variety of products developed and issued by its centers, institutes, and offices: National Center on Birth Defects and Developmental Disabilities, National Center for Chronic Disease Prevention and Health Promotion, National Center for Environmental Health, National Center for Health Statistics, National Center for HIV, STD, and TB Prevention, National Center for Infectious Diseases, National Center for Injury Prevention and Control, National Immunization Program, National Center for Occupational Safety and Health, Epidemiology Program Office, and Public Health Practice Program Office.

Statistical data from the *2001 State Health Profiles* series can be downloaded from the "Data Warehouse" page. This state-by-state annual publication provides the most current data on childhood health, vaccination coverage, prenatal care, environmental and occupational health, infectious and chronic diseases, and mortality. Print copies for individual states may be ordered from the Epidemiology Program Office.

Centers for Medicare and Medicaid Services [CMS] http://cms.hhs.gov/default.asp?fromhcfadotgov=true

Health care recipients and providers will find on the CMS's Web site description of programs and services, statistical data, laws and regulations, and local contact information pertinent to Medicare, Medicaid, and the State Children's Health Insurance Program (SCHIP).

Resources on Special Health Topics

2000 Epidemiologic Profiles of HIV/AIDS in Michigan (Michigan Department of Community Health, 2000)

This annual publication reports statewide and regional number and distribution of HIV/AIDS and cases of sexually transmitted disease by race, sex, age group, and mode of transmission. The profiles include a description of the HIV/AIDS epidemic among children, teenagers, and young adults, along with sections on different sexual behavioral groups and on rural versus urban issues.

Cancer Incidence in Massachusetts, 1994–1998, by Susan T. Gershman (Massachusetts Department of Public Health, 1999)

This report provides standardized incidence ratios for 23 types of cancers in the cities and towns of Massachusetts. Copies can be requested by contacting the Massachusetts Cancer Registry at MDPH, Mass. Cancer Registry, 6th Floor, 250 Washington Street, Boston, MA 02108-4619. Telephone: 617-624-5646, fax: 617-624-5697. It is also available online at http://www.state.ma.us/dph/bhsre/MCR/98/supplement/supplement98.htm.

The Oral Health Crisis in Massachusetts: Report of the Special Legislative Commission on Oral Health (Massachusetts General Court, 2000)

This report was mandated by the Massachusetts legislature's Health Access Act of 1997. A special commission investigated and reported on oral health status in the Commonwealth. The report is used by legislators, health care workers, researchers, and the public. It is available online at http://oralhealthcommission.com.

Resources on Consumer Health

CAPHIS [Consumer and Patient Health Information Section] (Medical Library Association) http://caphis.mlanet.org/directory

http://caphis.mlanet.org/consumer/index.html

This source provides consumer health information to librarians, the public, and others. The Web site includes a directory of consumer health libraries that is searchable by subject area and/or individual state. Directory listings include a description of the library and its holdings, contact information, hours of operation, and catalog and Web site information. The "Web sites You Can Trust" section provides a listing of the top 100 health care Web sites recommended by the MLA, including MedlinePlus, Healthfinder, National Women's Health Resource Center, and Ask NOAH About: Men's Health.

PERC Pathways [Patient Education Resource Center] (Comprehensive Cancer Center, University of Michigan) http://www.cancer.med.umich.edu/learn/percpathways.htm

These pathways are intended for newly diagnosed patients and their families. Users can select topics from three drop-down menus for adult cancers, childhood cancers, and cancer topics. Each entry lists downloadable fact sheets, informational Web sites, newsletters, articles, listservs, and organizations. Choices include all types of topics on cancer.

Resources on Injuries and Safety

Youth Risk Behavior Surveillance—United States, 2003 (Centers for Disease Control and Prevention, 2004) http://www.cdc.gov/mmwr/PDF/SS/SS5302.pdf

This resource from the Youth Risk Behavior Surveillance (YRBS) program of the National Center for Chronic Disease Prevention and Health Promotion reports on unintentional and intentional youth and young adult health-risk behaviors, including those that contribute to injuries, tobacco use, alcohol and other drug use, sexual behaviors, infection, unhealthy dietary behaviors, and physical inactivity. Data come from a national school-based CDC-conducted survey as well as state, territorial, and local school-based surveys. This is an MMWR doc available in both HTML and PDF formats, reachable from the YRBS homepage (http://www.cdc.gov/HealthyYouth/yrbs/index.htm), which also carries the questionnaire for 2005. This home page includes state fact sheets and a Power Point slide set for 2003 data.

Fast Stats A to Z [individual state data] http://www.cdc.gov/nchs/fastats/map_page.htm

This report summarizes mortality and morbidity statistics state by state and nationally. It provides information on births, deaths, marriages, divorces, and leading causes of death in two age groups: 10–24 years and 25 and older. It also reports on risk behaviors leading to death, including injuries, alcohol and other drug use, tobacco use, sexual behaviors, and physical activity. Each report is fairly detailed (20–50 pages) and the data is less than two years old.

Medical Guidelines: The Lead-Exposed Worker
(Commonwealth of Massachusetts, Department of Labor and Workforce Development, Division of Occupational Safety) http://www.state. ma.us/dos/leaddocs/Lead-MedGuide.htm

This online pamphlet explains lead standards and discusses the medical management of lead-exposed workers. It is geared to physicians and the medical profession. The Division of Occupational Safety, at http://www.state.ma.us/dos, provides similar pamphlets on other topics, such as asbestos, indoor air quality, and mine safety.

Resources for Special Populations

Resources for Children

Children's Mental Health Services: A Parent's Guide
(Idaho Federation of Families for Children's Mental Health, 2001)

This booklet is a practical resource for parents of children with serious emotional disturbance. There are highlights from the Children's Mental Health Services Act, followed by three sections: referrals, services/ rights and responsibilities, and agency contacts. Within each of the sections, information is provided for the State Department of Education, the Department of Health and Welfare, the Department of Juvenile Corrections, and the Idaho Federation of Families for Children's Mental Health.

Kids Count in Michigan 2000 Data Book: County Profiles of Child and Family Well-Being (Kids Count in Michigan project, 2000)

This book includes a section on asthma among Michigan children, discussing the causes, effects, risks, and interventions. Each county profile includes two tables: one on background and one on trends in child well-being. The background table provides the latest demographic data, including racial composition, statistics for teenage pregnancy rate, child care and

early education, family support, health care, children with disabilities, and juvenile justice. The trends table covers economic security, child health, child safety, adolescence, and education.

The "Kids Count in Michigan" project publishes other reports that provide the most current information on Michigan children with national comparisons. One such annual report with a focus on mothers and newborns in large urban centers is listed below.

The Right Start in Michigan's Largest Cities: The Status of Mothers and Babies in Michigan's 28 Largest Cities (Kids Count in Michigan project, 1990–2000) http://www.milhs.org/media/EDocs/ LargestCitiesSum03.pdf

Statistics include 10-year indicators of health for mothers and babies, including measurements such as the percentage of teen births, the percentage of births to unwed mothers, and the percentage of low-birth-weight babies. The Web site includes a profile of Detroit at http://www.milhs.org: select Kids Count, Right Start, cities, Detroit.

Similar publications can be obtained from individual states' Kids Count projects or from the National Kids Count project.

Resources for Women

Ohio Women's Health Clinics: Resource Guide 2000
(Ohio Department of Health, Office of Women's Health Initiatives)

This guide lists a selection of clinics, health care services, and health care providers in the Ohio area for women and children with limited income and insurance coverage. The guide includes information on health care plans and health insurance options such as a state health insurance plan offering free coverage for children up to age 19. This guide is not comprehensive and covers only the most common health issues. Contacts for various agencies and organizations are listed for additional resources.

Women of Color Health Data Book: Adolescents to Seniors (National Institutes of Health, 1998)

This report provides health data for Native American, Hispanic, black, and Asian American women. It is divided into three major sections: factors affecting the health of women of color, health assessment of women of color, and issues related to improving the health of women of color. References are provided at the end of each section. The report presents comparative data for various health conditions among different ethnic groups and among the same ethnic groups residing in different counties or cities of states where these groups are prevalent.

Resources for Men

African-American Health Initiative: Striving Toward a Healthier Future (Michigan Department of Community Health)

This trifolded brochure contains succinct facts on leading medical conditions specific to African American men and boys. The primary intent is to increase health-risk awareness and promote quality of life. Individual brochures are available on each of the leading health risks for African American men, such as heart disease, stroke, cancer, HIV/AIDS, and unintentional injuries.

Resources for the Elderly

Resource Directory for Older People in Maine (Bureau of Elder and Adult Services [BEAS], Maine Department of Human Services)

Older citizens of Maine can find here a wealth of publications relevant to medical conditions, health and mental health services, legal services, tax services, various assistance programs, and issues such as bioethics, age discrimination in employment, and consumer fraud.

Resource Directory for Older People (National Institute on Aging) http://www.nia.nih.gov/health/resource/rd2001.htm

This national resource has extensive links to all kinds of agencies and organizations. Most national agencies and organizations have state or regional affiliations that can be contacted for information on services available locally.

Know Your Rights: Your Medicaid Care and Coverage in a Nursing Home (Michigan Department of Community Health)

This booklet is of value to residents of nursing homes. Seven sections address many of their questions and concerns over rights, responsibilities, Medicaid coverage, services and supplies not covered by Medicaid, and a list of agencies. The FAQ section is very helpful and treats major issues in an easy-to-follow format. This publication may be complemented

by *Senior Citizens and Long-Term Care*, released by the Michigan Legislature. It supplies information on Medicaid eligibility and application, Medicare coverage, selection of nursing homes, and rights of nursing home residents.

Statistical Resources

Statistical Information on Older Persons (Administration on Aging) http://www.aoa.dhhs.gov/aoa/stats/statpage.html

This site provides links to statistical information on older populations in the United States. It includes "A Profile of Older Americans: 2000," a summary brochure that reports on key statistics on older Americans in 12 subject areas, including income, poverty, and housing. It also provides links to statistical tables, indicators, slides, and references from the *Older Americans 2000*.

Older Americans 2000: Key Indicators of Well-Being (Federal Interagency Forum on Aging-Related Statistics) http://www.agingstats.gov/chartbook2000/default.htm

This report gives detailed information on population, economics, health status, health risks and behaviors, and health care. Demographic profile data obtained from the Current Population Survey (CPS) conducted by the Census Bureau is also included. Statistical information includes data on centenarians, mobility, voting, foreign-born older Americans, projections to 2050, gender, minorities, grandparents and grandchildren, and housing. This is an excellent starting place for statistical information on older Americans for researchers, academic library users, and the general public.

HCUPnet [Healthcare Cost and Utilization Project] (Agency for Healthcare Research and Quality) http://hcup.ahrq.gov/HCUPnet.asp

This site helps users find and compare statistics on hospitals at the national, regional, and state levels. Data are extracted from the Nationwide Inpatient Sample (NIS), a stratified probability sample of approximately 20 percent of U.S. community hospitals, and the State Inpatient Databases (SID). A custom table is created for the user. The FAQ page gives the following examples of what HCUPnet can do for the user: What is the mean length of stay for patients with diabetes? What are the mean total charges for male versus female patients with hypertension? What percentage of patients with septicemia die in the hospital? Does this vary by age group? Does it vary by type of insurance? Does it vary by type of hospital or region of the country?

Users can select their query scope: national data, children's hospital data, national trends, or state data. Users can also specify whether they want general information on hospital stays or data on specific conditions and procedures. Researchers and health care professionals will find this a source of valuable information.

MEPSnet/IC [Medical Expenditure Panel Survey–Insurance Component] (Agency for Healthcare Research and Quality) http://www.meps.ahrq.gov/MEPSNet/IC/mepsnetic.asp

This resource provides national statistics and trends about health insurance. The information comes from the Medical Expenditure Panel Survey (MEPS), a national probability survey focusing on the costs and utilization of medical care in the United States. Survey data are from 1996, 1997, and 1998. Users can select whether they want information on employers, employees, or premiums. Additional options include the ability to specify firm size ranges, industry groups, ownership categories, age of firms, states, and Census divisions. Query results can be saved or downloaded. This resource is useful for policymakers, health care administrators, businesses, and researchers.

Bureau of the Census http://www.census.gov

A host of statistical information can be found through the Census Bureau Web site, including 2000 Population and Housing data, Economic Census data, Census block maps, and voting maps. The Bureau's resource, American FactFinder, allows users to view population, housing, and business statistics from the Decennial Census, the American Community Survey, and Economic Census reports and surveys. A good example is statistical information provided by the "Publications: Population" page, at http://www.census.gov/prod/www/abs/popula.html#income. Users can generate geographic comparisons and maps from population and housing data and from Economic Census data.

American Factfinder http://factfinder.census.gov/servlet/BasicFactsServlet

There are three main ways to use this Census Bureau resource. Users can type in a keyword search or a geographic keyword search and get a list of tables, maps, industry reports, and product listings. The second way is to use the "Start with Basic Facts" box. Users select either a table or map, then a suggested topic from the drop-down menu (e.g., race, population, age), then a geographic range (e.g., United States or a city or town). The corresponding quick table or thematic map will appear. The third way to access data is to select specific data sets from the Decennial Census, American Community Survey, and Economic Census reports and surveys. This option allows users to make their query very specific and choose whether they want summary information or detailed information. Tables and maps can be downloaded and printed.

Ambulatory Health Care Data (National Center for Health Statistics [NCHS]) http://www.cdc.gov/nchs/about/major/ahcd/ahcd1.htm

This resource contains data sets from the National Ambulatory Medical Care Survey (NAMCS), a general survey of ambulatory medical care services in the United States, and the National Hospital Ambulatory Medical Care Survey (NHAMCS), which focuses its collection of data on ambulatory care services in hospital emergency and outpatient departments. The site includes links to data highlights, including physician office visits, outpatient department visits, emergency department visits, sports injuries data for children and young adults, and ambulatory care data for 2000. Users can also download data set and documentation files from 1973–1999 NAMCS data and 1992–1999 NHAMCS data. This site also provides access to a PDF file of all NAMCS/NHAMCS publications and downloadable NCHS reports.

National Archive of Computerized Data on Aging [NACDA] (National Institute on Aging) http://www.icpsr.umich.edu/NACDA/index.html

The National Institute on Aging provides the largest library of electronic data on aging in the United States. Researchers can download data and produce cross-tabulations, descriptive statistics, and frequencies for selected studies using the archive's data analysis system, including *National Hospital Discharge Studies* (1994–1997), a longitudinal study on aging, and the *National Health and Nutrition Examination Survey II: Mortality Study*, 1992. Researchers can search for data by keyword or browse by subject. Each study is represented by an abstract that includes the study accession number, title, principal investigator, summary, extent of collection, extent of processing, series name, series description, data type, time period, date of collection, data source, data format, notes, sampling, universe, and bibliographic citation. Data can be downloaded and pages can be printed in a friendly format. The "Recent Updates and Additions" section lists studies that have been added within the previous 90 days. A selection of *Rand Family Life Surveys* is also included.

Substance Abuse and Mental Health Data Archive (Substance Abuse and Mental Health Services Administration [SAMHSA]) http://www.icpsr. umich.edu/SAMHDA/welcome.html

This archive database is for the use of primarily researchers, academics, policymakers, and service providers. Data files, documentation, and reports are available for downloading. Some of the data sets allow users to conduct analyses using an online data analysis system. Similar to the NACDA, it is also being archived by the Inter-university Consortium for Political and Social Research at the University of Michigan. Researchers can search by keyword or browse holdings by subject or study number. Sample subjects include health behavior in school-aged children, national pregnancy and health survey, and a D.C. Metropolitan Area drug study. Study abstracts contain the same fields as abstracts within NACDA.

Substance Abuse and Mental Health Statistics (SAMHSA) http://www.samhsa.gov/oas/ oasftp.cfm

SAMHSA provides information on the prevalence and incidence of substance abuse and mental health problems in the United States. This resource provides access to reports based on several major data collection systems: the *National Household Survey on Drug Abuse*, the *Drug Abuse Warning Network*, the *Drug and Alcohol Services Information System*, and other substance abuse treatment studies. Data can be accessed via links to short reports, state data, just-released reports, and recently released reports. A substance abuse facility locator is available and searchable by state.

Directory of Health and Human Services Data Resources (U.S. Department of Health and Human Services) http://aspe.hhs.gov/datacncl/datadir

This directory attempts to cover all major data collection systems sponsored by HHS. It can be used by policymakers, administrators, researchers, and the public to obtain information about various data collection systems. Each system is described in the following way: title, acronym, agency or program, description, race/ethnicity, data limitations, status (frequency of data collection and present status), how to access data, Web site, and contact person.

Data collection systems are arranged under major agencies and offices and then by program or sub-agency. Major agencies include the Office of the Secretary, Administration for Children and Families, Administration on Aging, Health Care Financing Administration, Agency for Healthcare Research and Quality, Centers for Disease Control and Prevention, Food and Drug Administration, Health Resources and Services Administration, Indian Health Services, National Institutes of Health, and Substance Abuse and Mental Health Services Administration.

CONCLUSION

There is a wealth of health information readily available to users in digital and print formats. Good starting points for finding information about your topic are with the U.S. Department of Health and Human Services and the National Institutes of Health sites listed in the General Web Sites section of this chapter.

The general public will be well served by consulting the directories profiled in this chapter. In addition, the public can often find answers to their questions by consulting reference librarians or community information databases at their public library or local hospital library.

Researchers and health professionals will want to consult agency Web sites, databases, statistical resources, and state libraries and federal agencies. Most of the resources available via the Internet provide contact information for follow-up.

CHAPTER 11
Finding Information on Crime and Criminals

Michael J. Kaminski and Dan Stanton

MAJOR TOPICS COVERED

MAJOR RESOURCES COVERED

INTRODUCTION AND OVERVIEW

Merriam-Webster's defines *crime* as "an act or the commission of an act that is forbidden or the omission of a duty that is commanded by a public law and that makes the offender liable to punishment by that law" (Collegiate Dictionary, 11th ed.). Because crime is defined with relation to *public* law, one would assume that information on crime and criminals would be readily available to the public and it is. The criminal justice system is a complicated response to the criminal act, an ever-evolving morass of people and policy. Information is readily available; the needs of the user determine what sources to investigate. There are a number of factors to keep in mind when beginning a search.

What is exciting is that with the explosion of electronic information, intellectual access and virtual access are available through Web pages and library online catalogs. As a result of the ability to use Geographic Information System (GIS) software in this arena, local access to information about crime and criminals is undergoing a revolution. Crime data can be organized in electronic databases and superimposed on maps made available through a police department's Web site. Sex offender information, sometimes even accompanied by photos, is also loaded into local databases and readily accessible on the Web. A 1997 Bureau of Justice Statistics study found that 35 percent of local police departments provided citizens with routine access to crime statistics by this means. For departments serving 100,000 or more, this percentage went up to 80 percent (Wartell and McEwen). These statistics and many more can be found in a report entitled *Privacy in the Information Age: A Guide for Sharing Crime Maps and Spatial Data*, published in July 2001 by the Crime Mapping Research Center of the Office of Justice Programs, a division of the U.S. Department of Justice. Guidelines for making crime-map information available to the public are provided and clearinghouses that have developed standards are listed.

Local police and sheriff's departments are making heavy use of new technology to provide the public with key information on crime and criminals, and even with the U.S. Justice Department providing numerous reports concerning local crime information available on the Web, many helpful sources of information remain in traditional print format. Many states publish annual reports on crime, usually based on participation by various local police agencies in the Federal Bureau of Investigation's (FBI) Uniform Crime Reports (UCR) program. Partnerships exist between government and academia to provide access to information such as the online provision of the Justice Department's *Sourcebook of Criminal Justice Statistics*, by the State University of New York at Albany. Many local governments utilize action plans for dealing with crime that were published prior to Web access and are available at libraries, especially those with local government documents collections. For a selective list of libraries with local documents collections, see page 318 of the *Directory of Government Document Collections and Librarians*.

Directory of Government Document Collections and Librarians (Congressional Information Service, 7th ed., 1997)

This directory is compiled by librarians active in GODORT (Government Documents Round Table), a group within ALA (American Library Association). This directory is compiled by surveys sent to Depository libraries throughout the country to collect information about their government-documents collections. It is the most comprehensive source of information about these libraries in existence. There is a directory of federal Depository libraries available through the GPO Access Web site, but it does not include information about state, international, foreign, or local government Depositories. The directory contains listings of libraries and include lists of libraries in the above categories, as well as some additional categories such as special collections, library-school instructors, state data centers, personal-name index, and association and government offices. The list of local government-documents collections begins on page 318. It refers to entries in the main section of the directory that include information such as the name, address, telephone number, and fax number of the library. Information about the collections, subject specialties, Depository information, and staff are included. Information such as public or private, fee or no fee, and circulation and interlibrary loan information is provided.

The particular local sources we highlight serve as examples of similar resources that may exist in other locations or jurisdictions. One can find local information on crime and criminals at three different levels and from four different types of sources. The levels are local, state, and national. The types of sources are government, private nonprofit organizations, commercial publishers/media, and academia.

Obviously local information should be obtainable through local sources, but with crime and criminal information, much of the data that are compiled within the jurisdiction get aggregated and analyzed further up the line at the state and national level. The prime example of this is the UCR program of the FBI, a bureau within the U.S. Department of Justice. These reports contain analytical information that is quite valuable because the data are collected at the local level.

GENERAL RESEARCH GUIDES

The following resources take the user through the research process from the initial topic selection to the identification of potential sources and their effective use to in-depth examinations of specific or specialized resources. Keeping in mind that criminal justice sources include books, journals, newspapers, government documents, statistical reports, and bibliographies—in print and online—these resources cover thousands of potential sources of information by type and subject area

Criminal Justice Information: How to Find It, How to Use It, by Dennis Benamati et al. (Oryx Press, 1998)

This publication is valuable to a variety of users because it explains the research process, provides an excellent array of print sources, and moves into the present and future by addressing the electronic information explosion and how both research resources and research methods are evolving. The preface mentions the ability of the modern researcher to work in "isolation" (translation: anywhere outside of the traditional library). The authors stress the importance of authorities—individuals or institutions (including publications)—that are recognized in the specific topical areas. The publication then reviews various reference sources, both general and specific, such as statistical or international sources. The final subject listing of Web sites is no longer particularly helpful. As if to demonstrate the pitfalls of online research, although the book was published in 1998, this section contains a number of bad links. Hopefully the user will be versed enough in research techniques to find a selective list of useful sites. A simple Google search (at http://google.com) will often retrieve the correct URL.

Criminal Justice Research in Libraries and on the Internet (Greenwood Press, 1997)

This publication is another good starting point for persons interested in attempting thorough research in criminal justice. This brings the excellent 1986 work *Criminal Justice Research in Libraries: Strategies and Resources* up to date by integrating electronic resources into the mix. This publication stresses the interdisciplinary nature of criminal justice and delves into research details providing information that would be useful to the advanced researcher or information professional. The book is set up to take the researcher through the planning stages, into specific types of sources and formats and the best ways to utilize them, and finishes with a section dealing with specialized areas such as legal and international research. The appendices are helpful in providing background information and resources such as Library of Congress subject headings (LCSHs) and major reports in criminal justice.

Because of the amount of criminal justice information available from the federal government (a book in itself), this chapter will describe some of the agencies that research, fund, and support criminal justice initiatives in the United States, as well as examples of the types of resources available. (Other, nonfederal national-level sources will be dealt with in later sections.) As crime exists in all facets of our society, resources on crime are not limited to criminal justice agencies in the federal government. For topical Internet searching of federal electronic resources, we sug-

gest FirstGov, at http://www.firstgov.gov, the federal government's general electronic portal; and Google at http://www.google.com/unclesam, a component of the powerful Google search engine limiting results to government domains. For assistance with further investigation, understanding, and access to federal resources, we strongly recommend contacting your local or regional federal Depository library, which is responsible for collecting and managing federal information (http://www.access.gpo.gov/su_docs/locators/findlibs/index.html).

United States Department of Justice
  http://www.usdoj.gov

The Department of Justice (DOJ) was established in June 1870 and is the law enforcement branch of the federal government, with a responsibility to every citizen of the United States. The DOJ fulfills its responsibilities in myriad ways. A listing of the many subagencies within it can be found at http://www.usdoj.gov/02organizations/02_1.html. Some of these components, such as Community Dispute Resolution (Office of Justice Programs), at http://www.ojp.usdoj.gov/eows/cdr, and Community Oriented Policing Services (COPS), at http://www.cops.usdoj.gov, are evidence that the DOJ is also very busy at the local level in ways that might not be apparent. Other agencies are also described and hot links provided to their Web sites.

DIRECTORIES/LISTS

Many of the sources mentioned in this chapter publish directories of information. Some of the resources offer information in the form of lists or searchable databases.

National Directory of Law Enforcement Administrators: Correctional Institutions and Related Agencies (National Public Safety Information Bureau, annual)

This publication (in its 37th edition) is written primarily to facilitate communications between law enforcement professionals, although the comprehensive information is valuable to anyone seeking to contact law enforcement agencies around the country. The directory boasts over 43,000 entries for departmental profiles and professional contacts, which include the chief or director's name, title, address, phone and fax numbers, number of sworn officers, and the population served. Information is presented alphabetically, by state and agency, and is updated annually.

State of California, Department of Justice—Directory of Services (State Attorney General's Office, 2000) http://caag.state.ca.us/ag/publications/directory.pdf

This state directory consists of a listing of the primary staff responsible for the provision of service, an alphabetical listing by subject matter of the services, and a brief description of services, with agency contact information. A listing of appropriate forms and agency publications follows. To further assist in locating a needed service, the index contains a detailed cross-reference of all subjects contained in the directory. It is published in paper and also available at the Web site.

Arizona Criminal Justice Agencies Directory (Arizona Criminal Justice Commission) http://acjc.state.az.us/pubs/services/2003ACJCdirectory.pdf

This is an example of a directory that lists many local government law enforcement agencies, including state offices, sheriffs and jails, police departments and precincts, courts, prosecutors, public defenders, federal agencies, and tribal agencies. This directory continues to be published in paper as well, and may be available at local public, academic, and law libraries with state government documents collections.

While most people approach the search for information to answer a simple question or find out what resources are available for a particular problem/issue, *research* takes information seeking to a higher level by attempting a systematic and (implicitly) thorough examination of data. The goal of research is to posit new knowledge by filling in information gaps or altering existing theories. Research has been made both easier and more complicated with the electronic age. It is easier, via speedy electronic searches through large databases, as opposed to the manual searching of one print index at a time. Searching is more complicated because of the sheer amount of information available to/from anyone with a computer and modem, and in the variety of ways that electronic databases function by following citations and using contact information and links to raw data, the researcher is encouraged to do further research. State government is a particularly good resource for directory and contact information.

STATISTICAL RESOURCES

At the national level, data collected by the state and localities are aggregated and summarized and become the baseline by which all data are compared. There is also strength in numbers. Once again, it is imperative that the user investigate the authority and credibility of the source, because information is easily manipulated and national credentials do not guarantee objectivity or the ability to draw sound conclusions from data. Also, changes in parameters for reporting can skew statistics terribly. This could involve changing age ranges or the definition of a reportable offense.

Bureau of Justice Statistics [BJS] http://www.ojp.usdoj.gov/bjs

The BJS was established in 1979 and is the United States' primary source for criminal justice statistics; online data are available from the early 1990s. BJS is responsible for collecting, analyzing, publishing, and disseminating crime-related information at all levels of government. The home page provides links to summary and detailed statistical information on a variety of crime, criminal, and justice topics. The summary information is useful for getting the big picture concerning crime in the United States. The reports section provides an abstract of the detailed information in a specialized crime area (e.g., corrections populations, police use of force), press releases of the report, Acrobat and ASCII files of the report, links to the raw data sets, and links to related Web sites. A link to "The Justice System," http://www.ojp.usdoj.gov/bjs/justsys.htm, provides an excellent explanation of the sequence of events in the criminal justice system. An alphabetical list of report titles is offered, with many reports broken down to the state jurisdiction level and sometimes lower. There are also links to outside sources of statistics for those who wish to dig deeper. Some recent examples of BJS publications are listed below.

Crime in the United States, Annual (FBI, annual) http://www.fbi.gov/ucr/ucr.htm#cius

This publication, the statistical culmination of law enforcement data collection at the city, county, and state levels, provides both a macro and a micro view of reported crimes. In terms of national statistical publications, this is the biggie. Although participation in the UCR program is voluntary, more than 17,000 law enforcement jurisdictions nationwide submit information. The reports are valuable snapshots of the nation, as these jurisdictions correspond to 254 million Americans, or 94 percent of the population. Because of jurisdictional differences in criminal codes, the data are not directly comparable (what is a felony in one place may turn out to be a misdemeanor in another). To get around this, the FBI report utilizes a crime index that generalizes reported offenses into universal categories. These categories are divided into violent crimes (murder and nonnegligent manslaughter, forcible rape, robbery, and aggravated assault), property crimes (burglary, larceny-theft, motor vehicle theft, and arson), and hate crimes. The only consistent correlate used in this report is population size. Any further investigation would need to take a myriad of factors (population density, economic conditions, citizen attitudes, etc.) into account before drawing conclusions. However, this publication still provides the most comprehensive listing of criminal statistics available since its inception in 1930. The data are presented in charts and tables, and are generally aggregated, with various temporal and geographic breakdowns. In addition to reported crimes, the publication presents information for offenses cleared via arrest, data on persons arrested, motor vehicle theft, and law enforcement personnel by locale. Several appendices give more detail regarding the process of putting this report together. How reported crimes are dealt with is given in another source, the *Sourcebook of Criminal Justice Statistics,* which is available for free at a Depository library, for sale in paper from the GPO bookstores, and online from the Web site listed below.

Sourcebook of Criminal Justice Statistics (Office of Justice Programs [OJP], Bureau of Justice Statistics, annual) http://www.albany.edu/sourcebook

This publication of criminal justice data is from a variety of governmental and nongovernmental sources. The data have been compiled by the Utilization of Criminal Justice Statistics project, located at the University of Albany since 1973. Whereas *Crime in the United States* focuses on reported crimes, the *Sourcebook* deals with the disposition of crime and with societal attitudes. The *Sourcebook* presents data in the form of tables and figures that are divided up into six sections: characteristics of criminal justice systems, public attitudes toward crime, nature and distribution of known offenses, characteristics and distribution of persons arrested, judicial processing of

defendants, and persons under correctional supervision. Each table includes source information for citation purposes for easy follow-up. Although most information is for states or the nation, there are some tables with city and regional information. One example is for crime rates for cities with over 100,000 population. An annotated list of sources and references is included, as is contact information for publishers of the data used. Appendices provide definitions of terms and summaries and methodologies of surveys used. Because some of the data come from opinion polls and surveys of those involved in the criminal justice system, the *Sourcebook* allows insight into the *perceived* status of criminal justice in the United States, providing an interesting perspective on the quantitative data. The publication is available for free at a Depository library, for sale in paper, and online at this Web site. Earlier editions of the *Sourcebook* are available on CD-ROM at Depository libraries and from the Bureau of Justice Statistics: http://www.ojp.usdoj.gov/bjs/sourcebook.htm.

Law Enforcement Management and Administrative Statistics, 1999: Data for Individual State and Local Agencies with 100 or More Officers (OJP, Bureau of Justice Statistics, 1999) http://www.ojp.usdoj.gov/bjs/abstract/lemas99.htm

This publication is the fifth and most recent report for the Law Enforcement Management and Administrative Statistics survey of all state and local agencies with at least 100 full-time sworn personnel. It is essentially a business report on law enforcement agencies, based on surveys returned from more than 700 state and local agencies nationwide. The surveys cover various subject areas: personnel (including salaries and expenditures), community policing, operations, information systems, and written policies. The data are reported in tables that break the information down by state, with further breakdown by county and specific agency. Commercial publishers, university social science departments, and private nonprofit organizations often produce crime and criminal-offender information independent of government agencies. These provide an alternative, if not always objective, viewpoint. Often they will take government information and try to add value to it. They usually accomplish this by reorganizing the data in subject-oriented fashion, often combining information links to or from several different sources in one location. These and other methods have the effect of making the resources more user friendly, so to speak, and enhance access to the information. Below are examples of a few resources that fit into this category.

Crime in America's Top Rated Cities: A Statistical Profile (Universal Reference Publications/Grey House, 2000)

Many people looking for local statistical information on crime and criminals are individuals about to relocate, businesspeople interested in locating a company, or simply people who are concerned about the crime situation in their city. They are likely to turn to one of several commercially produced sources. One of them is this publication. While using information from some private agencies, such as the National Center for Prosecution of Child Abuse and the Anti-Defamation League, the main sources for this volume are the UCR, the *Sourcebook of Criminal Justice Statistics*, and various DOJ reports.

In addition to summary information regarding UCR index crimes, this publication gives a quick snapshot of statistics on illegal-drug crimes; hate crimes; correctional facilities; inmates and HIV/AIDS; the death penalty; handgun, alcohol, and hate crime laws; anti-crime programs; the chances of becoming a victim; and whether or not there is legislation in place for requiring the identification of released sex offenders. It does this for 76 larger U.S. cities in the year-2000, third edition.

The reader is cautioned not to make comparisons between cities based on the information in this book. The data are based solely on population size, which is only one correlate for understanding the phenomenon of crime. While the FBI warns that such comparisons "often create misleading perceptions which adversely affect cities along with their residents," some other print sources do make such comparisons. One such is *City Crime Rankings*, from Morgan Quinto Press (Lawrence, Kansas). While this reference book ranks 300 cities nationwide, a host of larger notable cities (e.g., Pittsburgh, Chicago, Philadelphia) are missing from the comparison.

Justice Research and Statistics Association [JRSA]
http://www.jrsa.org/index.html

JRSA is a national organization of State Statistical Analysis Center directors, criminal justice professionals, and researchers from government, academic, and private institutions. It conducts research and provides training and technical assistance on a variety of criminal justice topics. Its Web site provides links to research, programs, and publications that JRSA has undertaken, localized research that individual states have done, and links to each state's Statistical Analysis Centers. The publication described below is published by the organization.

Crime and Justice Atlas (Justice Research and Statistics Association, 2001 update) http://www.jrsa. org/pubs/index.html

This publication provides a state-by-state breakdown of significant trends and initiatives in crime, justice, and expenditures over the past 20 years, with a focus on sentencing and corrections policies. While it is difficult to compare data state to state because of variations in the definitions of crimes and in prosecution and sentencing policies, it is helpful to be informed by the past while planning for the future. Since the JRSA exists to assist policymakers and administrators in using statistical information to make decisions, this is a great summary source for those interested in getting the broad picture as well as those interested in looking at a particular state. The 2001 update provides national-level summary information from 1960 to 1999 for violent crime, property crime, drugs, juveniles, prisons, and parole/reentry, along with a general summary of state crime legislation for the year 2000.

Crime Data Sources in Criminal Justice: How Crime Data Is Collected, Analyzed, and Put to Use http://faculty.ncwc.edu/toconnor/data.htm

This Web site is useful for the university student studying criminal justice information in that it brings together a plethora of links to criminal justice agencies of the government. These links are organized under three subject headings: Comprehensive, Topical, and State-by-State. It also points to tutorials in basic statistical concepts, which are useful in understanding crime data analysis. Examples of these tutorials are *Guide to Crime Statistical Analysis* and *Advanced Statistics for Criminology/Criminal Justice*.

NATIONAL, STATE, AND LOCAL RESOURCES

National

Office of Justice Programs (U.S. Department of Justice) http://www.ojp.usdoj.gov

Regarding DOJ relevance at the local level, the OJP figures prominently. Since its creation in 1984 by the

Justice Assistance Act, it has worked to form partnerships with federal, state, local, and tribal agencies and national and community-based organizations to develop, operate, evaluate, and improve programs dealing with crime prevention and control, criminal and juvenile justice, knowledge of crime-related issues, and assistance to crime victims. The OJP provides funding support, training, and technical assistance to local law enforcement agencies. It also conducts research, evaluates existing programs, and collects and publishes statistical information. It works through its five distinct but interrelated bureaus, each of which deserves mention. The Bureau of Justice Assistance (BJA) provides leadership and support of local criminal justice strategies. The Bureau of Justice Statistics (BJS) collects and reports crime and justice system statistics and assists state and local governments with statistical data. The National Institute of Justice (NIJ) administers and reports research to increase knowledge of effective practices and develops tools and technologies to assist criminal justice programs in the field. The Office of Juvenile Justice and Delinquency Prevention (OJJDP) assists in the development and utilization of effective prevention programs and an organized response to child victimization and juvenile delinquency through national leadership and support (states often have their own juvenile justice subdivisions). The Office of Victims of Crime (OVC) supports crime victims through compensation and other assistance programs designed to promote justice and foster healing. The OJJDP and OVC will be dealt with under Topical Resources. These agencies are described in more detail in their subject-related section.

Bureau of Justice Assistance (Office of Justice Programs) http://www.ojp.usdoj.gov/BJA

This agency provides information and funding to the law enforcement professional or the community activist, as well as information and funding for dealing with crime at the community level. There are links for funding opportunities, training, and technical assistance, publications highlighting effective real-world programs implemented across the country, and information about BJA-affiliated conferences. Links are provided to several federal programs that assist local law enforcement professionals with funding and/or informational resources to improve their ability to do their jobs. Links are also provided to nongovernmental organizations whose missions support improved criminal justice systems and safer communities. The following publication is a recent example from BJA.

The Role of Local Government in Community Safety
(OJP, Bureau of Justice Assistance, 2001)
http://www.ncjrs.org/pdffiles1/bja/184218.pdf

This publication highlights the trend of community members working in conjunction with local governments to assist in the provision of public safety. Community safety has evolved into a basic human right, and local leaders are constantly looking for ways to improve the situation for their locale. This report stresses leadership as the responsible and driving force for change in the criminal justice system and examines recent developments from around the world, provides a framework for addressing community safety, examines issues that complicate the process, and highlights specific real-world programs that are considered exemplary attempts at working within the community safety framework.

National Institute of Justice (U.S. Department of Justice) http://www.ojp.usdoj.gov/nij

The NIJ is the research and development arm of the DOJ, tasked solely with researching crime control and justice issues. The NIJ provides knowledge, technology, and tools that state and local criminal justice professionals can use in addressing their crime-related issues. Links to publications are broken down by topic (law enforcement, courts, corrections, science and technology, investigative sciences, drugs and crime, victims, crime prevention, international, and research and evaluation) and then by year of publication. Links are also provided to a variety of NIJ-sponsored programs, ranging from the Arrestee Drug Abuse Monitoring (ADAM) program, which studies the links between drug use and crime, to the Violence Against Women and Family Violence Research and Evaluation (VAW&FV) program, which promotes the safety of women and family members and attempts to improve the criminal justice system's response to these crimes.

Mapping and Analysis for Public Safety (Office of Justice Statistics)
http://www.ojp.usdoj.gov/nij/maps

Formerly the Crime Mapping Research Center, this is another useful source of local information. It explains the significance of crime mapping as a tool used by law enforcement professionals at all levels and contains links to jurisdictions that have this type of data available online.

National Criminal Justice Reference Service [NCJRS] http://www.ncjrs.org

The NCJRS serves as a clearinghouse for information offered through its federal partner agencies—the OJP (which includes the five agencies outlined above) and the Office of National Drug Control Policy, based in the executive office of the president. The Web site offers access to many reports having to do with corrections, courts, drugs and crime, international crime-related issues, juvenile justice, law enforcement, victims of crimes, and statistics. Many of the services and resources are available for free (including shipping of up to five items) to the general public. Some items, such as the *Community Policing in Action* video, are available for a fee. In addition to past reports, the NCJRS offers opportunities to stay current via e-mail newsletters and other electronic mailing lists.

State

At the state level, information on crime and criminals is available from several different areas: the attorney general's office (which is separate from the executive branch at the state level), the governor's office, and independent boards and commissions. Each state has a different emphasis on the information provided by these agencies, but the descriptions below should apply to most states.

At the attorney general's office, one can find the numbers and statistics on crime, victim's services information, crime prevention programs, and reports on various hot topics like hate crimes and sex offender registries.

The governor's office is usually responsible for dealing with oversight of corrections and public safety. Most states have a department within the executive branch with this responsibility. Some states provide a separate department for juvenile justice. The state police and/or highway patrol reports to the governor. These agencies may also fall under what is called a Department of Public Safety. A few governors in states like Georgia and Pennsylvania are sponsoring a Geographic Information System (GIS) clearinghouse, such as the one at http://gis.state.ga.us/Clearinghouse/clearinghouse.html, which confirms the trend toward publishing crime maps and related statistics on the Web.

Most states use the data in the monthly UCR submissions as the basis for their official annual crime reports. These reports carry names like *Crime in Texas*, or *Uniform Crime Report: The Commonwealth of Pennsylvania*, or *The State of Tennessee: Uniform Crime Report*. Aside from some introductory text and descriptive information, these reports use easy-to-read graphics, tables, charts, and summaries to convey a greater degree of detail than the national report from the FBI. In the case of Texas, the final and most extensive chapter of the report provides a listing of index crimes by individual jurisdiction. It should be noted that these are data regarding crime information that was *reported* to the police in each state, not necessarily the actual amount of crime committed, as some instances go unreported. Like the national report, there is a section providing information about the law enforcement personnel employed in the state, and the number of times they were assaulted or killed in the line of duty.

Crime in Texas (Texas Department of Public Safety)

The state reports also provide additional data on crimes beyond the simple UCR index list (homicide, sexual assault, robbery, aggravated assault, burglary, larceny-theft, vehicle theft). Texas, for example, provides separate summary data on family violence and campus crime and data for selected nonindex crimes like drug abuse, weapons violations, DUI (driving under the influence), and drug seizures. Information on hate or bias crimes is now required as part of the UCR and is made available in the state reports as well. In Texas, incident-based reporting (IBR), which is a more detailed system that has not yet caught on in a big way, is converted to summary form and included in this report. With only 50 law enforcement agencies in Texas reporting IBR data at this time, compared with 956 for UCR, there was no separate publication for this information as of 2001.

Criminal Justice Policy Council Biennial Report to the Governor and the 77th Texas Legislature: The Big Picture in Adult and Juvenile Justice Issues (Criminal Justice Policy Council, January 2001)

This report contains extensive numbers, summary information, and trend analysis that busy legislators need in order to get a handle on the overall criminal justice picture and to make informed policy decisions. For these same reasons it is valuable to researchers and the general public as well. It starts by reviewing, in outline form, the present policies and past accomplishments of the legislature. It proceeds to outline where the Council believes the legislature's attention needs to focus, and finally makes concrete recommendations and requests for appropriations. It does all this through the use of outlines and easy-to-follow charts, graphs, and tables, thus packing a lot of useful information into a single report.

Arizona Criminal Justice Commission [ACJC] http://www.acjc.state.az.us

The ACJC was created by state statute in 1982 to assist in the administration and management of criminal justice programs in Arizona. It is responsible for assisting with service areas including legislation/policy/grants, drug control and system improvement, criminal justice records, statistical analysis center, and victim services. The Web site provides links to Arizona state and local criminal justice agencies and programs as well as federal Web sites. The ACJC is important as the administrator of federal funds and as the collector/analyzer/reporter of criminal justice statistics and other information for the state of Arizona. Convicted-offender information is also available on the state level. The information made available is in line with the particular state's open records act. Currently some states are making this information easily available over the Web, while others provide a discussion of the applicable law and telephone numbers to request such information.

Florida Department of Corrections http://www.dc.state.fl.us/inmateinfo/inmateinfomenu.asp

This site may be an indicator of the direction in which the availability of the Internet will lead many agencies. It provides standard personal information about the offender as well as a photograph, the facility in which he or she is detained, the cell number and inmate number, the crime for which the inmate is being held, incarceration history, and information on possible release dates. There is also a list of prison escapees since 1990.

State of Texas, Sex Offender Database (Texas Department of Public Safety) http://records.txdps.state.tx.us/soSearch/soSearch.cfm

Title 42, chapter 136, subchapter VI, section 14071 of the U.S. Code requires state attorneys general to es-

tablish guidelines for programs that require persons convicted of a criminal offense against a child to register their place of residence so that communities may be notified of their presence. Many states have mounted extensive Web sites for the purpose of notification. However, each contains a strongly worded disclaimer about the information presented. The burden of responsibility for the use of the information contained in the database is leveled squarely on the user in order to leave law enforcement free of liability.

Local

Whenever a police officer is dispatched, there is an immediate paper trail that becomes publicly available government information. The majority of the time, calls for service do not result in the reporting of a crime, but rather deal with noncrime events like a cat in a tree, false burglar alarms, or a citizen requesting police assistance. According to the San Antonio, Texas, Police Department, for every 100 calls for service, 10–20 will involve minor crimes and another 10 will deal with serious UCR index crimes (homicide, sexual assault, robbery, assault, burglary, theft or vehicle theft). No matter what the circumstances, if you want to find out why a police car stopped two doors down from you in the middle of the night on a certain date, you can consult the list of neighborhood calls for service at your local police department, obtain a case number, and request a copy of the report. There is usually a small charge associated with this service.

Police departments in most urban areas have sophisticated Web sites from which anyone with a computer can obtain statistical information and basic facts. What previously involved a time-consuming and sometimes costly trip to the police department can now be accessed with a few keystrokes. Crime mapping and other information on the Web can facilitate cooperation with other agencies. There are indeed some problems with providing crime and criminal information in this manner. These problems deal mainly with privacy issues, especially privacy for sexual assault victims. While specific point information is generally available in paper copies of crime reports, there has traditionally been an informal agreement to not post such information for mass dissemination. The Supreme Court has endorsed this notion, in *U.S. Department of Justice v. Reporters Committee* (489 U.S. 749), and so to avoid the many privacy issues involved with providing crime data and statistics on the Web, some departments choose to limit the information to an aggregate, rather than provide specific point information. In other words, they'll give the neighborhood or even perhaps the street, but not a particular house number (Wartell and McEwen).

The following are some exemplary police department Web sites that provide crime mapping and statistical data:

The San Diego, California, Police Department
http://www.sannet.gov/police

This department was one of the first in the country to provide static crime maps and summary information about crime over the Web. Its site includes crimes by neighborhood for 2000 and 2001, crime rates per 1,000 population, historical crime data, and rates for the entire city dating back to 1950, in addition to college and university crime data. It also provides the most recent 30 days of information by neighborhood and a photo listing of the "top 10 most wanted" in the San Diego area. What really sets the San Diego area apart is that all law enforcement agencies—federal, state, and local—in the county of San Diego have joined together to create the first regional interactive crime-mapping Web site, Automated Regional Justice Information System, at http://www.arjis.org. Users can create customized crime maps and/or reports based on a particular date, time, neighborhood, or type of crime. The interface has three categories—crime and disorder, arrests and citations, and vehicles and traffic. The information is used by law enforcement for tactical analysis, investigations, statistical information, and crime analysis. It appears to be the wave of the future for keeping the citizenry informed as well.

The San Antonio, Texas, Police Department
http://www.ci.sat.tx.us/sapd/?res=1024&ver=true

This site, one in the latest generation of Web design, is very user friendly in that it provides detailed information to the public on how to search for crime information both at the Web site and through more traditional means. It is a prime example of how local law enforcement is attempting to draw the public into a useful partnership with police to more effectively understand and solve community crime problems. Regularly updated static crime maps based on data for the UCR are posted, as well as specific information and trends related to sexual assault, domestic violence, and historical trends dating back five years.

University of Tampa Campus Crime Report
http://www.ut.edu/directory/administration/crp2000.html

All colleges and universities must make their crime data publicly available, in accord with the Campus Security Act of 1990. Noncompliance leads to disqualification from participation in federal student loan programs. While some local police departments provide this information on their Web sites, the individual school or its police or security department is the best place to access this information.

The University of Tampa, like most schools, makes this information available on its Web site, along with a brief but helpful explanation of the corresponding law, and with links to other pages related to campus safety. For examples of attitudes toward crime and statistics from schools around the country, see http://nces.ed.gov/surveys/ssocs.

It is unclear how widespread the trend is, but there are examples of private media sites providing access to crime mapping services:

NewsOK.com (KWTV, Channel 9, Oklahoma City)
http://www3.kwtv.com/television

This TV news site provides a somewhat quick and dirty lookup of crime data based on a provided address. The data are limited to an established aggregate level in order to protect privacy rights. The availability of this information directly from police department Web sites, in more complete and detailed form, may be leading the media to discontinue duplication of this service.

Inmate information is undergoing a similar revolution. Now many agencies are providing inmate information lookup services over the Web. While information is still limited to individual inmates, one usually needs little more than a last name, or partial last name, to gain access to publicly available information on particular offenders, such as age, date of birth, height, weight, the particular crime committed or charged with, the particular court the inmate appeared in, and possible release dates.

San Diego, California, Sheriff's Department
http://www.co.san-diego.ca.us/cnty/cntydepts/safety/sheriff

Along with a 10 most wanted list for the county, this site provides "Booking Log," "Who's in Jail," and "Arrest Warrants" lists. These are searchable by last name, but are not browsable.

BCSO [Bexar County, Texas, Sheriff's Office] Sex
Offender Listing http://www.co.bexar.tx.us/
BCsheriff/Sex%20Offenders/portal.htm

Under the most recent law, state attorneys general
are responsible for implementing programs that notify
the public of the residence of released sex offenders, so
state databases are likely to be the most thorough and
up-to-date. Bexar County's database posted on the Web
is an example of what some local authorities are under-
taking. Hyperlinked zip codes of the unincorporated
areas of the county take one to a photo with address
and descriptive information on each convicted offender. Some are ranked as to their risk (low, moderate,
high) of repeat offending. This is an excellent source
for those wanting historical information on what has
been done in a particular area and how concerned citizens in that area view the problem. Many libraries with
federal and state documents collections also collect an
array of such local government documents. They are a
good starting point for researching the local political
scene in terms of crime and criminals.

TOPICAL RESOURCES

Victims

Office for Victims of Crime [OVC]
http://www.ojp.usdoj.gov/ovc

The OVC was established in 1984 through the Victims of Crime Act and is charged with overseeing federal programs that assist victims of crimes. As of
January 2002, the OVC Web site was dominated by
news and resources related to the September 11, 2001,
tragedy, widely interpreted as producing a nation of
victims. Other helpful links provide contact information for state victim assistance and compensation programs that administer local victims programs funded
by the federal government. OVC also provides links to
training and technical assistance opportunities in
areas as diverse as children who witness violence,
hate crimes, and sexual assault. An alphabetical list of
links by crime type is available to assist victims of
specific-circumstances crimes (such as campus crime
or workplace violence). A range of OVC publications,
available online or for order in print, are offered to assist crime victims themselves, as well as the people
and institutions whose lives are touched by victims of
crime. A list of resources for international victims is
provided because, as we have seen over and over,
crime (and its victims) has no boundaries.

Prevention

*Preventing Crime: What Works, What Doesn't, What's
Promising* (U.S. DOJ, Office of Justice Programs,
1997) http://www.ncjrs.org/works/wholedoc.htm
http://www.ojp.usdoj.gov/nij/pubs-sum/
171676.htm (1998 Summary)

In 1996 Congress mandated that the attorney general provide an evaluation of the effectiveness of DOJ
crime prevention grants of over $3 billion annually to
state and local law enforcement agencies and communities. The evaluation needed to be independent of
the government and scientific in nature. The University of Maryland's Department of Criminology and
Criminal Justice was selected to perform the research
and presented its findings in 1997 after a review of
over 500 prevention-program evaluations. This report
is useful for assessing whether existing (or future)
community crime prevention programs are worth the
resources. Many of the prevention programs evaluated are common in communities across the country:
extra police patrols in high-crime areas, Drug Abuse
Resistance Education (DARE) campaigns in schools,
neighborhood watch programs, proactive drunk driving roadchecks, battered women's shelters, etc. The
results were classified into four categories: what
works, what doesn't, what's promising, and what's
unknown. Programs that work were judged to prevent
crime or reduce risk factors in the social settings in
which they had been evaluated; the findings could be
generalized for other similar settings. Programs that
don't work were reasonably certain to fail to prevent
crime in the social settings evaluated. Programs that
are promising were those where evidence was not
conclusive enough to generalize that they would
work, but further attempts and studies could support
that conclusion. Programs whose effectiveness was
classified as unknown were those that fell outside the
other categories usually due to the inability to evaluate results properly.

National Crime Prevention Council [NCPC]
http://www.ncpc.org

NCPC had its start in the late 1970s as a public service advertising campaign envisioned by the FBI director and featuring "McGruff, the Crime Dog,"
enjoining citizens to "take a bite out of crime." The
advertising campaign was so successful that NCPC
was founded as a nonprofit organization whose goal

was to assist in the prevention of crime at the individual and community level

The Web site provides a number of informative and action-oriented links through which individuals and communities can learn, plan, and act on stopping crime through prevention. Children and teens are special prevention populations that NCPC attempts to assist through specific programs for youth and for their caregivers. An online library is available with information in the form of bibliographic citations or hot links to articles such as "Neighborhood Watch Gets Residents Prepared" (http://www.ncpc.org/ncpc/ncpc/ ?pg=2088-6106), Web sites on various topics, ordering information for NCPC publications, and the monthly newsletter, the *Catalyst*, a fitting title for an organization that invites the nation to action, as individuals and as community members.

Juveniles

Office of Juvenile Justice and Delinquency Prevention http://ojjdp.ncjrs.org

The OJJDP has its origin in the Juvenile Justice and Delinquency Prevention Act of 1974 and subsequent amendments and is responsible for assisting with the specialized needs of the youth population in the criminal justice system. The Web site provides links to statistical information, resources on grants and other funding, and resources on a variety of topics, including parenting and geographic areas. Links are provided for initiatives being attempted and the local jurisdictions making the efforts. Also provided are links to full-text publications, OJJDP-sponsored events, and other information such as the "Drug Free Communities Support Program" (http://ojjdp.ncjrs. org/dfcs/index.html).

FOR FURTHER READING

Wartell, Julie, and J. Thomas McEwen. "The Problem of Crime Mapping and Data Confidentiality." In *Privacy in the Information Age: A Guide for Sharing Crime Maps and Spatial Data*, 1–5. Washington, DC: U.S. Department of Justice, National Institute of Justice, Crime Mapping Research Center, 2001. http://www.ncjrs.org/pdffiles1/nij/ 188739.pdf (accessed September 10, 2004).

CHAPTER 12
Finding Local Government Map Resources

Mary Martin

MAJOR TOPICS COVERED

Introduction
General Map Resources
  Guides
  Directories
Online Resources/Web Sites
  General Web Sites
  Specialized Web Sites
  Specialized/Topical Map Resources
  Gazetteers
  Special Use Maps
Map Collections
  Libraries
  Depositories
  Publishers/Catalogs

MAJOR RESOURCES COVERED

Maps for America: Cartographic Products of the U.S. Geological Survey and Others
The National Map: Topographic Mapping, USGS Geo-Data, and Aerial Photographs and Satellite Images
Guide to U.S. Map Resources
The World Map Directory: A Practical Guide to U.S. and International Maps

Facsimiles of Maps and Atlases: A List of Reproductions for Sale by Various Publishers and Distributors
International Map Trade Association Membership Directory
USGS National Mapping Information
MapQuest
Maps.com
City Map Sites
MAGIC
Columbia Gazetteer of the World
New England Gazetteer
U.S. Gazetteer
Geographic Names Information System
National Atlas of the United States
Sanborn Fire Insurance Maps
Map Collections in the United States and Canada: A Directory
Map Libraries on the World Wide Web
Directory of Government Document Collections and Librarians
Ordering U.S. Geological Survey Products
Thomas Brothers
TopoZone.com

INTRODUCTION

Maps are used for a wide variety of purposes. A map could be needed to find the location of a city or town, street or business. One could be looking for an airport, a train station, or a port of a river or bay. Maps offer countless possibilities for looking for information. You would use one to get somewhere, look for something, plan something, or get a general idea of what a place is like. Searching for maps of any kind is both an overwhelming and a rewarding experience. There are thousands of maps available for all geographic areas and time periods. Among the many types of maps are street maps, parcel maps, planning maps, topographic maps, and orthophoto maps. When looking for a map of a local geographic area, a map can often be found at the local Automobile Club or at a local library. The largest mapping authority is, of course, the United States Geological Survey, and now that most map information is digitized, most maps are creating by using digitized data. The Geological Survey and its new mapping agency, the National Imagery and Mapping Agency (NIMA), provide much of the digitized data available. Other agencies that create maps are the Bureau of Land Management, the U.S. Forest Service, the National Park Service, the Army Corp of Engineers, the Defense Mapping Agency, the National Ocean Survey, and many others. State, county, and city government agencies also produce maps. Some of the sources that produce maps available for local geographic information are described in further detail.

Another major source of maps is the commercial map publishers. There are commercial map producers that sell maps, and some that make them available for free. Major map publishers include Rand McNally Inc.; the American Automobile Association; gasoline companies such as Mobil Oil, Exxon, and Chevron; and Thomas Brothers. Some publishers such as MapQuest and MapLink advertise and sell maps from a Web site. Nonprofit societies such as the National Geographic Society and the Sierra Club also have maps available.

GENERAL MAP RESOURCES

Guides

Maps for America: Cartographic Products of the U.S. Geological Survey and Others, by Morris M. Thompson (3rd ed., U.S. Geological Survey [USGS], 1987)

This resource by a retired cartographer of the USGS describes and explains maps and their uses, from the development of mapping in America to the publication of the book. It contains a brief historical perspective and descriptions of kinds of maps and kinds of map data. There are detailed descriptions and diagrams of what natural and cultural features appear on maps, with lots of illustrations and explanations. Boundaries are explained in a chapter, and there are special chapters on topographic maps, geologic mapping, land use maps, and space-age maps. The National Ocean Service merits a special chapter, as its mapping activities are so extensive. The National Park Service and the Bureau of Land Management create and publish maps of vast territories held by the federal government. For example, the Coconino National Forest in Arizona is a vast tract of land managed by the federal government. The Defense Department, of course, has extensive mapping activities for its purposes. In 1974, the National Cartographic Information Center was established to make cartographic data more readily accessible to the public. At the time when Thompson's book was published, it may not

have been anticipated that a user could sit at a computer in her home and have topographic maps drawn and available to her in a matter of seconds.

Products of other commercial and geographic organizations are briefly described, but because of the date of the book, digitized mapping is discussed only in terms of future development. This resource is very useful in describing particular maps and their features and is easy to read, with numerous photographs and examples. There is a subject index, a limited list of agency addresses, and a glossary of terms. This book was a Depository item and should be held by Depository and map libraries.

The National Map: Topographic Mapping (2001), *USGS GeoData* (2000), and *Aerial Photographs and Satellite Images* (1995) (U.S. Geological Survey)

These are several in a series of pamphlets put out by the USGS that describe some of the maps and mapping services available from the agency. There are descriptions of the data collected, what kinds of maps are currently being generated, and where that particular technology is going in the future, along with examples of applications of the data, information on how to obtain them, descriptions of products and software, and Web addresses of where to obtain further information. The USGS Web site is detailed in a separate section in this chapter.

Guide to U.S. Map Resources (American Library Association, 1990)

This resource is a fairly comprehensive listing of map libraries and collections, with detailed information including addresses, telephone numbers, contact persons, collection strengths, holdings, chronological coverage, hours of service, and services available to the public. The book is arranged geographically by state, then alphabetically by city. Each entry is numbered, and there are extensive indexes of Earth Science Information Centers and libraries/institutions.

Although dated, the book is still valuable for locating libraries and collections, although telephone numbers and contact numbers have probably changed in some places. It also contains no e-mail or Web page addresses. Updated information can be found in some of the directories available on Web sites.

Directories

Directories are useful for determining what maps are available and where to locate them. There are many map directories, some covering a particular area and some a particular topic, such as historical maps of New England or nautical maps.

The World Map Directory: A Practical Guide to U.S. and International Maps, by Aaron Maizlish and William Tefft (Map Link, 1992–93)

This volume is a directory of map sources organized by geographic area. The publisher is a retailer and wholesaler of maps. The directory is comprehensive, listing many sources other than Map Link (of course, Map Link may be the easiest way to get the map). The name of the place is indexed, and under that section in the book is a listing of map resources available for that place. Information listed includes the map name, the Map Link code, the price, the scale, and the date of the map. For example, an entry looks like this:

Maine: Cities

Bangor	2.50	na	nd	ARO BANGOR
Bangor, Brewer	2.50	na	nd	DELO BANGOR
Portland, Greater	2.50	na	1987	ARO PORTLAND
Portland, Greater	2.50	na	nd	DELO PORTLAND

This directory is good for determining what map is available for a particular geographic area, a task that is difficult unless you travel to that area—and even then!

Facsimiles of Maps and Atlases: A List of Reproductions for Sale by Various Publishers and Distributors, compiled by Barbara R. Noe (Geography and Map Division, Library of Congress, 1980)

Although this publication is dated, it is obviously of great value, as the Map and Geography Reading Room of the Library of Congress uses it for reference. Although current maps are relatively easy to find, historical maps can be much more difficult to locate. Not only do places and place names change over time, but also geographic and man-made features. This makes the process more complicated. First, the date and general location need to be determined, and then one can decide where would be the best place to look for the map.

Although Web directories update this book, it is significant that one of the largest map library collections in the world considers it an important reference source. It lists outlets and retailers for map purchase

by name and has a geographic arrangement. An example of a map for sale is that for Jefferson County, Kentucky, in 1858 (reprinted 1978), published by the G. T. Bergman company of New York City. This map shows names of property holders, division lines of farms, position of houses, churches, schoolhouses, roads, watercourses, distances, and topographic features of the county. Actual dimensions are listed, along with the price, $18.75.

This resource would be useful if one wanted to purchase a map. It possibly might not be available in a library nearby, and buying it is actually the easiest way to obtain the map. It wouldn't be the easiest way to find a current map.

International Map Trade Association Membership Directory (IMTA, 1997–98)

This is an extensive directory listing of members of the International Map Trade Association, arranged geographically by world area, state, country, and city, with each member organization listed alphabetically after that. Although it contains no addresses, it gives telephone numbers that may or may not be accurate. There is also a listing by name. The organization or any of its member retailers would be a major resource in any particular geographic area. This directory is updated periodically.

ONLINE RESOURCES/WEB SITES
General Web Sites

USGS National Mapping Information (U.S. Geological Survey) http://mapping.usgs.gov

This is the official Web site for the USGS, the largest mapping service in the world. Information is available on all types of maps it creates. Access to an online atlas, described below, and the Geographic Names Information Web site are general reference tools. A fairly new product is the National Map, which provides a full range of services related to maps from the United States. The site provides access to digital maps by allowing a user to view USGS Maps and Aerial Photo Images Online, at http://mapping.usgs.gov/partners/viewonline.html. There are so many maps available from the USGS and its partners that filtering through all of the information on the Web site takes considerable effort. It is possible to view maps of particular areas online, usually from a more specialized Web site, such as MAGIC at UConn (see the profile below). The USGS Web Site provides very sophisticated images such as satellite and remote sensing, aerial photographs, and Digital Raster graphics. There is a selection of maps available for downloading and viewing, but the program warns that it requires additional software to actually view the maps. In the future, the USGS is planning to provide a service that will create a type of map vending machine—the Survey and Wildflower Productions, a San Francisco–based digital map company, are exploring new technology that will let a user walk into a USGS office and print a customized topographic map from a self-service kiosk. The Web site allows users to download and view maps of differing geographic subjects, but a certain amount of knowledge about software applications is required. It also includes links to maps, aerial photographic resources, digital cartographic resources, digital satellite data, and software product retailers. This Web site provides comprehensive information about all maps and mapping services available from the USGS.

MapQuest http://www.mapquest.com

MapQuest allows a map to be created and printed and also provides driving directions from one point to another anywhere in the United States. First the address of the starting point is entered, and then that of the destination. If the addresses can be located in the database, then driving directions are generated. A map can be created and printed at several different magnifications. This service is primarily for travel or business, and the maps are not really detailed. It is possible to navigate from one place to another on the maps, but the directions do not always provide the shortest route possible. For example, if directions are requested for 325 N. Indian Hill Boulevard, Claremont, California 91711, a corresponding map is generated. This is a useful Web site, particularly if only general directions and orientations are needed. Yahoo Maps, http://maps.yahoo.com, provides a service similar to MapQuest. Both are designed for general directions. Yahoo provides maps for some countries in Europe and the United Kingdom.

Maps.com http://www.maps.com

This company was founded in 1991 as Magellan Geographix. Maps.com the company provides mapping solutions to the business-to-consumer, business-to-business, and business-to-education marketplaces. Maps.com the Web site is a combination of content

and commerce offerings, which attracts over 2 million unique users per month and consistently ranks among the most-visited travel Web sites.

Specialized Web Sites

City Map Sites http://www.lib.utexas.edu/Libs/PCL/ Map_collection/map_sites/cities_sites.html

The Web site is actually a part of the Perry-Castañeda Library Map Collection at the University of Texas at Austin. Most entries are direct links to general Web sites that provide city maps and links to actual city Web sites that have maps for that particular city. For instance, the map for Anchorage, Alaska, is a street map (of moderate detail, showing major streets and landmarks) provided by Alaska Information Services. The city-map link for White Rock, New Mexico, created by Virtual Los Alamos, is more complete. It includes roads by type and name, major points of interest, such as churches and schools, and recreational places like golf courses and parks. An interesting entry of note is a historical map of Buffalo, New York.

The listings on this Web site are alphabetical and international in scope. The site is updated regularly and is a good place to check, although the numbers of cities included is limited.

MAGIC [Map and Geographic Information Center] (University of Connecticut, Homer Babbidge Library) http://magic.lib.uconn.edu

This Web site has been created and maintained by the map librarian at the University of Connecticut (Storrs, Connecticut) and is actually a research center that provides access to spatial data, primarily for the state of Connecticut. It has digitized maps down to the state level, county level, town level, quad level, the Hartford MDC (Metropolitan District Commission), New England, and the United States at scales of $1° \times 2°$ 1:250 000 and $30' \times 1°$ 1:100 000. If these symbols are unknown or confusing to you, there is a link to the online version of the *Dictionary of Abbreviations and Acronyms in Geographic Information Systems, Cartography, and Remote Sensing*, at http://www.lib.berkeley.edu/EART/abbrev2.html#nos. The site also contains information about historical map scans, geospatial software, Geographic Information System (GIS) tips, and help. It is of specific use to those looking for information about the state of Connecticut. Other states are developing similar resources, and those that do are located by using a map directory organized by state such as the USGS Web site.

Specialized/Topical Map Resources

Specialized map resources assist in the use of general map resources and may focus on a particular type of map. The type of map could be a topographic map, showing land surface features of an area, or a property map, showing boundaries of a property or of the building structures on a property. Specialized map resources are usually created for a specific purpose, for which they are most useful, although they may sometimes reveal other useful things.

Gazetteers

Gazetteers, although not actually maps, are alphabetical listings of place names that provide the user with the map location of the particular places. These places include countries, regions, provinces, states, counties, cities, towns, islands, lakes, mountains, deserts, seas, rivers, canals, peninsulas, capes, and other geographic features. Information is included about name pronunciations and variant spellings, population, geographic and political boundaries, resources, longitude/latitude/elevation, trade, industry, agriculture, and minerals and other natural resources, as well as national environments. Often featured are specialized items such as railroads, irrigation works, river lengths, communication networks, historical and archaeological points of interest, cultural institutions, monuments, battles, and popular attractions. In fact, gazetteers usually provide information not obtainable from maps. They can be worldwide, such as the three-volume-set *Columbia Gazetteer of the World*, or as geographically focused as the *New England Gazetteer*.

Columbia Gazetteer of the World (Columbia Press, 1998)

These three volumes compose one of the most comprehensive resources of a very large geographic area. It includes every incorporated place and county in the United States, as well as several thousand unincorporated places, special-purpose sites, and physical features. It is noteworthy that this gazetteer lists many local places and features of all the countries of the world.

The names used rely heavily on those supplied by the U.S. Department of the Interior's Board of Geographic Names. A sample entry is that for Bamberg, South Carolina (one of three entries for the name *Bamberg*):

Bamberg, town (1990 pop. 38,430), Bamberg co., S Central S.C., 17 mi/27km SSW of Orangeburg; 33° 17″ N 81 (degrees) 01″ W., site of Bamberg Job Corps Center. Mfg. includes machinery, commercial printing, textiles. Agriculture area for soybeans, grains, cotton, watermelon and dairying.

This resource is very helpful in determining which of several places with the same name would be closest to the correct one. It is now available online for subscription at http://columbiagazetteer.org.

New England Gazetteer (Heritage Books, 1997)

This particular edition of this publication is a facsimile reprint of the fourth edition of *The New England Gazetteer*. It contains descriptions of all the states, counties, and towns in New England, along with descriptions of the principal mountains, rivers, lakes, capes, bays, harbors, islands, and fashionable resorts within that territory, all alphabetically arranged. It was first published in 1839. This resource is a historical one and could be a guide to places that no longer exist or that have changed names or locations.

U.S. Gazetteer (U.S. Census Bureau) http://www. census.gov/cgi-bin/gazetteer

This Web site is an online version of a gazetteer that is designed to identify places to view with the TIGER (Topologically Integrated Geographic Encoding and Referencing) map server. It then can be helpful in obtaining Census data from the 1990 Census Lookup. A simple search page functions by name and state abbreviation or by a five-digit zip code. The files used for this service are the U.S. Gazetteer Place and Zipcode files and are used in the USGS Geographic Names Information System (see profile below). These files are available for free from the Census Bureau, at http://www.census.gov/geo/www/gazetteer/places.html, and are available for downloading. An example is provided on how to interface with the server from your own Web page.

Geographic Names Information System [GNIS] (U.S. Geological Survey) http://geonames.usgs.gov/ gnishome.html

The GNIS, developed by the USGS in cooperation with the U.S. Board on Geographic Names (BGN), contains information about almost 2 million physical and cultural geographic features in the United States. The federally recognized name of each feature described in the database is identified, and state, county, and geographic coordinates make references to a feature's location. The GNIS is our nation's official repository of information on domestic geographic names.

A search engine allows a search of the database by name that can be modified by providing different pieces of information such as state, county, feature name, or elevation. There are good help resources for the searches that are useful. Many place names are known to local dwellers, but may not be official. For example, on a search of "Mt. Baldy," a common name for San Antonio Peak in the San Gabriel Mountain Range of Southern California, the only "Mt. Baldy" that comes up is a Mt. Baldy in Humboldt County, in Northern California. "Mt. Baldy Trail" comes up in San Bernardino County, but not Mt. Baldy. Luckily, the help feature of the Web site suggests using alternate phrases and words. This is an easy way to search a huge database, and retrieval produces a list much like one would find using the paper version of the title. (The most comparable version would be the *National Gazetteer of the United States of America: United States Concise*, 1990.) By contrast, the *Columbia Gazetteer* is a much more up-to-date paper gazetteer.

National Atlas of the United States (U.S. Geological Survey) http://nationalatlas.gov/index.html

This atlas does not provide links directly to the local geographic level, but it does provide links to services that do maps of county boundaries and specialized features such as dams and land-cover characteristics. To reach smaller geographic levels and complex detail, it has a "Map Layers Warehouse," http://www.nationalatlas.gov/atlasftp.html. Here are links to downloadable maps of metropolitan areas, hydrologic districts, the Public Land Survey System, railroads, public aquifers, and others. Using the maps requires that certain software be downloaded, and directions are provided. Software producers and sales are also linked.

Special Use Maps

Historical Maps

Sanborn Fire Insurance Maps http://www.sanbornmap.com

These maps were produced by the Sanborn Map Company between 1880 and 1950 to provide accurate, current, and detailed information to the fire insurance industry for risk assessment purposes. The company mapped over 12,000 U.S. towns. The maps were revised periodically in order to be accurate and suitable for the intended use. This series of revisions provides the historical researcher with invaluable neighborhood snapshots. The maps typically show a bird's-eye view of a community at the scale of 1 inch = 50 feet. At this scale, it is possible to show each building in outline. The original maps were color coded to indicate each building's exterior construction material. A complex set of symbols—initials, numerals, an assortment of lines, circles, and squares—is used to describe a building's use, composition, and appearance.

Although these maps are older, they are useful for historical purposes and for purposes in areas that have not changed much since the turn of the nineteenth and twentieth centuries. Catalogs and index listings for the Sanborn maps are available, such as *Fire Insurance Plans in the Library of Congress: A Checklist*, published in 1981 by the Library of Congress. A library will often list its holdings of Sanborn maps also, and the Center for Research Libraries in Chicago has a large collection of them.

MAP COLLECTIONS
Libraries

Map Collections in the United States and Canada: A Directory (4th ed., Special Libraries Association, 1985)

This directory is dated, but it still serves as a valuable resource for locating map collections. Map collections must be substantial in size to be included in this directory, and it is rather unlikely that a map collection would cease to be substantial because it is dated. It is actually more likely that the collection would become more significant for historical reasons. This directory does refer to only paper map collections, as it predates the widespread availability of digitized map sources. The collections are housed primarily in libraries in educational institutions, universities, and large public libraries. There are entries for selected corporate libraries also. The directory is geographic by state, with entries organized by city. Contact information provided includes names, addresses, and telephone numbers, and descriptive information is given about the size of the collection, types of maps owned, subject specialization, special cartographic collections, whether or not the collection is cataloged, whether the collection is in a Depository, and what the reproduction capabilities are. The title, name, and subject indexes are extensive. Although there does not appear to be an updated version of this publication, most libraries should have it.

Map Libraries on the World Wide Web
   http://map.lib.umn.edu/map_libraries.phtml

This Web site at the University of Minnesota's John R. Borchert Map Library has a listing of map library organizations and map libraries worldwide organized by world area and county. The map library organizations include MAGERT (the Map and Geography Round Table of the American Library Association) and the Western Association of Map Libraries (WAML). Links to library map collections include the Penn State University Maps Library, http://www.libraries.psu.edu/maps. This Web page has links to descriptions about the Online Library, GIS assistance, paper maps, and other relevant links. By selecting "Links" and "Interactive Mapping," there is a list of links to resources such as the Census Data Browser, the Demographic Data Viewer, and PASDA, Pennsylvania's Official Data Clearinghouse. Under the paper maps section, there are links to atlases, topographic maps, and aeronautical and nautical charts. There are also links to road maps and old parcels, land ownership, and land-use maps. The link for online maps displays additional links to sites such as the Geography Network, the National Geographic Printable Maps Web site, and the GNIS Web site. This Web site is well organized and useful. Other Web sites vary in how they are organized and provide varying degrees of comprehensiveness. The Penn State Web site is quite complex, yet provides clear directions of where to access certain types of map resources. Under the paper maps section, there are links to atlases, topographic maps, and aeronautical and nautical charts. There are also links to road maps and old parcels, land ownership and land use maps. The link for online maps displays additional links to sites such as the Geography Network, the National Geographic Printable Maps Web site, and the GNIS Web site. This Web site is well organized and useful. Other Web sites vary in how they are organized and provide varying degrees of comprehensiveness.

Depositories

Directory of Government Document Collections and Librarians (8th ed., Government Documents Round Table/American Library Association, 2001)

This directory is a comprehensive source of government documents collections. Map libraries are included only if they are also government Depositories, of which there are actually only a small number (about 1,300), but many of which have substantial map collections. In fact, the list of collections of maps consists of a section in the index of this directory for USGS maps, listed in alphabetical order. The index listing actually refers to the entry in the directory that lists information such as name and address, telephone and fax numbers, e-mail and home page addresses, brief descriptions of collections and subject specialties, and access and photocopying information.

Publishers/Catalogs

Large Map Publishers and Distributors

Earth Science Information Center (U.S. Geological Survey) http://mapping.usgs.gov/esic/esic_index.html

This Web site provides information about map distributors, in many of the states, that sell maps in paper format.

Ordering U.S. Geological Survey Products http://mapping.usgs.gov/esic/to_order.html

In contrast to the Earth Science Information Center, this Web site is primarily for purchasing map data in digital format. It has extensive information on how to order topographic maps from both the USGS and commercial sources. Information is available about types of products such as printed maps and map indexes, aerial photographs, satellite images, geospatial and other digital data, publications, CD-ROMs, and software.

Specialized Map Publishers and Distributors

Thomas Brothers http://www.thomas.com

Thomas Bros. Maps is best known for the *Thomas Guides*, which are excellent street-map volumes with a specialized format. They are highly accurate, as company representatives keep abreast of latest construction and development in many heavily populated areas. *Thomas Guides* are available as handy, spiral-bound map books for car or office. As a companion, an additional product, the *Thomas Guide Digital Edition* CD-ROM product for the personal computer is available. *Thomas Guides* are published for cities and localities in California, Washington,

Oregon, Arizona, Maryland, Virginia, and Nevada, and the area in and around the District of Columbia. Each of the map editions uses the distinctive Thomas Bros. Maps "Page and Grid" system, which makes navigating quick and easy. Another unique feature of the *Thomas Guides* is that, at least up until the early 1990s, the company has produced an edition with Census tracts superimposed on the street maps. This provided an easy way to find out which streets were in certain Census tract areas. New Census tracts will be redrawn beginning in 2004, and it has not yet been announced whether or not the maps will include the Census tract lines in the future.

TopoZone.com http://www.topozone.com

TopoZone is a recreational and professional map publisher and distributor. It works with the USGS to prepare maps for commercial distribution. The two have also worked together to produce the first interactive topographic map of the entire United States. TopoZone serves maps on the Web site and also provides interactive mapping services to partners like Maps.com, MapQuest, Trails.com, and others. It is an excellent Web source for custom digital topographic data sets for Web, GIS, and computer-assisted design/drafting applications. These mapping services grow more sophisticated every day. This is a very dynamic area in which to be involved.

CHAPTER 13
Finding Information on Parks and Museums

Ann Ellis and Joan Goodbody

MAJOR TOPICS COVERED

MAJOR RESOURCES COVERED

INTRODUCTION

Throughout the world there are thousands of parks and museums located in cities, countries, and rural areas that enrich the lives of people by providing cultural and educational materials and opportunities for recreation and relaxation. Information about parks and museums can be found in a variety of resources, which vary in format, scope, and quality. This chapter focuses on some of these resources, beginning with general sources of information for parks and museums, followed by regional and specialized sources.

Using directories and other materials available for getting information on local parks and museums can be a tedious experience. The Internet makes it much easier to find such information, but it is still difficult to find the real treasure troves.

Many commercial sites and publications are available, including the Fodor's, Frommer's, and Michelin guides and Web sites. Among the most specialized are the Hunter Guides, useful resources covering subjects such as African American, wilderness, and Jewish travel. *Off the Beaten Path* guides are also good sources for unusual and very specialized targets. All of these provide basic starting points for learning about the museums and parks that are available and making travel plans to visit them.

A search on the Internet will turn up some information through chambers of commerce and state, county, and city sites. A search using "museum" or "park" and the city name may also be useful in unearthing informative sources, but yet more searching may be necessary afterward. Local, regional, state, or county organizations can provide information and are also good sources for gathering further details. Finally, write to the closest historical society, state park, information center, town/city hall, or county court house and ask for information or publications for that area.

GENERAL RESOURCES FOR PARKS AND MUSEUMS

General guides, directories, and Web sites, both commercial and government, provide the basics for finding information on all types of parks and museums. The organizations that represent the different types of parks and museums can also help in establishing what is available in any given area. Because most parks and museums are under the direction of government organizations, they are apt to be listed under an organizational heading.

Directories for parks and museums typically include the names in alphabetical order, often grouped by region or type. Brief descriptions of the features of each facility are included, along with additional information about planning a visit, such as pricing, telephone numbers or Internet addresses, and other helpful facts.

Commercial Guides and Web Sites

Begin a search for general information for parks and museums by consulting material in basic sources such as commercial guidebooks and Web sites. These sources typically provide concise and accurate information and are updated to provide current data on a regular basis.

Guidebooks featuring specific points of interest often include histories of parks or museums and describe many other features and points of interest. Guidebooks are frequently published as part of a series and come in many forms, from many publishers. These can be a good starting point for looking into parks and museums. Some of the major publishers are listed below. Any of the publications issued can be helpful, and many are available in the local library or can be purchased from a favorite bookstore.

Frommer's http://www.frommers.com

Frommer's is one of the major producers of commercial travel guides. Its Web site has many options—bookstore, message board, vacation ideas, tips/resources, etc. It is kept up-to-date, but the links for some areas do not always work. Many of the Frommer's publications deal with a specific region of the

country or a specific city and are published annually. Other Frommer's publications are updated less frequently and range from topics about specific parks to "dollarwi$e" guides to "gateway" guides.

Frommer's Yellowstone and Grand Teton National Parks, ed. by Eric Peterson (Frommer's, 2002)

This publication is an example of a gateway guide. It contains essential material including maps and highlights of the most distinguishing features of each park. Costs, directions, and other vital information are included. It is available for sale on the Frommer's Web site.

Fodor's http://www.fodors.com
　http://www.fodors.com/ebooks

This travel guide series is one of the best known. Fodor's books and e-books present travel information in a unique way. The coverage is selective and includes choices for all budgets, including things to see and do and places to stay and to eat. Travel experts who live in the place you plan to visit provide the advice. The Web site format is ideal for travelers; it is easy to read, interactive, and accessible from any computer linked to the Internet.

Fodor's Complete Guide to America's National Parks (11th ed., Fodor Travel Publications, 2000)

This is an excellent printed source. The guide covers each of the 384 sites under National Park Service jurisdiction. It has photographs and maps and shares the lively format of the typical Fodor's publication.

Another title, *Fodor's Road Guide USA, National Parks of the West*, 2002, is a more specialized treatment of the subject of National Parks, focused on the West.

Michelin Guides http://www.viamichelin.com

These deal with areas within the United States or within cities. Many of these guides are small in size, travel well, and contain good maps. The published versions are updated frequently, and the Web site is kept up-to-date.

Hunter Guides http://www.hunterpublishing.com

The Hunter Guides are primarily specialty guides. They include guides for unique or unusual places, such as battlefields (by area or war), or specialized groups (see the Betsy Sheldon book profiled next). So-called adventure guides discuss museums, parks, ecological tourism, and specific areas such as the Chesapeake Bay and Florida Keys. They can be purchased from the publisher or bookstores.

Jewish Travel Guide, by Betsy Sheldon (Hunter Publishing, 2001)

This book is for travelers interested in Jewish history and culture. It includes listings of sights and resources and is a concise, easy-to-use handbook for those who want to explore the best in Jewish sightseeing and travel. It provides a directory that includes synagogues, community centers, kosher restaurants, Judaica shops, lodgings, and Jewish establishments. The book contains complete contact information for individual listings along with colorful descriptions and little-known facts.

Chesapeake Bay Adventure Guide, by Barbara Radcliffe Rogers and Stillman Rogers (Hunter Publishing, 2001)

This book presents a look at one of the country's most visited regions: Maryland, Washington, D.C., and Virginia's Eastern Shore. It highlights activities for outdoor enthusiasts and those interested in natural surroundings and is available from the publisher.

Web sites sponsored by commercial enterprises are an excellent way to find information for parks and museums. Because they are produced electronically, they are usually updated in a timely manner and can provide the most up-to-date information available.

State Travel and Tourism Offices http://www. sirlinksalot.net/travel.html

This is a comprehensive site with an alphabetical listing and links to state travel and tourism offices. Information includes addresses, telephone numbers, fax numbers, and links to the state Web site. Additional links are to national parks in the state, Frommer's for the state, and an Internet search for the state.

GENERAL ORGANIZATIONS AND ASSOCIATIONS

Organizations and associations such as state park associations and local, state, or national groups that support a topic or area and are usually not for profit promote and/or sponsor parks and museums. They often publish guides and create Web sites that advertise and provide a variety of information to highlight their affiliates. The Web sites often provide links to members' own Web pages and to related areas of interest. The sites are usually updated frequently and can provide the most up-to-date information available.

Directory of History Organizations in the United States and Canada (15th ed., American Association for State and Local History/Alta Mira Press, 2001)

Since 1936, this directory has come to be regarded as a standard resource for those working in state and local history. It is a comprehensive listing of historical agencies, museums, sites, programs, and other types of organizations. This latest edition updates, expands, and adds entries to provide information on almost 13,000 history-related organizations and programs in the United States and Canada. Useful cross-reference guides provide ways to locate information.

Farm Museum Directory: A Guide to America's Farm Past (Stemgas Pub. Co., 1998)

This resource is a book compiled in cooperation with the Association for Living Historical Farms and Agricultural Museums, Inc. It provides interesting information related to the preservation of the historical aspects of agriculture throughout North America, including illustrations, locations, and hours of operation of historic farms and museums.

The Official Museum Directory, 2002 (National Register Publishing, 2001)

The "OMD" is an authoritative resource that provides essential information on America's diverse museum community. This unique reference supplies accurate and up-to-date facts on museums, historic sites, zoos, and parks, and is available in many libraries and bookstores.

The Online Chambers: Online Chambers of Commerce Internet Services http://www.online-chamber.org

This Web site identifies chambers of commerce in the United States, Canada, and countries around the world. Chambers of Commerce often provide information about museums and parks as local attractions to promote tourism. Other resources on this Web site include links to the American Chamber of Commerce

Executives, Chambers of Commerce Directory, and International Chambers of Commerce.

Museums Hotlist http://sln.fi.edu/tfi/hotlists/ museums.html

The Franklin Institute Science Museum in Philadelphia produces a series of "Hotlist" Web sites. Included is a "Museums Hotlist," which features a directory of Web sites of museums worldwide and has links to science centers and museums, natural history museums, and other cultural institutions.

Art Hotlist http://sln.fi.edu/tfi/hotlists/art.html

This site features a directory of Web sites on art, with links to information on art museums such as the Getty Museum, the High Museum in Atlanta, the Andy Warhol Museum, and the San Francisco Museum of Modern Art, as well as images of works by and biographies of famous artists, such as Frank Lloyd Wright, Salvador Dalí, and Francisco Goya.

MUSÉE http://www.musee-online.org

MUSÉE is a nonprofit organization that works with cultural institutions around the world to provide services to museums, schools, and the general public. Its mission is to enhance cultural awareness, advance education at all levels, and stimulate public interest in cultural institutions. It presents a directory of museum collections, including art, science, and history collections, as well as information on zoos, archaeological collections, and aquariums. It profiles a different museum every day and offers access to Web site reviews of specific museums arranged alphabetically, a museum directory arranged by topic or alphabetically, and direct links to many museums' Web sites.

Sierra Club Guides to the National Parks (Stewart, Tabori, and Chang, 1996)

These series of guides, by region, are published and revised on a regular schedule. Check the Sierra Club Bookstore, at http://www.sierraclub.org/books, your local bookstore or library for the availability of a particular geographic location. If you go to the site, it provides information about availability for purchase. Many of these lists can be found at your local library.

After basic data for parks and museums have been located, a library catalog may be consulted for more detailed information about individual places. A link to

LibWeb, http://sunsite.berkeley.edu/Libweb, an online directory of library Web servers, may be useful in locating libraries online and checking their catalogs for holdings.

A good way to begin a library catalog search is by using the subject function to locate the topic "parks" or "museums," followed by the geographic location. This search will retrieve more specific information than a directory or guidebook can provide. A catalog search by the proper name of the site not only will retrieve information about it, but also may provide direction to further sources.

The following two sections of this chapter are arranged to provide separate information for park and museum guides, directories, and Web sites. Examples of the types of sources to look for are noted, although more are available in bookstores and libraries and on the Internet.

PARK RESOURCES

ParkNet (U.S. National Park Service) http://www.nps.gov/parks.html

This federally sponsored Web site provides a way to find parks by name or interest and includes information on how people can volunteer to be tour guides, campground workers, park assistants, etc. It has links to each of the parks within the national system and provides historical information, a nature and conservation link, and educational services. It also includes a link to the park service online bookshop where you can search for any of its publications.

AmericanParkNetwork http://www.americanparknet work.com

This Web site highlights what are considered to be the premier parks and cultural wonders, with a finder link to each. It is a comprehensive online guidebook for premier locations such as Acadia, Colonial Williamsburg, Mount Rushmore, and Yosemite. As of 2003, the Web site was undergoing a redesign.

Guides

National Geographic Guide to the State Parks of the United States (2nd ed., National Geographic Society, 2004)

This publication from the premier commercial outdoors source includes information for the best parks as recommended by state park agencies in the United

States. The guide includes photographs and maps. This and many other publications are available from the National Geographic Society Web site, http://www.nationalgeographic.com.

National Park Service Camping Guide, by William Herow (Roundabout Publications, 2001)

This resource includes information for campgrounds in national parks and recreation areas, national monuments, lakeshores, scenic rivers, seashores, historical parks, and preserves.

Directories

Parks Directory of the United States and Canada: A Guide to Nearly 5,000 National, State, Provincial, and Urban Parks in the United States and Canada, ed. by Darren Smith (Omnigraphics, 1992)

This book provides information about national parks, forests, wildlife refuges, state and selected urban parks in the United States, and national parks in Canada. Listings are grouped into several main sections according to type of park. The sections on state parks include maps to help pinpoint their location. Entries provide complete contact information, including addresses and telephone numbers, size, location, facilities, activities, special features, and special events. More than 3,600 Web sites and 1,000 e-mail addresses are included. A section of color maps for national parks, forests, trails, wildlife refuges, marine sanctuaries, and Canadian national parks completes the book.

MUSEUM RESOURCES

While the examples in this section by no means represent an exhaustive list, they provide a good idea of the types of resources available for museums.

Most museum guides and directories are produced by not-for-profit organizations and associations or by commercial sources. Some of these have already been profiled. Other resources of these types are listed below. Remember that these are just a few examples. Also, always check with the local chamber of commerce, visitor center, or county or city offices for further information.

Guides

Art Gallery Directory: A Guide to Art Galleries and Museums across the USA (W3Commerce, Inc., 2000) http://www.Art-Gallery-Directory-Online.com

This guide is published in book form and on the Internet. It presents an overview of American art museums and galleries, as well as of some lesser-known art spots of interest. The Web site has searchable listings for many cities.

Kuban's Guide to Natural History Museums on the Web http://members.aol.com/fostrak/museums.htm

This Web guide is compiled by the Natural History Museum of Los Angeles County and features a directory of Web sites on museums and cultural resources throughout the world. This site allows users to directly add links to other sites.

Museums in the USA http://vlmp.museophile.com/usa.html

This Web site includes an alphabetical listing with links to over 1,000 specialized museums covering a variety of interests. The links have short descriptions of each site. There are categories of links such as the most visited sites; new sites; and sites by museum name, topic, or state. They include children's museums, science museums, history museums, multidisciplinary museums, and art museums.

Directories

Art Museum Directory http://www.amn.org

This is the official Web site of the world's leading art museums and provides free access to information about their collections, exhibitions, and services. It includes an alphabetical listing, the Art Museum Image Consortium (AMICO), which features an illustrated search engine of more than 50,000 works of art, and the official exhibition calendars of the participating art museums.

Museum Computer Network http://www.mcn.edu

This Web site has links to over 1,000 international museum and museum-related Web sites in alphabetical order. This site can be used more effectively if the name of the institution is known. For example, in 2002, under "Phillips Collection: The First Museum of Modern Art," there was a description of then-current exhibitions as well as a description of "Jacqueline Kennedy's Washington: A Citywide Celebration" in Washington, D.C., that summer.

MuseumSpot http://www.museumspot.com

This guide to museums and other cultural information provides information about many types of museums. It also links to other museum-related Web sites and includes a newsletter feature. If you are an art or museum enthusiast, curator, educator, student, historian, or librarian, this site is for you. MuseumSpot is a free information resource center that simplifies the search for useful museum information on the Web. A user of the site can locate museums by city, state, country, name, and topic; explore museums by type; search for exhibits by artist; and access educational and industry resources.

Museums, Arts, and Interests
http://www.awa.com/arts.html

This Web site is produced by Downtown Anywhere, Inc. It features links to a wide range of sites, including ArtNetWeb, an international community of artists; museums such as the Smithsonian's Ocean Planet Online, Chicago's Field Museum of Natural History, San Francisco's Exploratorium, the U.S. Holocaust Memorial Museum in Washington, D.C., and the Krannert Art Museum in Champaign, Illinois; and online cultural exhibits.

Museums on the Web
http://curry.edschool.virginia.edu/curry/class/
Museums/Teacher%5FGuide/Hotlist/home.html

John Bunch presents a web directory of museum Web sites as part of "Going to a Museum? A Teacher's Guide." The directory lists a reviewed selection of museums. Categories of museums include art, science, history, natural history, cultural, and miscellaneous. This is not an exhaustive list from this Web site, but rather a small sampling of the wealth of information currently available there. But it could be a starting place for teachers looking for online museum resources. The Curry School of Education at the University of Virginia provides the directory online.

SPECIALIZED TOPICAL RESOURCES FOR PARKS AND MUSEUMS

These sources can help you find unusual or theme-oriented activities. Some of the more interesting are children's activities, museums by topic, tours by topic, and activities and events by topic. Many of these can be found in state, county, and municipal information resources or are provided by organizations that deal with the specific topic. Examples include festivals (watermelon, corn, cotton, boll weevil, ice cream, etc.), African American tours or museums, Jewish museums, natural history museums, zoos for specific animals, and many, many more.

After basic data for parks and museums have been located, the next step can be to consult specialized directories and guides for more detailed information about individual places.

By Location

Look for sources of information for parks and museums that are limited or grouped by geographic location. Resources that deal with museums and parks by location typically include the names in alphabetical order within each region or area. Brief descriptions of the features of each facility are included, and additional information about planning a visit, such as pricing, telephone numbers, or Internet addresses, may be included.

Frequently, guidebook series are also grouped by region, or by groups of states, and make it fairly easy to find information for many areas of interest, which are located near each other. These guidebooks are designed to be especially helpful to travelers but are also helpful to others who wish basic information about parks and museums.

California Museum Directory: A Guide to Museums, Zoos, Botanic Gardens, and Historic Buildings Open to the Public (2nd ed., California Institute of Public Affairs, 1992)

This directory covers 1,200 institutions. Entries provide name, location, mailing address, telephone, hours open, tours available, whether admission is charged, publications issued, and concise but thorough descriptions of collections. Listing is by location, and indexes are included. The book is available from the Web site for the California Institute of Public Affairs, an independent, nonprofit, nonpartisan organization devoted to improving policymaking on complex public issues (http://www.interenvironment.org/cipa/publications.htm).

Exploring Missouri's Legacy: State Parks and Historic Sites, by Susan L. Flader and Oliver Schuchard, with John A. Karel (University of Missouri Press, 1992)

This book describes many of Missouri's parks and historic sites with text and photographs that focus primarily on natural and cultural resources and related recreational venues. It is also a comprehensive review of Missouri natural and cultural history. The book includes an index, map, color illustrations, and black-and-white illustrations from archival sources.

Florida State Parks: A Complete Recreation Guide, by Michal Strutin (Mountaineers Books, 2000)

According to the author, Florida has one of the nation's top three state park systems, in terms of the number of parks and total annual visitors. Abundant ecological habitats host a diverse array of wildlife and vegetation for visitors to explore. This directory covers Florida's natural and historical parks, preserves, and recreational areas and is illustrated with more than 100 photographs and 80 maps. The book includes user-friendly tables that list each park's amenities.

The New England Museum Guide, by Leigh Grossman and Jamie Johnson (Swordsmith Books, 2001)

This is a guide to a wide variety of New England museums. It describes where they are, their hours, directions, and what to look for at each. In addition, it has descriptions of 600 museums and contact information for over a thousand more. It includes indexes by state, town, subject, and highway.

Official Guide to Texas State Parks, ed. by Laurence E. Parent and George Zapple (Texas Parks and Wildlife Press, 1997)

This book is the only official and complete guide to the state parks of Texas. It includes information from the Texas Parks and Wildlife Department; describes the attractions of each park; and gives details about camping and lodging facilities, types of recreation offered, and addresses and phone numbers for more information. The parks are grouped into seven geographic regions within the state of Texas. The book has locator maps and color photographs.

Oregon State Parks: A Complete Recreation Guide, by Jan Gumprecht Bannan (2nd ed., Mountaineer Books, 2002)

This book profiles 110 of Oregon's state parks and is illustrated with photographs and reference maps. It includes information on how to get to Oregon's state parks; camping, hiking, swimming, fishing, cycling, and year-round attractions available at the parks;

plants, wildlife, history, and geology information; and park hours, fees, reservations, and regulations.

By Topic

For the researcher who is interested in a special type of museum or park, sources are available to provide the information needed. Listed below are some examples of these.

African American Historic Place, ed. by Beth L. Savage (Wiley, 1996)

This is a book that contains information about 800 black historic sites in 42 states, Puerto Rico, and the Virgin Islands. Included are homes of famous black people and information for schools, hospitals, clubs, colleges, forts, and cemeteries. The listings include brief descriptions and addresses of the historical sites. The book is readily available at your favorite bookstore.

African American Museums http://www. blackmuseums.org

This site has an alphabetical listing of its member museums, with links to many of them, as well as links to information on the organization, such as the projects it supports, its history, and its meetings. Some of the site links are not always active.

America's National Battlefield Parks: A Guide, by Joseph E. Stevens (University of Oklahoma Press, 1990)

This is an example of a guidebook featuring information on a specialized topic. This richly illustrated book contains stories about particular battles fought in the U.S. national parks and presents self-guided walking and automobile tours that are coordinated with National Park Service tour maps. Maps portray battlefield troop movements and depict present-day roads, trails, and visitor facilities. The book is indexed and alphabetically arranged. It is available at many libraries, on NetLibrary, and for purchase from your favorite bookstore.

Civil War Battlefields: A Touring Guide, by David J. Eicher and John H. Eicher (Taylor Publishing Co., 1995)

This book is a comprehensive, illustrated tourist guide designed for students and casual researchers. More than 40 separate battles are described, along with traveler's information, maps, and suggestions for lesser-known itineraries. This book is readily available at bookstores and libraries.

The Amusement Park Guide: Coast to Coast Thrills, by Tim O'Brien and James Futrell (4th ed., Globe Pequot Press, 2001)

This is a useful guidebook to amusement parks in North America that covers more than 290 park locations. It describes what to see and do and includes descriptions of rides and roller coasters, statistical information, illustrations, and an index.

Empire State Railway Museum's 36th Annual Guide to Tourist Railroads and Museums, 2001 (Kalmbach Books, 2001)

This illustrated annual publication lists over 450 museum names and addresses. It lists information for train rides and fares and contains some coupons. Again, it is readily available in libraries and bookstores.

Historic Monuments of America, by Donald Young (Portland House, 1990)

This coffee table–type book presents the reader with the opportunity to tour and relive American history, not only in words but also through photography. It illustrates views of historical monuments ranging from Valley Forge and Gettysburg to the mansions of Gilded Age millionaires of the late nineteenth century. Arranged by region, this survey explores many significant landmarks. Designed for the history buff, the student, and those wishing to reacquaint themselves with the American story, the book includes authoritative historical facts and inspiring imagery.

On Exhibit: Art Lover's Travel Guide to American Museums, ed. by Judith Swirsky (Abbeville Press, 2000)

This guide has over 750 listings for American art museums, a directory of permanent collections, and a calendar of special exhibitions. It is organized by state and city. There is information about hours, ticket prices, accessibility, and facilities.

Religious Sites in America: A Dictionary, by Mary Ellen Snodgrass (ABC-Clio, 2000)

This book lists 160 diverse religious sites in the United States, from cathedrals to storefront churches

to retreats. Each entry describes its history, sacred architecture, current activities, location, and layout, along with telephone and fax numbers, e-mail addresses, and Web site information. Also highlighted are the beliefs and practices of the group that worships at the site. The book includes a glossary and photographs for many of the entries.

The Zoo Book: A Guide to America's Best, by Allen W. Nyhui (Carousel Press, 1994)

This book lists, by category, the top 53 American zoos in the United States. In addition to describing each zoo's featured exhibits, special attractions and exhibits are highlighted. Smaller zoos, aquariums, and other places that display animals are also listed with brief descriptions. Although the focus is on American zoos, summary information for noteworthy zoos in Canada, Mexico, Europe, and other areas of the world is included. For ease of use, the book is indexed. It is available at libraries and bookstores.

Air and Space Museums. http://www.aero.com/museums/museums.htm

This Web site lists these museums alphabetically by state or by name. It includes contact information for each museum via mailing address and telephone number and provides a listing of museums in Canada and worldwide.

Aviation Museum Locator http://www.aero-web.org/museums/museums.htm

Through this Web site, users can locate museums in the United States, Canada, and the United Kingdom. The main page is arranged by state and/or country. Those links provide alphabetical listings and rankings for the museums, which also link to each location providing contact information. The site is maintained by the Aviation Enthusiast Corner (http://www.aero-web.org/air.htm), which offers information on air shows and events, aviation history, and aviation records.

Voice of the Shuttle: Libraries and Museums http://vos.ucsb.edu/index.asp

This research-oriented site presents a directory of library and museum Web sites, compiled by Alan Liu as part of the *Voice of the Shuttle* humanities resource. This topically arranged database includes links to research libraries, public libraries, museums, general resources, and sites on research and projects related to computerizing libraries and museums.

Fire Museum Network http://firemuseumnetwork.org

The International Association of Fire Chiefs (IAFC) has created this Web site to promote the interests of those who preserve the artifacts and the history of fire service. It contains a directory of museums in the United States and Canada, the current issue of a newsletter, and information on membership in the Network. The site posts contact information and includes an online membership form. There are links to the home pages of the IAFC and fire museum.

Ephemeral

Many additional resources are available for the researcher who is interested in knowing where to find more information for parks and museums.

Besides the traditional materials discussed in this chapter, look for city or town Web sites, maintained by chambers of commerce or local government agencies, which often provide links to parks or museums that fall under their jurisdiction.

Examples:

City of Rochester, Minnesota
 http://www.ci.rochester.mn.us/park

This is a link to Rochester's Department of Parks and Recreation. This Web site includes information for visitors and newcomers alike. Categories include parks, trails, golf, shelters, forestry garden plots, recreation activities, outdoor pools, and beaches. Links to information about various indoor facilities are included.

Taos, New Mexico http://www.taosgov.com

Along with several other history and culture-related links, there is a link to a guide to the museums of Taos (http://taosvacationguide.com/history/MAT/index.php). It provides information about seven museums in the Taos area.

Brochures are also helpful in finding out about parks and museums. These are usually bright, artistically designed advertisements that provide basic information about sites of popular interest. They can frequently be found in local libraries, tourist centers, chamber of commerce offices, and local business establishments. The National Park Service publishes an extensive and comprehensive series of brochures that are available at federal Depository libraries and at each national park and can be ordered through the Park Service Web site.

Larger museums usually publish catalogs of their collections and will also publish catalogs of special exhibits that are at the museum on a temporary basis. These catalogs often appear as booklets and may be available only from the museum. The contents of these may vary significantly, from a basic listing of the items in the collection to provision of full-color illustrations and descriptions of the items. A search of bookstores and library catalogs may enable the user to locate some of these.

RESOURCES FOR ADDITIONAL RESEARCH

MuseumStuff.com http://www.museumstuff.com

This Web site explores thousands of museum links to search for museums, virtual exhibits, and fun and games. It is also searchable by type of museum or popular search terms. Categories such as organizations, articles, and current events about museum activities and exhibits are described.

America's National Parks: The Spectacular Forces That Shaped Our Treasured Lands, by Paul D. Schullery (Dorling Kindersley Publishing, 2001)

This is a lavishly illustrated book describing the features of 55 of the diverse national parks throughout the United States. Parks are categorized according to the particular physical and geological forces that created them. The book features color photographs and topographic maps that highlight important landmarks and travel routes throughout each park, and a comprehensive index is included. Available from Amazon (http://www.amazon.com).

America's National Scenic Trail, by Kathleen Ann Cordes, Steven Elkinton, and photographer Jane Lammers (University of Oklahoma Press, 2001)

This general guide is arranged by and describes each of the eight regional national scenic trails. It provides background and touring information, lists points of interest for each trail, and includes trail maps, photographs, references, and an index.

The Great American Wilderness: Touring America's National Parks, by Larry H. Ludmer (Hunter Publishing, 2000)

This travel guide provides detailed information about 53 national parks and monuments arranged alphabetically by name. Each chapter begins with an introduction to the park and its features, directions to the park, admission fees, the area's climate, contact information, touring information, and special activities. The book contains photographs, maps, and an index.

Great City Parks, by Alan Tate (Routledge Press, 2001)

Great City Parks is a study of 20 public parks in a number of major cities in North America and western Europe. Organized by country, the book discusses park origins, designers, design principles, current management practices and use, and proposals for future use. The text is based on park visits and interviews with park management organizations and includes plans and color photographs. It is available from Amazon (http://www.amazon.com).

Our National Parks (Reader's Digest Association, 1997)

This guide combines photographs with informative text. It covers the histories, geological features, and wildlife of America's unspoiled paradises. It has photos and color illustrations that depict plants and animals in their native habitats, panoramic vistas, and extraordinary natural phenomena.

Atlases

Refer to a good highway atlas as a basic way to locate parks and museums. Consult atlas legends to determine how the features are marked. Parks, landmarks, and public buildings such as museums are specially coded, and street or highway information is included to help you navigate your way to the site.

2002 Road Atlas: United States, Canada and Mexico (Rand McNally & Co.)

This popular, reliable atlas is a redesigned standard reference book that includes updated highway maps and enhanced information on points of interest, including maps of national parks.

For more information on maps, please see the chapter on Map Resources.

Encyclopedias and Indexes

Consult encyclopedias for general overviews of parks and museums. Look for information under the name of the site or the geographic location, or in a general section about parks or museums. Examples of comprehensive encyclopedias include *Encyclopedia Britannica*, *Grolier*, and the *Columbia Encyclopedia* (published by Columbia University Press). The online versions of these encyclopedias contain hyperlinks to related or associated sites, enabling you to easily do a multilevel search of resources. Some of the encyclopedias will link to an online bookstore, if your search reveals no results.

When researching data for parks and museums, do not overlook indexes and abstracts, which are located in libraries and on library Web sites. These resources will guide you to magazine, journal, and newspaper articles about various sites. Using standard indexing terms and, in the case of electronic indexes, powerful search engines, these sources will lead you to information about museums and libraries. Some of the materials identified in the indexes are available in the library, while others are available through interlibrary loan or document delivery programs.

The following are examples of typical electronic indexes and abstracts but do not represent an exhaustive listing. Depending upon the size and scope of the library, there may be many more indexes and encyclopedias to choose from.

Wilson Web http://www.hwwilson.com/ Documentation/WilsonWeb/tecfaq7.html

This source is available in many libraries and has several databases, including *Art Abstracts*, *Humanities Abstracts*, and *Readers Guide*, all good sources for getting information on parks and museums.

EBSCo (Elton B. Stephens Co.) http://www.ebsco.com/home

The Web site of this reputable Birmingham, Alabama–based information service is another multiple index site that many states use for their state online library resource. Check for it at your local library.

FirstGov http://www.firstgov.gov

FirstGov is a government site that can be used from any computer and indexes over 47 million Web sources. The user can limit a search to a specific state or to federal government information, or both. The Web site can be used to gather information on parks and museums as well as any other government information. When the main page is opened to the search box in the top left-hand corner, enter the name of the park, area, or state interested in with "park" or "museum" (do not use the word *and* or symbol +, since the program does that automatically). Then choose either "federal" or "both" to include the states. This will get you a list of Web sites, with short descriptions of each.

FirstSearch http://www.oclc.org/firstsearch/
 index.htm

This source is available in many libraries and has several databases, including WorldCat, the Monthly Catalog of Government Publications (U.S. Government Printing Office), ArticleFirst, and in many libraries, ERIC (Educational Resources Information Center). These are all good sources for getting information on parks and museums and their programs.

FOR FURTHER READING

Anchorages and Marine Parks: Coastal Guide to Anchorages and Marine Parks on the West Coast, by Peter Vasilopoulo. Vancouver, BC: Seagraphic Publications, 1998).

Indiana State Parks: A Guide to Hoosier Parks, Reservoirs and Recreation Areas for Campers, Hikers, Anglers, Boaters, Hunters, Nature Lovers, by John Goll. Saginaw, MI: Glovebox Guidebooks of America, 1995.

Museum Properties Directory. Washington, DC: National Society of Colonial Dames of America, 1998. Colonial Dames publishes this directory on a regular basis, usually no less than every few years. It includes listings for historic buildings and museum properties.

The National Directory of Theme and Amusement Parks: 400 Fun-Filled Attractions for Youngsters…and the Young at Heart. New York: Pilot Books, 1977.

U.S. Military Museums, Historic Sites and Exhibits, by Bryce D. Thompson. Falls Church, VA: Military Living Publications, 1992.

Wisconsin Travel Companion: A Guide to History along Wisconsin's Highways, by Richard Olsenius and Judy Zerby. Minneapolis: University of Minnesota Press, 2001. This book focuses on both familiar and little-known historic sites in the state of Wisconsin.

CHAPTER 14
How to Find Local Governmental Information on Education

Mary Martin

MAJOR TOPICS COVERED

MAJOR RESOURCES COVERED

INTRODUCTION

It seems that local government information resources related to education are available in as many variations as jurisdictions. Governance of education is within the provenance of several geographic and political jurisdictions. The federal government is responsible for supplying funding for many programs, such as the free school lunch program. The state government controls funding for such programs as special education of disabled children. Much of the remaining responsibility for education falls to local government agencies such as county and district school boards.

As with most information gathered and made available by the government, where one would find the information is directly related to who collected it and how and where it was reported. If one is looking for statistics on the number of students enrolled in a grade at a certain school, the answer could be in statistics of local or state departments of education. To find information about jurisdictional boundaries of school dis-tricts to determine which school a child would be assigned would probably be available only from the local school district office. Or to find out whether there is a private school in the neighborhood, one might need to consult a directory of private schools published by the state. It is important to know where the information might be located in order to actually find it. Information on education is available from all levels of government: national, state, county, and district or city.

OVERVIEW OF TYPES OF SOURCES

Resources on education at the local governmental level are available in varied formats. While at one time it was always useful to begin by referring to paper indexes and catalogs, the preponderance of these resources in electronic format justifies the inclusion of Web sites in the General Web Site Indexes category. There will also be descriptions of detailed references to Web pages within Web sites that have more specific information resources. The resources are organized by type, providing information about whether a source is available in electronic format also or exclusively. To begin by reviewing paper resources and end with the sources available in electronic format makes good sense. However, there are instances when beginning by looking at Web resources also makes sense, as it could save a trip to a library or office.

The broadest category of resources is, of course, statistical compendiums such as the *Digest of Education Statistics*. Unfortunately, this wonderful resource rarely contains information below the state level. It is important to remember here that information and statistics are *collected* at the local level but not always *published* at that level. The information certainly is compiled somewhere and may often be obtainable if you know where it is stored. There is a very large database of educational resources published by the Educational Resources Information Center (ERIC), published in paper as well as electronically, on CD-ROM and online.

There are also directories of schools, districts, personnel, resources, students, and such. Both published and unpublished information is available from government agencies. Unpublished information can often be obtained by contacting the government agency directly, as in the case of the National Center for Education Statistics, a state agency such as the California Department of Education, or a local school district office.

Topical resources such as special education resources, personnel directories, and data resources on a subject are also published. Full-text data files are often maintained at various levels of government and can be rich sources of statistical information, such as scores on competency exams for a particular school. If a school district does not have a Web site or make data files available electronically, information can also be obtained by writing or calling a school district office and requesting it.

Finally, there are resources available through the Internet, such as electronic databases maintained by the National Center for Education Statistics or the California State Department of Education, as well as Web sites maintained by a school district or a particular school. Local government agencies often publish guides to services specific to the local areas. For example, a county or school district might publish a board of education directory or guide to education services. There are also local governmental Web sites that provide links to information about individual cities, towns, and counties. These Web sites can provide general information about a county or link to specific resources, such as the district or even school Web

page. For example, when connecting to the New Jersey State Department of Education Web site, there are links to general information as well as to sites for individual schools.

Details on how to find and use these resources are provided below. As previously mentioned, the interconnectivity of resources makes them more difficult to use but provides more opportunities for access and use.

General Web Site Indexes and Catalogs

A good place to start is with a large education organization or publisher, many of which maintain extensive Web sites as well as databases and catalogs of publications. These catalogs are now available online as well as in paper. There are very large Web sites created by agencies that also have subagencies with additional resources available.

ED.gov (U.S. Department of Education)
  http://www.ed.gov/index.jsp

This Web site is a great resource for a wide range of information. It encompasses everything from general information on programs such as the "Town Meeting on Reading 400, Reading and Writing Activities for Children" and "Find a College, K–12 School, or Library" to a section on research and statistics. There are links to "Blue Ribbon Schools" and "After School Grants," a public school and district locator, and "21st Century Community Learning Centers." Of special note is the "Nation's Report Card." Department of Education publications can also be ordered online from the ED Pubs Web site, http://www.ed.gov/pubs/edpubs.html.

Some changes have occurred in the U.S. Department of Education. One example is that the Office of Educational Research and Improvement (OERI) was abolished, and a new agency organized, the Institute of Educational Sciences, which has designed its own Web site, at http://www.ed.gov/about/offices/list/ies, and funds ERIC. ED.gov provides links to the ERIC database, which is described in detail below. The Web site provides a searchable database, with abstracts and ordering information. This Web site is useful for general information on contacts, grants, funding, and similar topics.

National Center for Education Statistics [NCES]
  http://nces.ed.gov/index.html

At this subagency of the Department of Education can be found more detailed statistical information at the local district level than is made available at ED.gov. The Projects with Partners section (http://nces.ed.gov/partners) provides links to many government agencies that provide statistics, such as links to FedStats, First.gov, and searchable locators of public and private schools. There are links to full-text statistical reports, although most of them are on the national level only. For example, the *Digest of Education Statistics* and the *Condition of Education* are both available online through this NCES Web site but do not have much data down to the local level. The most recent editions are not always available online, or links from older to current editions are not always clear. Information such as that included in these sources can sometimes be found at Web sites of individual state departments of education.

The NCES site also links to other publications that might be of interest and provide a national view of very local problems. One such publication is the *Indicators of School Crime and Safety*, at http://nces.ed.gov/pubs2003/schoolcrime. Unfortunately, only aggregate statistics are provided for the United States. A greater challenge, of course, would be to find statistics by school district or school. More details on this is provided in the chapter on Crime and Criminals. The NCES also has a catalog of publications available for purchase. Its Web site is an excellent resource for finding local governmental statistics.

NCES Electronic Catalog http://nces.ed.gov/pubsearch/index.asp

This is a valuable source of information on electronic publications compiled from surveys conducted by the U.S. Department of Education. It allows searching by keyword, product, name of survey, and release date. For example, a keyword search using "district data" brings up a list on which the first publication is *Nested Structures: District-Level Data in the Schools and Staffing Survey*. This report presents a number of arguments for the increased importance of within-state district-level data in systematic assessments of changes in the organizational structure of schools. One difficulty is that it is not obvious which products and surveys have information down to the local area level. It often requires looking at the files or the tables of contents of files to determine at what geographic level data are provided.

There are some resources such as the Common Core of Data, described in further detail under Specialized Resources/Full-Text Data Files, that do provide local-level data.

Resources in Education and Current Index to Journals in Education (Educational Information Resources Clearinghouse, monthly)

Depository libraries receive this publication free, and many academic libraries have subscriptions. Published since 1966, it provides access to citations with abstracts for over 780 journals and documents in the field of education. Program descriptions, research and development reports, and unpublished documents are in education and related fields such as counseling, psychology, and the social sciences. These publications are part of a microfiche collection that is purchased by most large academic libraries. Journal citations must be retrieved from the journals as they are published and owned by a library.

ACCESS ERIC: Educational Resources Information Center http://www.eric.ed.gov

ERIC maintains this Web site to provide access to its database of citations and abstracts, as well as full-text versions of many of the publications. A document delivery option is provided by the ERIC Document Reproduction Service (http://www.edrs.com/default.cfm), from which any ERIC document can be purchased. Some of these publications are also available in electronic format, in a national education database that, during its lifetime, was sponsored by OERI. A search of the terms "California" and "test scores" retrieved a number of publications, such as "Five Cities, One Vision—CORAL: Linking Communities, Children and Learning," which provides an assessment of the progress of a five-city collaborative effort in after-school child care. Evaluation instruments included standardized test scores for students.

A certain subset of the ERIC collection is made available for free through the Depository library program. These consist primarily of reports completed under government contract. ERIC can have information on reports and studies done in local schools, such as the CORAL initiative described above. The government often contracts with educators and schools to do reports in various areas. The reports that are prepared under government contract are available through the Depository library program and will be available from this Web site. Most ERIC reports are actually issued in microfiche, and many large academic libraries have the collection, which comes with commercial purchase of the database. The *Directory of ERIC Resource Collections* provides information about institutions and organizations that provide online access (including Internet) or CD-ROM access to the ERIC database, maintain sizable collections of ERIC microfiche, and subscribe to and collect ERIC publications. The *Directory* is available online at http://searcheric.org.

NCES Common Core of Data; Information on Public School and School Districts in the United States [National Center for Education Statistics] http://nces.ed.gov/ccd/ccseas.asp

Most states have fairly extensive Web sites that provide connections to the state department of education and also publish data down to the district and school level. The NCES CCD Web site provides a direct linking list of all state department of education Web sites. There are links to several Web sites in some of the states, and each state department of education often provides data files of school and student performance tests. Using the NCES Web site, it is possible to connect to the Alabama State Department of Education site, then to the 2004 Accountability Reporting System (http://www.alsde.edu/Accountability/preAccount ability.asp) to find these types of data files. The Web site utilizes a nice, user-friendly search form that allows selection of a particular school for a report. The report provides information on academic status and scores for various grades on the Stanford Achievement Tests, high school exit exams, writing tests, and ACT tests. There are also indicators such as enrollment by race, ethnicity, and sex; projected dropout rate; enrollment in special programs; number of students receiving free lunches; and expenditure per student. The statistics provided appear to vary from state to state but are obviously drawn from similar sets of databases on a standardized type of questionnaire. Many states provide links to these data and under many different names. Another example of a state Web site that can be accessed from the NCES site is the California State Department of Education. This is another example of how such a Web site is designed and implemented.

California State Department of Education
http://www.cde.ca.gov

This Web site has tabs on its home page that are very helpful. For instance, extensive data are provided under "Finance & Grants." Under "Data & Statistics" are links to school performance and academic performance, including data on Scholastic Aptitude Test (SAT) results. Another feature is the School Ac-

countability Report Card, http://www.cde.ca.gov/ta/ ac/sa, which is a performance indicator, reported by school and measured by the state, that includes expectations of decreasing dropout rates, meeting student assessment goals, and reducing class sizes and teaching loads. There are links to demographic and school enrollment data via the DataQuest search engine, which allows you to create your own reports from the academic performance index (API), overall and course enrollments, graduates, dropouts, staffing, ESL (English as a second language) learners, and Stanford 9 test data. The reports are available for schools, districts, counties, or statewide. Demographic data files are compressed files (in DBF format) that may be downloaded and provide complete data from the California Basic Educational Data System, the U.S. Census, and private schools. A list of California public schools with addresses and legislative status is available. Demographic reports are viewable, along with reports of trends in demographic data for California public schools (K–12). Reports available from DataQuest are being expanded at this site. Most of the state Web sites have links to local district education departments and schools.

Davis School District (Utah)
http://www.davis.k12.ut.us
Alameda Unified School District (California)
http://www.alameda.k12.ca.us

A quick search on an Internet search engine yielded over 600,000 hits for "school district." These two county school-district Web sites exemplify the results that can be obtained. The site for the Davis School District (Farmington, Utah) has a full row of tabs across the top of the home page and other links down the side; is accessible by student PINs and IDs; and contains information for parents on calendars of events, opportunities for community support, news, and a link to the District Information System. The Web site of the Alameda Unified School District, based in the city of the same name, is efficiently laid out by a variety of tabs and links, including a detailed map in PDF format, which allows magnification up to 800×. Another link is to the 2002–2003 School Accountability Report Card, http://www.alameda. k12.ca.us/SARC_home.htm, which gives important statistics on particular schools such as student enrollment, student attendance, ethnicity, class size ratio, free or reduced lunches, and staff instructional minutes per day. The information is similar to that found on the

Common Core of Data, and the data probably were gathered from that source or from the report the school district prepared for the data submission to the Common Core of Data survey.

Statistical Compendiums

The most popular sources of statistical information about education are compendiums. One is compiled by the National Center for Education Statistics, and another by Bernan, a specialized government publications publisher. These statistical compendiums offer a wide array of statistics on various educational measures. They are created from the same set of data and are identical, with one major exception, described below.

Digest of Education Statistics (National Center of Education Statistics, annual)

Although information is rarely provided in detail down to the county, district, or city level, many times statistics for the greater geographic jurisdiction can still be valuable. For example, the *Digest* lists statistics on topics such as teacher/pupil ratio and expenditures by state, but it has very limited statistics by local area. One it does contain is "Selected statistics on enrollment, teachers, graduates, and dropouts in public school districts enrolling more than 15,000 pupils, by state: 1989 and 1996"—this table, alphabetically by state and school district, lists overall enrollment, enrollment by race, number of teachers, teacher/pupil ratio, number of staff, percentage of dropouts in grades 9–12, number of high school graduates, and number of schools. Another statistical table is of "Revenues and expenditures of public school districts enrolling more than 15,000 students," showing revenue by source of funds (federal, state, local); current expenditure per pupil; and expenditures on instruction, capital outlay, interest on school debt, and totals. The data published in the *Digest* are indicative of the fact that all of these data have been gathered and compiled on the school level but published selectively, on primarily the national and state levels in statistical compendiums such as these. In the *Digest*, as in most other U.S. government statistical compendiums, each table lists a source of data. To obtain statistics down to the local-area level, the original source can be consulted. Most of these sources are data files available for free from the NCES Web site, or on CD-ROM at a Depository library. Also, individual states, counties, and school districts have compiled data for their particular area and have made them available via the

World Wide Web. For details on these sites, see the section in this chapter on Specialized Resources/Full-Text Data Files.

Education Statistics of the United States (Bernan Press, Inc., annual)

This book is available at a reasonable price. Although it duplicates much of the information in *Digest of Education Statistics*, it is an alternative source. It adds some county-level statistics such as population, percentage by age, number of school districts, number of schools and level, and level of students by school, along with characteristics of students such as percentage with Individual Education Programs, percentage receiving free lunch, and percentage by minority group. This information has been gleaned from the Common Core of Data, the Public School District Financial Survey data file, and U.S. Census Bureau data. Data, therefore, is available down to the county, district, and school level, although it must be extracted from the database and compiled into tables usable by the average researcher.

More detail may often be obtained by contacting the national or state agency. The *Digest* publishes tables of information for larger geographic areas, but you will still have to go to the state or local agency to find more information.

Directories

Directories of education resources are another popular and useful information source. For local education resources, a directory might be published by a national agency such as the Department of Education or a local governmental agency such as a board of education. Directories usually have information such as addresses, names, and basics such as listings of expenditures and support services.

Local Education Agency (School District) Universe Survey Data
http://nces.ed.gov/ccd/pubagency.html

This resource is a listing of directory-type information on public schools from the Common Core of Data database. It provides a complete listing of every education agency in the United States responsible for providing free public elementary/secondary instruction or education support services, as well as basic information about all education agencies and the student populations for which they are responsible. These files are available back to 1992 and provide various types of information—names, addresses, telephone numbers, county codes, locale codes, and type of agencies: regular local school district, local school district component of a supervisory union, supervisory union administrative center, regional education service agency, state-operated institution, and federally operated institution. Student data include membership counts for such categories as ungraded, total pre-K–12, special education, graduates and high school completers, etc., and breakouts for dropouts by grade, sex, and race.

New Jersey School Directory
   http://www.state.nj.us/njded/directory

More specifically, this is a link from the home page of the New Jersey Department of Education Web site. It is organized first by county and then alphabetically by district or school. It should be easy to use as long as one knows the name of the city or school district being searched for. This is not always as easy as it sounds. One city's schools may actually belong to a larger school district with a different name. There is no easy solution to this problem, except to ask someone on the city level for that information. It might be possible to look at a map for a particular school district, but such maps are not readily available on the Internet. The local public library is a possibility and real estate and rental agents usually provide this information if you are moving to a new area. But the best way is to call the district office, provided you have its contact information. By clicking on the link for "School District," selecting "Atlantic" from the drop-down county menu, and typing in a keyword, let's say, "Vocational," you get the Atlantic County Vocational School District.

California Public School Directory (California Department of Education, annual)

There are also the old-fashioned paper directories such as this. It contains listings on members of the state board of education, various state agencies and officials, and special institutions and curriculum centers, as well as schools and school districts by county and special schools and associated officials, centers, and programs. Information includes address, telephone number(s), and names of principals only. A code number in the common county-district-school coding system is provided, specific to the state of California and of some significance. There is an alphabetical index of school and community college districts and an alphabetical index of schools and institutions

of higher learning. Personnel are listed in an alphabetical index. A geographic index to schools and school districts would probably be helpful. If the name of the school or person is not known, it may be difficult to find them (especially in a state the size of California). There might be a county directory of school districts, if the school district falls within the confines of the county.

Small Schools Directory: A Directory of Small and Charter Schools in the Chicago School System (Business and Professional People for the Public Interest, annual)

This is an example of a smaller, focused directory. The compiler is a private organization addressing the issue of schools from other than a strictly geographic, hierarchical arrangement. Presumably this directory would be a resource for parents looking to send their child to an alternative to a traditional public school.

TOPICAL RESOURCES

Certain resources may provide information on a specific topic, such as a particular school that would not be found in the general resources.

Key Statistics on Public Elementary and Secondary Schools and Agencies: School Year 1997–98 (National Center for Education Statistics, 2001)
   http://nces.ed.gov/pubs2001/2001304.pdf

This report presents detailed information from the 1995–96 and 1994–95 Common Core of Data about the approximately 16,000 local education agencies and 87,000 public schools operating during that time period. Topics include the number, size, and location of schools and school districts; enrollment in schools by grade; selected student characteristics; high school completers; dropouts; numbers of instructional, support, and administrative staff and staff ratios; and revenues and expenditures. Much of the information is broken out by school, or district data is reported. The appendix includes tables for the 1994–95 school year. This file was released on October 14, 1999. A free copy is also available from ED Pubs.

National Public School Locator and School District
   Locator http://nces.ed.gov/ccd/schoolsearch
   http://nces.ed.gov/ccd/districtsearch

These locators will enable you to find the correct name, address, telephone number, NCES ID number, urbanicity (rural, large city, etc.), and other student and teacher information for public schools or school districts for school year 2001–2002 as reported to NCES by state education officials in each state. This site also has information for E-Rate applicants (this is a discounted rate for Internet service available to schools and public libraries). There is also a listing of new schools and districts for 2001–2002 and 2002–2003. This represents unedited state data submissions and will be updated as new data are received. A search engine allows school or district names. This feature is very helpful for finding these codes.

School District Demographics (National Center for Education Statistics) http://nces.ed.gov/surveys/sdds/index.asp

This Web site links to both the Census 2000 School District Demographics and the Census 1990 School District Demographics. These two links appear to have replaced the former School District Data Book. The Census 2000 link allows comparisons between two school districts; for example, by selecting "Citrus County School District" in Florida and "Lake Forest School District" in Delaware, an interesting comparison table can be created.

The School District Data Book, compiled by NCES, was an electronic library containing social, financial, and administrative data for each of the 15,274 school districts in the United States for 1989–90. Census 1990 School District Demographics is an education database and information system. It contains the most extensive set of data on children, their households, and the nation's school systems. The volumes on U.S. data by state contain detailed 1990 Census school-district special tabulation data for the state and each of its districts and counties. The Profiles section allows access to data on every school district in the United States and enables you to retrieve data in a preorganized format at the URL listed. Access is actually provided by the Oregon State University Library server. You can also download the order form in PDF format (8KB) and fax your order for the School District Data Book (44 disks, $300 in 2004) to the Census Bureau Web page at http://www.census.gov/mp/www/rom/msrom6i.html.

The NCES has prepared an update to these data. The Bureau of the Census has produced special tabulation files using the basic record files of the 2000 Decennial Census of population and housing by school district. These tabulation files contain aggregated data describing attributes of children and households in school districts. Of primary interest is the total person record developed specifically for children 3 to 19 years of age, not the high school graduate.

SPECIALIZED RESOURCES/FULL-TEXT DATA FILES

Common Core of Data [CCD]: Information of Public Schools and School Districts in the United States http://nces.ed.gov/ccd

This is another NCES program, a comprehensive, annual, national statistical database of information concerning all public elementary and secondary schools (approximately 87,000) and school districts (approximately 16,000). The data set includes files such as Public Elementary/Secondary School Universe Data: 1987–Present, Local Education Agency (School District) Universe Survey Data: 1986–Present, and Local Education Agency (School District) Universe Survey Longitudinal Data File: 1986–95. Also included are data from the State Nonfiscal Public Elementary/Secondary Education Survey Data: 1995–Present, National Public Education Financial Survey Data: 1995–Present, Early Release Files, and the CCD Data Archive (at International Archive of Education Data). An example of data contained in the Public Elementary School Data file are number of classroom teachers, number of students per grade, and whether or not free lunch is available. Also included are numbers of students by five broad racial/ethnic categories: American Indian/Alaskan Native, Asian/Pacific Islander, Hispanic, black, and white.

There are also files containing financial data. The primary purpose of the National Public Education Financial Survey Data is to make available to the public on an annual basis state-level collection of revenues and expenditures for public education of grades prekindergarten through 12. Revenues and expenditures are audited after the close of the fiscal year and are then submitted to NCES by each state education agency. Beginning with fiscal year 1989, detailed fiscal data on all public revenues and expenditures within states for regular pre-K–12 education has been collected. This is not a great amount of data, but it is available for every public school in the United States. The Common Core of Data files are available on the NCES Web site and also on CD-ROM at Depository libraries. The data files are quite large and need unzipping. They still will not fit on a standard floppy disk.

They would have to be downloaded to a hard drive with enough memory. CCD is not available in paper.

ED TABs (National Center for Education Statistics, 1995) http://nces.ed.gov/pubsearch/bytype.asp?pubtype=012

These are a series of reports produced from the CCD. They include tabulations of series that are available for sale from the NCES Web site. These are more manageable if downloading and unzipping the files is too cumbersome. The reports in the series are available for sale from NCES on CD-ROM and many can be downloaded as PDF docs or browsed from this Web site. Examples are *E.D. TAB: Advanced Telecommunications in U.S. Public Elementary and Secondary Schools, K–12* (in which comparisons from a previous survey conducted one year earlier are presented and then compared one year later) and *E.D. TAB: Advanced Telecommunications in U.S. Public Elementary and Secondary Schools, 1995*, among a long list of others from 2004 back to 1990 to be found on the Web site, not all of them online. The home page of each report lists authorship and has other links, including general ordering information for a paper volume or CD-ROM.

Schools and Staffing Survey http://nces.ed.gov/surveys/sass

The Schools and Staffing Survey (SASS) is the nation's largest sample survey of the characteristics and conditions of America's public and private schools and the teachers and principals who work in them. It is a good resource for tracking school accountability. Conducted by NCES, SASS offers a source of data for policymakers, educators, education researchers, and the general public. SASS is representative of K–12 teachers, principals, schools, and school districts at the state and national levels. SASS provides state-reliable data on public schools and affiliation-reliable data on private schools. It collects data from every charter school in the United States and every school operated by the Bureau of Indian Affairs. SASS users can analyze data across various components of the survey—using NCES restricted data; they can link teachers and principals to their schools, and schools to their school districts. The Schools and Staffing Survey is available on CD-ROM or the 1999–2000 version is downloadable for free at the ED Pubs Web site.

Private School Universe Survey http://nces.ed.gov/surveys/pss

With increasing concern about alternatives in education, the interest and need for data on private education has also increased. NCES has made the collection of data on private elementary and secondary schools, which is comparable to the Common Core of Data universe survey for public schools, a priority. The purposes of this data-collection activity are to build an accurate and complete list of private schools to serve as a sampling frame for NCES surveys of private schools and to generate data on the total number of private schools, teachers, and students in the universe. This survey is conducted every two years, beginning with the first collection during the 1989–90 school year and proceeding in 1991–92, 1993–94, 1995–96, 1997–98, and 1999–2000 and every two years thereafter. The Web site says that the 2001–2002 version is currently being edited.

GRANTS AND FUNDING OPPORTUNITIES

There are good resources for finding information on grants and funding opportunities, but these are often known primarily to specialists in educational development. It is very helpful to have general information sources available on grant monies to schools and school districts.

ED.gov (U.S. Education Department) http://www.ed.gov/index.jsp

There is a wealth of funding information available at this site, which provides links to Web pages allowing one to check for information on Discretionary Grant Application Packages and General Administrative Regulations for Ed Grants. Funding opportunities are further delineated under such sponsors as the Office of Bilingual Education and Minority Languages Affairs (OBEMLA) and the Safe and Drug-Free Schools program. This site is useful for information about grants that are awarded and managed on the national level. There is also a page that allows searching for contacts by state.

OSEP Grant Opportunities and Funding (Office of Special Education Programs) http://www.ed.gov/fund/grant/apply/osep/index.html

On this Web site are links to program descriptions of grants specifically for children with disabilities, with application forms and instructions. Information on certifications, disclosure requirements, and performance evaluation reports are available. Local school officials will be able to print forms and review what kinds of information will need to be provided for the grant application process, which is very complex. Using this site is a helpful way to get information quickly and easily begin the process. This resource leads to more specific sources of funding at the school-district level.

Catalog of Federal Domestic Assistance (U.S. Office of Management and Budget) http://www.cfda.gov

This publication is available at most large Depository and public libraries. It is also available for free online at this Web site. As the basic reference source for federal assistance programs, the primary purpose of the *Catalog* is to assist users in identifying them, obtaining general information on a program, and meeting its specific objectives. In addition, the intent of the *Catalog* is to improve coordination and communication between the federal government and state and local governments.

The *Catalog* provides the user with access to programs administered by federal departments and agencies in a single publication. Program information is cross-referenced by indexes of functional classification, subject, applicant, deadline(s) for program application submission, and authorizing legislation. These are valuable resource tools, which, if used carefully, can make it easier to identify specific areas of program interest more efficiently. Other sections of the *Catalog* provide users with information on programs added and deleted since the last edition, a crosswalk of program numbers and title changes, regional and local offices, intergovernmental review requirements, definitions of the types of assistance under which programs are administered, proposal writing, grant application procedures, and additional sources of information on federal programs and services. Also included are two charts on how to use the *Catalog* to locate programs of interest.

Programs selected for inclusion in the federal assistance database are defined as being any function of a federal agency that provides assistance or benefits for a state or states, territorial possession, county, city, other political subdivision, grouping, or instrumentality thereof; any domestic profit or nonprofit corporation, institution, or individual, other than an agency of the federal government. Of special interest is a listing of contact persons in the state for local government officials and the general public.

Grants: Corporate Grantmaking for Racial and Ethnic Communities (National Committee for Responsive Philanthropy, 2000)

This source is unique, with a focus on applying for grants based on ethnic/racial criteria. Of course, these criteria would apply to grant applications on the local governmental level. Most ethnic and racial communities are in cities and towns.

The publication lists grant statistics by industry and company, with additional information about revenue and profits. Corporations are listed by the ethnic or racial group to which they donate, and the resource has charts and tables that list further details on how corporations spend their money. This enables one to see what corporation might be most likely to award a grant based on a specific need. Racial/ethnic profiles are broken down into categories such as amounts awarded, number of recipients, number of donors, average grant, major interest areas funded, most generous donors, most generous industries, least generous industries, and top recipients by number of grants. For example, the top corporate giving industry for African Americans has been the insurance industry; for Hispanics, the leisurewear and sports equipment industry. Another interesting statistic states that only half the companies awarded funds to Native Americans, and the computer industry was the top giver.

There are entries for individual corporations that list the company's business, what portion is racial or ethnically based, details about the grants, giving preferences, racial/ethnic beneficiaries, contacts, and application procedures. There is a feature called "If You Approach Toyota, Remember This," which gives some helpful tips specific to Toyota. An example is: "Grant requests to the corporation contributions program of $5000 or less are directed to the employee contributions committee. Other requests are sent to community relations." Application procedures list information about deadlines, whether the form is available, who the personnel contacts are, the anticipated wait, and whether unsolicited proposals are accepted.

Most large corporations are profiled, such as Ford Motor Company, Bank of America, PepsiCo, Sara Lee, Chevron, Metropolitan Life Insurance Company, and Calvin Klein. Two major industries with poor records on reporting grant making are professional sports and the media/entertainment. There is also a listing by metropolitan area; for example, for San Antonio, there is a summary of total funding, grants, average grant size, geographic parameters, significant characteristics, interest areas, types of support, and a list of companies with awards given. For example, Hispanics as an ethnic group have received the bulk of the grants, and grants to education were almost four times that given in any other area. The biggest corpo- rate giver in San Antonio was May Department Stores. Lastly, there is a list of grants by corporation, listing the category, organization, name, city, state, racial/ethnic group(s) awarded, and amount. This is very useful information if one is looking for possible funding sources.

CHAPTER 15
Finding Environmental Information

Darcy Carrizales and Jim Church

MAJOR TOPICS COVERED

MAJOR RESOURCES COVERED

INTRODUCTION

Finding environmental information at the local level can be a daunting task. Environmental issues compose a wide variety of diverse topics. Some issues overlap, while others have nothing in common with one another. Add to this the fact that information covering local areas can be collected by the federal, state, or local government and disseminated by a completely different source, and the task becomes even more challenging. This chapter should help to alleviate some of the difficulties encountered in researching local governmental information about the environment.

When searching for environmental information, it is important to define what kind of information you are looking for. Keep in mind that some information may be found among reports in a related area. Environmental health data are often found along with those of hazardous waste materials. Similarly, environmental justice resources can be found in the company of environmental law. Laws and regulations often require specific reports to be produced by federal agencies, cities, states, towns, and industries. Searching for these regulations can aid in the discovery of what reports are produced and where that information can be accessed.

Although the focus of this chapter is on finding local sources, with environmental data it is important not to overlook information compiled at the national level. National agencies, such as the Environmental Protection Agency (EPA) and the United States Geological Survey (USGS), collect data directly from small geographic areas and collaborate with local agencies to retrieve local area information. This can result in databases and detailed reports that contain information down to the state, city, and even zip code level. Contacting local government departments and agencies and doing research in the local library can be a great help in locating some types of materials. Keep in mind that although the government may require that certain reports be produced, it may rely on local governments to do the collecting and dissemination of the data.

This chapter provides just a small sample of resources that are available on such topics as planning, public policy, numeric and spatial data, maps, law, regulations, pollution, toxic substances, industrial waste, and other topics. Materials such as these can be found in many cities, townships, and states throughout the United States.

Some recent changes have reduced access to documents due to security concerns after the September 11, 2001, terrorist attacks. It is unclear whether these changes will be permanent or other solutions will allow this information to be disseminated again. Currently several agencies have pulled information from their Web sites. Examples of withdrawn documents include several water-resource reports from the USGS, the New Jersey Department of Environmental Protection's Community Right to Know Program's Web site, and the interactive maps from the International Nuclear Safety Center.

GENERAL GUIDES AND RESOURCES

Directories

A good government directory can be an excellent starting point in the search for local environmental information. The best ones will include current contact information for government agencies, local organizations, and public officials. Don't hesitate to pick up the phone and contact your local city or county environmental agency. Unfortunately, many environmental directories get published, continue for a year or so, and then cease, never to be heard from again. All too often the environmental directory in your local library will be out of date. Some of the better resources are listed here, but when in doubt, investigate your local city or county agency Web sites and libraries, and take advantage of the e-mails and telephone numbers provided.

The Environmental Resource Handbook (Grey House Publishing, 2002)

This encyclopedic resource is one of the more comprehensive environmental directories in print and includes listings of associations and organizations, research centers, educational programs, legal information, "green city" rankings, consultants, publications, electronic resources, and state and local government agencies. Also included are statistical annexes and rankings for a variety of environmental indicators at the state, county, and city levels. The publisher's claim that no other resource on the market provides as much current environmental information is surprisingly credible, and detailed geographic, subject, and entry indexes make this source particularly easy to use.

National Environmental Directory (Harbinger Communications, 1995, annual) http://www.environmentaldirectory.net/default.htm

This digital directory, available on the Internet and a selection of CD-ROMs, lists more than 13,000 organizations in the United States associated with environmental issues and education. It is probably the most comprehensive environmental directory available, in terms of the total number of entries. The free Internet version is searchable by organization name, geographic location (city, state, and zip code), environmental keyword, and subject category. The CDs, or software programs, which cost only $50 each, offer enhanced search and download features and cover the following regions: New England, the Central Atlantic, the Great Lakes, the Pacific Northwest, Hawaii, and California.

State and Local Gateway: Environment/Energy (U.S. Environmental Protection Agency) http://www.epa.gov/epapages/statelocal

This Web site, intended as a tool for state and local officials, contains descriptions of best practices of local governments, resources for government officials and planners, environmental training information, state and local environmental news, and guides to environmental laws and regulations. Also included are contact information and Web links to EPA regional offices and state environmental agencies. An annotated topical reference section covers environmental Internet resources in 15 different categories, including air, community development, human health, water, natural resources, and research and technology. EPA also publishes several directories in print, including *National Directory of Volunteer Environmental Monitoring Programs* and the *Pollution Prevention Directory*.

Environmental Libraries

If you live in or close to a large city, chances are the local government or EPA will have an Environmental Library close by. They are staffed by library professionals with expert knowledge of their local jurisdictions, so be sure to ask for help. These specialists not only can assist you in finding the correct resources, but can also put you in touch with knowledgeable individuals in state or local government.

EPA Regional Libraries http://www.epa.gov/natlibra

The EPA divides the United States into 10 regions, whose libraries are among the best collections of local environmental information in the United States. Each library houses EPA reports, books, journals, and government documents on nearly all aspects of the environment, including hazardous waste, pollution prevention, sustainable development, environmental justice, the history of the environmental movement, and many other topics. The EPA Online Library System, at http://www.epa.gov/natlibra/ols.htm, also offers a collection of databases with citations for the holdings of most EPA libraries. It also includes holdings of EPA documents available through the National Technical Information Service (NTIS) (also searchable on FedWorld at http://www.fedworld.gov). To locate an EPA regional library near you, see the "Link to EPA Libraries" home page at http://www.epa.gov/natlibra/libraries.htm.

City and County Libraries

County and city governments may have their own environmental libraries, so check the directory or Web site of your local government. Environmental departments may be scattered throughout the local bureaucracy, so be persistent in tracking down the right office: environmental agencies have widely divergent names like "environmental services," "natural resources," and "planning and land use." A good exam-

ple is the City of San Diego Environmental Services Department Library (http://www.sannet.gov/environmental-services/geninfo/library.shtml), which houses materials on landfills, solid waste, environmental management, recycling, and legal information. Piper's State and Local Government on the Net Web site, at http://www.statelocalgov.net/index.cfm, is a quick way to reach Web pages for similar sources in your area.

Often universities with environmental programs will have libraries that contain significant collections on the environment. An example of this is the University of Oregon, which has created the Web site Local Area Data for Oregon: A Bibliography of Sources, http://libweb.uoregon.edu/govdocs/localdat.html. This guide to state and local sources contains large sections about ecology, hazardous substances, recycling, environmental impact statements, public lands, and water. The bibliography includes both print and online sources and provides the call numbers for items found in the library at the University of Oregon.

Historical Societies and Archives

Environmental archives and historical societies have extensive collections of primary source materials on the environment, including local government information. For a comprehensive search for environmental archives in the United States, the Library of Congress has the most comprehensive Web site.

Archives of Industrial Society [AIS] (University of Pittsburgh Archives Service Center) http://www.library.pitt.edu/libraries/archives/ais.html

These archives house 626 primary source collections on the development of urban industrial society, particularly environmental history and the urban environment. The collections deal chiefly with Pittsburgh and western Pennsylvania, but because of the industrial importance of the region, much of the material is of national interest. Historical records of local government agencies are well represented, including government records from the city of Pittsburgh and Allegheny County, as well as Environmental Action Foundation records, historic land use and coal mining maps, a WQED-TV Three Mile Island video collection, and selected primary sources from England and Canada. The Web site offers an impressive list of searchable and browsable finding aids, including 210 guides to archival collections on the history of the greater Pittsburgh area.

Harvard University Environmental Information Center (Harvard College Library Science Center) http://hcl.harvard.edu/environment

This information center includes the Environmental Science and Public Policy Archives, a collection of primary source materials documenting the evolution of the environmental science and public policy movement from the mid-1960s to the present. Collections include correspondence of governmental and nongovernmental participants during environmental policy deliberations. The center also features a virtual gateway to environmental research via its Web site at http://environment.harvard.edu.

Environmental Design Archives (University of California, Berkeley, College of Environmental Design) http://www.ced.berkeley.edu/cedarchives

This archive contains nearly one hundred primary source collections documenting the built environment from 1890 to 1990, including correspondence, reports, drawings, photographs, and artifacts. The focus is the San Francisco area, but information on projects throughout California and the United States are included. Selected finding aids for the collections are available on the Online Archive of California under "UC Berkeley Finding Aids," at http://www.oac.cdlib.org. Finding aids are listed by name of the collection donor (e.g., Simpson [Horace G.] Collection, 1907–1917) so some exploration is needed for first-time users.

Indexing and Abstracting Databases

One excellent source of information at the local level is in specialized indexing and abstracting databases. Many of these are not free, and even those that allow free searching charge a fee for a copy of the document, electronic or paper. Several very specialized databases are described below.

Environmental Sciences and Pollution Management (Cambridge Scientific Abstracts) http://www.csa.com/csa/factsheets/envclust.shtml

This database provides environmental citations and abstracts from over 1,000 journals, conference proceedings, books, and reports. An extraordinarily comprehensive system, it contains subfiles in the areas of water resources, pollution, agricultural and environmental biotechnology, aquatic environmental quality, ecology, environmental engineering, environmental

impact statements, toxicology, and health and safety science. This is perhaps the most complete environmental database available and is the system of choice for any research library or organization that can afford the price.

Environmental Issues and Policy Index http://www.epnet.com/government/enpolindex.asp

Formerly the Environmental Knowledgebase, the Environmental Issues and Policy Index is now published by EBSCo Information Services. This is the electronic version of the print *Environmental Periodicals Bibliography*, and as of December 2001 contained over 640,000 citations to environmental articles dating from 1973. The database is a broad-based, interdisciplinary product that covers the full range of social, political, and philosophical issues involving the environment, including air, energy, science and industry, land resources, conservation, agriculture, pollution, and health. Approximately 1,000 journals are included in the complete system, and over 400 are currently indexed. Journal titles are browsable alphabetically by title, subject, publisher, and country.

Elsevier Science Direct http://www.sciencedirect.com

Many commercial databases index scientific journals, but the excellent search features of Elsevier Science Direct—which includes subject limits and searching by keyword and references—make this online journal collection an abstracting and indexing database in its own right. The system contains the full text of more than 1,000 Elsevier journals in the life, physical, medical, technical, and social sciences, including earth and planetary sciences, energy and power, and the environment. An environmental query using keywords and local geographic locations can yield very fruitful results.

PLANNING AND LAND USE DOCUMENTS

Planning and land use documents offer a rich supply of local environmental information, particularly environmental impact reports (EIRs), which are required by law to comply with the standards and procedures of state and local environmental quality acts and guidelines. EIRs are often deposited at city and county libraries, so a search in your local public library catalog may locate them. Unfortunately, not all libraries have the resources to acquire, process, and catalog these documents, and there are usually no depository agreements under which they are obliged to retain them.

The only real clearinghouses for local environmental documents may be the county or city clerk's offices, which are required by law to comply with each state's public records management act. Typically, this legislation stipulates retention schedules for public documents. The matter is complicated by the fact that plans may be stored in planning and land use offices or closed-stack storage facilities that offer limited public access. The user may need to know in advance the city or county resolution or project number of the report in question; general subject requests may be refused. Another issue is that local governments may not be required to permanently archive this material; public-records retention schedules vary according to the type of document and level of government

Fortunately, more information has begun to surface on the Internet, which presents both new opportunities and new challenges. Documents made available for public review may be posted (often temporarily) on clerk or planning and land use Web sites and advertised in local newspapers. Selected State Data Centers also offer full-text environmental planning and land use documents online.

Local Planning Documents

*Journal of Planning Literature, Incorporating the
    CPL Bibliographies* (Sage Publications, quarterly)

The Council of Planning Librarians (CPL) produces this thorough bibliography of the local planning literature, previously issued as a monographic series with individual titles such as "Environmental Discrimination," "Waterfront Revitalization," and "Habitat Conservation Plans, 1984–1994." Since 1996 the bibliographies have been incorporated into *the Journal of Planning Literature*, and local environmental documents are included. Searching can be tedious, as the bibliography retains a traditional subject-oriented classification (without a print or electronic index), so this source is best used by those striving for comprehensiveness in specialized areas. It is also available electronically through Sage Publications, http://www.sagepub.co.uk/journal.aspx?pid=105676.

Geographical Abstracts: Regional and Community
    Planning via GEOBASE (Elsevier Science, 1980)
    http://www.oclc.org/firstsearch/databases/details/
    dbinformation_GEOBASE.html

GEOBASE is one of the more confusing products on the market because it offers such a disparate collection of subfiles. Although offered by several other publisher/vendors, the Online Computer Learning Center's (OCLC) *FirstSearch* version includes the following categories: ecology, geology, geomechanics, oceanography, physical geography, international development, and human geography. Only the last two categories deal with the planning literature, corresponding to publications indexed in the print *International Development Abstracts* and *Geographical Abstracts*. Once the user figures this out, the database offers a surprisingly rich store of books and journal abstracts in planning and land use, much of it region specific. This is a much overlooked, surprisingly useful database that is one of the most valuable indexing and abstracting databases for planning literature.

California Environmental Resources Evaluation System [CERES] (California Resources Agency)
    http://www.ceres.ca.gov

CERES is an online network that integrates state, local, and national environmental resources and makes them available to a wide range of users. Sources are browsable by geographic area, including cities, counties, bioregions, and watersheds, as well as by organization, theme, and data type. The strength of the system lies in its ability to quickly steer the user toward specific resources at the local level—for instance, a person searching for data on local invasive plant species can select the appropriate geographic region and browse by theme to uncover full-text reports, project descriptions, and local government contacts, including names, phone numbers, and e-mail addresses. The system also includes the California Land Use Planning Information Network (LUPIN), at http://ceres.ca.gov/planning/index.html, which focuses on planning and land use documents, spatial data, regulations, and special-districts information not easily obtained elsewhere. Interfaces that allow users to combine subjects ranging from the hydrosphere to health care with data types like aerial photographs, digital archives, bibliographies, and government reports makes this site among the most effective environmental research tools in the nation.

San Diego Association of Governments
    http://www.sandag.org

The San Diego Association of Governments (SANDAG) is a joint-powers agency created by the local governments of San Diego County. The organization adopts plans for growth, transportation, environmental management, housing, air quality and conservation in the San Diego region, many of which are available full-text on the Internet. The Web site also features the "San Diego Data Warehouse," at http://cart.sandag.org/dw, and online interactive mapping systems (http://cart.sandag.org) that are unique sources of community and neighborhood data and have been nationally recognized. The "Demographic & Economic Mapping System" will create custom maps.

Environmental Impact Reports

EIRs (also called environmental impact statements) provide detailed analysis of the environmental effects of a proposed land use project, including air and water quality, geology and soils, drainage, hazardous materials, light and noise, and aesthetics. Most EIRs include detailed maps, photos, and statistical data intended to illustrate significant irreversible environmental changes that may be effected by a development project. In high-growth regions, EIRs are legion, particularly since governments typically require that both draft and final reports be printed and distributed.

CEQAnet Database (California Governor's Office of Planning and Research) http://www.ceqanet.ca.gov

The California state government established a clearinghouse in 1973 to receive and distribute environmental documents according to the California Environmental Quality Act (CEQA). This online database contains environmental documents submitted to the state for review since 1990. Entries provide summaries of EIRs, negative declarations, and other types of CEQA and National Environmental Policy Act documents. Coverage at the local level is impressive, if not comprehensive. For information prior to 1990, the California EIR Monitor (http://ceres.ca.gov/topic/env_law/ceqa/guidelines/art16.html) notices amendments to CEQA guidelines and listings of draft EIRs by county, project number, title, description, location, and contact information from 1973 to 1988.

Digital Library Project: Documents Collection (Chesire II) (University of California, Berkeley) http://elib.cs.berkeley.edu/docs

This is a substantial full-text digital collection of documents, maps, articles, EIRs, pamphlets, bulletins, and county plans dealing with the California environment and is one of the many outstanding components of the UC-Berkeley's Digital Library Project. Government agency sources include the California Department of Water Resources, the California Department of Fish and Game, the San Diego Association of Governments, and many others. Chesire II is the name of the search engine (http://elib.cs.berkeley.edu/cheshire), touted as a next-generation online catalog and full-text retrieval database that enables users to search additional digital collections and catalogs, ranging from the Library of Congress to the *CIA World Factbook*.

POLLUTION, TOXIC SUBSTANCES, AND HAZARDOUS WASTE

The Emergency Planning and Community Right-to-Know Act (EPCRA—also known as Title III of the Superfund Amendments and Reauthorization Act) was created to help plan for chemical emergencies and provide information to the public about chemicals used, stored, and released in communities. EPCRA and other environmental legislation, such as the Clean Air Act (CAA), have made it easier for the public to find information on hazardous waste and pollution in a particular area by requiring certain industry groups and federal facilities to report data.

Databases, Encyclopedias, and Guides

Chemicals in Your Community (U.S. Environmental Protection Agency) http://www.epa.gov/swercepp/ep-publ.htm#chemicals

A PDF version of a pamphlet produced by the Office of Solid Waste and Emergency Response, this document is a great starting place to find out where to uncover environmental information about local communities. It explains what data the EPCRA and CAA collect and the limitations the data have. The booklet contains contact information and methods for obtaining data from various agencies, Internet sites, and organizations not affiliated with EPCRA or CAA.

Toxic Release Inventory [TRI] (U.S. Environmental Protection Agency) http://www.epa.gov/triexplorer

This database contains annual reports on chemicals released by industry groups and federal facilities that are required to report under EPCRA. Release reports, waste transfer reports, and waste quantity reports are the three types of TRI reports that can be produced. Within reports, data can be grouped into five categories: facility, chemical, year, industry type, and geographic area. Reports can be made as specific as the zip code level. The most recent data included in TRI are from 1999, but any updated reports can be found in Envirofacts, at http://www.epa.gov/enviro/html/ef_over view.html. Another site, Scorecard.org, http://www. scorecard.org/env-releases/us-map.tcl, combines TRI data with information on the potential health hazards of toxic substances, indicating what chemical releases may be of the greatest health dangers.

TOXNET: Toxicology Data Network (U.S. National Library of Medicine) http://toxnet.nlm.nih.gov

TOXNET also provides access to the TRI. In addition to TRI information, it provides links to a number of other toxicology databases, such as the Integrated Risk Information System (IRIS), which focuses on human health risks associated with toxic substances. The Web site provides an assessment of hazards and gives information on over 500 specific chemicals. Several other toxicology-based databases are provided. The Right to Know Network's (RTK Net) Environmental Databases, at http://www.rtknet.org/ rtkdata.html, has a similar site that provides access to various databases covering the environment, housing, and sustainable development.

Superfund: National Priorities List (U.S. Environmental Protection Agency) http://www.epa.gov/ superfund/sites/npl/index.htm

This site lists national priorities for cleaning up land that has been exposed to hazardous waste. Locations of Superfund sites are displayed by state on maps or are available in lists arranged by EPA region. The site lists the dates places were listed on Superfund and when and if they have been deleted from the priorities list. Clicking on the name of the Superfund site brings up a site description, cleanup progress, and the types of threats and contaminants present. For similar information, *Toxic Waste Sites: An Encyclopedia of Endangered America* (ABC-Clio, 1997) is an encyclopedia that summarizes the history and cleanup (or planned cleanup) of over 13,000 Superfund sites. Information about legal actions taken and the parties responsible for the contamination is also provided. The Web site allows searching for Superfund cleanup sites on the national priorities list by state.

State and Local Sources

The federal requirements for reporting certain environmental hazards have resulted in the creation of

Local Emergency Planning Committees and State Emergency Response Commissions. They develop emergency response plans at the local level and receive annual reports from industries required to report by law.

In addition to federally mandated reporting, states also often have their own requirements regarding pollution and toxins. State and local agencies, such as the Nebraska Department of Environmental Quality or the St. Louis City Division of Air Pollution Control, often are in control of or have the knowledge of state and city regulations. EPA regional Web sites are another good source for state and regional information.

Some local areas have become famous for their environmental troubles. Love Canal and Hinckley (made famous by Julia Roberts in the movie *Erin Brockovich*) have a plethora of Web sites, books, articles, and even movies created about them. A search in the local library catalog or browsing at a bookstore can uncover many of these materials. Additionally, searching the catalog of a library near a polluted site or checking with its special collections librarian can also unearth information about those sites that you may not find elsewhere. Superfund sites usually set up a records repository at a local library or with a local agency. These contain documents about the project, and their location can usually be found in the Superfund National Priorities List.

Water-Resources Investigations Reports (U.S. Geological Survey) http://water.usgs.gov/pubs/wri

Water-Resources Investigations Reports include data and interpretive reports specific to local areas. The reports are usually quite technical in nature and display extensive charts, graphs, tables, and maps. Often the reports are a collaboration between the USGS and state or local agencies or other federal agencies. Examples of just two titles are (1) *Delineation of Discharge Areas of Two Contaminant Plumes by Use of Diffusion Samplers, John's Pond, Cape Cod, Massachusetts, 1998* and (2) *Ground-Water Quality and Susceptibility of Ground Water to Effects from Domestic Wastewater Disposal in Eastern Bernalillo County, Central New Mexico, 1990–91.* Published for over 20 years, reports can be found in many Depository libraries or ordered from the USGS, and selected cases from 1973 can be found at the Web site.

Danger All Around: Waste Storage Crisis on the Texas and Louisiana Gulf Coast (University of Texas Press, 1993)

Studies of Texas and Louisiana Gulf Coast waste storage sites are used to emphasize the impacts of petrochemical industrial facilities and waste storage sites on the environment. Although the majority of the book deals specifically with these two states, the broader context of environmental waste is provided and conclusions are drawn about overall environmental protection, public health, and safety. Regulatory information is also given for the national and state levels.

Texas Superfund Program (Texas Natural Resource Conservation Commission) http://www.tnrcc. state.tx.us/permitting/remed/superfund

Similar to the Superfund National Priorities List, this Web page is exclusive to Superfund sites in Texas. It gives the mission of the Superfund program and the laws that regulate it. The site is updated every 30 days when new information is available. Other states have similar sites. The Hazardous Materials and Waste Management Division of Colorado's Department of Public Health and the Environment maintains a Web page for the federal Superfund sites in Colorado (http://www.cdphe.state.co.us/hm/sf_sites.asp).

NUMERIC DATA

Environmental data differ from much of the numeric information generated by government agencies in that it is tabulated according to natural, rather than human, boundaries. Such areas include hydraulic regions, air basins, watersheds, and single-point sources like reporting stations and industrial facilities, as opposed to Metropolitan Statistical Areas (MSAs) or Census tracts. The majority of the data are on the Internet, although print sources can be consulted for quick reference. The advent of Geographic Information Systems (GIS) technology has revolutionized users' ability to interpolate data taken from single observation points and construct environmental models, according to varying climatic conditions. Because much of the data are seasonal (even hourly), print sources represent only a snapshot of conditions at a certain point in time. The following sources are representative of some of the better federal, state, and local tools that provide current and historical environmental data at the local level.

Federal Sources

National Air Quality and Emissions Trends Report (Environmental Protection Agency, 1978, annual)

This print report (SuDoc: EP4.22/2) on ambient air quality covers emissions and concentrations of particulate matter, sulfur dioxide, carbon monoxide, nitrogen dioxide, ozone, hazardous air pollutants, and lead from 1978 to the present. Pollution data are recorded at federal, state, and local monitoring sites in urban and suburban areas. This is one of the more convenient and useful data resources (print or otherwise) in the field of local environmental policy, as it presents a snapshot of critical air quality and emissions data by MSA over time. A condensed version of the data from 1990–1998, entitled the *National Air Pollutants Emissions Trends Report*, is available at http://www.epa.gov/ttn/chief/ publications.html#reports.

Environmental Industry of the United States: Overview by State and Metropolitan Statistical Area (U.S. Department of Commerce, 1997, semiannual)

Statistical profiles of the environmental sector of the economy are provided for all states and 49 MSAs. Revenues and employment are displayed by environmental industry segment. Each industry segment includes sections that cover services, equipment, and resources. Information in these sections is then subdivided further. An overview of statistics for the United States is provided and data for each state as a percentage of the United States are given. Data provided are from 1997. SuDoc identifier is C 61.2:IN 8/7/.

Envirofacts Data Warehouse and Applications (U.S. Environmental Protection Agency) http://www.epa.gov/enviro

To date, this Web site is the EPA's best attempt at providing a user-friendly gateway for environmental data applicable to the local level. Some of the data include information on industrial facilities, hazardous waste, Superfund sites, toxic releases, water permits, drinking water, and more. Users can retrieve data to generate reports or create maps from a variety of interactive mapping applications. Data are frequently available for cities, counties, and even zip codes. More than one database can be queried simultaneously and there are a host of advanced user options available.

EPA AIRData (U.S. Environmental Protection Agency) http://www.epa.gov/air/data/index.html

This statistical Web site offers data on concentrations of air pollutants for cities, towns, points, and mobile sources, as well as emissions estimates of hazardous air pollutants. The "Data" section directs the user to the National Emission Inventory database, http://www.epa.gov/air/data/neidb.html, which provides emissions data by point sources, facility emissions, and even Standard Industrial Classification (SIC) code. The "Monitors" section measures prevailing levels of air pollution in cities and towns across the United States. A section on state/local contacts, http://www.epa.gov/air/data/contsl.html, lists individuals in state, county, and city environmental agencies who manage air pollution data in their jurisdictions.

State Sources

These state and local resources are examples of the types of information you may be able to find in your locality, although data availability varies considerably. Some states offer substantial amounts of local data, while others offer little. There seems to be little pattern nationwide, despite the environmental significance of region: Colorado has relatively little environmental data online, while Maryland features some excellent, state-of-the-art numeric databases at the Maryland Department of Natural Resources Data Sets Web site, http://together.net/~bspatial/duck/samples.htm. Some states post daily or even hourly data on the Web, while others post summary data only.

California Data Exchange Center [CDEC] (California Department of Water Resources) http://cdec.water.ca.gov

The CDEC collects, stores, disseminates, and exchanges hydrological data from hundreds of rain, snow, temperature, wind, atmospheric pressure, humidity, and stream stage sensors operated by over 50 federal, state, and local government agencies. Data are available in real time, hourly, daily, monthly, and historically. Included among the seemingly inexhaustible supply of hydrological data sets from this site are current river conditions, snow pack levels, river stages and flows, reservoir data, satellite images, river and tide forecasts, and numerous full-text reports.

California Air Quality Database [ADAM] (California Air Resources Board) http://cdec.water.ca.gov

These air quality data are derived from hundreds of air quality monitoring stations throughout California, which measure ozone and air pollution (particulate matter) concentration levels, including the number of days in which pollution levels exceed EPA standards.

Data are available statewide, by air basic, air pollution control district, county, and monitoring site; hourly, daily, and weekly. A variety of software modeling tools are available, including programs for calculating health risk assessments, emissions inventory models, and meteorological models.

Local Sources and State Data Centers

Much environmental data obtainable from local governments is available at the state and federal levels; however, there are some exceptions. A rule of thumb is that when looking for local data of any sort, investigate your closest State Data Center. These are cooperative programs between the states and the U.S. Census Bureau that make local data available via a network of state and local governments, universities, and libraries. A description of the program, with a listing of State Data Centers, is available on the U.S. Census Bureau Web site, at http://www.census.gov/sdc/www.

County of San Diego Air Pollution Control District (County of San Diego, Air Pollution Control District) http://www.sdapcd.co.san-diego.ca.us/air/air_reports.html

This site contains numeric data on ozone levels and air toxins for specific regions in San Diego County. Ozone level data are reported hourly by air contaminant levels (nitrogen dioxide, nitric oxide, hydrocarbons, carbon monoxide, and sulfur dioxide, along with wind speeds and temperatures) and are archived daily. Another feature is the emissions calculation procedures, http://www.sdapcd.co.san-diego.ca.us/emission/emission.htm, which presents detailed emissions information from local facilities, public notification and health risk assessments of local industries, and reports of local environmental studies.

Hazardous Materials San Diego (County of San Diego Land Use and Environment Group, Dept. of Environmental Health) http://www.sdcounty.ca.gov/deh/hmd

This Web site includes a database on hazardous waste materials produced by business establishments in San Diego County. The system can be searched by establishment name, zip code, city, street, and establishment number. It supplies information on types of waste generated (e.g., metal sludge, infectious waste) and what, if any, environmental hazards are associated with the company's waste materials.

SPECIALIZED MAPS, ATLASES, AND SPATIAL DATA

Atlases and Maps

Maps and atlases can be used to display a variety of environmental information. Federal and state agencies are often the creators of these visual resources, which provide information down to the state, city, and sometimes zip code level.

Environmental Atlas (U.S. Environmental Protection Agency) http://www.epa.gov/ceisweb1/ceishome/atlas

The Environmental Atlas is a collection of maps that include environmental information about land, water, air, and population issues. The data are collected from federal, state, and local governments. The site is easy to use and includes detailed information about where and how the data were obtained. There are four primary sections: USA Maps, State and Regional Maps, Learn about Maps and Data, and About the Atlas. The national maps are a visual summary of data collected from the entire United States. In some cases Hawaii and Alaska are excluded. Smaller geographic regions are shown by state or EPA region.

EnviroMapper (U.S. Environmental Protection Agency) http://www.epa.gov/enviro/html/em/index.html

EnviroMapper differs from the EPA's Environmental Atlas by allowing maps with specifically chosen information to be created and displayed at the national, state, and county level. Brownfields, Superfund sites, and watersheds are some of the information that can be mapped. EnviroMapper also includes mapping of the Environmental Monitoring for Public Access and Community Tracking (EMPACT) program, which provides real-time environmental data collected from cities across the country.

HUD Environmental Maps E-Maps (U.S. Department of Housing and Urban Development [HUD]) http://www.hud.gov/emaps

Like EnviroMapper, HUD's E-Maps allows users to create their own maps. HUD compiles these maps using environmental data from the EPA and community data of its own. This combination allows users to see environmental aspects in even small portions of a city. Users can then click on parts of the map's legend to indicate which items they wish to display.

SanGIS (joint-powers agency of the county and city of San Diego) http://www.sangis.org

SanGIS provides access to regional geographic databases for the county and city of San Diego. A map gallery provides ordering instructions for printed versions of the maps. Interactive maps are available by subject, including natural features, utilities, and conservation planning areas. As with the HUD Environmental Maps, interactive map users can choose which types of data they wish to display.

Texas Oil Spill Planning and Response Atlas (National Oceanic and Atmospheric Administration, 1998)

This CD-ROM contains maps and data that indicate environmentally sensitive areas in order to help plan for the event of an oil spill. Although not created to be environmental data, these maps contain information on habitat, biological resources, human and animal populations, and shoreline sensitivity. Sixty-seven detailed maps are provided that cover the upper coast of Texas from the Texas-Louisiana border to the Matagorda Bay. This CD-ROM is one of a series of Environmental Sensitivity Index atlases, which are available for over 20 states and regions and in a variety of formats, including paper, PDF, and GIS datasets. GIF formats of some maps can be found on the National Ocean Service Mapfinder Web site (http://oceanservice.noaa.gov/mapfinder).

GEOGRAPHIC INFORMATION SYSTEMS DOWNLOADS

GIS is a computer system that uses hardware, software, and trained personnel to retrieve, store, analyze, and display spatially referenced data. It is useful for researching environmental data not only because of its mapping abilities, but also because of its analyzing and modeling abilities. Data of different types can be layered on top of each other, as long as they both use the same coordinate system. This would allow users to simultaneously display the locations of toxic Web sites along with reported incidences of cancer. Worst-case-scenario data can also be input into GIS in order to analyze the possible repercussions of certain actions. The uses of GIS with environmental data are practically endless. Land use planning, natural resource management, watershed analysis, toxic site locations, and health issues are some examples of data commonly analyzed, modeled, or mapped by GIS.

National Geospatial Data Clearinghouse (Federal Geographic Data Committee) http://www.fgdc.gov/clearinghouse/clearinghouse.html

This site provides the ability to search over 250 spatial data servers that offer digital geographic data for use primarily with GIS. Some sections of this clearinghouse can be searched separately. The EPA's Geospatial Data Clearinghouse, http://www.epa.gov/nsdi, and the USGS Geospatial Data Clearinghouse, http://nsdi.usgs.gov, provide access to the spatial datasets used by their Web sites either for free or for a cost. Many nongovernmental sites also offer downloadable information about the environment. At MapCruzin.Com, of the Clary Meuser Research Network, you can download free digital maps or purchase more complex maps (http://www.mapcruzin.com/download_mapcruz.htm). The GIS DataDepot (http://www.gisdatadepot.com) offers a similar service.

National Resources and Environmental Management (University of Rhode Island) http://www.edc.uri.edu

The cooperative extension program at the University of Rhode Island, along with several other sponsors, has created this Web site, which organizes and displays links to other Internet sources containing environmental data about Rhode Island for use with GIS systems. Access to data about the state as a whole is given, and individual regions and towns are also covered. Furthermore, the site furnishes sections of specific topics, such as wildlife and land and water.

Community and Environmental Geographic Information System (Houston-Galveston Area Council [HGAC]) http://www.h-gac.com/HGAC/Departments/Community+and+Environmental/default.htm

HGAC dedicates a section of its Web site to Geographic Information Systems. This site is divided into several parts, including the "Community & Environmental Planning GIS" page. GIS data are downloadable as either Arc Export or Arc View shape files using FTP (File Transfer Protocol). Recycling, solid waste, and water quality data are some of the topics covered. Community data on railroads, highways, lakes, etc., are also available. Coverage includes over 10 counties in Texas.

CHAPTER 16
Planning and Zoning

Shawn W. Nicholson and Brian W. Rossmann

MAJOR TOPICS COVERED

Introduction
General Guides and Sources
  Guides
  Dictionaries and Encyclopedias
  Bibliographies and Abstracts
Topical and Specialized Resources
  Laws and Regulations
  Maps
  Departments, Boards, and Commissions
  Planning Reports

MAJOR RESOURCES COVERED

Comprehensive City Planning: Introduction and Explanation
Planning in the USA: Policies, Issues and Processes
The Planner's Use of Information: Techniques for Collection, Organization, and Communication
Community Planning: An Introduction to the Comprehensive Plan
The Citizen's Guide to Planning
A Glossary of Zoning, Development, and Planning Terms
Plannerese Dictionary
Encyclopedia of Urban Planning
Urban Planning, 1794–1918: An International Anthology of Articles, Conference Papers, and Reports
Sage Urban Studies Abstracts
Albany Law School Government Law Center Bibliography of Planning Resources
Land Use Law and Zoning Digest
Antieau on Local Government Law
Zoning and Planning Law Handbook
Cyburbia
Seattle Public Library Municipal Codes Online
Ordinance.Com
Index to Current Urban Documents
Report
PlannersWeb

INTRODUCTION

Human beings have been planning cities and towns since the dawn of human civilization. Whenever groups of buildings have been built close together, inhabitants of these communities have discussed and argued about what structures, parks, and roads should be allowed to be placed in relation to each other. However, as a legal process and professional activity, planning came into existence only in the twentieth century. Before the First World War, urban planning was largely an ancillary function of the architects designing the buildings. Since then an entire planning profession has emerged; one could essentially think of this profession as one of city or urban architects who concern themselves with the development and orderly growth of urban and rural areas.

Planning exists primarily to protect property. If an individual purchases a piece of property and builds his dream house on it, he needs some assurance that his neighbor is not going to build a factory or shopping center next door. Since the 1920s the primary mechanism to achieve this goal in planning has been zoning, which the *Glossary of Zoning, Development, and Planning Terms* defines as "[t]he division of a city or county by legislative regulation into areas, or zones, which specify allowable uses for real property and size restriction for buildings within these areas." Thus, if one purchases a piece of property in a neighborhood that has been zoned "single family" (typical for suburbia), only structures intended to be lived in by families can be built there; one would not need to fear that a supermarket, apartment building, or some other commercial building might be built next door.

Urban areas will typically hire professional planners to plan their cities or towns. Small towns may have only an individual working for them, while large cities may have entire departments dedicated to planning. The planners will be responsible for—among other duties—formulating and articulating an area's master plan, zoning ordinance, community renewal program, subdivision ordinance, and capital improvement program. Anyone wishing to begin searching for information regarding planning and zoning in his or her community will almost certainly need to begin with acquiring a copy of the master plan, zoning ordinances, and zoning maps.

The master plan (or comprehensive plan or general plan) is a long-range plan, which is intended to guide growth and development of a community or region; it is one that includes analyses, recommendations, and proposals for the community's population, economy, housing, transportation, community facilities, and land use. The zoning ordinance (or zoning code) is enacted by city council under state law that sets forth regulations and standards relating to the nature and extent of uses of land and structures; it is consistent with the master plan of the community. Typically, it will include zoning maps, which graphically show the zoning district boundaries and classifications within the community as detailed in the zoning ordinance. These three documents will frequently evolve and change, sometimes from year to year. In most cities or towns they will be available to the public at city hall or the city's planning department. Often local public libraries or college and university libraries will also maintain copies in their collections. Increasingly some municipal governments are making their master plans or ordinances available on the Internet (some suggestions on locating these are given below); however, the only way of ensuring that one has the most current plan or ordinance in hand may still entail a trip to the local planning department.

Another form of information that will more often than not be essential in learning about a community's planning activities are the minutes from meetings held by planning departments, boards, and commissions. Some municipal governments are beginning to place these on their Web site; but again, they may be available only in hard copy at the local city hall planning office.

Much of the planning and zoning information available for a community will still be available only in the individual communities. This can make it difficult to research areas without traveling there personally. Moreover, the type of local government may determine what type of documents are prepared by whom in a local municipality: for example, the master plan may be prepared initially for a planning board, a development administrator, or for a mayor or city manager—similar information may be found at different offices from municipality to municipality. A thorough understanding of the local government's structure will be most helpful in tracking down planning and zoning documents.

GENERAL GUIDES AND SOURCES

It is important to gain a necessary amount of background knowledge about a subject before tackling specific issues. The resources in this section indicate what information planners and other users of planning and zoning documents might need, how that information is defined and used, and where citations and abstracts to planning and zoning information might be found.

Guides

Comprehensive City Planning: Introduction and Explanation, by Melville Branch (Planners Press, 1985)

This volume serves as a general introduction to the planning process and answers basic questions from a planning perspective, defining what a city or town is and explaining the procedures to follow in planning one. This volume covers subjects such as urban growth and its consequences, the circumstances affecting urban development, who plans cities, and how it is done. Although dated, it is still a classic in its categorization of the planning process. It is available at special libraries and is for sale from the publisher or Amazon.com.

Planning in the USA: Policies, Issues and Processes, by Barry Cullingworth (Routledge, 1997)

This title offers an extensive introduction to the policies, theory, and practice of planning. Topics covered include land use regulation; transportation, housing, and community development; public attitudes to planning property rights; environmental planning and policies; growth management; and planning and governance; with a subject index and extensive bibliography. It is available from the publisher and from Yankee Book Peddlers.

The Planner's Use of Information: Techniques for Collection, Organization, and Communication, by Hemalata Dandekar (Hutchinson Ross Publishing, 1982)

Despite being somewhat dated, this guide offers useful instruction on field methods of collecting primary information and survey methods for planners. Information from secondary sources such as the Census and other statistical sources is also addressed, along with practical analysis methods.

Community Planning: An Introduction to the Comprehensive Plan, by Eric D. Kelly and Barbara Becker (Island Press, 2000)

This book introduces community planning and focuses on the comprehensive plan: "a tangible representation of what a community wants to be in the future." Its primary purpose is to serve as a teaching text for introductory planning classes and as such it provides a good overview of the field and process of planning.

The Citizen's Guide to Planning (California Governors Office of Planning and Research, 2001) http://www.opr.ca.gov/planning/PDFs/citizens_planning.pdf

This publication provides a guide to ordinary citizens who are seeking information about planning. There are sections on state and local planning, the general plan (which usually applies to local governmental entities), zoning, ordinances and regulations, etc. There is a glossary of terms and a bibliography. It offers useful advice on obtaining information in these areas and other relevant topics. An example of a zoning map from the PDF file is provided at http://www.opr.ca.gov/planning/PDFs/citizens_planning.pdf. This publication is available from the California State Office of Planning and Research Web site, at http://www.planning.org/publications/overview.htm.

Dictionaries and Encyclopedias

A Glossary of Zoning, Development, and Planning Terms, by Michael Davidson and Fay Dolnik (American Planning Association, 1999)

This book contains a list of terms with definitions that has been compiled by the American Planning Association (APA) with input from its membership and other professional planning associations. Planners deal with a very wide breadth of knowledge regularly, much of which falls outside the immediate profession of planning. This book covers definitions from—but not limited to—the professions of architecture, civil engineering, environmental science, landscape architecture, law, public works, real estate, and transportation engineering. This publication is available from the APA Web site, at http://www.planning.org/publications/overview.htm.

Plannerese Dictionary, by Richard B. Stephens (Urban and Regional Planning College of Environmental Design, California State Polytechnic University, 1994)

An irreverent look at planning and zoning definitions, this book provides the levity that every profession/discipline needs. In a simple alphabetical structure, the author provides humorous, irreverent, and at times simply silly definitions for common terms and phrases in the planning field. As an example, look at the author's parody of a Monopoly board.

Encyclopedia of Urban Planning, ed. by Arnold Whittick (McGraw-Hill, 1974)

This is a comprehensive encyclopedia on planning that is international and historical in its scope. It contains a large number of plans, photographs, and illustrations, which make this work valuable. This source is unparalleled in its coverage of international planning information, and despite being a bit dated, remains the first place to look for planning information from other countries. This classic can be found in many college and university libraries.

Bibliographies and Abstracts

Urban Planning, 1794–1918: An International Anthology of Articles, Conference Papers, and Reports, by J. W. Reps (Cornell University, 2001) http://www.library.cornell.edu/Reps/DOCS/homepage.htm

This Internet-based bibliography culls English-language primary source documents about how urban planning developed—techniques, theories, and principles—internationally from 1794 to 1918. Each entry is a link to the full text of the document. The site is in HTML but does provide some scanned sketches and drawings. The user is helped by the pithy editorial headnotes commenting on the author and the contents of the selected text. The site may be searched by keyword or browsed by author or time period or as an alphabetical list.

Sage Urban Studies Abstracts (Sage Publications, 1973–) http://www.sagepub.co.uk/frame.html? http://www.sagepub.co.uk/journals/details/j0105.html

Contains complete bibliographic information and abstracts for scholarly books, articles, pamphlets, speeches, and government publications. Access to the citations is made easy through the author and subject indices. *Abstracts* is published quarterly. Although content is expansive, the topical coverage of planning and zoning is well represented. This resource will be found at most major research libraries.

Zoning: Recent References, by Mary A. Vance (Public Administration Series—Bibliography, P-2756/ Vance Bibliographies, 1989)

This unannotated bibliography provides an alphabetical list of books and periodicals dealing with zoning from the mid-1980s. Its focus is difficult to discern, but coverage does include local zoning issues. Although limited in timeframe and lacking any annotations, this source stands out for its targeted, if not comprehensive, coverage of the zoning literature. Other works, like *Sage Urban Studies Abstracts*, are better organized and possess greater currency, yet they lack the depth of zoning resources that this bibliography offers.

Albany Law School Government Law Center Bibliography of Planning Resources, by Trudy Menard (West Publishers, 2002)

This publication, once available at the Law School Web link, connected to an online bibliography of planning publications arranged geographically by state. The entries are arranged alphabetically by author and/or agency within the state. Examples include, from Georgia, the Department of Community Affairs, Office of Coordinated Planning, *Why Plan? A Guidebook for Local Planning*; and from Maine, the Maine Department of Conservation, Eagle Lake Management Unit, *Public Reserved Lands System, Unit Management Plan*, March 1990. This bibliography is included in the 2002 edition of the *Planning and Zoning Law Handbook*, which can be purchased from Thomson/West publishers at their Web site, http://

west.thomson.com/store/product.asp?product%5Fid= 14854727.

TOPICAL AND SPECIALIZED RESOURCES
Laws and Regulations

The focus of this section is on locating planning and zoning laws, whether produced by courts, legislatures, or city councils. A zoning or planning ordinance is a legal document setting forth the parameters upon which physical development in a town may be based. Although some of the discussion here may be duplicative of the more general look at laws, regulations, and courts in other chapters (for example, chapters 5–7), the focus on planning and zoning bears repeating. By and large, a wonderful array of targeted print volumes and expansive subscription-based electronic tools exist to locate law-related material for zoning and planning.

Land Use Law and Zoning Digest (American Planning Association, 1949–, annual)

This monthly publication contains synopses and commentary of important judicial decisions and legislative developments in federal, state, and local jurisdictions pertinent to zoning, taxation, and environmental regulation. It draws relevant, broadly applicable examples from around the United States. An annual index is included in the last issue of the year to make searching easier. This publication will be available at law and major research libraries. It is also available from the APA Web site, at http://www.planning.org/publications/overview.htm.

Land Use Law Update in Michigan, by T . S. Decker and the National Business Institute (National Business Institute, 1999)

Covering all aspects of state law pertaining to land use and planning, this is an easy-to-use reference source. It is updated via pocket part frequently to reflect any changes in law, both judicial and statutory. The most recent edition provides some necessary background on federal laws, such as the Endangered Species Act, that may have special application to local jurisdictions. Because of its focus on a single state (Michigan, in this case), the researcher is greeted with a much greater comprehensiveness than in works such as *Land Use Law and Zoning Digest*. The National

Business Institute publishes a volume of land use law updates for nearly every state and is likely found in a major research library.

Antieau on Local Government Law, by Sandra M. Stevenson (2nd ed., Matthew Bender, 1997)

This loose-leaf service covers all aspects of local government law, including land use. Part 8 contains six chapters across a range of topics, from urban redevelopment to local planning master plans. Its main function is to bring into clarity these functions through definitions, analysis, and thorough footnotes. For example, the section on spot zoning gives a detailed definition and some examples of its validity or invalidity from various states, while giving complete citations of court decisions in the footnotes. The loose-leaf nature guarantees continual updates to the topical areas. This work is available from the publisher at http://www.bender.com/bender/open.

Zoning and Planning Law Handbook, by F. A. Strom and Clark Boardman (Clark Boardman Co., 1981–)

Published since 1981, this annual provides a practical overview of pertinent issues relating to land use law. The editors make fine use of example cases from all jurisdictions (local to federal) to shed light on their analysis. Similar to *Land Use Law and Zoning Digest*, this work strives for broad applicability in its discussions.

Zoning and Planning Deskbook, by Douglas W. Kmiec (2nd ed., West Group, 2001)

This highly specialized legal work provides technical expertise on obtaining permits, initiating hearings, and working to reverse adverse decisions. Access to the broad topical coverage is easy through the detailed index. Although similar in nature to the *Zoning and Planning Law Handbook*, this work is not quite as friendly to the lay user. Many law libraries will own a copy of this handbook.

Growing Smart Legislative Handbook http://www.planning.org/guidebook/Guidebook.htm

An outgrowth of the APA's Smart Growth project, an effort to replace planning and zoning statutes from the 1920s, this guidebook provides commentary on legislative alternatives and on implementation of new statutes. Drawing on a variety of state statutes, the commentary lays out the pros and cons of various legislative alternatives. Model statutes are present for users to use in their own practice. This publication is available for free electronically (PDF or HTML) from the publications page http://www.planning.org/publications/overview.htm, http://www.planning.org/guidebookhtm/table_of_contents.htm, or for purchase from the Association.

LexisNexis http://www.lexisnexis.com

Westlaw http://www.westlaw.com/about

Each of these commercial subscription services contains major archives of federal and state case law as well as continuously updated statutes of all 50 states. However, each is limited in its coverage of local law sources, though. Nevertheless, state law does have particular bearing on local-level laws, as much of the case law dealing with planning and zoning will begin as a local or regional issue. It is, therefore, possible to take advantage of these databases to find case law with relevant bearing on local jurisdictions.

A growing number of planning and zoning codes are finding their way online, via the Internet. These can be found using the search engines, such as Google (http://www.google.com). Some examples of the freely available (or personal subscription–based) codes are described below.

City and County Codes Online http://www.bpcnet.com/codes.htm

All listed codes are published and maintained on the Web by Book Publishing Company (BPC). This publisher has been purchased by LexisNexis. Thirty states are present. The number of codes varies from 1 for Hawaii to over 100 for California. The site is easily navigated through its simple alphabetical listing. It is refreshing to see statements about currency on the first page of all the codes. The user needs to be mindful that BPC holds the copyright to these codes.

Cyburbia http://www.cyburbia.org

The link to this Web site contains a comprehensive directory of Internet resources relevant to planning, architecture, and, as the site managers say, "the built environment." This site also offers a large searchable directory of zoning ordinances and regulations. Each entry links to the Internet site of the municipal or county jurisdiction, thereby creating the possibility of broken links. Ordinances are in HTML or PDF format.

Municipal Code Corporation [MCC]
http://www.municode.com

MCC provides codification, indexing, and publishing services. Its Web site offers a list of freely available codes and minutes. Arranged alphabetically by state and then by municipality, the links are easy to navigate. Presently, 14 states and nearly 50 jurisdictions are represented. All of the information is present on this site, so there is less concern about stability of links. Currency of the information may be limited, however. Also, due to the broad scope of the site, the links are not limited to planning and zoning, and a user may be confronted with much extraneous material.

Seattle Public Library Municipal Codes Online
http://www.spl.org/default.asp?pageID=
collection_municodes

This site offers freely available Internet-based city and county codes. The layout is simple, alphabetical by state and then by local governmental jurisdiction. Each entry links to the top-level code, meaning that the entire code is displayed. Therefore, some digging is necessary to find the appropriate section on planning and zoning. The site is lacking in comprehensiveness but does direct the user to other sites offering similar services.

Ordinance.Com (Jungle Lasers LL) http://www.
ordinance.com/default.asp

This subscription service provides zoning information for New Jersey, Connecticut, California, Washington State, Rhode Island, Massachusetts, and the New York City, Philadelphia, Washington, D.C., and Chicago metropolitan areas. The ordinances from Ordinance.com are not official versions; rather, they are intended for planning purposes. The layout provides easy movement between sections, links to defined words, and easy importation of data for computer-assisted drawings or spreadsheets.

Maps

As the chapter on map resources in this book demonstrates, a spate of online and paper mapping resources for and about local government exists. Geographic representation is quite important to adequately conceptualize zoning districts. A zoning district is a portion of the territory of a county or city within which certain uniform regulations and requirements apply and are codified in an ordinance. A zoning map is simply the map adopted by the appropriate government entity to represent the entity's districts. In addition to the obvious need for mapping of zoning districts, it is clear that maps of all varieties are invaluable tools for planners.

Although no one place has compiled and made available a complete set of zoning maps for all counties, townships, and municipalities, many of these jurisdictions have placed their maps on the World Wide Web. Any of the popular search engines will index and help retrieve many of these maps. Two caveats: First, many maps may be in PDF and therefore elude some search engines, so use appropriate steps to locate these; and second, the user needs to be aware that often these free maps are for informational purposes only and that official maps must be purchased or requested from the appropriate government body. For instance, the zoning map of Nevada, Iowa, is presented at http://www.ci.nevada.ia.us/PDF%20Forms/NevadaZon.pdf.

Despite the advances in Internet technology and the efforts of libraries, the vast majority of zoning maps remain under the care of each city, township, or county, often at the respective bodies' clerk's office. Retrievability of copies will vary from locale to locale and may incur a nominal charge to cover printing and distribution. See the earlier discussion about how to contact your jurisdiction.

Another type of map that may be quickly overlooked but provides a tremendous amount of necessary information for a planner is a soil survey map. The Soil Survey series published by the United States Department of Agriculture and other agencies provides invaluable information on land capability, productivity, wildlife habitat, classification of soils, and environmental plantings, to name a few. The Natural Resources Conservation Service within the Department of Agriculture maintains a Web site of full text soil surveys; consult http://www.nrcs.usda.gov/programs/soilsurvey. As of this writing, 49 states and two regions are present on the ever-expanding site. The balance of states and territories' soil surveys may be found at most federal Depository libraries.

Departments, Boards, and Commissions

Planning offices are usually composed of full-time government officials and are responsible for the following activities: administration of the planning and zoning code, development and maintenance of the master plan and staff support for various boards (zoning appeals, etc.). On the other hand, planning commissions and/or boards are composed of volunteers drawn from the community. The duties are, however, quite similar, including creating master plans; preparing comprehensive programs for capital improvements; reviewing site plans, subdivisions, special use permits, rezoning requests, the widening and extension of streets, and the development of park space; and developing new zoning standards.

Despite the wide application of the work of planning offices and boards and commissions, their agendas and minutes are often the only indication of future planning and past decisions. Although no one place has a complete collection of agendas or minutes for the nearly 90,000 local governmental jurisdictions, many counties, cities, and townships have begun to place their minutes and agendas on the Internet. Dover Township, New Jersey, at http://twp.dover.nj.us/agendas.htm, is representative of a governmental unit that simply places the current agenda in a plain HTML file and provides no archiving for previous agendas or minutes. Others (e.g., City of East Lansing, Michigan, http://www.cityofeastlansing.com) may maintain an archive of agendas and minutes going back a year or more. Some cities (e.g., Bozeman, Montana, at http://bozemanmt.virtualtownhall.net/subscriber.html) have offered additional services like e-mail updates for their agendas and minutes. What is clear is that there is no uniform method of distributing agenda and minutes, over the Internet or otherwise. As with other items, retrievability of copies of agendas and/or minutes will vary from locale to locale and may incur a nominal charge to cover printing and distribution. The Internet has expanded access somewhat. The few sites that offer the broadest coverage across multiple jurisdictions are exemplified by the MCC Web site (see the profile above for Municipal Code Corporation) and the site listed below.

Index to Current Urban Documents (Greenwood
    Publishing Group, Inc., 1990–) http://www.
    urbdocs.com

This index is available in print or online (via subscription) and offers access to the reports and research generated by local government agencies. Occasionally, the minutes of zoning departments, boards, or commissions are indexed. Older documents were part of a microfilm set and may be viewed via that medium. Work has begun to offer Internet access to indexed documents. This is an ongoing process, however, and the coverage in the database for minutes is limited. Many more libraries have access to this publication in print than in electronic form.

Planning Reports

From bicycle paths to new subdivisions, planning reports cover a huge array of subjects. They look at natural resource issues, cultural issues, and how a proposal melds with existing structures and services. These reports will typically include photos, sketches, and tabular data. Often state legislation will specify how a master plan for a local jurisdiction is to be prepared, adopted, modified, and implemented. There are a variety of ways to locate planning reports. Library Online Public Access Catalogs (OPAC), professional associations and groups, the Internet, and clerk's offices each offer access to planning reports.

Library OPACs, particularly at academic institutions that support programs in planning and design, will lead a researcher to a set of professionally produced reports for surrounding communities and major metropolitan areas. In addition to the professionally produced reports, many libraries will collect student-produced reports. The student reports are valuable because they often tackle geographic areas and/or subject matter that will not have been covered by any professional report.

Professional bodies like the APA not only produce reports that have a wide interest, but make it easy for researchers to find these reports through detailed indexing. The APA's Planning Advisory Service Reports described below offer a good example.

Report (American Planning Association, Planning
    Advisory Service, 1978–)

Published eight times per year, these reports cover a broad range of topics relevant to city, county, and state planning agencies, developers, and consultants. The reports place an emphasis on solving problems and use a plethora of examples to show how planners have dealt with common planning issues—from housing development to rewriting a zoning ordinance. There is an annual index that accompanies this set.

PlannersWeb (Planning Commissioners Journal)
    http://www.plannersweb.com

A privately owned and maintained Web site such as PlannersWeb will also provide decent access to planning reports. Until recently, PlannersWeb offered a comprehensive listing of planning reports. At this writing, the site was not available and no confirmation could be obtained about its future. PlannersWeb does, however, offer the Sprawl Guide: Reports on Sprawl and Related Topics, http://www.plannersweb.com/sprawl/home.html, which provides links to full texts of planning reports directly related to sprawl. For reports not available in full text, complete contact information is provided so that they may be obtained from their producer. An example of a report is under the topic "Problems: Land Consumption and Threat to Farmland," and one of the reports is *Protecting Farmland on the Edge: What Policies and Programs Work?*, by Jerry Paulson of the American Farmland Trust, Center for Agriculture in the Environment.

Like many other items in this section, a clerk's office may be the only place to get a copy of a master plan for a local jurisdiction. These plans are comprehensive by nature, tying together social, political, and economic elements. Retrievability will vary from jurisdiction to jurisdiction, so contacting the relevant office is the best approach. However, a researcher may want to turn to the Internet to see if a master plan or other planning reports of interest have been scanned or otherwise made available by the jurisdiction. For example, Marion, Iowa's Park Project, http://cityofmarion.org/parks/lowe_park, and Stamford, Connecticut's Master Plan for the City, http://www.ci.stamford.ct.us/PlanningBoard/MasterPlan.htm, are freely available on the Internet. Again, as some reports may be in PDF, use appropriate searching techniques to locate these often-elusive documents.

CHAPTER 17
Finding Information on Transportation and Public Works

Mark Anderson and Mark Gilman

MAJOR TOPICS COVERED

MAJOR RESOURCES COVERED

INTRODUCTION

Discussed in this chapter are transportation and public works topics—airport operations, roads, bridges, highways, tunnels, mass transit systems, solid waste management, sewerage treatment, snow removal, asset and fleet management, urban forestry, and building maintenance. Key legal and statistical resources will also be highlighted, together with resources from selected federal, state, and regional government agencies.

Public works and transportation professionals are often guided in their work by handbooks, standards, and other publications produced by their respective professional associations. For the convenience of the reader, tables with Internet addresses for these associations and for government agencies are appended below.

As emphasized elsewhere in this book, the organization of city and county governments differs greatly from one locality to another. For the purposes of this chapter, public works and transportation have both been rather broadly construed. In many cities, some of the functions will be allocated to freestanding units and not grouped within a designated transportation and public works department.

GENERAL TRANSPORTATION AND PUBLIC WORKS RESOURCES

A generally useful strategy for uncovering research in transportation and public works is to identify the relevant professional associations and regulatory agencies, both of which frequently engage in publication or at least in the dissemination of materials developed by others. Moreover, publication often takes the form of technical reports, with limited distribution. Such documents are typically available for purchase, for only a limited time, directly from the issuing agency or association. Copies of older works are found in very specialized library collections. Fortunately, some excellent finding tools are available. For documents published in the past decade or so, there are bibliographic databases accessible via the Internet. For earlier periods, there are printed bibliographies.

General Web Sites

The following Web sites are ones that the transportation researcher will find especially useful. The first section includes specialized search engines and Web-based directories.

American Public Works Association [APWA] http://www.apwa.net

In addition to the usual things one would expect to find on the Web site of a professional association, the APWA site provides a directory of annotated links to the Web sites of national, state, local, and other organizations. Select "Resource Center" on the menu bar. Then select from a list that includes such topics as asset management, emergency management, right of way management, street sweeping, transportation, urban issues, utilities, and water resources. For example, selecting "transportation" as a main topic and "air quality" as a subtopic takes one to entries for 1000 Friends of Oregon and the EPA Transportation Air Quality Center. The entry for each organization includes a description of its mission and a link to its Web site. APWA also monitors proposed federal legislation.

American Association of State Highway and Transportation Officials [AASHTO]
http://www.aashto.org

All 50 state departments of transportation along with the District of Columbia and Puerto Rico are represented in AASHTO, a nonpartisan organization through which state governments coordinate interstate transportation and environmental protection–related policies and projects. It concerns itself with air, public, highway, rail, and water transportation. AASHTO reviews, analyzes, and comments on state and local legislation and regulations. It also formulates and recommends standards for transportation plans and materials. Other useful features of the AASHTO Web page include a page of links to all state Department of Transportation (DOT) Web sites and a section with commentary on proposed national transportation-related legislation. AASHTO's current publications may be ordered online from a catalog at www.aashto.org/publications/bookstore.nsf. The best features of this site are the links to state DOTs and the summaries of current legislative issues.

DOTBOT (U.S. Department of Transportation)
http://search.bts.gov/ntl

DOTBOT is an online search engine, maintained by the National Transportation Library, which provides indexing to publications and information currently available on U.S. Department of Transportation agency Web sites. The description in the FAQ section asserts that DOTBOT includes 110,000 documents on 190 different Web sites. This appears to be something of an understatement. For example, a search using the Boolean construction "air and quality" produced 971,478 hits. The document list include press releases, decisions of regulatory agencies, full-text online reports, and much more.

TRIS Online [Transportation Research Information Services] (U.S. Bureau of Transportation Statistics, National Transportation Library)
http://199.79.179.82/sundev/search.cfm

The National Transportation Library, the premier repository of transportation-related information in the country, created this free online index. The half-million bibliographic records in the TRIS database represent books and conference proceedings, articles from some 470 transportation-related journals, government reports, research in progress, and more. The government publications include reports by state and federal agencies, environmental impact statements, technical reports generated by government-funded research at universities and research laboratories, and congressional committee reports and hearings. Chronological coverage dates from the 1960s to the present. TRIS does not index newspapers, newsmagazines, or wire-service articles. Most bibliographic records are accompanied by exceptionally well written, descriptive abstracts. When a publication is available online, the document includes a link to the full text. If a document is available for purchase from the National Technical Information Service (NTIS), a link connects the user to ordering information in the NTIS catalog.

INFOMINE (The Libraries of the University of California) http://infomine.ucr.edu/cgi-bin/search?govpub

INFOMINE is a database with some 20,000 annotated links to university-level research and educational tools on the Internet, including databases and search engines, electronic journals and conference proceedings. The URL above will access the "Government Information" section of INFOMINE. All the Web resources indexed are cataloged and have Library of Congress subject headings (LCSHs) attached. The list of all LCSHs used is accessible, with each heading being hotlinked to the resources. Or the whole database can be keyword-searched for terms appearing in the title or annotation. A sample search with the term "AMTRAK" produced five annotated links, AMTRAK's official Web page, a California DOT page describing AMTRAK service in that state, the Los Angeles Union Station Web page describing AMTRAK, a bibliographic record for the National Transportation Atlas on CD-ROM, and a page of links to selected Congressional Research Service Reports posted by the office of Congressman Christopher Shays of Connecticut.

National Technical Information Service [NTIS] (U.S. Department of Commerce) http://www.ntis.gov

NTIS's most important product is its library of microfilm masters of technical reports from government agencies and research and academic institutions. It includes an excellent selection of National Transportation Safety Board (NTSB) Reports. A free online index is available, which includes bibliographic records and ordering information (but no abstracts) for technical reports produced since 1990. For a fee, NTIS can reproduce hard copy of any report one finds in the NTIS index. Because the legislation that established NTIS mandates that the service operate at a profit, its comprehensive index—containing bibliographic records, abstracts, and ordering information for reports dating back to 1964—requires a subscription fee. Many titles of national scope provide good detail in relation to local areas.

World Wide Web Transportation Library (U.S. Department of Transportation, Bureau of Transportation Statistics) http://www.bts.gov/virtualib/index.html

This far-ranging directory comprises topically arranged links to Web sites of government agencies, advocacy groups, and others. The scope is international, and the collection includes subjects of popular interest (e.g., National Public Radio's "Car Talk" program). Each of several hundred Web sites is listed under one or more of 13 indexing terms. Some of these, like "air travel," "cycling," and "rail," are straightforward. The focus of others, like "miscellaneous" and "research," appears somewhat ambiguous. There is a good deal of overlap and duplication.

Guides/Directories

TranStats: The Intermodal Transportation Database (Bureau of Transportation Statistics, U.S. Department of Transportation) http://www.transtats.bts.gov

This product consists of transportation-related GIS (Geographic Information System) data and transportation-related geospatial data for the United States and includes transportation networks, transportation facilities, and other spatial data used as geographic reference. The data are contributed by a number of cooperating federal agencies. Note: As a result of the events of September 11, 2001, the National Transportation Atlas was removed from this URL. Selected files may still be downloaded from http://www.bts.gov/gis/download_sites/ntad02/maindownload.html. The BTS (Bureau of Transportation Services) Web site has additional capabilities such as the Shapefile Download Center, designed to create customized maps and zipped Environmental Systems Research Institute (ESRI) shapefiles of the National Transportation Atlas databases. There are three ways to download the shapefiles: the entire U.S., selected states, and by using an interactive mapping tool to select any area of interest. The older databases can also be accessed on CD-ROM at various federal Depository libraries. To locate the nearest Depository, see http://www.access.gpo.gov/su_docs/locators/findlibs.

Sources of Information in Transportation (4th ed., Special Libraries Association, Transportation Division, 1990)

Researchers interested in transportation literature before 1990 will find this comprehensive, 10-volume bibliography, featuring detailed annotations, an essential resource. Individual volumes cover general transportation, air transportation, shipping, railroads, trucking, inland water transportation, pipelines, highways, urban transportation, and intercity bus lines. Parts or all of this set can be found at many major university libraries and transportation research collections. Coverage includes monographs, serials, research reports, and more.

Management of Local Public Works: Municipal Management Series (International City/County Management Association, 1989)

Published in cooperation with the American Public Works Association, this volume forms part of the highly regarded series of *green books*. Designed to function as a textbook, this volume introduces the basic principles of public works and the "management skills needed to plan and implement effective public works programs and service delivery." Exceedingly well produced, it serves both the novice looking for a general introduction to the field and the seasoned professional seeking an authoritative statement on a particular facet.

GOVERNMENT REGULATION
Federal/State/Regional Agencies

Delving deep into myriad federal, state, and regional Web sites reveals a wealth of resources, including full-text publications, databases, and statistics. The U.S. Department of Transportation (USDOT), the U.S. Department of Energy, and the U.S. Environmental Protection Agency (EPA) are the main entities considered here. Though it is technically an arm of USDOT, owing to the scope of its resources, the Federal Highway Administration (FHWA) is given independent consideration. There is drawn together a representative cross-section of agencies and offices in a table that appears below.

Agency Name	Sub-unit	URL
Association of Local Air Pollution Control Officials (ALAPCO)	***	www.cleanairworld.org
Association of Metropolitan Planning Organizations (AMPO)	***	www.ampo.org
Department of Energy (DOE)	***	www.energy.gov
	Center for Transportation Analysis	www-cta.ornl.gov/cta/
	Clean Cities	www.ccities.doe.gov
	Fuel	www.energy.gov/transportation/sub/fuel.html
	Heavy Vehicles	www.energy.gov/transportation/sub/heavy.html
	Innovation	www.energy.gov/transportation/sub/innovation.html
	Safety	www.energy.gov/transportation/sub/safety.html
	Office of Transportation Technologies	www.ott.doe.gov
Department of Transportation (DOT)	***	www.dot.gov
	Bureau of Transportation Statistics (BTS)	www.bts.gov
	Federal Aviation Administration (FAA)	www2.faa.gov/
	Federal Highway Administration (FHWA)	NOTE: Treated separately, below.
	Federal Motor Carrier Safety Administration (FMCSA)	www.fmcsa.dot.gov
	Federal Railroad Administration (FRA)	www.fra.dot.gov/site/

Agency Name	Sub-unit	URL
	Federal Transit Administration (FTA)	www.fta.dot.gov/
	Maritime Administration (MARAD)	www.marad.dot.gov
	National Highway Safety Traffic Administration (NHTSA)	www.nhtsa.dot.gov
	Surface Transportation Board (STB)	www.stb.dot.gov/
	United States Coast Guard (USCG)	www.uscg.mil/USCG.shtm
Environmental Protection Agency (EPA)	***	www.epa.gov
	Office of Air Quality Planning & Standards	www.epa.gov/oar/oaqps/
	Office of Solid Waste (OSW)	www.epa.gov/epaoswer/osw/
	Office of Transportation & Air Quality	www.epa.gov/OMSWWW/omshome.htm
	Office of Underground Storage Tanks	www.epa.gov/oust
	Pollutants / Toxics	www.epa.gov/ebtpages/pollutants.html
	Wastes	www.epa.gov/ebtpages/wastes.html
	Water	www.epa.gov/ebtpages/water.html
Federal Highway Administration* (FHWA)	***	www.fhwa.dot.gov
	Asset Management	www.fhwa.dot.gov/infrastructure/ asstmgmt/index.htm
	Federal Motor Carrier Safety Administration	www.fmcsa.dot.gov
	National Center for Statistics & Analysis	www-nrd.nhtsa.dot.gov/departments/ nrd-30/ncsa/
	National Highway Institute	www.nhi.fhwa.dot.gov/default.asp
	National Highway Safety / Traffic Safety Administration	www.nhtsa.dot.gov/
	Office of Bridge Technology	www.fhwa.dot.gov/bridge/
	Office of Pavement Technology	www.fhwa.dot.gov/pavement/
	Planning, Environment & Realty	www.fhwa.dot.gov/environment/
	Traffic Calming	www.fhwa.dot.gov/environment/tcalm/
	Turner-Fairbank Highway Research Center	www.tfhrc.gov/
	Volpe National Transportation Center	www.volpe.dot.gov/
National Association of Regional Councils (NARC)	***	www.narc.org
State and Territorial Air Pollution Program Administrators (STAPPA)	***	www.cleanairworld.org
Transportation Research Board (TRB)	***	www.nationalacademies.org/trb/

Table 17.1 SELECTED GOVERNMENT AND QUASI-GOVERNMENTAL AGENCIES
Note: FHWA is actually a subunit of the US DOT. However, because of its scope and importance, we are treating it here as if it were a separate agency.

In the case of the EPA, rather than link to separate administrative units, it simply points toward thematic pages that have been thoughtfully provided by that agency. As administrations change, budgets are adjusted, reforms undertaken, and priorities reshuffled, agencies predictably undergo reorganization. The point is to emphasize and to some degree reveal the rich resources provided through these agencies, which function not merely as regulators but also as clearinghouses and coordinators of research. Indeed, the federal government has spawned, across the years, its own network of research institutes and laboratories, many of which are prolific publishers.

Directory of State Departments of Transportation (Federal Highway Administration)
http://www.fhwa.dot.gov/webstate.htm

The Web pages of the various state DOTs frequently provide state, county, and local data that have been extracted from various national data collection programs in formats more conveniently accessible to the end user. In addition, local transportation-related information that is not available on the USDOT pages is often available at these Web sites. Travelers and commuters can usually find information on local weather and road conditions, construction schedules, and state traffic laws and regulations. State GIS systems map data on such things as collisions and annual average daily traffic volumes for state highways and local roads. Contractors can usually find a section on "Doing Business with the State DOT," which provides information on approved materials, state contracting regulations, and programs for contracting with minority- and women-owned firms.

National Association of Regional Councils [NARC]
  http://www.narc.org

Most counties and municipal governments participate in regional councils of government. These voluntary associations give local planning officials at different government levels a forum in which to coordinate land use and economic development plans. California has 28 regional councils. Colorado has nine, the most active of which is the Denver Regional Council of Governments. Regional councils typically maintain Web sites from which meeting agendas and publications are available. Demographic and economic data for the region and for individual member counties and cities are often posted. NARC maintains a comprehensive list of links to its member regional councils' Web sites at http://www.narc.org/links/cogslist.html. NARC serves as an advocate to the U.S. Congress for local government on a wide variety of issues and provides current information on transportation legislation and regulations. The NARC Web site carries full-text reports and other documents, in addition to meeting information and member information.

Association of Metropolitan Planning Organizations
  [AMPO] http://www.ampo.org

Under the terms of a series of federal laws, designed to facilitate regional planning of transportation systems, more than 300 metropolitan areas identified in the population census have been required to create Metropolitan Planning Organizations (MPOs). In about half of these metropolitan areas, the MPO is a component of a regional council of government. In other cases, it is an independent agency. Arguably, AMPO's most useful information product is its annual *Profiles of Metropolitan Planning Organizations*, a directory of the MPOs that constitute its membership, along with information about the parameters of its

various jurisdictions, structural compositions, air quality status, and program activities. Some MPOs are also councils of government, such as the Dallas–Fort Worth area's North Texas Council of Governments, online at http://www.dfwinfo.com.

Law and Regulation

GPO Access http://www.gpoaccess.gov/index.html

Individuals interested in federal regulatory activity often consult the Web site of the regulatory agency directly to find its latest decisions. A more systematic method is to monitor the *Federal Register* (FR), a daily chronicle of federal government activities in all agencies. Proposed new regulations and amendments to existing regulations are first published in the FR, as well as notices of public hearings that agencies frequently hold to elicit public comment on proposed rule changes. The FR also informs grant seekers of the availability of federal financing for local public works projects. The full text of the FR, updated daily going back to 1994, is available free through GPO Access, maintained by the U.S. Government Printing Office (GPO).

FindLaw http://findlaw.com

Privately maintained but free to the end user, this is a one-stop portal for the widest range of legal information. At the federal level, it contains links to the United States Code, FR, and the Code of Federal Regulations. It also maintains searchable databases of U.S. Supreme Court decisions from 1893 to the present and decisions of circuit courts of appeals from 1996 to the present. Links are also provided to the Web pages of all the various federal district courts and courts with unique jurisdictions, from which full-text decisions are usually available. At the state level, it maintains links to all the online state statutory (as distinct from administrative) codes. FindLaw also has a legal subject index. Under "Legal Subjects," click on "Transportation Law" to bring up a page of links to resources such as the Web pages of law firms and legal consultants who specialize in transportation law. State laws and municipal codes are also available online here.

TEA-21 (Federal Highway Administration)
  http://www.fhwa.dot.gov/tea21/index.htm

The Transportation Equity Act for the 21st Century (TEA-21) was enacted June 9, 1998, as Public Law 105–178. It authorizes federal surface transportation programs for highways, highway safety, and transit through 2003. The Web site, maintained by FHWA, is a collection of federal documents and data tables that illustrate the impact of TEA-21 since its passage. The site lacks a search engine for all the documents concurrently, but fortunately the number of documents is small enough that this is not a major deficiency. Access is provided through a list of eight reasonably straightforward indexing terms. Under "Legislation," one finds the full text of TEA-21 and the report of the conference committee that accompanied it to the floor of both houses of Congress. Click on "Fact Sheets" to find news releases describing some of the projects funded by TEA-21. Under "Publications" is a bibliography of related government reports, some linked to ordering information and some linked to the full-text online version.

A Citizen's Guide to Transportation Decisionmaking
http://www.fhwa.dot.gov/planning/citizen/
citizen1.htm

This online document, produced by FHWA, is designed to provide background information to citizens who wish to influence state and local transportation decisions, calling upon the provisions for citizen involvement laid down in TEA-21. The focus is on motor vehicle transportation on streets and highways and the language is nontechnical and jargon free. It describes the structure and function of state and local government agencies and how decisions are made. This document would be useful for citizens who, as individuals or as part of an advocacy group, wish to have an impact on the planning process.

SPECIALIZED/TOPICAL RESOURCES
Roads and Highways

Highway Capacity Manual (Transportation Research Board, 2000)

An affiliate of the congressionally chartered National Academies, the Transportation Research Board, http://www.nationalacademies.org/trb, publishes this massive tome, which provides guidance to traffic engineers and planners for analyzing levels of service with respect to different sorts of roadways, from bicycle paths to multilane freeway systems. It is available in both metric and U.S. standard measurement versions and accompanied by a CD-ROM offering supplementary material. The scope of the work concerns mainly the United States.

Trip Generation (Vols. 1–3). *Trip Generation Handbook: An ITE Recommended Practice* (Institute of Transportation Engineers)

The Institute of Transportation Engineers (ITE) publishes standards, manuals, and handbooks for transportation modeling, highway capacity, traffic control devices, transit planning, and similar issues. Traffic engineers and planners are often called upon to engage in demand forecasting. For this purpose, standard trip-generation tables, plots, and equations published by the ITE are used to gauge the projected effects on traffic flow of placing different sorts of facilities along a roadway. For example, a library or a public hospital of a certain size generates, on average, a predictable volume of car trips. This is vital to know when projecting demand for roadway capacity planning.

Mass Transit

Federal Transit Administration (FTA) http://www.fta.dot.gov

A division of USDOT, the FTA regulates and provides information resources in relation to the various modes of mass transportation, especially bus and intraurban rail.

Amtrak http://Amtrak.com

Legally known as the National Railroad Passenger Corporation, Amtrak began operations in 1971 and over the next 12 years took over the few remaining commercial intercity passenger services. Its official Web site is the best place to find out about Amtrak schedules and fares or to make reservations. One can also find links to congressional reports, testimony regarding Amtrak's current operations, and technical reports regarding the future of high-speed rail in America.

Greyhound http://Greyhound.com

For much of rural America, the only transportation alternative available, aside from private automobiles, is the Greyhound bus company and its regional affiliates. Schedules and fares, along with other information about its operations, are available from its corporate Web site.

Paratransit in America: Redefining Mass Transportation, by Robert Cervero (Praeger, 1997)

Cervero, who is known mainly for his advocacy of regional governance structures, explores in this book all those "flexibly routed bus, van, or small-vehicle services not (generally) driven by the passenger." While paratransit services in the United States are usually thought of in conjunction with transporting the physically disabled (see 47 CRF Subtitle A, Part 37), Cervero's conception of the possible role for such services is far ranging. This book deserves to be in every collection oriented toward transportation issues for the way in which it rounds out the picture of what we normally think of when we hear the term *public transit*. Its scope is global.

Whether negotiating the downtown of a strange city, moving through a crowded airport, or speeding along a winding turnpike, people in unfamiliar environments require signs and other aids to render their trips legible and help them to reach their destinations. Consultants range from purveyors of signage systems to architects and environmental psychologists. The foremost thinker in this area is Kevin Lynch, whose works laid the groundwork for the field. Even though his books are mostly out of print, they are worth the effort to seek out.

ITS America http://www.itsa.org

Intelligent Transportation Systems (ITS) comprises a number of technologies, including information processing, communications, control, and electronics. Its objective is to apply these technologies to our transportation systems in order to save lives, time, and money. ITS America monitors federal, state, and local transportation policies. The Web site serves as a clearinghouse for news on these issues and about local ITS projects. It is an excellent place for industry insiders and the curious public to track government- and industry-related developments within the United States.

Manual on Uniform Traffic Control Devices
    [MUTCD 2000] (Federal Highway Administration) http://mutcd.fhwa.dot.gov

"The MUTCD contains standards for traffic control devices that regulate, warn, and guide road users along the highways and byways in all 50 states. Traffic control devices are important because they optimize traffic performance, promote uniformity nationwide, and help improve safety by reducing the number and severity of traffic crashes." Local transportation officials make heavy use of this standard resource.

Bicycling and Pedestrians

In 1991, Congress passed landmark transportation legislation that set a new direction for transportation policy. The Intermodal Surface Transportation Efficiency Act recognized the importance of bicycling and walking in creating a balanced transportation system, and which require their own distinctive infrastructure and planning. TEA-21, signed into law in 1998, extended most of this legislation and authorized federal transportation funding through 2003.

The Online Pedestrian and Bicycling Information
    Center http://www.walkinginfo.org

This is undoubtedly the best portal for information on everything from design and engineering to education and enforcement of local ordinances. For example, in the interests of creating a safer environment for pedestrians: Should local police target jaywalkers or motorists who fail to yield at pedestrian crossings? Should only the most egregious violators be targeted, or would a zero-tolerance policy work better? What approach is most effective?

Bicycle Transportation: A Handbook for Engineers,
    by John Forester (2nd ed., MIT Press, 1994)

This provocative and pathbreaking study applies recognized principles of transportation engineering to cycling, which according to the author, "heretofore has suffered only superstitious emotionalism." In addition to setting forth an argument on behalf of taking cycling seriously, this book addresses practical subjects like road design, pavement condition, and the history of government regulation.

Airport Operations/Management

Office of Airline Information [OAI] (U.S. Department of Transportation, Bureau of Transportation Statistics) http://www.bts.gov/oai

OAI provides "uniform and comprehensive financial and market/traffic statistical and economic data on individual air carrier (airline) operations and the air transportation industry." Some of the data sets included on this Web site are "Fuel Cost and Consumption," "U.S. International Air Passenger and Freight Statistics," and "Airline On-Time Statistics."

Airline On-Time Statistics (Bureau of Transportation Statistics) http://www.transtats.bts.gov

This is a searchable database of airline departure times, delays, cancellations, and diversions. The data cover the years 1997 to 2004 and is searchable by airline, origin, and destination airport. There is a box on the right that has flight delays.

Domestic Airline Fares Consumer Report: Passenger and Fare Information (U.S. Department of Transportation) http://ntl.bts.gov/DOCS/l-dafcr.html

This quarterly report began publication in 1996. It presents data on airfares charged by carriers for top origin and destination city pair markets. At the time of this writing, the October 2001 issue and earlier editions were available in PDF format online.

Air Travel Consumer Report (U.S. Department of Transportation, Office of Aviation Enforcement and Proceeding) http://airconsumer.ost.dot.gov/english/problems.htm

This monthly publication reports statistics regarding passenger complaints about such things as mishandled baggage, flight delays, and cancellations. Data are available by airline and airport. Monthly reports from 1998 to 2004 are available in PDF format at the Web site.

Harbor and Port Authorities

American Association of Port Authorities [AAPA] http://www.aapa-ports.org

This trade association represents more than 150 public port authorities in the United States, Canada, Latin America, and the Caribbean. Its annual directory, *Seaports of the Americas*, is a comprehensive guide to seaports and port authorities of the Western Hemisphere. Incidentally, most of the public port authorities that comprise the membership of AAPA maintain individual Web pages, and the Web site contains a comprehensive list of links. Typically, a local port authority Web page will contain local airport and seaport information, schedules, and maps. Weather and tide information is usually available, along with tariff schedules and local planning documents.

MERMAID (Texas A&M University, Texas Transportation Institute) http://maritime.tamu.edu

This one-stop portal to maritime information provides access to admiralty law, statistics, trade data, government agencies, corporate resources, maritime law, and more. It is perhaps the single best place to access international maritime–related information on the Web. Links are well organized and carefully annotated. You may either browse by categories or use the "Treasure Search" feature to find information using keywords.

Snow Removal

Winter Maintenance Virtual Clearinghouse (Federal Highway Administration) http://www.fhwa.dot.gov/winter/index.html

This Web site is a comprehensive clearinghouse for winter maintenance research and technology activities. Selecting the "Library" header in the left-hand column frame will take the user to a bibliography of FHWA technical reports on de-icing and other winter road-maintenance programs. Currently, not many records are listed. A few are hot-linked to electronic online versions. The arrangement is by publishing agency, not by subject.

Guide for Snow and Ice Control (American Association of State Highway and Transportation Officials, 1999)

This guide discusses what is needed for a successful snow and ice control program, including "the importance of involving other jurisdictions, the media, emergency management services and the public in developing policies and practices to provide the level of service." Ordering information is available from the AASHTO Web site.

Environment/Land Use

Clean Air Handbook (Government Institutes, 1998)

This book covers the Clean Air Act and its 1990 amendments, providing a broad overview of regulatory requirements and developments through the time of publication. This is a very useful tool for gaining an overview of this complex area. Chapters covered include "The Federal-State Partnership," "The 1990 Amendments," "Air Quality Regulations, State Implementation Plans, and the Nonattainment Program," "Control Technology Regulation," "Operating and Preconstruction Permitting Programs," "Acid Deposition Control Program," "Hazardous Air Pollutants," "Regulation of Mobile Sources of Air Pollution,"

"Stratospheric Ozone Protection," "Enforcement and Judicial Review," and "Current Regulatory and Legislative Trends." Municipalities have to cope with these issues or stand to lose their federal highway funding.

Smart Growth Online (U.S. Environmental Protection Agency and the International City/County Managers Association) http://www.smartgrowth.org

Smart Growth initiatives seek to reconcile local quality-of-life issues with economic development. This Web site is a clearinghouse for news and commentary on local projects and also has a library of links to other online Smart Growth resources. The Smart Growth Resource Library includes many full-text documents, like *Profiles of Local Clean Air Innovation: Empowering Communities to Meet the Air Quality Challenges of the 21st Century* and *Location Efficient Mortgages*.

Urban Sprawl: A Reference Handbook, by Donald C. Williams (ABC-Clio, 2000)

In recent years there has been a rich harvest of books on urban sprawl, and there is no better guide to that literature than this excellent handbook. It covers not only monographs and serials, but also associations and even a section with biographies of leading figures in movements such as the so-called New Urbanism. For example, just how should one set about the business of again creating those compact, pedestrian-friendly, convivial neighborhoods that are the focus of so much nostalgia? Do current zoning codes even permit that kind of development? Here is where to turn for answers to just that kind of question.

Transportation Resource Exchange Center [T-REX] (University of New Mexico) http://trex-center.org

This source indexes documents, databases, and links to the "people, organizations, and programs that are involved in the transport of radioactive materials." T-REX is a national repository of expertise on all kinds of issues having to do with the transport of these materials.

STATISTICAL RESOURCES

There are so many databases and statistical repositories that contain information useful for transportation and public works that it is simply not feasible to highlight all of them. The approach taken in this section is to focus on meta-sites and tools useful in ferreting out often-hidden statistical resources. Note that the Bureau of Transportation Statistics coordinates the data-collection activities of other USDOT agencies. It also supplements those activities with its own surveys and inventories.

FedStats http://www.fedstats.gov

This Web site can be used to access statistical data currently available on federal agency Web sites. Statistics appear on agency Web pages in a variety of formats—one-page news releases, full-text online statistical compendia, databases with raw data attached to an agency search engine, etc. FedStats accommodates users with different needs or levels of sophistication. If the agency that produces the data is known, FedStats has an alphabetical list of the most important statistical agency URLs. Following the links labeled "MapStats" or "Statistics by Geography" provides demographic, economic, and other statistical profiles for U.S. states, regions, counties, cities, congressional districts, and judicial districts. The "Statistical Reference Shelf" is a collection of online full-text versions of the major statistical compendia (*Statistical Abstract of the United States, National Transportation Statistics, 2000*, etc.). Many agencies post the raw data files from their surveys and statistical gathering programs on servers and connect them with a search engine, so users can create their own tables and conduct their own analyses. FedStats has a collection of links to many of these databases under the label "Data Access Tools." There is also a feature that conducts keyword searches of more than 70 statistical federal agency Web sites concurrently.

Nationwide Personal Transportation Survey (U.S. Department of Transportation, Office of Highway Policy Information) http://www.fhwa.dot.gov/policy/ohpi/nhts/index.htm

The Nationwide Personal Transportation Surveys (NPTS) were conducted by the U.S. Census Bureau between 1969 and 1983, and by the FHWA in 1990 and 1995. FHWA is currently working on a successor report, the *2001 National Household Travel Survey*. Survey questions include number and types of motor vehicles and bicycles in a household and travel habits of residents. Data from the 1995 survey are currently being analyzed and reported in publications such as *Travel Patterns of People of Color, Bi-*

cycle and Pedestrian Programs, Women's Travel Issues, and others. Online versions of some of these are linked to the above Web site, where the users will also find reports, data tables, and other information from all of these surveys.

Vehicle Inventory and Use Survey (U.S. Census Bureau) http://www.census.gov/econ/www/viusmain.html

This Web site presents data from a national survey conducted every five years since 1963 and formerly called the Truck Inventory and Use Survey, issued as part of the Economic Census. It counts the number and characteristics of private and commercial trucks registered in the United States on July 1 of the survey year. Statistics include characteristics such as weight, length, number of axles, type of use, miles driven, and commodities (including hazardous materials) hauled. Data are available for states, counties, and Metropolitan Statistical Areas (MSAs).

Fatality Analysis Reporting System (National Highway Traffic Safety Administration, National Center for Statistics and Analysis) www-fars.nhtsa.dot.gov

This is a searchable online database of reports of all fatal accidents involving a motor vehicle collision with another motor vehicle, a non–motor vehicle, a pedestrian, or a stationary object. Data are extracted by state DOT officials from medical examiner reports and police accident reports. Variables include number of crashes by time location and circumstances (including alcohol involvement), age, race, sex, previous records of drivers, and demographics of passengers and victims. Data are available for states, counties, and MSAs from 1994 to the present.

LIBRARIES/PROFESSIONAL ASSOCIATIONS

Libraries

DOT Library (U.S. Department of Transportation) http://dotlibrary.dot.gov

Noteworthy features of this site are the bibliographies covering a range of issues related to transportation, such as policy, planning, environment, law, and aviation safety and security. Also useful is "Putting the DOT Puzzle Together," a collection of Web sites and points of contact throughout USDOT headquarters. These are topically arranged under major categories: administration mission and history; consumer issues/customer service; education; environmental and hazmat (hazardous materials) issues; legal; libraries and information centers; publications; regulation and certification; safety and security; and statistical information. Frequently contacted individuals and offices—such as the phone number at the Federal Aviation Administration for reporting aircraft noise—are drawn together in one convenient location.

National Transportation Library (U.S. Department of Transportation, Bureau of Transportation Statistics) http://ntl.bts.gov

The National Transportation Library was established in 1998 through TEA-21 and serves as a repository of materials from public, academic, and private organizations. Home of the TRIS database, described above, and a digital library, this is the U.S. government's premier outlet for transportation-related information.

Name of Resource	Creator / Maintainer	URL
Boating Accident Report Database	US Coast Guard	www.uscgboating.org/stats.htm
Fatality Analysis Reporting System (FARS)	National Center for Statistics and Analysis	www-nrd.nhtsa.dot.gov/departments/ nrd-30/ncsa/fars.html
Highway Statistics	Federal Highway Administration	www.fhwa.dot.gov/ohim/ohimstat.htm
Lock Performance Monitoring System	US Army Corps of Engineers	www.iwr.usace.army.mil/ndc/lpms/lpms.htm
National Transit Database	Federal Transit Administration	www.fta.dot.gov/ntl/database.html
Waterborne Commerce Statistics Center	US Army Corps of Engineers	www.iwr.usace.army.mil/ndc/wcsc/wcsc.htm
Vehicle & Equipment Information	National Highway Traffic Safety Administration	www.nhtsa.gov/cars/

Table 17.2 SELECTED STATISTICAL REPOSITORIES AND/OR DATABASES

National Transit Library (U.S. Department of Transportation, Federal Transit Administration) http://www.fta.dot.gov/ntl/index.html

This site provides access via a set of browsable indexes to information about transit best practices, education, databases, funding, legal issues, planning, policy, procurement, publications, research, and safety.

Directory of Transportation Libraries and Information Centers, by Susan C. Dresley (7th ed., John A. Volpe National Transportation Systems Center, 1998) http://199.79.179.78/tldir

In addition to the expected contact information, such as telephone numbers, staff names, e-mail addresses, URLs, hours of operation and interlibrary loan policies, this document—available for downloading as a PDF file—includes a wealth of useful information, including notes that highlight each institution's subject strengths and special collections. Beginning with the seventh edition, the directory provides coverage of Australia and New Zealand, Europe, Central and South America, and Asia, in addition to the United States and Canada. An eighth edition is in progress as of this writing.

Harmer E. Davis Transportation Library (Institute of Transportation Studies [ITS], University of California at Berkeley) http://www.lib.berkeley.edu/ITSL/index.html

The ITS Library at UC Berkeley carries an extensive collection of more than 150,000 volumes and 2,500 serials covering all transportation-related issues. The collection is especially strong for research in air transportation, urban transportation, traffic engineering, railroads, and San Francisco Bay area transportation issues. The library Web site managers maintain a cataloged directory of external links to transportation resources at http://lib.berkeley.edu/ITSL/transres.html. Subjects include catalogs and databases, dictionaries and encyclopedias, and community transportation links. Select "For Kids" and find links to Web resources developed by state and federal agencies, the American Automobile Association, and others, with educational activities at kindergarten through middle school levels that students, teachers, and parents might find useful and fun.

Northwestern University's Transportation Library http://www.library.northwestern.edu/transportation

Considered to be one of the largest transportation libraries in the world, the Transportation Library at Northwestern "has information on transportation (air, rail, highway, water, pipeline), law enforcement and police management, and environmental impact assessment." It also publishes the quarterly *Current Literature in Traffic and Transportation*, a national review.

Professional Associations

Engineering standards and handbooks, periodicals, and technical reports tend to be published by the professional associations that conduct or coordinate research in everything from pavement and bridge construction standards to formulas used in the maintenance of water quality. Engineering handbooks and standards are generally published by professional associations and tend to be expensive. Nonetheless, the professionals in the public works and transportation departments who rely on these manuals to guide their work often consider the information they contain indispensable.

Name of Association	Acronym	URL
Air & Waste Management Association	A&WMA	http://www.awma.org
American Academy of Environmental Engineers	AAEE	http://www.enviro-engrs.org
American Association of Airport Executives	AAAE	http://www.airportnet.org
American Association of Port Authorities	AAPA	http://www.aapa-ports.org
American Association State Highway & Transportation Officials	AASHTO	http://www.aashto.org
American Bus Association	ABA	http://www.buses.org
American Concrete Pavement Association	ACPA	http://www.pavement.com
American Concrete Pipe Association	ACPA	http://www.concrete-pipe.org
American Consultant Engineers Council	ACEC	http://www.nspe.org
American Council of Engineering Companies	ACEC	http://www.acec.org
American Institute of Architects	AIA	http://www.aia.org

Name of Association	Acronym	URL
American Planning Association	APA	http://www.planning.org
American Public Health Association	APAHA	http://www.apha.org
American Public Power Association	APPA	http://www.appanet.org
American Public Transportation Association	APTA	http://www.apta.com
American Public Works Association	APWA	http://www.apwa.net
American Road & Transportation Builder's Association	ARTBA	http://www.artba.org
American Society for Testing & Materials	ASTM	http://www.astm.org
American Society of Civil Engineers	ASCE	http://www.asce.org
American Society of Highway Engineers	ASHE	http://www.highwayengineers.org
American Traffic Safety Services Association	ATSSA	http://www.atssa.com
American Water Works Association	AWWA	http://www.awwa.org
Asphalt Institute	AI	http://www.asphaltinstitute.org
Associated General Contractors of America	AGC	http://www.agc.org
Association of Iron & Steel Engineers	AISE	http://www.aise.org
Association of Nature Center Administrators	ANCA	http://www.natctr.org
Association of State & Territorial Solid Waste Management Officials	ASTSWMO	http://www.astswmo.org
Association of State Floodplain Managers	ASFP	http://www.floods.org
Equipment Maintenance Council	EMC	http://www.equipment.org
Insurance Institute for Highway Safety	IIHS	http://www.hwysafety.org
Intermodal Association of North America	IANA	http://www.intermodal.org
International Right of Way Association	IRWA	http://www.irwaonline.org/
Institute of Transportation Engineers	ITE	http://www.ite.org
International Association of Emergency Managers	IAEM	http://www.iaem.com
International Bridge, Tunnel & Turnpike Association	IBTTA	http://www.ibtta.org
International City / County Management Association	ICMA	http://www2.icma.org/main/sc.asp?t=0
International Erosion Control Association	IECA	http://www.ieca.org
International Facility Management Association	IFMA	http://www.ifma.org
International Society for Concrete Pavements	ISCP	http://iscp.tamu.edu
Laborers-Employers Cooperation and Education Trust	LECET	http://www.lecet.org
Lincoln Institute of Land Policy	LILP	http://www.lincolninst.edu/index-high.asp
National Asphalt Paving Association	NAPA	http://www.hotmix.org
National Association of Corrosion Engineers	NACE	http://nace.org/nace/
National Association of County Engineers	NACE	http://www.naco.org/affils/nace/news/index.htm
National Association of Fleet Administrators	NAFA	http://www.nafa.org
National Association of Regulatory & Utility Commissioners	NARUC	http://www.naruc.org
National Association of State Chief Information Officers	NASCIO	http://www.nascio.org
National Association of State Telecommunications Directors	NASTD	http://www.nastd.org
National Contract Management Association	NCMA	http://www.ncmahq.org
National League of Cities	NLC	http://www.nlc.org/nlc_org/site/
National Parking Association	NPA	http://www.npapark.org
National Precast Concrete Association	NPCA	http://www.precast.org
National Ready Mixed Concrete Association	NRMCA	http://www.nrmca.org
National Roadside Vegetation Management Association	NRVMA	http://www.nrvma.org
National Society of Professional Engineers	NSPE	http://www.nspe.org
National Stone, Sand & Gravel Association	NSSGA	http://www.nssga.org
North American Power Sweeping Association	NAPSA	http://www.napsaonline.com
Public Fleet Supervisors Association	PFSA	http://www.pfsa.org
Public Technology, Inc.	PTI	http://www.pti.org/elib/publish/defaulthome.asp
Snow & Ice Management Association	SIMA	http://www.sima.org/index2.cfm?poll=phase1
Society of Municipal Arborists	SMA	http://www.urban-forestry.com
Solid Waste Management Association North America	SWANA	http://www.swana.org/default.asp
Urban Land Institute	ULI	http://www.uli.org
Water Environment Federation	WEF	http://www.wef.org
World Road Association	PIARC	http://www.piarc.inrets.fr

Table 17.3 SELECTED PROFESSIONAL ASSOCIATIONS/INDUSTRY ASSOCIATIONS/RESEARCH CENTERS

CHAPTER 18
Budgets, Taxes, and Revenue Sources

Anna Levy and Deborah Mongeau

MAJOR TOPICS COVERED

MAJOR RESOURCES COVERED

INTRODUCTION

Currently, there are 87,000 local governments in the United States—counties, municipalities and townships, special districts and school districts—all dealing with the major challenge of maintaining fiscal health in a rapidly changing and complex environment. According to the U.S. Census Bureau data compiled for 1996 (http://www.census.gov/econ/overview/go0400.html), state and local government general revenue exceeded $1.2 trillion.

In 2001, the *Municipal Year Book* noted that "local governments in the United States [raised] more than 65 percent of their own revenues, with the property tax—at about 26 percent of total revenues—making up the largest portion of their own-source income" (67). The rest of their funding is obtained from various other sources, including sales tax revenues, local income taxes, user fees, miscellaneous charges, and grants-in-aid from the federal and individual state governments.

The Internet has revolutionized the way people gain access to information about local government finances (financial statements, statistical data, fiscal records, etc.), which was once available only through exhaustive research. Any information or service that can be made available over the Web will be provided at a fraction of the cost of transactions taking place between human beings over a government counter. In the past several years, many states and localities have vastly upgraded their information technology infrastructures and have pushed the use of the Internet in schools, public libraries, and other public places where potential users can gain access to Web-based government services and publications, including financial reports and statistics, budgets, and tax information.

Challenges of the twenty-first century continue to inspire local governments in finding creative ways to pay for the computer power they need to manage their financial information. For example, New York City's Independent Budget Office has a service allowing taxpayers to get an itemized tax receipt showing how much they contributed to various government activities. Information technology will continue to hold the key to meeting some of the most pressing challenges governments face with their finances—from financing public infrastructure projects to making revenue collection both efficient and fair.

Responsible accounting of public funds and property dictates the necessity to preserve state and local government financial records. Fiscal records are preserved mostly because of their fiscal value, and sometimes because of their potential archival value. The chief fiscal officer of the county or municipality reviews adequate retention periods for financial records. Some fiscal records, such as tax records (i.e., poll—capitation, or head—taxes, property taxes), may have been considered for permanent preservation. For instance, lists of polls provide the only comprehensive source of names of adult males for the early colonial period, before the initiation of decennial censuses. The majority of methods of public levy are still documented in the records of county and municipal governments. Large quantities of tax records have been preserved in local government archives, and their historical value can hardly be underestimated.

Given the demanding expectations of managers of local governments, researchers, students, and the gen-

eral public, there are a great variety of resources that represent and explain the complex world of local government finance. The majority of these sources are published by government agencies at the federal and state level, but also by the local governments themselves. Each source is aimed at a specific audience and produces a different viewpoint of the same fiscal picture. For this reason the sources in this chapter are arranged primarily by issuing agency.

FEDERAL GOVERNMENT RESOURCES

Among the most important resources for financial analysis of local governments are those covering population and governments, income and taxes, labor market and prices. The Bureau of the Census, within the U.S. Department of Commerce, is the primary source of data on population and governments. The principal agency that collects income data is the Bureau of Economic Analysis of the United States Department of Commerce.

Federal Agency Resources

Census Bureau

Federal, State and Local Governments
   http://www.census.gov/govs/www

Census Bureau programs are in fact the major source of general information on state and local government finances other than the governments themselves. These programs are collectively represented on this Census Bureau Web site. The Census Bureau has conducted a Census of Governments at five-year intervals since 1957 and an annual survey for the intervening years, both of these programs covering local government finance.

Census of Governments (U.S. Census Bureau, 1997)
   http://www.census.gov/govs/www/index.html

The Census of Governments, the most thorough and comprehensive source of information on the finances of all state and local governments, is taken for years ending in 2 and 7, as required by law (13 U.S.C. 161). It used to be published only in paper, but since 1997 is also available on the Census Bureau Web site, in PDF format. "Government Finances," one of the major subject areas covered by this Census, includes statistics on government financial activity in four broad categories: revenue, expenditure, debt, and assets. Internet files and viewable tables cover state and local governments and employee retirement systems of state and local governments.

Printed reports of the Census of Governments that cover local government finance include *Finances of County Governments*, *Finances of Special District Governments*, *Finances of Municipalities and Township Governments*, *Compendium of Government Finances*, *Public Education Finances*, and *Employee Retirement Systems of State and Local Governments* (SuDoc no. C 3.145/4:). The statistics in these publications cover local revenues and expenditures by state and by localities grouped by population size. Revenues and expenditures are subdivided by source of revenue and by category of expenditure. *Finances of County Governments* and *Finances of Municipalities and Township Governments* also list revenues and expenditures for all counties in the United States and all municipalities with populations of over 25,000. *Finances of Special District Governments* give the revenues and expenditures for individual special governments that exist independently of other local governments but do not include school districts. *Public Education Finances* includes revenues, expenditures, and indebtedness of school districts that are not part of a larger county or local government. The *Compendium of Government Finances* is a summary of all of the data that appear in the above publications. *Employee Retirement Systems of State and Local Governments* lists the contributions and payments of retirement systems of local governments that are larger than $20 million. Some 2002 data is beginning to appear at http://www.census.gov/govs/www/cog2002.html.

Annual Survey of State and Local Government Finances http://www.census.gov/econ/overview/go0400.html

Periodic surveys of state and local government finances have been conduced by the Census Bureau from 1902 to 1952. Since 1952, the Bureau has started to conduct a survey of state and local government financial activities as authorized by law (13 U.S.C.182). Reported data are for each government's annual accounting period that ends on or before June 30 of the survey year, with months covered varying by government. Data collection begins each October and continues for about 12 months. It includes revenue, expenditure, financial assets, and debt of all state and local governments in the United States. Revenue data include taxes, charges, interest, and other earnings. Expenditure data include total by function (such as

education and police protection) and by accounting category (such as current operations and capital outlays). Debt data include issuance, retirement, and amounts outstanding. Financial assets data include securities and other holdings, by type. Over 400 different budgetary accounts have been standardized, providing for a uniform accounting structure, which made possible the comparison of state and local government finances. Tables provide summary data on financial activities covering state and local, state-only, and local-only governments. Finance reports include revenue by source, expenditure by function, indebtedness, and financial holdings.

The survey has been available on the Census Bureau's Web site since 1993, and the reports consist of viewable tables and data files that users can download. Data from the survey are available about 12 months after the survey year.

Prior to 1993, the print version of the survey was published as a collection of reports. Those dealing with local government finances are *City Government Finances in* [*year*] (SuDoc no. C 3.191/2–5:) and *County Government Finances in* [*year*] (SuDoc no. C 3.191/2–7:).

Summary of State and Local Government Revenue (quarterly) http://www.census.gov/govs/www/qtax.html

This survey has been conducted continuously since 1962 and offers quarterly estimates of state and local tax revenue, as well as detailed tax revenue data for individual states. Data for the current quarter as well as for the previous 12 months are given. Since 1994, the data have been available on the Web in both viewable tables and spreadsheet files. The Web version also includes historical data back to 1989 in some cases. Prior to 1994 the print version was titled *Quarterly Summary of Federal, State and Local Tax Revenue* (SuDoc no. C 3.145/6:).

Education Finance Survey (1977–, annual) http://www.census.gov/govs/www/school.html

This survey is a joint effort by the Census Bureau and the National Center for Education Statistics (NCES) to provide statistics about the fiscal year finances of all public elementary and secondary public school systems. The data from the survey have been published as *Public Education Finances Reports* since 1977. From 1957 to 1977, school expenditure data were collected and published as part of the annual public finance survey. Data include revenue by source (local property tax, monies from other school systems, private tuition and transportation payments, school lunch charges, direct state aid, and federal aid passed through the state government), expenditure by function and object (instruction, support service functions, salaries, and capital outlay), indebtedness, and cash and investments. Beginning with the survey for 1992, content was expanded at the NCES's request. New data items include direct state aid for 11 types of programs (such as general formula assistance, staff improvement, and special education). The *Public Education Finances* tables, released about 18 months after the reference fiscal year, contain national and state aggregated data for major components of school system revenues, expenditures, debt, and assets. They also provide similar detail, per pupil, for school systems with enrollments larger than 15,000. Statistical tables for 1997 and after can be viewed and downloaded from the Web site.

Consolidated Federal Funds Report: State and County Areas (annual) http://www.census.gov/govs/www/cffr.html

In this PDF-only series, volumes before 2000 had the title *Consolidated Federal Funds Report* [CFFR] *for Fiscal Year: State and County Areas*. This report is a representation of federal government expenditures in state, county, and subcounty areas of the United States, as well as the District of Columbia and U.S. outlying areas. In 2001, the Census Bureau introduced the CFFR Online Query System, intended to supplement the resources available through the main pages, where one can find summary displays as well as downloadable data files with federal expenditure information. Complementary features of the query system include interactive searching, according to geographic location and functional expenditure category, for specific federal agency and program expenditures. As on the other Web pages, data are available for the federal fiscal years 1993 to the present.

Bureau of Economic Analysis (BEA)

National Income and Product Accounts of the United States http://www.bea.gov or http://www.stat-usa.gov

BEA analyzes government spending and surpluses as part of the National Income and Product Accounts (NIPA), used to determine the gross domestic product.

The data coverage (SuDoc no. C 59.11/5:) is from 1929 to the present. Detailed estimates of several components in the state and local government sectors are published annually. The historical estimates for most of the NIPA tables are available on the BEA's Web site or the Stat-USA Web site.

Survey of Current Business (monthly, 1921–) http://purl.access.gpo.gov/GPO/LPS1730

The *Survey of Current Business*, BEA's monthly journal, contains estimates of income for the entire nation, including gross national/domestic product and personal income. Every year, in its April or May issue, it publishes an article on fiscal position estimates for states and local governments, entitled *State and Local Government Fiscal Position in* [*year*]. Issues of the *Survey of Current Business* from 1998 to the present can be accessed via the agency's Web site.

National Center for Education Statistics http://nces.ed.gov

A *school district*, by census definition, is a type of local government. It may be part of a municipality or even a stand-alone governmental entity. Being supported by the variety of revenues available for public education, a school district's fiscal policy is likely to be subjected to intense scrutiny. Certain data, such as per pupil expenditures, are also expected to be placed in political and social contexts when compared with other school districts and even other states.

NCES publishes surveys and research and development reports on school district finance in the United States. Common Core of Data (CCD), http://nces.ed.gov/ccd, is the NCES primary statistical database of all public elementary and secondary schools and school districts. The CCD surveys collect data annually about all public schools, all local education agencies, and all state education agencies throughout the United States. One of a set of five surveys sent to state education departments is *School District Fiscal Data*, which includes revenues by source and expenditures by function and enrollment. The *National Public Education Financial Survey* is the other component of the CCD collection of surveys.

A number of fiscal reports are among the publications of NCES Common Core of Data, such as the annual *Statistics in Brief: Revenues and Expenditures for Public Elementary and Secondary Education*. NCES also publishes research reports (some of them reviewed below) on political and social issues of financing public education, such as *Disparities in Public School District Spending* and *Inequalities in Public School District Revenues*. NCES publications and data products can be easily located by doing a customized search on the NCES Electronic Catalog, http://nces.ed.gov/pubsearch.

Inequalities in Public School District Revenues: Statistical Analysis Report http://nces.ed.gov/ pubsearch/pubsinfo.asp?pubid=98210

This report examines variations between school districts and across states in the quantities of the various types of revenues received for educational programs and services. It builds on some of the analysis techniques introduced in an earlier NCES publication, *Disparities in Public School District Spending, 1989–1990* (1995). While that report focused primarily on public education expenditures for the 1989–90 school year, this one provides detailed information about how much money is received through alternative funding sources at the federal, state, and local levels for different types of students, districts, and communities for the 1991–92 school year.

Selected Papers in School Finance (National Institute of Education, 1974–, annual) http://nces.ed.gov/ pubsearch/pubsinfo.asp?pubid=2001378

This publication, available from 1997 on the NCES Web site, is an annual collection of research papers. Publication was suspended after 1977 and resumed in 1994. The papers, targeting school policymakers as well as education researchers, address advances in topics on school finance, such as measuring inflation and adjusting for it; the emergence of a new focus upon spending at the school and district level; private sources of funding for public education; and a review of the state of the art of assessing educational productivity.

U.S. Advisory Commission on Intergovernmental Relations [ACIR] http://www.library.unt.edu/gpo/ ACIR/acir.html

From 1959 until Congress disbanded it in 1996, ACIR studied the relationship between federal, state, and local governments and fostered communication among all levels of government. It published numerous reports on all aspects of intergovernmental relations, including finance. ACIR was succeeded by a private-sector organization, the American Council on Intergovernmental Relations, which acquired the inventory

of its predecessor's reports. More information on ACIR and its publications may be found at the University of North Texas Web page, "Government Agency Cybercemetery," which is located at the above URL.

The three major publications of ACIR on local government finances are briefly reviewed here. *Significant Features of Fiscal Federalism* is an annual survey (1976–) that describes in table format the state and local tax policies, rates, deductions, and credits for each state. It lists local revenues and expenditures by state, provides data on the county governments that levy the tax, identifies states with significant levels of participation by municipalities, and shows various patterns of state restrictions on local government tax and expenditure powers.

It is known that federal funds are channeled to localities either directly or through the states. The major publication covering this topic is the ACIR's *Catalog of Federal Grant-in-Aid Programs to State and Local Governments: Grants Funded FY*, also an annual publication (1974/1975–1989), which provides data on intergovernmental transfers as a percentage of municipal revenues. Some historical data were given for the purpose of comparison. *Characteristics of Federal Grant-in-Aid Programs to State and Local Governments: Grants Funded* [for FY 1991–95], a biennial serial publication, continued the catalog.

Attitudes of taxpayers toward taxes and spending often influence how much governments can tax and spend, as reflected by an annual ACIR survey, *Changing Public Attitudes on Governments and Taxes: A Commission Survey* (1981–1994). It reports on the results of a public opinion poll on tax fairness and public confidence in the government at the federal, state, and local levels. In some years questions were asked on special topics such as taxes for local public works projects and local sales taxes. The appendix lists the actual questions that were asked of the respondents.

Internet Resources

Federal government Web sites can be extremely useful for research in local government fiscal activities. Listed below are some of the most comprehensive, official U.S. gateways to all government information, described in more detail in earlier chapters of this book.

FirstGov http://www.firstgov.gov/Government/ State_Local/Grants.shtml#financial

This site is an easy-to-search, free-access official Web portal for the U.S. government designed to give users a centralized place to find any kind of information from local, state, and federal agency Web sites. Government Gateway, http://www.firstgov.gov/Government/Government_Gateway.shtml, is one of the major sections of this Web site, providing one-stop access to information about federal assistance programs for state and local governments, acquisition and procurement, financial management, and taxes.

Library of Congress Internet Resource Page: State and Local Governments http://lcweb.loc.gov/global/state/stategov.html

This site lists meta-indexes and other government information locators having to do with state and local government. Nonprofit and commercial sites are included as well as official sites. For links to local government sites, however, it is not as complete as the popular Web site State and Local Government on the Net, http://www.statelocalgov.net/index.cfm, described in an earlier chapter.

FedSales.go http://www.firstgov.gov/shopping/shopping.shtml

This site is the official U.S. federal portal for all official government surplus property sales and auctions. This database includes all government asset sales worldwide, including state and local government unclaimed and surplus property (financial and real estate assets). It provides complete alphabetic listing by state.

GENERAL COMMERCIAL SOURCES

There are numerous sources produced by private publishers that offer information on local government finance. The source listed below represents added value to the primarily statistical data provided by federal government agencies.

Directories

Directory of Incentives for Business Investment and Development in the United States: State-by-State Guide (3rd ed., Urban Institute Press, 1991)

According to the National Association of State Development Agencies, some states have authorized the use of tax abatements, the most popular incentive, by local governments to attract businesses and increase their tax base. This directory summarizes state by state the incentives used to attract business to that state. The statutory provisions in the states governing the use of tax abatements are given as well as contacts for more information. While this directory lists incentives granted by the state governments, some of the tax abatements, such as property tax reductions, can have an impact on the local government tax base.

Bibliographies

In the previous decades a few attempts have been made at compiling bibliographic guides to local government documents, including city/county budget publications and annual financial reports, thus complementing Greenwood Press's *Index to Current Urban Documents*. (The index is described in detail in the chapter on General Indexes and Bibliographic Resources.)

Municipal Government Reference Sources: Publications and Collections (R. R. Bowker, 1978)

This source concentrates on large urban areas, arranged by state and, within the state, by municipality. It offers a detailed overview of publications of a given city. Though some information is dated, this volume is still prototypic, highlighting the kinds of documents available.

Urban Finance and Administration: A Guide to Information Sources, by Jerry McCaffery (Gale Research, 1980)

This bibliography evaluates sources about all aspects of city finance from the 1950s to 1978. The sources evaluated cover the topics of revenues, expenditures, debt structure, budgeting, financial decision making, innovative financial programs, and urban fiscal crises. The emphasis is on scholarly studies and professional journals, but there is a section on reference resources. While dated, this is a good source for locating classic studies on urban finances and mid-twentieth-century urban financial conditions.

Periodicals and Newsletters

The periodicals and newsletters listed below are good sources for finding current information on issues and trends in local government finances.

City Fiscal Conditions (National League of Cities [NLC], 1986–, annual) http://www.nlc.org/nlc_org/site/programs/research_reports/index.cfm

Its former title was *City Fiscal Conditions and Outlook for Fiscal…* Current reports are available for download on the NLC Web site as Adobe PDF files. Printed copies of these and other recent NLC research reports are available from the NLC Publications Center, at nlcbooks@pmds.com.

This annual survey of city officials from over 300 cities covers in detail the status of current fiscal conditions and the outlook for the coming fiscal year. The results are broken down by type of revenue and expenditure and by city size and region.

Governing (*Congressional Quarterly*, 1984–)
http://www.governing.com/srchgov.htm

Governing is a monthly magazine that targets executive and financial officials of the state and local governments but is also useful to journalists and companies that provide products and services to local governments, as well as involved citizens with an interest in the governments closest to them. Topics covered include a variety of public finance and economic development issues on the state and local levels. Current and past years' issues (January 1995–present) of this magazine are searchable online for free in addition to news and other current information, on this Web site.

Government Finance Review (Government Finance Officers Association, 1985–)

A bimonthly official publication, this periodical publishes articles on a broad spectrum of topics relating to the management of state and local government finances. Some issues are devoted to a particular topic such as public school finance. It is indexed by the *Public Affairs Information Service Bulletin*.

Municipal Finance Journal (Panel Publishers, 1980–)
http://hws.wichita.edu/kpf/journal.asp

This quarterly is the only professional journal devoted to municipal securities and state and local financing. Articles are mostly scholarly and provide timely analysis, cutting-edge research, and creative ideas on public securities, tax-exempt bonds, infrastructure financing, and state and local finance. There are also articles describing innovative programs, analyzing current issues and trends. Articles may include such topics as the financial impact of borrowing costs and the impact of e-commerce on local sales taxes. Tables of contents from 1989 (vol. 10) to the present

may be found on the Web site of the Hugo Wall School of Urban and Public Affairs, Wichita State University.

Nation's Cities Weekly (National League of Cities, 1963–)

This is the official weekly publication of the NCL (called the American Municipal Association from 1962 to 1964). *Nation's Cities Weekly* was formed after merging with *City Weekly* in 1978. Starting with volumes for 1964, it includes the section "American Municipal News," previously issued as a separate publication. Topics covered by some of the special issues include city budgets, finances, and economic development.

Public Finance Review (Sage Periodicals Press, 1997–)

This scholarly journal (called *Public Finance Quarterly* from 1973 to 1996) includes articles on local government finance. The articles emphasize financial policies especially as they relate to current issues and problems in governments. This journal has been indexed by ABI/INFORM from October 1975. Online access to abstracts and full-text articles is available by subscription through the Online Computer Library Center's (OCLC) FirstSearch Electronic Collections Online, http://www.oclc.org/oclc/menu/eco.htm, and EBSCo, http://www.ebsco.com.

Nonprofit Organizations

Most of these are nonpartisan as well as nonprofit and are based within one state. The membership comes primarily from the business community, but other concerned citizens and local government officials are usually welcome. These organizations assume a watchdog role over government fiscal policies, especially with regard to taxes and spending. Listed below are examples of these organizations.

New York

Citizens Budget Commission [CBC] http://www.cbcny.org/

The CBC is a nonpartisan, nonprofit civic organization devoted to influencing constructive change in the finances and services of New York City and New York State government. It was founded in 1932, a time of great fiscal crisis, when a group of distinguished civic leaders decided to start a research organization that would analyze the city's finances, evaluate the management of city government, report on these matters to its members, and recommend improvements to municipal officials. In 1984, CBC expanded this analysis to the fiscal affairs of state government. A list of its publications (mostly in PDF format) is available on the CBC Web site, at http://www.cbcny.org/publications1.htm.

Pennsylvania

Pennsylvania Economy League [PEL]
    http://www.pel-central.org

PEL was founded in 1932 to promote better government and economic development in Pennsylvania. It offers advice and technical support to local governments to promote sound fiscal management. This state nonprofit organization was quite prolific in preparing educational reports for citizens of Pennsylvania in the past decades. Just to name a few: in 1982, *Fiscal Outlook for the School District of Philadelphia: Revenues and Expenditures for Fiscal 1983–1986 and Financing Plan for Balanced Budgets*; in 1991, *Citizens' Guide to the Philadelphia Budget*, 3rd edition; in 1993, *Philadelphia Revenue and Expenditure Comparisons: Five Year Comparison of Philadelphia and Ten Competitor Cities*. Many of the current reports are available on PEL's Web site.

Rhode Island

Rhode Island Public Expenditure Council [RIPEC]
    http://www.ripec.org

RIPEC was established to promote fiscal responsibility and effective government in Rhode Island. For over five decades, RIPEC has influenced the agenda for government accountability. RIPEC publishes reports on such topics as local tax structure, local government finances, and public school finances. Two annual reports, *How Rhode Island Compares: State and Local Taxes and Expenditures* and *How Rhode Island Schools Compare*, use statistical data to show how well Rhode Island does compare with other states and highlights the areas where the state could improve. The current issues of these reports, as well as most of the other individual reports, are available on the Government Finance Officers Association Internet publications page at https://www.estoregfoa.org/ScriptContent/Index.cfm.

Trade Associations and Professional Societies

These organizations provide resources that allow finance officers to be more effective. The resources can take the form of conferences, training workshops and materials, and consultative services, as well as publications and Web sites. Listed below are the major national organizations for local government finances, with an example of a state organization.

National

Government Finance Officers Association http://www.gfoa.org

The Government Finance Officers Association, established in 1906, is the major professional association of state/provincial and local finance officers in the United States and Canada. The Association provides training, computer software, and consulting services to its members and to governments. It publishes *Government Finance Review*, a major periodical on government finance; several newsletters; and a number of technical reports. Information on the Association's publications may be found on its e-store site, https://www.estoregfoa.org/ScriptContent/Index.cfm.

National Association of Local Government Auditors
    http://www.nalga.org

This is a professional organization devoted to improving local auditing practices and providing a forum for issues that concern local government auditors. The Association's Web site includes selections from its journal, *Local Government Auditing Quarterly*, and a database of over 1,500 audit reports.

New York

New York State Government Finance Officers Association http://www.nysgfoa.org

Founded in 1978 as a not-for-profit professional organization, the membership of this association numbers more than 1,230. Its mission is to promote and improve professional management of state and local government finances throughout New York State. The association conducts training seminars, holds an annual conference, monitors government finance–related bills before the state legislature, and publishes a newsletter.

Comprehensive Web Sites

These Web sites provide convenient access to a wide variety of links to state and local government information.

Search Systems (Pacific Information Resources)
http://www.searchsystems.net

Produced by Pacific Information Resources, this site claims to be the largest collection of free public records on the Internet, with access to over 6,300 databases. Records include property tax and tax assessor records, unclaimed property listings, Uniform Commercial Code filings, and farm subsidy recipient data (provided by the Environmental Working Group Farm Subsidy Database, 1996–2000). Arrangement is by state and then by locality, but keyword searching by type of record and locality (including zip codes and congressional districts) is also available.

State and Local Government on the Net
http://www.piperinfo.com/index.cfm

This site, provided by Piper Resources, offers links to all official state and local government sites. Local government Web sites are included if they have ".ci" or ".co" in their domain name. Arrangement is by state with links to state agency and local government Web sites. Keyword searching is available, but the search is conducted only on the site name rather than the whole page, so some sites may not turn up in the list of results.

Electronic discussion groups, also known as listservs, constitute a powerful communication tool for elected officials.

MuniNet Internet Listserv
http://www.sec.state.vt.us/othersites/muninet.htm

One of the keys to improving financial management in local governments is the increasing ability for financial professionals to communicate on a daily basis with one another in newsgroups and forums in which one can quickly post and receive answers and solutions to questions and problems encountered in daily work. The MuniNet Internet Listserv, maintained by Peter Brownell from the Department of Continuing Education at the University of Vermont, provides a forum for all municipal professionals to post questions related to municipal financial management, including accounting, bonds, revenues, taxation, budgets, fees, audits, and payroll. All messages are archived on the MuniNet site for easy viewing. The URL listed above gives directions for subscribing and posting messages to the listserv.

Localgov—Local Government Policy Discussion Group http://groups.yahoo.com/group/localgov

This list, sponsored by the Municipal Research and Services Center of Washington since 1995, covers a broad range of local government topics, including zero-based budgeting, citizen involvement in the budget process, and many others. It is intended primarily for local government officials, municipal leagues, and nonprofit associations to share information, innovations, and inquiries. There is no charge for subscribing. Any changes to the subscription can be done at any time by accessing the Yahoo Web site at the above address. There is an archive of previous messages, searchable by keywords.

STATE GOVERNMENT RESOURCES

State supervision of local government finance includes defining standards for performance of local government finance functions such as budgeting, accounting, and auditing; limiting local financial powers; and coordinating state and local units to avoid unnecessary duplication in carrying out different functions. Every state assigns these functions to different agencies within its organizational structure. Listed below are examples of the types of state agencies that carry out these functions and what resources they provide on local government finance.

Legislative Auditors

While the function of the legislative auditor is primarily to audit state programs and advise the legislature on fiscal policy matters, some local programs supported by state funding may be audited by a legislative auditor. Featured resources, listed below, are typical for the legislative auditors' publication activities related to local government finance.

California Legislative Analyst's Office [LAO]
http://www.lao.ca.gov

The LAO has been providing fiscal policy advice to the state legislature for more than 55 years, with an overview of the state's fiscal picture and identification of some of the major policy issues confronting the lawmaking body. Throughout the year, the LAO prepares special reports on topics of interest to the legislature, including school facilities financing, property tax administration, and budgeting for county welfare programs. Since 1996, most reports are available in electronic format (HTML or PDF) on the LAO's Web site, searchable under the topical link "Local Government" on the Publications Index page. Generally, reports are accessible on the Web site the same day they are released to the legislature. Any publication that is not available electronically may be obtained from the LAO (925 L Street, Suite 1000, Sacramento, CA 95814) by sending $2.00.

Maryland

Legislative Handbook Series (Maryland General Assembly, Department of Legislative Services, 1998)

Since the state legislature must consider and pass laws affecting local government finances, this series was produced to provide an understanding of local government finance structure so that well-informed decisions can be made. The full work comprises nine volumes, including volume 3, *Maryland's Revenue Structure*; volume 4, *Maryland's Budget Process*; and volume 7, *Maryland Local Government: Revenues and State Aid*. The text is very readable and is interspersed with sidebars, bullets, and numerous statistical tables. All of the information is well documented with bibliographical references, and the subject indexes make this series a good example of an in-depth but readable description of a state's local government revenue structure.

Minnesota

Minnesota Office of the Legislative Auditor [OLA]
  http://www.auditor.leg.state.mn.us

The OLA server includes history of the office and information about the Financial Audit Division and the Program Evaluation Division. Copies of reports released by the OLA are available in PDF format and include *Best Practices Reviews of Local Governments* and *Performance Budgeting*. An outstanding feature of this site is the numerous links to the federal, state, and Internet information resources that are of interest to auditors at all levels of governments.

State Comptrollers

In many states, the state comptroller's duties include supervision of the fiscal affairs and accounting policies of all local governments in a given state. In New

York State, this function is carried out by the Division of Municipal Affairs, which acts as liaison between the comptroller and the local governments.

In addition, state comptrollers may offer technical support to local governments in the preparation of their financial reports. Sources listed below feature publications frequently requested from the state comptroller's office.

New York

Office of the New York State Comptroller [OSC]
  http://nysosc3.osc.state.ny.us

This office provides numerous accounting, financial, and statistical publications and reports for use by local government officials and others interested in government issues and finance, as well as training newsletters and booklets. The "Frequently Requested Publications" Web page lists publications of interest to local government officials. The list provides information on the materials and links to publications that are available online or in PDF format.

One of the major publications listed on the Web site, *Special Report on Municipal Affairs: For Local Fiscal Year Ended in 1998* (released August 2000), the 90th in an annual series, is an authoritative and valuable reference tool for all who are concerned with the fiscally prudent operation of local governments. The report consists of statistical tables on revenues, expenditures, and debt for each municipality, school district, fire district, and joint activity in the state, with tables showing trends in local government statistics. It also includes information on special districts created or extended and consents granted for issuing and excluding debt. A valuable feature of this report is a historical overview of financial trends for New York's local governments. It can be found at http://nysosc3.osc.state.ny.us/localgov/muni/specrep/98/specrep.htm.

Education Departments

State Departments of Education not only produce data on public school finances but also analyze and compare the data so that taxpayers can see how individual school districts are doing. Resources listed below are examples of both types of data.

New York

New York Department of Education
  http://usny.nysed.gov/publications.html

The Department of Education produces numerous reports on public school finances both in print and as Internet resources. In addition, some of the data are available on the Department's Web site as raw data so that researchers and public officials may compile their own statistics. The Department's reports are available at the Web site and include statistical reports that are required by law, such as *New York, the State of Learning: A Report to the Governor and Legislature on the Educational Status of the State's Schools* (Office for Policy Analysis and Program Accountability, annual since 1987), which provides profiles of the major educational indicators, including expenditures and wealth ratio for each school district. The electronic version (in TIFF format) is made available via the New York State Library Scanned Documents Web page, at http://www.nysl.nysed.gov/scandocs. To access the report, search by the words in the title "New York the State of Learning." It is the last of 20 retrievals.

Analysis of School Finances, New York State School Districts, [year] (New York State Education Department, Bureau of Educational Finance Research, 2000–2001, annual) http://www.oms.nysed.gov/faru/Analysis/00–01/TEST2_02–03_Analysis_PDF.pdf

This source provides a detailed analysis not only of the revenues and expenditures of the school districts and Metropolitan Statistical Areas, but also compares the data by ranking percentile and by community wealth ratio. Historical data for the past five years are also given. The electronic version (scanned image in TIFF format) is available via the New York State Library Scanned Documents Web page listed above.

Pennsylvania

Selected Revenue Data and Equalized Mills for Pennsylvania Public Schools, [year] (Pennsylvania Department of Education, Bureau of Basic Education Fiscal Administration, Division of Child Accounting and Subsidy Research, annual) http://www.pde.state.pa.us/k12_finances/cwp/view.asp?A=3&Q=50956

This set of tables lists all revenues, both local taxes and state funds, collected by the school districts. The revenues are broken down by source of funds. A section on equalized mills shows the effective tax rate. Some tables include 10-year historical data. Reports for 1997/98 and later years are available on the Department's Web site.

Financial Control Boards

These agencies in many states are charged with the nuts and bolts of collecting and dispersing state funds. Therefore, they also monitor the finances of local governments as they may affect the financial health of the state.

Rhode Island

Report on Debt Management to the Public Finance Management Board, State of Rhode Island and Providence Plantations (Rhode Island Public Finance Management Board, Evensen Dodge Inc., 1997)

While emphasizing the state's debt, this report also analyzes the long-term and short-term debt of the city and town governments and ranks them by several criteria. The report concludes with several recommendations to the board on how the state can better manage its own debt and that of its local governments. This report represents a method that a state agency may use to monitor the financial activities of local governments in order to keep the state's own credit rating up.

Revenue Departments

These departments are charged with the collection of state revenues from all sources, including any assessments levied on the local governments for services rendered. A resource listed below is an example of government information available on state levies and distribution of state funds to local governments.

Massachusetts

Cherry Sheet: [year] City or Town Receipts (Massachusetts Department of Revenue, 1992–, annual)

Cherry Sheet: [year] Regional School Districts (Massachusetts Department of Revenue, 1990–, annual) http://www.dls.state.ma.us/CHERRY/index.htm

These two publications list how much state aid each local government is receiving. The *Cherry Sheet* serves notification by the Commonwealth to the local governments and school districts of the amount of state aid that was paid out and what assessments were levied. The *Estimated Cherry Sheet* is notification in the spring prior to the coming fiscal year of estimated state aid and assessments. Under each locality, the amount is broken down by program as well as by the total amount of aid/assessments. *Cherry Sheets* from 1995 to present may be found on the Web site.

State/Local Intergovernmental Relations Agencies

These agencies are charged with improving local governments by fostering good state/local government relations, technical support and consultation, and financial assistance; and administering community grants.

Colorado

Local Government Financial Compendium (Colorado Division of Local Government, 1966–, annual) http://www.dola.state.co.us/LGS/TA/ compendium.htm

This source is a good example of where to look for basic information on a local government's finances without a difficult search. It lists all sources of revenue for each municipal and county government, as well as all expenditures. Expenditures are listed by governmental function. Self-sufficient operations such as water and sewage companies are also included. There is also a section on indebtedness. The data are compiled based on one accounting model so that comparisons between communities can be made. The data are released about 15 months after the end of the year. Reports published after 1995 are available on the Web site.

LOCAL GOVERNMENT RESOURCES

Local governments themselves provide the most complete and detailed data on the state of local government finance. State laws defining revenue-raising powers of municipalities and counties, and most directly shaping local revenue policies, also in most cases require public disclosure and dissemination of relevant local financial information. Prior to the rise of the Internet, materials documenting this information were not published on a regular basis or widely distributed. Only the larger cities' management and financial agencies could develop impressive publication programs. For the smaller communities, the information research options were limited to appropriate local agencies or the federal and state resources discussed earlier in this chapter. Today the Internet has dramatically changed existing practices, allowing municipal and county governments to post financial, statistical, and budgetary statements on their official Web sites.

New York City is given as an example of what a large city has to offer, especially in view of this city's historic role in the budget movement, which is reflected upon in Jonathan Kahn's well-researched study *Budgeting Democracy: State Building and Citizenship in America, 1890–1928.*

The structure and mechanics of most modern municipal budgets can be traced back to the New York budget movement. While taxes have been levied for centuries, the concept of making governments accountable through a budget is barely a hundred years old. The author uses New York City, the first city to use modern accounting methods, as a model for the rise of the municipal budget as a means of government reform and explains how the budget evolved in New York City to make the city government accountable. The use of a budget as a tool for reform was so successful that the budget movement spread to other cities and states and ultimately to the federal government. Listed below are some resources available from New York City government agencies, as well as a few sample documents representing financial activities of the smaller municipalities and counties.

Local Budget Offices

The budget statement is a blueprint of what the local government expects in revenue and expenditures for the coming year. In most local governments, the initial responsibility for budget formulation rests with the executive (i.e., mayor), who submits a proposed budget to a governing body (i.e., city council) for legal approval. The budget is generally broken down into an *operating* budget (short-term expenditures) and a *capital* budget (long-term capital improvements). In most cases, annual budget reports are presented for three time periods: prior fiscal year, estimated figures for the current year, and proposed revenues and expenditures for the next fiscal year.

New York City

New York City Office of Management and Budget [OMB] http://www.ci.nyc.ny.us/html/omb/ html/budpubs.html

OMB, established in 1933 as the Bureau of the Budget and renamed in 1976, is responsible for assisting the mayor in developing and implementing the city's budget (for the 2003–2004 fiscal year, the city's operating budget is $47.8 billion) and for advising the mayor on policy affecting the city's fiscal stability and the effectiveness of city services. OMB monitors and forecasts the revenues and expenditures of the city, evaluates agencies' management improvement initiatives (including information technology purchases), conducts value engineering reviews of capital projects, and in cooperation with the Office of the Comptroller for the City of New York, issues bonds and notes in the public credit markets. Budget publications for the current fiscal year are available on the OMB's Web site in PDF. Although these files are large, they are also available for inspection at the OMB office.

Executive Budget of the City of New York for the Fiscal Year...(Mayor's Office, 1978–)

This annual publication was formerly the *Executive Capital Budget*. It primarily consists of three parts: a revenue budget for anticipated receipts, an expense budget for operating expenditures, and a capital budget for improvements to infrastructure, including mass transit, bridges and highways, and environmental protection. The executive budget is accompanied by the Message of the Mayor, which contains the highlights and objectives of the executive budget; descriptions of programs, the general fiscal and economic condition of the city, and anticipated aid from the federal and state governments; a three-year forecast for expenses; and a comparison of the prior year's budget with actual expenditures. The executive budget, Message of the Mayor, and 10-year capital strategy are available in local public libraries as well as in the libraries of local colleges and universities.

Expense Budget—City of New York (Mayor's Office, 1976–77)

This annual publication is continued by the *Budget of the City of New York: Capital Budget* and is merged with the New York City capital budget report to form the *Budget of the City of New York* (Bureau of the Budget). The *Expense Budget* shows the yearly projected expenditure for personnel, supplies, and other noncapital expenses, as finally adopted and certified by the mayor, the comptroller, and the city clerk and filed in the offices of those latter two officials.

Monthly Report on Current Economic Conditions (New York City Office of Management and Budget, 1992–)

Since New York City's economy is larger than that of many countries and also has a major impact on the U.S. economy, the OMB monitors economic indicators of the United States and New York City that will have an impact on the city's finances, such as unemployment and commercial office vacancy rates. This statistical report publishes these indicators for both the United States and the city with comparisons between the two. Some of the data are presented in graph format and some of the indicators are projected out to five years. Reports for the current fiscal year are available on the OMB Web site.

Independent Budget Office of the City of New York [IBO] http://www.ibo.nyc.ny.us

The New York City Charter directs the IBO to "enhance official and public understanding" of the city's budget and finances. IBO prepares various reports that are nonpartisan and informative, including short fiscal policy briefs and comprehensive reports on issues such as welfare law, bond acts being considered by voters, tax and other revenue proposals, and pending legislation. IBO also issues three annual reports as mandated by the city charter: *New York City's Fiscal Outlook*, an independent spending and revenue forecast; *Analysis of the Mayor's Preliminary Budget*; and *Analysis of the Mayor's Executive Budget*. IBO issues a newsfax, *Inside the Budget*, containing short articles on fiscal issues facing New York City as well as announcements of budget hearings and reports. All IBO reports are available to the public and are located on its Web site. The reports are searchable by date and by topic.

Local Comptroller's Offices

Local governments prepare financial statements to show how the budgeted resources have actually been spent. Comptroller's offices are responsible for preparing and publishing these statements. Financial statements also include infrastructure and other assets with long lives and show all of the resources available for the provision of public services. Many local governments publish annual financial reports that include retrospective data, in some instances up to 10 fiscal years, on general and special revenue funds and tax revenues by sources.

Los Angeles

City Controller's Annual Report (City of Los Angeles Controller's Office) http://www.lacity.org/ctr/ctrfr1.htm

This popularly written annual version of the city's *Comprehensive Annual Financial Report* presents its financial statements to the public. The report covers the audited handling of the prior fiscal year's revenues, expenditures, and debt load.

Tax Payers' Guide: Schedule of Tax Rates and Legal Requirements (County of Los Angeles Auditor Controller, 1931–)

This annual source provides county information on real property and property tax rates, payment of taxes, and the various tax levies for the county, schools, and special districts.

New York City

Comprehensive Annual Financial Report of the Comptroller for the Fiscal Year (New York City Office of the Comptroller, 1984–) http://comptroller.nyc.gov

This annual report gives very detailed financial statements showing all revenues, expenditures, and debt, as well as assets and liabilities. Chapter summaries of this report published after 1998 are available on the Comptroller's Web site, as are other published financial and audit reports. Copies of the full report are available from the Office (1 Centre Street, New York, NY 10007, (212) 380–8084, citizens@comptroller.gov).

Local Auditor's Offices

Auditors are responsible for seeing that generally accepted accounting practices are followed in all of the government's financial transactions. Resources for auditing and accounting standards are listed in the Audit and Accounting Standards section below.

Multnomah County, Oregon

Multnomah County Auditor's Office
    http://www.co.multnomah.or.us/auditor

This county auditor's office was the first to establish a home page on the Web. This site includes summaries of recent auditor's reports, an index of past reports, a profile of the office, and an auditor's column. The page is directed at Portland citizens with access to the Internet to let them know about the county auditor's office.

Monroe County, Indiana

Auditor's Links http://www.co.monroe.in.us/
    links.html

This site is a compilation of the laws governing the auditor's duties and the taxpayer's obligations concerning taxes, exemptions, and tax credits.

Tax Assessor's/Collector's Offices

The tax assessor is responsible for establishing an equitable method of determining the base for the property tax. The tax collector is responsible for collecting the property tax and keeping track of who has paid and who hasn't.

Oakland County, Michigan

@ccess Oakland http://ea2.co.oakland.mi.us/eap/
    index.cfm?Ua_Id=6DY7baaJ&Token_Id=ZNDIHbLR

A virtual warehouse of information on every piece of property was created in Oakland County. This site has eased the time-consuming task of combing public records. Records include all property tax information on individual parcels. There is also the capability to search all parcels by certain tax characteristics. The county gives access to delinquent-tax notices through the portal, as well as the entire registrar of deeds records, making this site the premier destination for such public information.

This very useful site is available only on a cost recovery basis; as a result, users are charged a fee for the information they use, to offset the cost of the database to the contributing communities.

SPECIALIZED AND TOPICAL RESOURCES ON LOCAL GOVERNMENT FINANCE

Sources of Municipal Debt Information

Tax-exempt municipal bonds are issued by local governments to finance their capital expenditures. When a bond is issued, the issuer is responsible for providing details as to its financial soundness and creditworthiness. This information is contained in what is known as an offering document, prospectus, or official statement. Rating agencies assign ratings to the bonds when they are issued and monitor developments during the bonds' lifetimes, which are meant to enhance their marketability. There are three major bond-rating firms that perform credit analysis on local governments: Moody's Investors Service, Standard and Poor's Corporation, and Fitch Investor's Service.

Mergent Municipal and Government Manual (Mergent, Inc., 2000–) http://www.fisonline.com

This annual publication was formerly *Moody's Municipal and Government Manual*, initiated in 1918. Moody's Investors Service has over 82 years of experience in analyzing tax-exempt municipal debt. All prior volumes are available on *Manuals on Microfiche—1909 to Date—Series M*. As each new manual is published, Mergent plans to add it to the microfiche collection. Beginning in the year 2000 all financial statements are shown in a separate volume (volume 4). These statements include the comparative financial statistics of the state governments, municipalities, and reporting entities shown as of the fiscal year end. The data may include tax rates, tax levies, and tax collection figures with percentages collected and bonded debt. Currently this manual maintains over 68,000 ratings on 16,000 municipal issuers, including the general obligations of governments, revenue bonds, and other municipal instruments. Descriptions of municipal securities offer certain provisions of the issue including security, purpose, sinking funds, and other protective features where available. Users of the manual are directed to *Mergent Municipal and Government News Reports*, which are published monthly and contain up-to-date information, including such items as securities offered, prospective security offerings, and rating changes.

In addition to the Mergent manual, other valuable sources of municipal bond information are publications by Bond Buyer (later the Thomson Financial Municipals Group), including historical studies (e.g., *The Guide to Municipal Bonds: The History, the Industry, the Mechanics*, 1991), statistical yearbooks on municipal bond sales by purpose, and municipal marketplace directories (listings of municipal financial services and stockbrokers). However, they appear to be available only in the largest libraries or through very expensive online subscriptions.

Sources of Historical Information

Local government financial information from prior years can provide a unique snapshot of the historical trends in public administration. Fiscal records produced by counties and municipalities document the actions of government and to some extent the lives of their citizens. Local tax records and real property records are among the most useful and most overlooked resources for genealogical and historical research. The following record series are commonly found in the county treasurer's office: *Tax Rolls/Real Estate and Personal Property* (rolls of taxes charged against real estate and personal property, showing to whom assessed, legal description of property, taxable valuation, school district number, amount of tax, fees, etc.), *Tax Collection Register* (record of tax collections, showing receipt number, name of townships, school district number, name of taxpayer, etc.); *School Land Sales* (records of sales of school land in the county, showing location and description of land, appraised value, name and address of purchaser, and purchase price).

Budgets and financial statements of counties, townships, cities, school districts, and drainage districts, showing the date, name, and number of the taxing unit, receipts and disbursements, floating and bonded indebtedness, estimates of receipts, and valuation of property, also yield valuable information for researchers.

In various municipal offices (e.g., the city clerk's office), other fiscal records may be found, like *Bond Register*, registers of payments made by cities on bond issues, or budget reports.

Researchers are encouraged to contact local historical societies and libraries in the geographic area they are researching (after consulting the holdings of the state archives). In some cases, records produced by a specific office may have remained in its custody.

Researchers and students alike often may be searching for reliable sources of historical statistics. Listed below are two of the very few sources available:

Historical Statistics on State and Local Government Finances, 1902–1953 (Bureau of the Census, 1955, State and Local Government Special Studies, no. 38. SuDoc no. C 3.145:38)

Annual statistics summarizing state and local revenue and expenditures are presented in this report. There are also several graphs depicting trends in state and local finances during the time covered. The strength of this report, prepared under the supervision of Robert F. Drury, acting chief of the Governments Division at that time, is the excellent description of the history of the collection of local government finance statistics by the Census Bureau and in what publications the detailed data may be found.

United States Historical Census Data Browser
http://fisher.lib.virginia.edu/census

The data presented here, in this joint project of Harvard University and the Inter-university Consortium for Political and Social Research, describe the people and the economy of the United States for each state and county from 1790 to 1960. Users select a Decennial Census year and then obtain the data by selecting from a list of demographic and geographic variables. The 1870 and 1880 Censuses include data on state and local property taxes and indebtedness.

Audit and Accounting Standards

Local governments must follow generally accepted accounting practices in keeping track of their finances. There are several organizations that establish standards for government accounting and provide a number of resources for both government officials and taxpayers. Listed below are some of the organizations and the resources that they provide.

United States General Accounting Office [GAO]
http://www.gao.gov

The GAO is charged with maintaining financial accountability for federal government programs, including grants and other funding programs to local governments.

Government Auditing Standards: Standards for Audit of Governmental Organizations, Programs, Activities, and Functions (U.S. Government Printing Office, 1994)

This revision of the *Government Auditing Standards* (the "Yellow Book") contains standards, often referred to as generally accepted government auditing standards (GAGAS), for audits of government organizations, programs, and activities. When the comptroller general issues a revised standard, the electronic version of *Government Auditing Standards*, available on the GAO Web site, will be immediately codified, with a periodic codification of the standards into printed-book format. This revised approach was adopted in order to provide more timely revision of the standards for emerging audit issues. Printed copies of the *Standards* (1994 revision) and subsequent amendments can be found in many federal Depository libraries, or purchased online from the GPO at http://www.gpo.gov.

Governmental Accounting Standards Board [GASB].
http://www.gasb.org/index.html

The GASB is a private, nonprofit body responsible for establishing and improving accounting and financial reporting standards for state and local governmental units. The board has produced numerous publications on government accounting for both public officials and taxpayers.

On its Web site, users will find information about various GASB publications, their prices and availability, and the newest releases, such as *Statement No. 34: Basic Financial Statements—and Management's Discussion and Analysis—for State and Local Governments*, which establishes new financial reporting requirements for state and local governments throughout the United States, and its accompanying publication from the board's *User Guide* series, *What You Should Know About Your Local Governmental Finances: A Guide to Financial Statements,* which explains in everyday language what information can be found in local government financial statements and what it means.

American Institute of Certified Public Accountants [AICPA]

AICPA is the major professional association for certified public accountants. It helps maintain professional standards by working with the GASB and other boards, providing consultation and technical support.

Audits of State and Local Governmental Units, With Conforming Changes as of May 1, 19…(American Institute of Certified Public Accountants/Commerce Clearing House, 1992–)

This audit and accounting guide presents recommendations of the AICPA State and Local Government Committee. These recommendations are used in the audits of the financial statements of state and local governments.

Specialized Web Sites

Tax and Accounting Sites Directory, State and Local Tax http://www.taxsites.com/state.html

This is a comprehensive index of Web-based tax and accounting resources. The directory is designed to be a starting point for people who are searching for tax and accounting information and services. There are links to governmental, professional, and commercial sites. The emphasis is on state government, but there are numerous links to local government resources.

State and Local Tax Policies: A Comparative Handbook (Greenwood, 1995)

This source compares tax policies for all 50 states and the local governments. The philosophy, administration, rates, exemptions, and limitations of all major types of taxes are presented. The political and social factors that influence tax policies are also discussed. The text is enhanced by numerous statistical tables comparing the various taxes and tax policies. While the emphasis is on taxes that the states traditionally use, there is a lot of detailed information on the taxes that the local governments levy as well.

State and Local Taxation and Finance in a Nutshell (West, 2000)

Though intended for an audience of first-year law students, this treatise may as well serve as a concise introduction to local government finance for public officials and interested citizens. The authors explain the sources of revenue, the type of taxes, and the patterns of spending. They offer a well-balanced discussion of the authority and legal limitations on collecting revenue and spending it, as well as on municipal debt financing. All the issues covered in this source are not only explained in legal terms, but are placed in the larger political and social contexts. References to appropriate legal sources and court cases enhance the usefulness of this excellent introductory material.

For Further Reading

Budgeting Democracy: State Building and Citizenship in America, 1890–1928, by Jonathan Kahn. Ithaca, NY: Cornell University Press, 1997.

Municipal Year Book 2001. Washington, DC: International City/County Management Association, 2001.

CHAPTER 19
Small Business Loans, Grants, and Financial Assistance

Sherry Engle Moeller

MAJOR TOPICS COVERED

Introduction
Small Business
  Guides
  Directories
Grants
  Libraries
  Guides
  Directories

MAJOR RESOURCES COVERED

The Foundation Center
Getting the Money You Need: Practical Solutions for Financing Your Small Business
United States Small Business Administration
Starting and Operating a Business: A Step-by-Step Guide
State and Local Governments on the Net
Small Business Sourcebook
Chamber of Commerce Directory
Online Chambers
Community Capital Development Corporation

Free Money for Small Business and Entrepreneurs
Online Orientation: The Grantseeking Process
User-Friendly Guide to Funding Research and Resources
Foundation Fundamentals: A Guide for Grantseekers
The "How To" Grants Manual: Successful Grantseeking Techniques for Obtaining Public and Private Grants
The Complete Guide to Getting a Grant
Catalog of Federal Domestic Assistance
Foundation Directory
GrantSelect
Guide to U.S. Foundations, Their Trustees, Officers, and Donors
A Guide to Funding Resources
"Finding Local Funding: A Guide to State Foundation Directories"
State and Local Funding Directories: A Bibliography
Community Foundations by State
Community Foundation Locator
Charitable Foundations Directory of Ohio
South Dakota Grant Directory
Foundation Grants to Individuals

INTRODUCTION

Resources for small business financial assistance and resources for grants are distinct from each other. Financial assistance for small business generally is in the form of loans or investment (equity). Most grants are intended for nonprofit organizations. There are some grants available for individuals and very few for small businesses. The small amount of grant money that is available for small business tends to be targeted to specific purposes, locations, or research and development. Assistance also may be available in the form of goods or services.

Loans are money that must be repaid. Usually loans are for a fixed period of time, with interest charged.

Collateral may or may not be required. Local banks and savings and loans often have special programs for lending to small businesses. They may work with state or local governments or with Certified Development Companies (CDCs). CDCs are locally organized nonprofit corporations set up to aid the economic development of the community. The United States Department of Agriculture Rural Business and Cooperative Service and the U.S. Small Business Administration (SBA) sometimes make direct loans to businesses. They also, however, fund nonprofit organizations and CDCs, who then loan the money to small businesses in their areas.

Outside investors are individuals or groups of individuals willing to provide funding for small businesses in exchange for partial ownership of the business. Venture capitalists are outside investors who are willing to invest in high-risk businesses, including new businesses. They may provide seed money to start the business or money for expansion or research.

The SBA works extensively with state and local governments and other entities to provide assistance to small businesses. It licenses and regulates Small Business Investment Companies (SBICs) and Specialized Enterprise Small Business Investment Companies (SSBICs) to provide assistance to small businesses. Both SBICs and SSBICs are privately owned and favor established businesses over startups. This assistance may be in the form of equity, loans, or management expertise. SBICs usually want equity in the company. SSBICs help small firms owned by minority groups. Many of the SBA's programs involve loans, lines of credit, or loan guarantees. Local Development Companies are locally organized entities that help arrange for SBA guaranteed loans. The SBA, in conjunction with state and local governments and local business communities, has established Small Business Development Centers (SBDCs) in every state. SBDCs usually are located on college or university campuses and offer training, information on business startups, and help in locating financial and other forms of assistance. The SBA offers special programs for businesses owned by minority-group members, veterans, and women. It also provides information about small business incubators developed to help new businesses during their startup periods.

The United States Minority Business Development Agency funds Minority Business Development Centers, Native American Business Development Centers, Business Resource Centers, and Minority Business Opportunity Committees. These centers provide management, financial planning, and technical assistance to socially or economically disadvantaged entrepreneurs. Although the centers do not make loans or grants, they assist in locating sources of funding and in preparing applications and proposals.

State Departments of Development offer many programs intended to stimulate the state economy. These departments receive both state funding and federal funding through community block grants. Some Department of Development programs are targeted toward specific communities or subgroups of those communities, while others are available throughout the state. The departments work cooperatively with local governments, business communities, and other organizations.

Local community development offices (county, city, or metropolitan area) try to attract and retain businesses. They work with private development companies to assist local businesses. These offices may offer incentives to new businesses such as tax credits, training, direct financial assistance, or assistance in locating funding sources and completing paperwork. A small business located in a Phoenix, Arizona, enterprise zone, for example, might qualify for a property tax reduction. The city's Small Business Development Program maintains an information line providing assistance and referrals regarding city licensing, certification, and taxes. The program also offers seminars and management and financial assistance.

Local chambers of commerce may offer or facilitate financial assistance. They frequently sponsor training programs targeted to the needs of local businesses. They also offer opportunity for local entrepreneurs to network. The Service Corps of Retired Executives (SCORE) offers free business counseling and low-cost training seminars. The local chapter of this organization may be able to provide assistance in determining appropriate financial strategies and in locating funding. There also may be minority or other special interest business groups operating in the area of interest. The Women's Network for Entrepreneurial Training, which provides mentors for women business owners, is an example of such a group.

Grants are funds given to the recipient. These funds do not need to be repaid. Grants generally are provided for a specific project or purpose. The grant seeker writes and submits a proposal. If the proposal is successful, the funds must be used for the purposes stated in the proposal. Formula grants are monetary allocations made to specific entities (states), based on a formula established by law or regulations. The money is used to fund ongoing activities. Project grants provide funding for a specified period of time, a particular project, or program. Research grants, demonstration grants, construction grants, scholarships, and fellowships are all subcategories of project grants. Block grants are funds provided by the United States government to states, regions, local governments, or other entities to fund groups of related projects. The state (or other entity) then uses the funds to meet local objectives. In some cases the funds are used to sponsor smaller grants or loans to organizations, businesses, or individuals.

Grants are funded through public or private funds. Public funds are obtained through government agencies. The National Foundation of Arts and the Humanities, for example, funds the National Endowment for the Humanities, the National Endowment for the Arts, and the Institute of Museum and Library Services through grants. Federal funds often are administered through state and local government agencies. Library Services and Technology Act grants are an example. These formula grants are given to state libraries, which then administer subgrants. Private funds are those provided by foundations, community groups, direct giving programs, and voluntary agencies. Private funds generally are aimed either at particular areas of interest (education, the arts) or toward a particular group of beneficiaries (geographic region, company employees).

The Foundation Center http://fdncenter.org

This is a nonprofit organization that organizes and disseminates information about foundations and corporate giving programs. Funded by foundations, the Center provides programs on grants and grant writing. It publishes a number of guides and directories in multiple formats. Foundation Center Libraries (discussed below) provide free public access to these resources. Publications and subscriptions to databases can also be purchased. A growing number of Foundation Center publications are freely accessible on its Web site. These include tutorials and topical reading lists such as "Proposal Writing Short Course," "African-American Philanthropy: A Bibliography and Resource List," and "Funding for Individuals: A Bibliography." The Center also provides links to more than 2,000 grantmaker Web sites. These annotated links are divided into four directories—private foundations, corporate grantmakers (includes foundations and giving programs), grantmaking public charities, and community foundations.

Many grants are administered through foundations. The Foundation Center defines foundations as nonprofit organizations whose primary purpose is to fund nonrelated organizations or in some cases individuals for charitable purposes. These purposes vary depending on the interests of the foundation, but may include arts and culture, education, research, social programs, along with other areas of interest to the foundation. Foundations are divided into two main categories, private and public. Private foundations, which generally receive funding from a single source, may be independent, corporate, or operating foundations. Independent foundations are funded by endowments from an individual, small group of individuals, or a family. Independent foundations are the largest category of

foundations. Grants usually are limited to fields of interest to the donor and frequently by geography. Corporate foundations are, as the title suggests, funded by companies through endowments and annual contributions. Corporate foundations often limit their giving to the geographic area in which the company operates or fields relating to the company's activities. Operating foundations, endowed by individuals or small groups of individuals, tend to fund their own programs rather than make grants. If grants are made, they are for purposes related to the foundation's programs. Public foundations are public charities. Like private foundations, their primary purpose is to fund nonrelated organizations and individuals. They receive funding from a variety of sources, including donations, grants from private foundations, and government monies. Community foundations make grants for educational, social, or other purposes within their defined geographic area. Other public foundations focus on specific segments of the population or fields of interest (*Foundation Fundamentals*, 1999).

Not all corporate giving is via foundations. Businesses also provide direct assistance to nonprofit organizations and individuals. Some companies match employee donations to nonprofit organizations. Businesses may provide gifts in kind rather than monetary support. Gifts in kind include the donation of goods or services. They may agree to sponsor special programs. Direct corporate giving, like corporate foundation giving, tends to be targeted toward the communities in which the company operates. Many companies set up programs targeted toward their employees and the families of employees. Information about this type of program can be found in selected Foundation Center publications (and on its Web site) and may be available on company Web sites or by contacting the company public relations office. International Business Machines (IBM) is an example of a corporation posting philanthropic information on its Web site, http://www.ibm.com/ibm/ibmgives.

Students and artists are the most common seekers of grants to individuals. The best place for students to start their search for financial assistance is at the financial aid office of the school they intend to attend. They might also look in the Educational Resources chapter of this book. Persons seeking funding for small business purposes should look at the resources discussed in the Small Business section of this chapter. Additional information on local funding to individuals may be available on local government Web sites.

When beginning a search for financial assistance, the searcher must first determine the purpose for which funds are needed and the desired type of assistance. Novice searchers may find it beneficial to acquire a basic understanding of terminology and advantages and disadvantages of each funding type before beginning a search for funding. The remainder of this chapter discusses resources useful for locating local sources of financial assistance. The resources are broken into two main categories, the first on small business resources and the second on grant resources. Each of these categories is subdivided into sections on guides and directories. The grants category also contains a discussion of libraries. The sections on directories provide annotations for a number of national directories as well as some examples of local or regional directories.

SMALL BUSINESS
Guides

Getting the Money You Need: Practical Solutions for Financing Your Small Business, by Gibson Health (Irwin Professional Publishing, 1995)

This book provides an overview of the types of financing available to small business owners. It includes information on loans, investment via venture capital, small business investment companies, and other forms of investment. The book also includes chapters on state and federal government assistance programs, focusing on SBA programs. Although there is scant mention of local resources, the book provides basic information about financial options for small businesses. Currently out of print, it is available in many libraries.

United States Small Business Administration
http://www.sba.gov

The SBA was established to help entrepreneurs establish and run small businesses. It provides financial and managerial assistance. The SBA home page provides links to local SBA offices, SBA regulated or sponsored programs, and information on starting and financing a business. Lists of CDCs, SBDCs, SBICs, and SCORE offices are available at http://www.sba.gov/gopher/Local-Information.

Starting and Operating a Business in [state]: A Step-by-Step Guide, by Michael D. Jenkins (Oasis Press, 1980–)

The first 10 chapters in each volume of this series (one volume for each state) provide general information about starting a business, with emphasis on federal resources. The 11th chapter provides state-specific information, including regional resources. It provides contact information for SBDC offices and business development centers for women and members of minority groups. Some volumes are out of print. Volume for the state may be available in a nearby library.

Directories

The government (blue) pages of the local telephone directory are a good place to begin a search for local community development offices. The titles of such departments vary considerably. Scan the city and county entries for departments of economic development, community and economic development, trade and development, or similar departments. Also look in the state section of the directory for local or regional offices of the state's department of development and in the federal section for closest the SBA office.

State and Local Governments on the Net
http://www.statelocalgov.net/index.cfm

This site provides links to county and city Web pages. Use this site to locate community economic development offices with a Web presence. The amount and type of information provided on Web pages varies considerably. Some local government sites provide detailed information about assistance programs for small businesses. Others provide merely contact information. These offices usually expect those seeking funding to make a personal visit. For example, the City of Phoenix Community and Economic Development Department can be located by selecting Arizona, cities, Phoenix, departments, then Community and Economic Development Department.

Small Business Sourcebook, ed. by Sonya D. Hill (15th ed., Gale, 2002)

Three hundred forty-one small business profiles make up the bulk of this two-volume publication. These profiles provide lists of resources useful for persons interested in starting or owning that particular type of business. These include references to publications relating to business startups, reference works, and trade periodicals. The profiles also include information on associations and other organizations and educational programs. The second volume includes state and federal government assistance sections. The state section consists of state-by-state listings arranged by sixteen subheadings: (1) Small Business Development Center Lead Office, (2) Small Business Development Centers, (3) Small Business Assistance Programs, (4) SCORE Offices, (5) Better Business Bureaus, (6) Chambers of Commerce, (7) Minority Business Assistance Programs, (8) Financing and Loan Programs, (9) Procurement Assistance Programs, (10) Licensing, (11) Incubators/Research and Development Parks, (12) Educational Programs, (13) Legislative Assistance, (14) Consultants, (15) Publications, and (16) Publishers. The section on federal government assistance includes contact information for local offices of federal agencies. This book includes a master index that lists in alphabetical order all entries from both volumes, primarily by state rather than local area. Available at many larger libraries, this resource also can be purchased from the publisher, at http://www.gale.com.

Chamber of Commerce Directory
    http://www.uschamber.org/Chambers/Chamber+D
    irectory/default.htm

Produced by the U.S. Chamber of Commerce, a nonprofit federation representing 3,000,000 businesses, 3,000 state and local chambers of commerce, 830 business associations, and 87 American chambers abroad, this directory is arranged by state. The title, address, and telephone and fax numbers for the state chamber of commerce are provided. Links lead to county and city chambers of commerce within the state. Chambers of commerce that are not members of the U.S. Chamber of Commerce are not included. If a chamber for the desired location is not found, look in the *Small Business Sourcebook* and Online Chambers.

As with the community development offices, the amount of information provided on chamber of commerce Web sites varies from simply contact information to access to online business tools and directories.

Online Chambers http://online-chamber.com/
    USA.html

This resource is an alternative source of state listings for chambers of commerce with an Internet presence. Links in Online Chambers are arranged by state, then alphabetically within the state. The site loads much more quickly than the Chamber of Commerce Directory. Online Chambers includes a number of chambers not included in the Chamber of Commerce Directory, but also omits many found in the former site. For example, for the state of Ohio, Online Cham-

bers links to 32 chambers, while the Chamber of Commerce Directory links to 41. Only 15 of the chambers are listed in both directories.

Community Capital Development Corporation
    [CCDC] http://www.ccdcorp.org/micro.htm

This Web site is an interesting example of one that is focused on one program and provides very specific information, such as the type of loan, interest rate, and amount that can be financed. It is an example of a microloan program. The CCDC is a private nonprofit organization that provides loans to small businesses in Central Ohio. Its microloan program provides loans to businesses with fewer than 10 employees. These loans can be used for working capital, inventory, or small equipment and are extended over a period of one month to six years.

Free Money for Small Business and Entrepreneurs, by Laurie Blum (4th ed., John Wiley and Sons, 1995)

This volume contains more than 700 entries for foundations, government agencies, and other entities providing assistance to small business owners. The book is divided into three sections. The first, "Program-Related Investments," consists of entries for foundations providing assistance for purposes relating to the foundation's objectives. The assistance may be in the form of grants, equity investment, loans, letters of credit, or donated services. The second section, "Flowthrough Funding," comprises entries for foundations providing cash awards, consulting, and technical assistance loans. Another section covers federal government assistance. Each of the first two sections is subdivided by state and by type of business. Entries include foundation (or other entity) name, contact person, restrictions or limitations on giving, focus (geographic locations of interest), amount given, assets, and application information. As this book is now somewhat dated, the searcher should verify information in it against other sources (such as those listed in the grants section of this chapter) before submitting applications. This book is available at many libraries or can be purchased from the publisher at http://www.wiley.com.

GRANTS

Libraries

The previously described Foundation Center is an umbrella organization founded to serve as an authoritative access point for information about foundations. It publishes numerous foundation directories in print,

CD-ROM, and online formats. Online files are available via subscription directly from the Center or through Knight-Ridder Information Services (formerly DIALOG). The Foundation Center has established five Center Libraries in the United States and more than 200 Cooperating Collections. Foundation Center Cooperating Collections are libraries or nonprofit information centers providing free public access to Foundation Center publications. They house additional related resources, particularly those with a local focus. Some libraries provide access to Internal Revenue Service form 990-PF (private foundation tax return information) for their state or region. These libraries may also provide workshops or training sessions. A directory of Foundation Center Cooperating Collections is available on the Foundation Center Web site, at http://fdncenter.org/collections/index.html. This directory is reproduced in many Foundation Center publications.

Many other libraries purchase copies of Foundation Center and additional resources relating to grant seeking and grant writing. A few of these publications are described below.

Guides

Online Orientation: The Grantseeking Process
  http://fdncenter.org/learn/orient/intro1.html

Particularly useful for novices, this tutorial introduces the reader to foundations, their operations, how to research possible funding sources, and the grant-writing process. It is one of many resources available on the Foundation Center Web site.

User-Friendly Guide to Funding Research and Resources http://fdncenter.org/learn/ufg/index.html

This resource, like the previous one, is available via the "Online Librarian" section of the Foundation Center Web site. Both resources, as do all Foundation Center publications, provide information about the Foundation Center, its publications, and services. The *User-Friendly Guide* complements the Online Orientation site, providing greater depth on some topics. It includes numerous references to additional sources of information and a glossary of frequently used terms. Unlike Online Orientation, which, as the name implies, is intended for online use, the *User-Friendly Guide* can easily be printed and read offline. (Print copies of the *User-Friendly Guide to Funding Research and Resources* are available at many libraries.)

Foundation Fundamentals: A Guide for Grantseekers, ed. by Pattie J. Johnson and Margaret Morth (6th ed., The Foundation Center, 1999)

This book provides an overview of the grant-seeking process. Arranged into 10 chapters, beginning with the definition of a foundation, this publication provides a more in-depth discussion than do Online Orientation and the *User-Friendly Guide to Funding Research and Resources. Foundation Fundamentals* serves as a how-to guide to using Foundation Center publications. It includes numerous figures illustrating sample searches of both print and electronic resources. Six appendices supply additional information, including a bibliography of additional resources, arranged by topic, a glossary of types of support, the Foundation Center's Grants Classification System and the National Taxonomy of Exempt Entities, directories of State Charities Registration Offices, Foundation Center Cooperating Collections, and resources produced by the Center.

The "How To" Grants Manual: Successful Grant-seeking Techniques for Obtaining Public and Private Grants, by David G. Bauer (4th ed., Oryx Press, 1999)

Provides step-by-step guidance in developing and submitting grant proposals. This publication is divided into three parts. The first part, "Getting Ready to Seek Grant Support for Your Organization," focuses on developing the project idea and documenting it. This section also discusses the differences between public and private funding sources. The second section, "Government Funding Sources," focuses on federal funding, although state and local funding sources are mentioned. Private foundations and corporate giving programs are discussed in the final section, "Private Funding Sources." The volume includes numerous charts, sample documents, worksheets, and other illustrative material. An annotated list of resources is included at the end of the volume. This volume does not provide as much depth in its discussion of Foundation Center resources as is found in *Foundation Fundamentals*. But it does discuss a number of resources not published by the Foundation Center. It is available in many libraries or for purchase from the publisher at http://www.greenwood.com/default.asp?SectionID=home&ImprintID=I1.

The Complete Guide to Getting a Grant, by Laurie Blum (New York: Poseidon Press, 1993)

This volume is written for individuals seeking grants. It includes sections on seeking a sponsor (non-profit organization), proposal writing, and types of available funding. Funding sources include foundations, corporate giving programs, government agencies, and donors. This volume is not a directory of funding sources. Rather, it describes procedures for seeking funds from fund-granting entities. This out-of-print resource is available in many libraries.

Directories

The majority of foundations limit their giving to specific geographic locations—states, counties, or even cities. Directories specific to states or regions are produced by a variety of publishers. In some states, the directories are published by government agencies. In other states, regional associations or commercial publishers produce them. The quality and contents of these directories vary considerably. Two examples of state directories are included below. Also included are a number of national directories. Numerous subject-specific directories (education, health and human services, etc.) are published each year. For an example of a subject-specific directory, see *Free Money for Small Business and Entrepreneurs* in the Small Business section of this chapter.

Catalog of Federal Domestic Assistance (Office of
    Management and Budget, annual)
    http://www.cfda.gov

Available in both print and online formats, the *Catalog of Federal Domestic Assistance* is a compendium of federal funding sources. The majority of these programs are designed for state, U.S. territorial, and local governments, along with groups and organizations (both profit and nonprofit). Very few programs provide funding to individuals, generally in the form of loans. Aid seekers may find that while they are ineligible to receive funds directly from the federal government, they may qualify for funding under the program via local organizations. Types of programs include formula, project, and block grants; direct payments, loans, insurance, training, and special services, among other forms of assistance. The online version offers several search options. To search specifically for grants, select "Find Assistance Programs," then "Find a Grant." The screen then displays grant categories.

The online version of this comprehensive resource is updated semiannually and is freely accessible. The annual print version is available at many libraries or can be purchased from the Government Printing Office, http://bookstore.gpo.gov.

Foundation Directory (New York: The Foundation
    Center, annual)

Published in two volumes, the first volume lists the 10,000 largest grant-making foundations in the United States; the second volume lists the 10,000 next largest. Each volume is arranged alphabetically by state, then by foundation name. Each entry includes the foundation's name and contact information, purpose, fields of interest, limitations (including geographic limits), application information, and other information about the foundation. Each volume contains seven indexes: (1) Donors, Officers, Trustees; (2) Geographic (the state and city housing the foundation's principal offices); (3) International Giving; (4) Types of Support; (5) Subject (fields of interest); (6) Foundations New to the Edition; and (7) the Foundation Name Index. It is also available in CD-ROM format and online via subscription and at most larger libraries. This directory can also be purchased from the publisher.

GrantSelect (Greenwood Press) http://www.
    grantselect.com

This is a subscription database including information about more than 10,000 grants available from nonprofit organizations, foundations, corporations, federal and state governments, educational institutions, and foreign sources. The basic search screen allows searching by keyword, state, and predefined subject heading. The advance search screen allows searching by keyword, geographic location, subject, program type, sponsor, title of grant, description, requirements, deadline, and restrictions. All entries include foundation (or entity) name, contact information, subject terms, and type of sponsor. There are links to additional information about the grant or granting agency, deadlines for application, restrictions, previous grants awarded, preferred population groups, and program numbers. The database can be subscribed to in its entirety or by segment: Arts and Humanities, Children and Youth, Community Development, Biomedical and Health Care, K–12 and Adult Basic Education, International Progress, and Operating Grants.

*Guide to U.S. Foundations, Their Trustees, Officers,
    and Donors*, ed. by David G. Jacobs and Melissa
    Lunn (Foundation Center, annual)

The 2001 edition contains 51,028 entries for private, corporate, operating, and community foundations. Many of the local foundations included in this directory are not covered by other print directories. Entries include legal name of the foundation and former name, if any, contact information, financial data, limitations on giving, employer identification number (EIN) assigned by the Internal Revenue Service, and the type of foundation. This directory is divided into two sections: the first lists private, corporate, and community foundations by state, then in descending order based on grants awarded. Operating foundations, which tend to award few grants, are listed in a second section. Three indexes are provided: Foundation Trustee, Officer, and Donor; Foundation Name Index and Locator; and Community Foundation Name Index and Locator. As with all Foundation Center publications, there is plenty of introductory material.

A Guide to Funding Resources, ed. by Robert Salmon (Rural Information Center, 1999) http://www.nal. usda.gov/ric/ricpubs/funding/fundguide.html

This is an annotated bibliography of resources related to grant-seeking and fund-raising processes. This publication includes a subject guide to grant funds as well as a nonannotated section on state directories of funding sources. A print version is available in federal Depository libraries.

"Finding Local Funding: A Guide to State Foundation Directories," by Marc Green (*Grantsmanship Center Magazine*, 2001)

This article discusses state and local foundation directories and provides annotated entries including contact and ordering information for 55 directories covering 40 states and the District of Columbia. It includes both state and regional directories. The *San Diego County Foundation Directory* (San Diego Foundation, Calif.) is an example of a resource included in this directory that is not listed in *A Guide to Funding Resources*. URLs for publisher Web sites are provided.

State and Local Funding Directories: A Bibliography http://fdncenter.org/learn/topical/sl_dir.html

This bibliography lists directories by state, then alphabetically by title. Entries include brief descriptive annotations and ordering information. Links to publishers' Web sites are provided in many entries. The bibliography also appears in print format in the first volume of *Guide to U.S. Foundations, Their Trustees, Officers, and Donors*, 2001 edition (Foundation Center, 2001).

Community Foundations by State
http://www.tgci.com/resources/foundations/ searchGeoLoc.asp

Produced by the Grantsmanship Center, this free Web site provides contact information: foundation name, address, telephone and fax numbers, and contact person name and title, as well as available links and e-mail addresses of community foundations. The entries are arranged by state (selected from an image map), then alphabetically by city.

Community Foundation Locator
http://www.communityfoundationlocator.org/ search/index.cfm

This free searchable database sponsored by the Council on Foundations allows users to search for community foundations by foundation name, region (east, central, south, or west), state, or zip code area served. The entries are similar to those in *Community Foundations by State*, including foundation name, address, telephone and fax numbers, and contact person. E-mail addresses and links to foundation Web pages are provided for some foundations.

Charitable Foundations Directory of Ohio (Ohio State Attorney General's Office, biennial)

This directory provides the foundation name, address, contact person, telephone number, charitable purpose, and assets of foundations in Ohio. Entries also include total dollar amount of grants reported in the foundation's last annual report to the attorney general. The 1999–2000 directory indicated that 2,676 out of 18,000 registered foundations funded grants. The directory is indexed by charitable purpose and by county. It can be purchased from the State Attorney General's Office.

South Dakota Grant Directory http://www. sdstatelibrary.com/grants/index.cfm

Produced by the South Dakota State Library, this searchable database is available free of charge on the Internet. It offers basic searching by foundation, grant name, or field of interest and advanced search capabilities. Entries include the foundation name, address, telephone and fax numbers, contact persons, purpose, field of interest, limitations, financial data, and information on application procedures. The database includes information on 293 foundations.

Foundation Grants to Individuals, ed. by Phyllis Edelson (Foundation Center, annual)

The 2001 edition contains entries for more than 4,300 private foundations providing at least $2,000 in support to individuals annually. The entries are arranged by the following topics: Educational Support (includes scholarships, loans, fellowships, and internships for secondary, undergraduate, and graduate study), General Welfare (grants, loans, and in-kind services paid either to the individual or to agencies rendering services to the individual), Arts and Cultural Support (fellowships, residencies, and welfare assistance and emergency aid), International Applicants, By Nomination Only, Research and Professional Support (PhD and above), Restricted to Company Employees (education and general welfare), and Restricted to Graduates or students of specific schools. Entries within each section are arranged alphabetically by foundation name and include the foundation name, address, contact person, limitations (frequently geographic), financial data, EIN number, type of foundation, application information, and program description. The volume is indexed by geography (state), company name, school, type of support, and foundation name. A bibliography of resources is included. (Bibliography also available on the Web at http://fdncenter.org/learn/topical/indiv.html.)

This chapter has covered just a few of the resources for finding financial assistance. Local governments wish to attract and retain businesses. They may provide loans directly or assist entrepreneurs in locating financial assistance. Federal and state agencies work with local governments and community organizations to provide assistance to small businesses. Numerous general and subject directories of grant-giving foundations are available. Most foundations limit their giving to specific geographic areas; thus using state or regional guides may facilitate searches for available resources. Local libraries often have small business and grants sections tailored to the communities they serve. Many libraries maintain Web presences. They can be found using directories such as Libweb, http://sunsite.Berkeley.edu/Libweb.

Index

About the Editor and Contributors

THE EDITOR

MARY MARTIN is currently the librarian for Business and Law at the Libraries of the Claremont Colleges in Claremont, California. She formerly served as Head of Government Publications at Claremont for 10 years and also worked in the Government Publications Department at the University of California at Irvine for 8 years. She received her MLIS from the UCLA School of Library and Information Science in 1989. She is active in the American Library Association's GODORT (Government Documents Round Table) and BRASS (Business Reference and Services Section). Mary has published several chapters in books and several articles in the area of government publications. One interesting piece is titled "What Pleasure Government Publications," in *Genre and Ethnic Collections: Collected Essays,* ed. Milton T. Wolf and Murray S. Martin, vol. 38 of *Foundations in Library and Information Science* (Greenwich, CT: JAI Press, 1996).

THE CONTRIBUTORS

HARRIET SEMMES ALEXANDER, Associate Professor, was a reference librarian at the University of Memphis for 25 years. She received her bachelor's degree from Arkansas State University, her master's degree from Memphis State University, and her Master of Library Science (MLS) from the University of Illinois at Champaign-Urbana. She has authored several articles and three books of literary criticism. In 1995 she received the Francis Neel Cheney Award recognizing her contribution to the world of books and librarianship from the Tennessee Library Association. She passed away in 2003.

MARK ANDERSON is Government Publications Librarian at the James A. Michener Library, University of Northern Colorado (UNC), Greeley, Colorado. He received his MLS from the University of Iowa in 1987. Prior to receiving his MLS, he held a variety of paraprofessional positions at the University of Iowa Main Library and Parks Library at Iowa State University. After receiving his MLS, he was Government Publications Librarian at Northwest Missouri State University, Maryville, Missouri, before coming to UNC in 1994.

MARIA CARPENTER is Research and Instruction Librarian and Advancement Program Manager at Northeastern University. She received her Master of Library and Information Studies (MLIS) from the University of Pittsburgh, School of Information Sciences. Prior to receiving her MLIS, she worked for the Cambridge Public Library in Cambridge, Massachusetts. There, she gained an appreciation for and interest in public access to information and resources such as government data and local agency information.

DARCY CARRIZALES, after obtaining a Master of Arts (MA) in International Studies from Ohio University and an MLS from Indiana University, worked for a year and a half as the Government Documents Librarian at Texas A&M International in Laredo, Texas. Currently, Darcy is the bibliographer for Government Documents at the University of Texas at San Antonio

JIM CHURCH is International and Foreign Documents Librarian at the University of California, Berkeley. Jim has worked at the University of California, San Diego (UCSD), where he was the State, Local and United Nations Documents Librarian and selector for Urban and Environmental Studies. Before UCSD Jim was the Economics and Intergovernmental Information Librarian at Yale, and prior to that the United Nations Collection manager at Princeton. He received his MLS from Rutgers University in 1997, where he specialized in government information and statistical data.

ANN ELLIS is the Head of the Bibliographic Control Department at the Stephen F. Austin State University Library in Nacogdoches, Texas. Her MLS is from the University of Pittsburgh. She has worked as a technical services librarian in academic, special, and public libraries, and as a high school librarian.

RICHARD GAUSE has been the Government Documents Librarian at the University of Central Florida since 1998. His previous 12 years were with the Orange County Library System (OCLS) in Orlando, Florida. Three of those years were in the OCLS Planning and Local Government Department, where he provided in-depth research for government staff from local municipalities, counties, and regional and state agencies. He received his MLS from Florida State University.

MARK GILMAN is Assistant Manager, Government Information Center at the J. Erik Jonsson Central Library, Dallas, Texas, where he also serves as Municipal Reference Librarian. Previously, he worked in special and academic libraries in Haifa, Israel; Denton, Texas; and Memphis, Tennessee. He earned his MLS from the University of North Texas and also pursued graduate study in urban anthropology at the University of Memphis.

JOAN GOODBODY has a bachelor of science degree in animal science from the University of Delaware, a Master's in Historical Administration from Eastern Illinois University, and her MLS from the University of North Texas. She worked as a Government Documents reference person for four years at Texas A&M before receiving her MLS. She is now at Michigan Technological University, Houghton, as the Government Documents Coordinator and Instruction/Reference Librarian.

SUZANN HOLLAND is the director of the Oskaloosa Public Library in Oskaloosa, Iowa. She previously worked for the Southeastern Library Service Area in Iowa as a consultant and the Milwaukee Public Library as a reference librarian. She received her MLS and MA in history from the University of Wisconsin–Milwaukee in 2000, with a concentration in archives.

DENISE JOHNSON is Interim Access Services Librarian, Reference and Government Documents Librarian, and Library Liaison to the Foster College of Business, Cullom-Davis Library, Bradley University, Peoria, Illinois. Denise received her MLS from the University of Illinois at Urbana-Champaign, Graduate School of Library and Information Science, and her Bachelor of Arts from the University of Illinois–Springfield.

MICHAEL J. KAMINSKI is Government Documents Librarian at the San Antonio, Texas, Public Library

and has a special interest in local government uses of Geographic Information Systems. He received his MLS from the University of Pittsburgh in 2000.

ANNA LEVY received her MLS from the Pratt Institute School of Information and Library Science in Brooklyn, New York, in 1993. Currently, she works as a Government Documents Librarian at the Brooklyn Public Library (Central Library). Since 2000, she has been teaching a Government Information Sources course at the Queens College Graduate School of Library and Information Studies (City University of New York).

MARIANNE MASON received her MLS from Indiana University (1988) and is currently the Federal Documents Librarian at the University of Iowa (UI) Libraries in Iowa City, Iowa. She also serves as an adjunct faculty member in the UI School of Library and Information Science and teaches a course in Government Information Resources.

SHERRY ENGLE MOELLER is an Assistant Professor and Government Documents Librarian at the Ohio State University Main Library. She received her Master of Science in Library Science (MSLS) from Clarion University of Pennsylvania and Master of Science from Mankato State University. She is a past president of the Government Documents Roundtable of Ohio.

DEBORAH MONGEAU received her MLS from Rutgers University. She has been Head of Government Publications and subject bibliographer for Government and Law at the University of Rhode Island Library, Kingston, for 16 years. Prior to her current position, she was a reference/government documents librarian in several public libraries in Rhode Island and Pennsylvania. Currently she is Chair of the Government Documents Committee of the Consortium of Rhode Island Academic and Research Libraries.

SHAWN W. NICHOLSON is Head of Government Documents at Michigan State University (MSU) Libraries. He received his MLIS from the University of Illinois at Urbana-Champaign, from which he also holds an MLIS. He also has an MS in political science. As bibliographer for State Documents and Sociology he has worked closely with faculty and students from the Department of Urban Planning and the Center for Urban Affairs at MSU.

BRIAN W. ROSSMANN graduated with an MA (classics) and MLIS from the University of Western Ontario. Since then, he has held professional positions with the federal government of Canada, Documents positions at Oklahoma State University and Rice University, and is currently Government Information Specialist at Montana State University, Bozeman. He has held various offices in the American Library Association's Government Documents Round Table.

MARIE-LISE SHAMS received her MSLS from Wayne State University in Michigan and is a member of the Medical Library Association's Academy of Health Information Professionals. She is presently an associate librarian at the University of Detroit Mercy and is the liaison for the School of Dentistry and the College of Health Professions.

DAN STANTON received his MLS from the University of Arizona in 1997. He currently serves as the Arizona Local Documents Librarian in the Government Documents and Maps Department of the Arizona State University Libraries. As the subject specialist for Arizona Local Government information, he is constantly exploring ways of identifying and accessing local government information. Working on this book allowed him the opportunity to explore this type of information outside of Arizona.